D1412031

CRUISING
IN A
NUTSHELL

By Tony Gibbs

PRACTICAL SAILING

PILOT'S WORK BOOK/PILOT'S LOG BOOK

POWERBOATING

SAILING: A FIRST BOOK

BACKPACKING

NAVIGATION

ADVANCED SAILING

THE COASTAL CRUISER

THE COASTAL NAVIGATOR'S NOTEBOOK

CRUISING
IN A
NUTSHELL

The Art and Science of
Enjoyable Coastwise Voyaging
in Small Auxiliary Yachts

~~~~~~~~~~~~~~~~~~~~~~~~~~~~~~~

by Tony Gibbs

Drawings by Nancy Behnken

W. W. NORTON & COMPANY
NEW YORK   LONDON

Published simultaneously in Canada by George J. McLeod Limited, Toronto.
Printed in the United States of America.

Library of Congress Cataloging in Publication Data

Gibbs, Tony.
    Cruising in a nutshell.

    Bibliography: p.
    Includes index.
    1. Sailing. 2. Yachts and yachting. I. Title.
GV811.G493 1983   797.1'25   83-42664

ISBN 0-393-03289-2

W. W. Norton & Company, Inc., 500 Fifth Avenue, New York, N.Y. 10110
W. W. Norton & Company Ltd., 37 Great Russell Street, London WC1B 3NU

for Elaine, Eric, and Bill

Contents

Introduction
to Coastal Cruising

Thanks to a multitude of intoxicating books, the cruising sailor has come to be seen—and to see himself—as a far-wandering adventurer, a crosser of trackless oceans. The truth is of course very different, if no less stimulating: Most skippers of small or large cruising yachts spend the majority of their time on the water daysailing, with an occasional overnight or weekend jaunt and maybe a once-a-season voyage for ten days or two weeks.

Furthermore, most of today's cruising sailors are seldom likely to find themselves out of sight of land, except at night or in fog—and there is a great difference between sailing where land is close but invisible and sailing where there is no land nearby. Many experienced high-seas voyagers freely admit that they are nervous only in close proximity to shore, and, having tried both types of cruising, I find coast-hopping harder on the nerves, more demanding (at least navigationally), and more rewarding.

For a variety of reasons, relatively few coastal sailors fully develop their talents, although such yachtsmen are sometimes more accomplished than they themselves realize. Collectively, however, they are too often intimidated or hypnotized by the romance of the open sea. In terms of skill as well as enjoyment, coastal cruising is potentially the equal of any other kind of sailing —but until its requirements are met, its potential won't be realized.

My previous book, *The Coastal Cruiser,* dealt with selecting, purchasing, and outfitting a small cruising auxiliary—thirty feet overall was the arbitrary upper length limit. My rationale was and is that a small cruising yacht is significantly different from a large one—not, perhaps, in terms of what one might accomplish in it, but in the manner in which a voyage is made. Despite the achievements of a few very talented and brave (and occasionally deranged) small-boat sailors, the twenty-to-thirty-footer is primarily a coastwise cruising vessel, designed and built for that kind of sailing. This truth becomes evident when one considers the degree of buttressing and rearrangement required in order to take such a vessel safely on an extended offshore voyage.

I am not, let me say right here, talking about "better" or "worse" boats. Most serious ocean cruising yachts are designed and constructed to take anything the ocean can dish out, and for an extended period. The result is that, in light breezes and coastal waters, many of them are clunks. The coastal cruiser, normally employed in good weather and relatively modest breezes, needs to be able to absorb a certain amount of punishment from the elements, but creating her to survive a hurricane just doesn't make sense.

What, then, is coastwise cruising? It's useful to work out a definition with some care, because that framework will to a considerable extent define the boat.

Well, as I said at the start, a good deal of coastal voyaging is in fact daysailing—leaving the slip or mooring for a day's enjoyment on the water, with the intent of returning home by nightfall. While under way, the boat may participate in a casual race—organized or impromptu—poke her way up a shallow stream, or drop anchor for a picnic.

Overnighting and weekending involve many of the same activities, except that more gear and planning and greater distances are usually involved. If the setting is a race, it will be hedged about with equipment requirements, and if it's a cruise, the cruiser may be mother to assorted dinghies and boardsailing craft.

The extended cruise, whether made alone or in company, imposes new stowage, sleeping, and distance-achieving standards. The element of navigation, till now an afterthought, becomes important, and the skipper may well begin to think seriously about the seaworthiness of his yacht, as he contemplates a bare stretch of coast with no port of refuge. At the same time, the cruiser must be more of a self-contained floating home than during shorter voyages, unless you're prepared to accept either a very primitive life-style or considerable added expense for room and meals.

We are not, however, talking about carrying supplies for more than a week at a time, and perhaps only fresh water is likely to run short with annoying frequency. The skipper of a coastal cruiser facing a three-day gale is more likely to worry about his supply of books and games than about his sea anchor and storm jib.

What sort of boat makes a good coastal cruising yacht? There are some general types that suggest themselves—as well as some others that seem sensible to avoid. Most important, at least to me, is that your cruiser be a good sailboat. If she does not perform well under sail, she will almost certainly be a failure, no matter what her other attributes. By the same token, a boat that sails very well can have any number of drawbacks and still work as a cruiser. The type of rig does not seem terribly important to me, as I have owned at various times a gaff-rigged catboat, two ketches, and several sloops. There is of course the question of cost, but if a given rig delights you, then that's all the excuse it needs.

Especially when buying their first cruising yacht, many people become so fixated on interior accommodation that they lose sight of everything else. In the American climate, sailing is still essentially an outdoor sport. You may spend a whole rainy day down below, and it's worthwhile giving thought to that possibility, but most of the time you'll be topside, and your boat's design should reflect that reality. The cockpit, for instance, should be able to accommodate your entire regular crew, and there should ideally be enough well-organized space so you can tack the boat without disturbing the people who are reading the Sunday paper. It will often be handy if there's enough exterior room so that one or more of the crew can get away from the rest—to sun themselves or read on the foredeck, perhaps. This pleasant feature was most apparent in a small catamaran sloop I once owned, where each of my sons had a bow pulpit of his own. At the same time, the cruising yacht should be capable of being sailed short- or singlehanded; unlike racing boats, most cruising auxiliaries are either perennially shorthanded or infested with landlubber guests. The ideal cruiser will function under either set of problems.

Many skippers insist on over-engining their cruisers—at least by my own standards. This is a case where one may go either way, according to taste. Or according to your boat's sailing qualities: A fast, handy sailboat needs an engine only to get through those inevitable flat calms or perhaps to thread her way into the most inaccessible corners of marinas, and a very small powerplant will save weight, space, and money. On the other hand, a boat capable of less than sparkling performance under sail may still be acceptable overall if she has an engine that can punch her into a headsea at close to hull speed, that can work her in and out of anchorages and other tight spots, and that can, as a side benefit, supply electrical power to create pressurized hot water, refrigeration, and other navigational and creature comforts.

I would suggest, if engine power is not important, that you obtain an engine capable at least of pushing your boat at hull speed in a calm. (Hull speed in knots is approximately equal to 1.25 times the square root of the waterline length in feet; thus, hull speed for a boat with a 16-foot waterline is about 5 knots.) Enough power to drive your boat at hull speed into a chop and a 15-knot breeze will probably be about as much as you can profitably use. Ian Nicholson's little *Boat Data Book* (see Bibliography) has tables for calculating the amount of power required by boats of various sizes and displacements, but it seems to me a demonstrable truth that all stock American auxiliaries with inboard power have at least enough horsepower and usually too much.

A large part of the attraction of cruising, I have long suspected, is that it gives adult males an excuse to play house in an acceptable setting. At the same time, manufacturers are now told by their marketing experts that it is the woman who clinches or breaks the sale, and as a result boat interiors have more and more come to resemble a man's idea of what a woman's house would look like if it were shoehorned into a boat. Aside from the fact that this is usually not good naval architecture, at least not in the size boat we are talking about, it isn't good house design, either; nor does it reflect very well on the intelligence of women, who are perfectly capable of telling the difference between houses and boats—perhaps more so than many men.

Within the severe space limits of the small cruiser, the following attributes are, I think, worth insisting on: good sleeping accommodations for your regular crew; adequate galley facilities for preparing breakfast and lunch and an occasional simple dinner; a head that is not too claustrophobic or depressing; a gathering place that can be shared by all hands at once, preferably sitting down; decent fair-weather ventilation throughout; and partitions of some sort so that people can have at least visual privacy. (On a small or even middle-sized yacht there is no aural privacy.) Anything beyond these basic parameters is a bonus: Take it and be grateful. And on many of the better small cruising designs, it is quite possible to achieve a good deal more than the basics, although no modern thirty-footer is going to be as spacious as a modern forty-footer. It is, however, true that a modern thirty-footer can have considerably more usable room both above and below than, say, a forty-five-footer of yesteryear.

There are also some false trails in cruising yacht design that ought to be avoided. Perhaps the most prevalent still—although many buyers have grown wise to it—is the provision of an absurdly large number of berths. Only a few years ago, twenty-six-footers that slept six or even seven were very popular; or at least they sold well, because I have my doubts about their popularity with the ultimate victims, the crew. A proper berth is only a berth and is just dead space when no one is sleeping in it. Don't get more berths than you know you'll need.

If a galley looks unworkable, it probably is. But at the same time, don't confuse a galley with a kitchen. Almost any waterside restaurant can prepare a better meal than you can turn out in a small cruiser's galley, and the sooner you accept this unpalatable truth, the happier everyone will be. Perhaps the most frequent use for your galley will be as a space to store, unpack, set up, and perhaps heat picnic meals.

"Almost" standing headroom is generally worse than an honest four-foot-eight. The small cruising yacht is one of the few places in the modern world where the shorter than average adult has an advantage. As someone who is just under average height—5'9"—I have full standing headroom in a considerably larger number of boats than does someone who is just on the far side of six feet, and my 5'6" wife has even more boats in which she can stand up. As long as there is one place below where you can stand upright, you probably have all the headroom you need, but do be sure that you have plenty of that more important commodity, full sitting headroom, in the places designed for you to sit.

For more detail I must refer readers to *The Coastal Cruiser*. As a concluding generality, let me urge people looking at cruising yachts for the first time to be as honest as possible about their own sailing ambitions—at least as they understand those vague stirrings. Look seriously at boats that have been popular in your sailing area for some time. While an energetic builder or dealer may be able to get a lot of his products into the water, they won't stay fashionable if they don't serve a purpose. Boats with a good local distribution have usually proven that they are right for the waters and winds that will be encountered, and there are few things sadder than an ocean cruising yacht wallowing through a light-air summer, or an ultralight racer that cannot leave the mooring without a reef.

Only a fool would talk about mastering the sea—or any body of water. What can be done is push back one's own limitations and those of one's boat. With knowledge and experience, a good sailor can actively enjoy the vast majority of his hours afloat and can cope with the unavoidable moments of uneasiness or fear. There seems to me a great difference between honest humility, the perception that no one can know all the answers, and a sense of inadequacy, when one cannot even define the questions.

Any experienced sailor knows that there are times afloat when nothing he can do will get him out of a tight spot unscathed. He also knows that there are considerably more times when any of half-a-dozen responses will be equally successful. With preparation, planning, and timely action, the expert sailor can go some distance toward avoiding the creation of needlessly difficult situations in the first place, while still enjoying the challenge of cruising under sail.

This book cannot make you an expert. I hope that it can delineate both the challenges and the problems, and suggest responses that you can tailor to your boat, your crew, and yourself, so that each successful cruise will bring a renewed sense of accomplishment and delight.

Five Coastal Cruisers

In *The Coastal Cruiser,* I included plans of and commentary on seventeen cruising yachts between twenty and thirty feet long, as a sort of cross-section of what was available to the buyer. This book is not a guide to boat buying —except, perhaps, by implication—but I've decided, after some hesitation, to append plans and descriptions for five more coastal cruising yachts, more to set the mood for the text that will follow than to provide anything in the nature of a market survey. (My own taste in cruising yachts seems always to have been across the grain of the market, anyway.)

The reader interested in more of this sort of thing may wish to consult my earlier book, the design sections of monthly boating magazines, the annual directory published by *Sail* magazine, or any of the dozens of design books compiled by writers over the years.

The boats described on the next ten pages are vessels that have seemed to me interesting in conception, proven in quality, and suggestive (at least) of the variety available in small cruising yachts today. Not one of them is perfect, because in this area there is no perfection; two are quite generalized in their appeal; the other three are somewhat more specialized. Each is the product of a great deal of thought.

Cape Dory 27

Designer: Carl Alberg
Builder: Cape Dory Yachts
160 Middleboro Avenue
East Taunton, Mass. 02718

LOA . . . 27'1"
LWL . . . 20'0"
Beam . . . 8'6"
Draft . . . 4'0"
Displacement . . . 7,500 lb.
Ballast . . . 3,000 lb.
Sail Area . . . 365 sq. ft.

If you like a traditional, no-nonsense look in an auxiliary sailing yacht, chances are that you'll respond to Carl Alberg's designs, which not only have that air but also share a strong family resemblance, from his early classic, the 28'6" Triton, to the Cape Dory 33, his latest design. The 27 is very much in the Alberg mainstream—full keel (of course), narrow by contemporary design standards, flat sheer, rather heavy for her size, and moderate in all other respects. She is a very clean-looking boat, both above and below, something that grows naturally out of Alberg's design and Cape Dory's engineering. There are no decorative excrescences, and if one had to come up with a one-word description, it might well be *sound*.

On deck, the 27 illustrates the conventional masthead sloop which was universal a few years back, but which has been replaced by three-quarter or seven-eighths rig in many small racing yachts and not a few cruisers. The aspect ratio—not quite 3:1 for the mainsail—is greater than it used to be in cruising yachts, but still not startling. The headsail sheeting is set up so that the working jib leads to blocks on a short track on the deckhouse, inside the shrouds, while the genoa track is outside, on the toerail, back toward the forward end of the cockpit. One small peculiarity arising from these locations is that the jib sheet will lead from its own block, back through the genoa block, and thence to the coaming-mounted sheet winch. The mainsheet is at the aft end of the cockpit, on a thwartships track, which is perhaps not the most effective arrangement mechanically, but which preserves a maximum of cockpit space, and that may well be the correct decision aboard a cruising yacht.

Below decks, the 27 is, because of her relatively narrow beam, rather small, but she will accommodate four easily, and a filler in the forward cabin should create a pleasant double berth. The table folding down from the bulkhead is undoubtedly the most sensible dining arrangement for a boat this size. The galley, while not large, is satisfactory for a small cruiser, although the occupant of the portside main cabin berth had better have feet of no more than average length, since they will be under the shelf that accommodates the two-burner alcohol stove. The decor generally is a nice combination of wood trim—for decks, bulkheads, and locker fronts—and well-finished white gelcoat to give an impression of roominess. A point worth noting is that ventilation, from hatches fore and aft as well as six opening ports, is exceptionally good. Power, as in all the Cape Dorys except the smallest, is a small diesel.

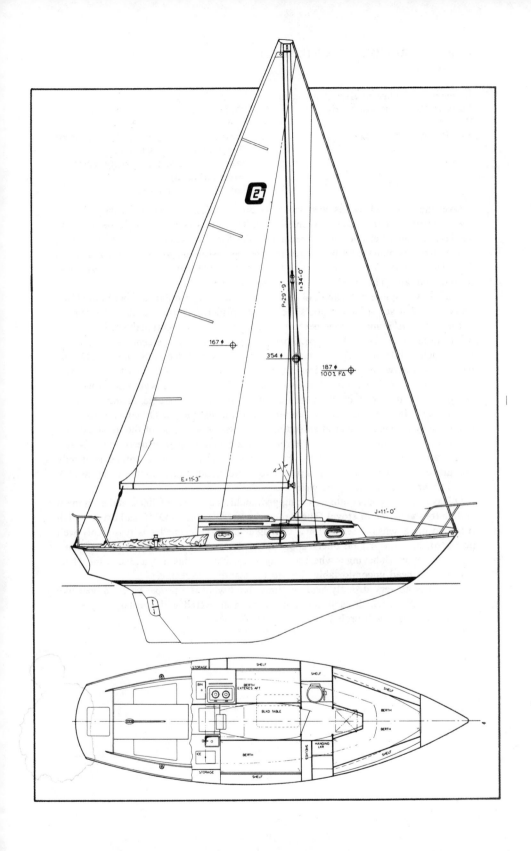

O'Day 28

Designer: C. Raymond Hunt Associates
Builder: Bangor Punta Marine
P.O. Box 991
Fall River, Mass. 02722

LOA . . . 28'3"
LWL . . . 22'11"
Beam . . . 10'3"
Draft . . . 4'6" (keel); 3'3" (centerboard)
Displacement . . . 7,300 lb.
Ballast . . . 2,350 lb. (keel); 2,725 lb. (centerboard)
Sail Area . . . 369.9 sq. ft.

Over the years, O'Day has been one of the great successes—and one of the relatively few survivors—in the popular yacht field. O'Day cruisers have always been roomy vessels that sailed well and that offered good value for their reasonable prices. The Hunt design firm has managed a family resemblance as distinctive as that of Carl Alberg's Cape Dorys, and if you are pleased by the look of one O'Day, you are probably going to like them all. (The reverse, of course, also applies.)

The LOA, displacement, and sail area of the 28 are very similar to those of the Cape Dory, but what very different boats they are. Consider, for example, the relative sizes of the two boats' mains and 100 percent foretriangles (the conventional way of measuring headsail potential). The Cape Dory's main is about 90 percent as large as its foretriangle, while the O'Day's main is only 70 percent as large as its foretriangle. The disparity in the two boats' real sizes comes from the differences in their beams (nearly two feet) and waterline lengths (nearly three feet). The 28's great beam has allowed her designers to put a berth on the port side that converts to a double, facing the single to starboard. In addition, extra beam amidships means that the O'Day can place her entire galley to port, instead of spreading it across the after end of the main cabin— and that, in turn, means that there is room for a generous quarter berth to starboard. Under way, the O'Day's extra floor space is not going to be an advantage, as it only provides extra room for things and people to rocket about, but at anchor or in the slip, the extra area will probably be welcome.

O'Day offers its boats quite well equipped, including sheets, lifelines, and even main and jib (but not head or stove). The standard powerplant is an OMC sail drive, which seems to me a sensible set-up for a boat like this—the propeller is reasonably well protected, and the engine offers good power for its size. One other option that's probably not worth having is wheel steering; in most boats this size, a man at the wheel will find his head uncomfortably close to the standing backstay.

If one has no very strongly held opinions about what is a proper yacht, a boat like the O'Day 28, in which each question has been answered with the largest possible audience in mind, will probably be quite satisfactory.

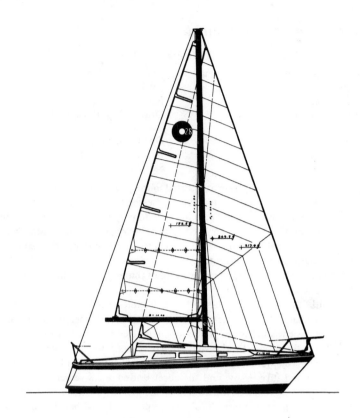

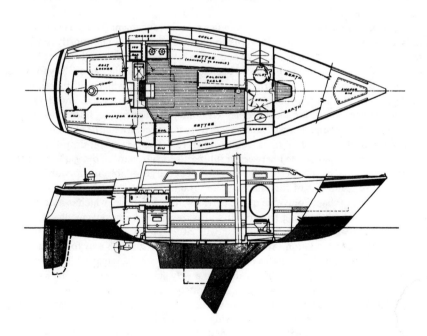

S2 9.2C Center Cockpit

Designer: Arthur Edmunds and S2 De-
    sign Group
Builder: S2 Yachts, Inc.
725 East 40th Street
Holland, Mich. 49423

LOA . . . 29′11″
LWL . . . 25′0″
Beam . . . 10′3″
Draft . . . 3′11″ (shoal keel); 4′11″ (deep
    keel)
Displacement . . . 9,800 lb.
Ballast . . . 4,000 lb.
Sail Area . . . 468 sq. ft.

The Slikkers family, who operate S2, started in the powerboat business, so they come to sailing yachts without a lot of the hangups possessed by people who have always been sailors. It took, let us admit, a good deal of nerve to put an unusual vessel like this one into production, and she will look very peculiar to a lot of people. (Interestingly enough, S2 also makes a "normal" version, the 9.2A, on the same hull, but the center-cockpit model is considerably more successful.) The 9.2C is not going to win any beauty contests, but she has, for the unprejudiced, a lot of things going for her, some apparent, some not so apparent.

To begin with, like all the S2s this one is well built, even overbuilt. The hardware is uniformly excellent and, as the S2 staff have become accustomed to the requirements of sailboats, equipment and fittings are better engineered than they were in some of the early S2s. The hull and rig, by the well-known cruising yacht designer Arthur Edmunds, are quite normal for an up-to-date boat. The fin keel and spade rudder will allow her to track well and turn easily, and the sheet leads are convenient for the crew in her cockpit. (A turning block at the aft end of the genoa track may be necessary with some jibs, to make a proper approach to the cockpit winch.) About the only drawback to the center cockpit is the increased difficulty of seeing under the foot of the genoa, when sailing close-hauled, but alertness at the helm and a window in the luff of the sail should minimize the problem.

The 9.2C's real novelty is, of course, in her cabin arrangement (which is not particularly unusual in larger boats). It seems to me at once original and mostly workable, providing exceptional privacy for two couples in a relatively small yacht. The aft cabin has a thwartships double berth and two big hanging lockers; in the passageway forward, on the port side, is a sizable surface, over the 15-hp. diesel, which will function adequately as a chart table, although there's not much clearance above it, and the setting may be claustrophobic for some people. The galley is an adequate, linear model, well to one side of the companionway, and across from it is a remarkable head compartment, with sink, toilet, and—of all things—a sit-down tub. The permanent drop-leaf table is reasonably large, and is sited between a full berth to starboard and a 5′4″ settee that could serve as a child's berth, if necessary. The large double up forward can be separated from the rest of the saloon by a curtain.

On passage, probably only one of the berths will be habitable, which is a drawback; the location of both hanging lockers aft will occasionally be inconvenient—it means, for instance, that wet foul-weather gear will either be tossed in the tub or tracked through the accommodation. And there are no sail lockers, which may force the choice of a roller-furling jib. But with this much said, the 9.2C is still a remarkable accomplishment, a boat that is a genuine home afloat in a very small size, and one that sails well enough, too. (Unless one's cruising is desperately constricted by shallow water, the deep-draft keel would be advisable, in view of the boat's considerable windage.) People who have experienced a good deal of living-aboard cruising, and who know that this aspect is what they like best, may well find the 9.2C a first-rate compromise.

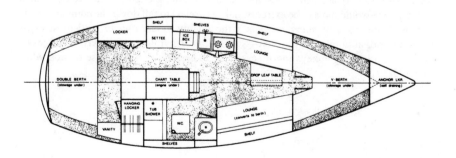

Mystic 30

Designer/Builder: Legnos Boat Building Company, Inc.
973 North Road
Route 117
Groton, Conn. 06340

LOA . . . 33'8"
LOD . . . 30'0"
LWL . . . 25'4"
Beam . . . 10'3"
Draft . . . 4'4"
Displacement . . . 9,500 lb.
Ballast . . . 3,000 lb.
Sail Area . . . 526 sq. ft.

The Mystic 30 is a development of an earlier Legnos design, which was known as the Mystic 10-3. That vessel was very similar to the 30, except for a snubbed bow and much longer bowsprit. Drawing out the bow about three feet has made a much shorter (and safer) bowsprit possible, with the same headsail arrangement. The Mystic 30 is, on deck at least, a conscious evocation of the past, and a very handsome one. Her silhouette calls to mind the large cruising catboats of yesterday, although her hull shape and underbody are very different. The rig is a more or less modern masthead cutter, of rather low aspect ratio. I am not really crazy about self-tending staysails on booms, as it seems to me that the hardware takes up a great deal of the foredeck, but this is an area in which opinions are strongly divided, and I certainly don't insist on mine. The high-clewed jib cries out for roller-furling—even with a pulpit to the end of the bowsprit, that's not a very comfortable place to work.

Below decks, the 30 is largely conventional in arrangement, but with a couple of remarkable touches. The small forward cabin has a skylight hatch and two ports to make it cheerful, as well as a couple of small hanging lockers. Sliding doors separate it from the main cabin, which has berths port and starboard, with lockers behind their backs. The decor generally is less woody than a lot of boats—white-painted surfaces, for the most part, with wood trim strips to set them off, and a wood deck and drop-leaf table. The galley is completely to port, and above the stove there is a pass-through port to the cockpit, big enough to handle a dinner plate. The head compartment is most unusual. Its door is the entire companionway ladder (mounted on a solid backing), which swings into the cabin. It looks a bit odd on a plan, but it works, and it utilizes to the fullest a part of the boat that is frequently slighted. From the head compartment a second door opens into the engine room—which is a real room on the 30, with a pair of seats, one each side of the small diesel, to make maintenance and repair work easier. My first reaction on seeing the 30's head compartment arrangement was that it made some extraordinary accidents possible, but after second thought, I came to the conclusion that one would have to be extraordinarily careless to fall down the companionway.

The Mystic 30 is in many respects a thoroughly modern yacht, and most of the suggestions of antiquity are just that—suggestions. Anything more overt would probably wind up looking hokey, and it seems to me her builders were wise to stop where they did.

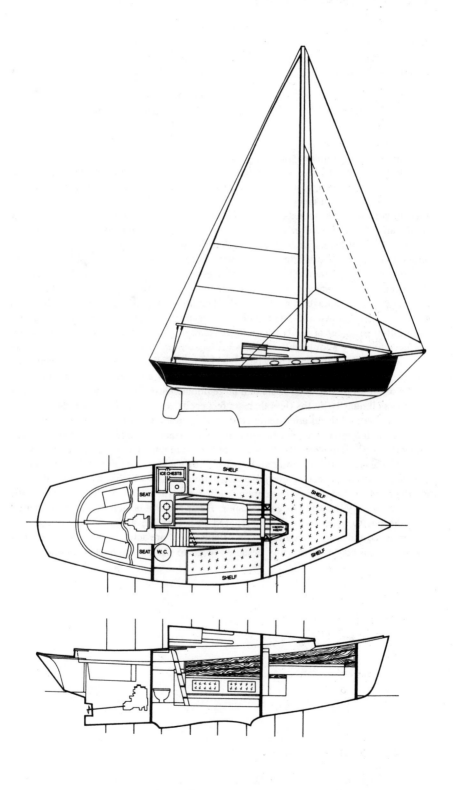

Stone Horse

Designer: S.S. Crocker
Builder: Edey & Duff
Mattapoisett, Mass. 02739

LOA . . . 28'3"
LOD . . . 23'4"
LWL . . . 18'4"
Beam . . . 7'1"
Draft . . . 3'7"
Displacement . . . 4,490 lb.
Ballast . . . 2,000 lb.
Sail Area . . . 339 sq. ft.

If the Mystic 30 aims at suggesting the past, the Stone Horse aims at replicating it
—with improvements. She was designed by the late S.S. Crocker, for wood construction, over forty years ago, and her revived version is true to all the good things in the
original. As for appearance, she is unabashedly a raised-deck boat, and you either like
them or you don't. The raised deck does permit an extraordinary amount of space below
decks, and if you believe in your heart that form follows function, you can make a
strong case for it here. The builders feel that the Stone Horse can be accurately called
either a sloop with two headsails or a cutter, but whatever you call it, there's more to
her than is first apparent. All the control lines—there are nine of them—lead back to
the cockpit, so that one can make, trim, or lower sail without going on the foredeck,
a considerable advantage in a small boat. (The jib is equipped with roller-furling and
the staysail has a downhaul.) The cockpit is exceptionally large, since its coamings are
right out at the sides of the boat, but because the footwell is fairly small, you should
not have to worry unduly about being swamped. Stone Horse is, of course, a full-keel
boat, with a large rudder. She may be driven by a small diesel, an outboard on a bracket
(which would, I think, be especially unsightly on such a vessel), or by sail alone.

The cabin arrangement consists of a large double berth forward, with a head under
it, two small quarter berths (less than six feet each), and a galley unit amidships. Two
seats, one over the head and one to starboard, give Stone Horse something that very
few boats under forty feet have got—a really comfortable place to sit and read. Stowage
under the berths is in fiber glass bins, so gear should remain dry, almost no matter what.
Stone Horse is a beautifully built and finished little yacht, to a standard that hasn't been
seen in many years, except in custom construction. Her very high price and resale value
are the result of that care and attention. Unlike, say, the O'Day or the Cape Dory, she
is a boat for only the knowledgeable sailor. He or she will be able to get out of her all
that she has to give, and will be prepared to accept the apparent compromises in
performance and accommodation—compromises that are actually recognitions of reality on a small boat that is really designed to go to sea and take what comes.

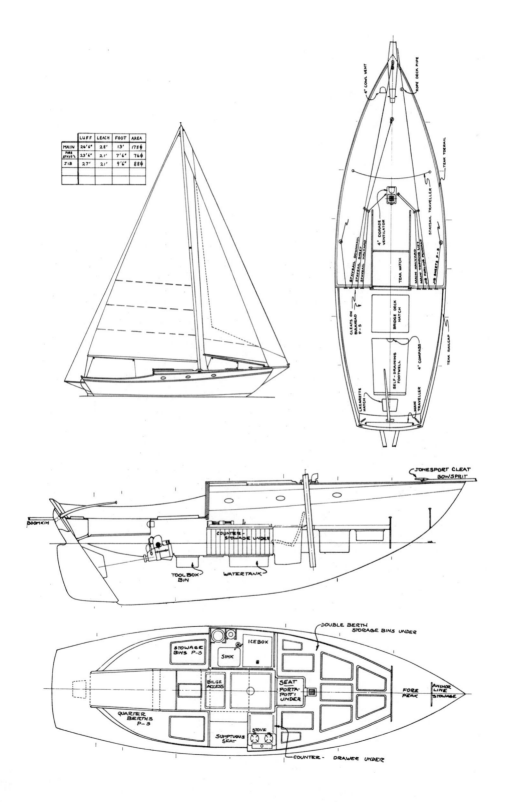

	LUFF	LEACH	FOOT	AREA
MAIN	26'6"	28'	13'	175½
FORE STAYS'L	23'6"	21'	7'6"	76½
JIB	27'	21'	9'6"	88¼

4" COWL VENT

ROPE DECK PIPE

TEAK TOERAIL

4" DORADE VENTILATOR

STAYSAIL TRAVELLER

STAYSAIL DOWNHAUL
STAYSAIL SHEET
STAYSAIL HALYARD

MAIN HALYARD
JIB TOPPING LIFT
JIB HALYARD
JIB SHEET P-S

TEAK HATCH

CLEATS ON BULKHEAD P-S

BRIDGE DECK HATCH

4" COMPASS

LAZARETTE HATCH

SELF-DRAINING FOOTWELL

MAIN TRAVELLER

TEAK RAILCAP

JONESPORT CLEAT
BOWSPRIT

BOOMKIN

COUNTER STOWAGE UNDER

TOOL BOX BIN

WATERTANK

DOUBLE BERTH
STORAGE BINS UNDER

STOWAGE BINS P-S

ICEBOX

SINK

BILGE ACCESS

SEAT PORTA POTTI UNDER

FORE PEAK

ANCHOR LINE STOWAGE

QUARTER BERTHS P-S

SUMPTUOUS SEAT

STOVE

COUNTER - DRAWER UNDER

CRUISING
IN A
NUTSHELL

I

~~~~~~~~~~~~~~

Preparing to Cruise

Cruising requires preparation, and while the duration of the voyage often determines the amount of planning, this isn't necessarily the case. A well-found cruising yacht, maintained in general readiness, will need only itinerary planning and provisioning for a weekend voyage; a racer that cruises only occasionally, however, may require the addition of considerable gear to make her livable.

Because so many variables may be involved, I've chosen to begin this discussion of preparing for cruising at the very beginning—getting to know a boat that's new to you, if not factory-new. Having checked the boat's major systems, broken in the engine and the instruments, and tuned the rig, the crew can then properly address cruise planning per se. And having polished your craft and set the boat up for cruising, it's then easy to plan the particular voyages.

Getting used to the boat

Treating your new boat like a toy unwrapped on Christmas morning seems an almost irresistible temptation to many Americans, including me. That a boat is nearly always delivered late only heightens the urge to have at her without any sort of coherent introduction to the vessel's hardware or tuning. My own suspicion, based on a hard backward look at the damage I've done to a succession of new and second-hand boats, suggests that the brand-new owner should arrive aboard wearing a pair of thumbless mittens, which he or she is forbidden to remove for at least a week.

Seriously, even the smallest cruiser is or ought to be the product of a great deal of careful design and engineering, and not all of it is apparent at first glance, even to an expert. Moreover, even though a marina or dealer may have billed you for something called make-ready, the chances are about one in three that the boat has some defect needing repair, adjustment, or correction, and you're likely only to aggravate any incipient problem by casually setting sail and heading out for a joy ride. Although it's less than welcome advice, my strong suggestion is that you set up a careful, organized get-acquainted program for your new—or second-hand—cruiser, followed by an equally thoughtful breaking-in curriculum. By doing so, you're far more likely to end your first month or so with a happy understanding of the boat and a good start on getting the most and best she has to give.

The first step in getting to know a boat is to be sure you've received everything you're entitled to. That means being on the scene when the boat's delivered, or when ownership changes hands, with a complete copy of the specification and/or order form in hand. Before you accept delivery, make sure you have the owner's manual and parts list for the boat herself, if the builder provides this kind of paperwork, and for the engine, head, stove, and every piece of electronic gear aboard. In their rush, boatyard workers who think they're familiar with the boats they service find manuals and paperwork just so much hindrance to their fitting-out operations, and throw them away right along with the cartons and wrapping paper. It can cost you weeks of correspondence later on to get a manual to replace the one that came with the boat. (If your purchase is second-hand, check with the seller or his agent as to which manuals and parts lists he has and which he's lost; as soon as the survey is completed, write the individual manufacturers for the missing literature.)

That's the easy part. Assuming your boat is supposed to be delivered in something approaching sailaway condition, you must now work out by observation what's there and what's not. Here are some for-instances: You have the anchor, the chain, and the rode; but do you have two shackles of the correct size to fit between anchor and chain and chain and rode? The mainsail is present and accounted for; but do you have shackles (and spares) of the correct size for halyard, tack, and clew? Are the winch handles the ones specified in the order form? If yours is a small inboard engine, does it have a hand crank? (It may all too often have a crank, while the engine installation makes it impossible to use that tool.) You may also find, often in a galley drawer, small metal parts of unknown function. Although it's entirely possible they have no use whatever, make certain that this is the case, and don't start off with assumptions either way. With an imported boat, it's more than likely that there will be little packages tucked away here and there. These probably belong to the importer, and represent informal catch-up shipments from his builder: One boat I bought from England arrived with a complete suit of working sails and tried my honesty nearly to its limit. Fortunately for my peace of mind, I'd already paid for and received a better suit of American-made sails, so I returned the extra main and jib.

As soon as you have the chance, go over the boat from stem to stern, keel to truck, and check every fitting, every switch. Make a defect list and have the problem items fixed before you even stir from the pier. If a fitting, especially a piece of sail-trim hardware, looks wrong, it probably is: The average yard worker is seldom disposed to walk back to the shop and get the right size clevis pin when the one in his pocket is nearly correct.

All this may sound unduly cynical, but it shouldn't. Half the time the mistakes will be in your favor, and most of them are the result of the breakneck speed with which the majority of boats are commissioned, often by personnel who have immense good will and little or no knowledge of the particular craft. If your yacht arrives in the spring, the harried marina owner is probably trying to get his regular customers' vessels launched, often in the teeth of contradictory, last-minute work orders, and his small band of skilled employees has been temporarily augmented (if he's lucky) by a handful of teen-agers and other relatives. Be patient but firm, and if your spirit can stand it, order the boat for delivery well before the fitting-out season in your area, or well after.

Upon the boat's arrival, the first thing you should compile is a list of every loose or detachable item aboard, with model and serial numbers if any, and sizes where applicable. Sit down with this list and check off those items that are consumable (like spark plugs or cotter pins) or likely to be lost (like clevis pins and winch handles). Before any of them disappears, breaks, or wears out, get spares and stow them in your spare-parts bag.

Next, gather up all the tools in the house and put them on the kitchen table. Discard the spares and broken ones and put the rest in a box. Take them down to the boat and check every fitting that might have to be unscrewed, tightened with a wrench, or otherwise adjusted, and ensure that you have a tool of the right size—and preferably rustproof—to deal with it. Check these tools against a master list of desirable tools (see Appendix 1), and create your tool kit then and there. At this stage, if there's a possibility that a given tool might be useful, hold on to it until you're sure one way or the other. Do not settle for tools that almost fit—a particular problem when more and more engines are built with metric nuts and collar fittings. Finally, assemble a complete set of lubricants, such as WD-40, oil, and grease.

Before you put anything on the boat, give the craft a complete cleaning from one end to the other, being especially careful to get at all the most difficult corners. If the interior and bilges are dry, start with a shop vacuum and when you've extracted everything you can reach, try to blast out the unreachable corners with a hose. By doing this you may (although I don't guarantee it) be able to eliminate one of boat ownership's darkest moments, the first time water infiltrates the bilge corners with the vessel well-heeled and brings down a torrent of scraps, shavings, metal filings, and fiber glass dust.

Rigging and tuning

With this preliminary work out of the way, and all the parts present and in working order, you're ready to rig and tune the boat. If there are instruc-

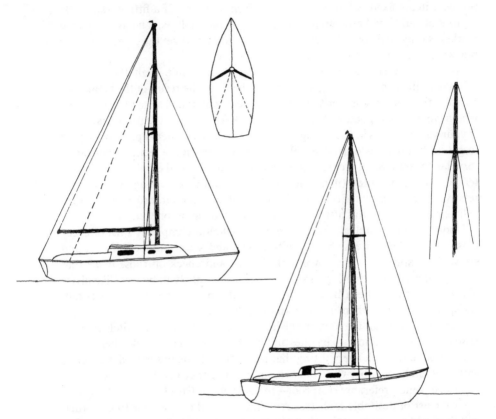

The normal standing rigging for small cruising yachts. The sloop at right has a mast-head forestay and backstay, paired upper shrouds, and paired forward and after lower shrouds (which run from the base of the spreaders to the chainplates on deck). Some smaller masthead-rig sloops have only a single pair of lower shrouds, leading from the spreader bases to the same chainplates as hold the upper shrouds, but forward and after lowers are a more secure and seamanlike arrangement. At left, the three-quarter (or seven-eighths, or five-sixths) rig, frequently seen on racer-cruisers. The backstay is often quickly adjustable at deck level, allowing the skipper to bow or straighten the mast. For serious cruising, running backstays (represented by dotted lines) are a good addi-tion, as the swept-back upper shrouds afford only limited support for the forestay.

tions, follow them, and if not, work slowly and use common sense. It cannot hurt to consult other skippers owning the same kind of boat. Nearly every type of stock cruising yacht starts off as a standard version and is then altered bit by bit to suit her successive owners' prejudices. Often the original is best, but equally often an imaginative or experienced owner will make changes that improve the vessel. Sometimes these changes or additions—a different main-sheet block, an unusual site for the steering compass—will be so idiosyncratic that only the perpetrator can get along with them, but it pays to look on them with an open mind.

In traditional cruisers with masthead sailplans, the primary objective of the initial rig tuning is to get the mast or masts straight in the boat and maintain that straightness, as much as possible, on the main headings—beat, reach, and run. Many of today's boats with fractional rigs can benefit from deliberate spar bending under certain conditions, but this bending is fore-and-aft, not athwartships, and the mast, to begin with, should be straight before sailing stresses are applied.

Different schools of thought exist as to the best way to approach initial tuning of a masthead rig; all I can say of my version is that it seems to work, and at least it's easy to remember. The whole system is based on having standing rigging progressively more taut (at rest) the higher on the mast it goes. Thus, the lower shrouds, backstay, and inner forestay can begin by being just hand-taut—no visible sag in the wire, but easily deflected by hand pressure. Upper shrouds and masthead forestay are slack. Make sure that the mast foot is square in its step, whether on the keel or in a socket on the cabin top. If the spar is keel-stepped, you should use reasonably hard but flexible wedges to hold it in place. Some people use wood, but most experts prefer hard rubber for this job. With the mast straight, no load, and only minimal support from the standing rigging, insert the wedges at the partners—the reinforced area where the mast goes through the deck—and drive them tight enough to stay put when the mast is stressed one way or another. To check that the mast is, at this stage, straight in the boat, lead a masthead halyard—preferably a wire one—down so that its end fitting just touches the deck at the main chainplates on one side, without strain. Now take it across to the corresponding chainplate on the other side. If the distance is exactly the same, the spar should be straight, but sight up the groove or track on the after side of the spar to make sure. If necessary, take up on one set of lowers or the other until the spar is truly straight, then carefully tighten the uppers and masthead forestay just enough to remove the slack, checking again to make sure the mast is perpendicular.

With upper and lower rigging hand-taut and the mast initially straight in the boat, check the leads of the rigging right down through the chainplates: The shrouds and stays should run in straight lines from the tangs on the mast through the turnbuckles at the lower ends of the wires, the toggles that help to line them up with the chainplates, and the chainplates themselves. The key point, if there can be said to be a single one, is the chainplate: It is a nonflexible element, and it's almost impossible for a builder to install it at the factory so that it will have a precisely linear alignment with the stay or shroud. The toggle takes care of this problem and allows for multiple angles of approach to the chainplate, according to the requirements of individual tuning. Your rig should have toggles for each turnbuckle—either separate or built-in—including those connected to the fore- and backstays, which might seem not to need them. But the forestay especially will have a pronounced sideways deflection with the boat hard on the wind in a breeze, and it will need the flexibility conferred by a toggle in order to take strain off the turnbuckle and tack fitting.

The designer of your boat may specify a degree of rake normal for the mast.

It will be expressed in the sail plan as inches or degrees of deflection aft at the masthead. The former is easy to measure, with the aid of a weighted main halyard dropped to a point on deck. Establishing the latter will require some plane geometry—ask your high-school son or daughter about right triangles; he or she will be flabbergasted to find that such things occur in real life. Obviously, the mast should be raked, if at all, after it is wedged. Now begin taking up on the upper shroud turnbuckles—a few turns on each, working first on one side, then on the other, and sighting up the mainsail track or luff groove after each complete cycle of turns. Remember that the rigging is a system and that each change will trigger a corresponding change in the element matching the one you have just tweaked. The upper shrouds should be taut, although this resists definition, especially since the term is relative to boat size as well as individual strength. If in doubt, do not tighten too much at this stage. The masthead forestay and backstay should be approximately as taut as the upper shrouds, but in tightening them be sure to preserve any mast rake you may already have injected.

Now pin all the turnbuckles, as otherwise they may back off under way, but open the cotter pins only just enough to hold them in place. It hardly needs saying that the turnbuckle-to-wire and turnbuckle-to-toggle clevis pins should now be cottered and taped—no further adjustment should be needed here, if the rigging is the proper size. (If, by the way, the shrouds and stays don't appear to be quite the correct length, try swapping the uppers, forestay, and backstay. In many cases, there is not much to choose in length among these four elements, and it's not unknown for the builder to attach them incorrectly. With the initial tuning done, the turnbuckles should have no more than half the length adjustment wound out of them.)

Tuning under way

Take the boat out and make sail, preferably on a day of reasonably brisk winds for your area. Hoist the main and largest jib the boat can handle for the weather (use other, similar-size boats as yardsticks), in a place where you will have room to beat, reach, and run for at least ten minutes per leg. You'll need a crew big enough in muscle and numbers to handle the sails while you attend to the adjusting. Remind the sheet tender that, with the turnbuckles untaped, he or she must be very careful in tacking or jibing, to avoid snags and consequent rips.

Begin close-hauled on either tack, using a masthead wind vane and shroud telltales as gauges. Don't worry too much about sail trim at this point, although your crew should avoid obvious, gross errors in sail shape or trim angle. With the boat settled down on a beat, sight up the mast to check alignment. Chances are that the leeward upper shroud will be visibly slack, the masthead arced off to leeward, and the headstay sagging terribly. Don't be downhearted. Take up on the windward upper until the mast is straight athwartships. If the whole spar bends to leeward, then both the uppers and lowers may be at fault. Don't try to correct everything at once, and do keep a written record of which shroud you've adjusted and how many turns it took.

Now come about and check athwartships trim on the other tack. If the masthead is hooked to windward, the windward lower shroud is probably too slack. It will probably require several tacks to get the same athwartships alignment on both tacks. When you've accomplished that, turn to the fore-and-aft tuning. The most common and visible problem here is a sagging forestay, which can have an effect out of all proportion to the amount of sag. Bear in mind that all forestays sag—they must, unless the rig is infinitely strong. The idea is to keep the degree of sag within decent limits. If the forestay sags badly and the mast is straight, then the problem is simple. Head up, drop the headsail, and take up on the forestay turnbuckle. Now make sail and try again. But if the forestay sags and there is a perceptible hook of the masthead toward the bow, chances are that the backstay needs attention. If the masthead hooks backward from the spreaders, the forward lowers may be too taut, but if the hook is at the top of the spar only, you may have created the problem by socking down on the backstay before tightening the forestay, and you will have to ease both of them and begin again.

Fractional rig

Boats with fractional rigs—that is, ones whose jibstays reach only seven-eighths or three-quarters of the way up the mast—are sometimes designed for deliberate mast bending, as a means of flattening and thus depowering the mainsail, which can be a desirable tactic in certain conditions. Not all fractional rigs, however, are designed for mast bending, and you may usually exempt any spar with jumper struts and stays—the spreaderlike arrangement between the top of the jibstay and the masthead.

Tuning the modern bendy rig calls for considerable tension on all the stays and shrouds except the adjustable backstay when at rest or off the wind. Although the details of tuning vary with the particular boat, here are some general guidelines.

Begin with the mast vertical in the boat, its heel flat on the step. If a degree of rake is called for, adjust the headstay turnbuckle until the proper amount of rake aft is present. (Rake, by the way, is the inclination, usually aft, of the straight spar, as opposed to pre-bend (see below), which is the amount of bend in the tuned spar at rest.) Uppers and lowers and fore- and backstay should all be attached, and the shroud turnbuckles taken up by hand to eliminate slack. Check to see that the spar is centered in the boat, using the main halyard in the fashion described earlier.

Now adjust the lower shroud turnbuckles as tightly as you can by hand, checking frequently to make sure the mast does not arc off to port or starboard. This done, alternately tighten the port and starboard uppers, using a wrench and spike, until you have the proper amount of pre-bend, which is usually expressed as the distance abaft the mast foot that the free-falling halyard's end will strike the deck.

Continue to tighten the lower shrouds, exercising care to keep the mast in column athwartships, until they are quite taut, and tighten the backstay turn-buckle hand-tight. You should now have the proper amount of rake and pre-bend, which will tend to look exaggerated when sighting up the spar. Take the boat out under sail, using the same testing techniques as for the masthead rig, and try her on several points of sail. If the wind is brisk, take up on the adjustable backstay to flatten the mainsail, and note that the forestay will necessarily sag off slightly. If there is too much sag in the forestay with the mast bent, you may have to resort to a cunningham in the jib luff, but if there is a lot of forestay sag without tension on the backstay, try taking up the forestay and the lower shrouds alternately, in such a way as to maintain the amount of rake and pre-bend already in the spar.

Because the bendy rig lives under considerable tension, and because many of the modern, fast boats that employ it are also very lightly built, you run some danger of distorting the hull if you overtension the rig. This will most frequently be apparent in the refusal of midships head or locker doors to close or open, and it means you've overdone.

With the mast initially set up, check the sails for approximate trim: They should have no gross wrinkles at the corners or along the foot of the main, no scalloping along the jib luff. It should be possible to pull luff, leech, and foot taut without coming to the end of the spar. It's not unknown for sails to be the wrong size, especially if you've received inexpensive "cruising" sails as part of the boat's option package. By the same token, if you have an older boat, the sails may well be stretched or blown by age or misuse. (We will deal with shaping the sails under way a bit later.)

The next move—and it will probably take the better part of a day—is to calibrate the boat's speedometer and tachometer, if you have either or both. This is best accomplished under power on a calm day, to eliminate unwanted variables. For organization's sake I've dealt with both operations in the next section, under engine break-in.

Crew assignments

You should now have a reasonably good idea of what's involved in tacking and jibing the boat, in getting set up for a sail, and in tidying up afterwards. It will be a good idea, while the various tasks are clear in everyone's mind, to sit down with your regular crew and work out assignments both for maneuvering and for housework. Since you will have been doing the tuning, it may be advisable to have another person in charge of taking notes about the various motions and tasks involved in maneuvering. Let me offer one opinion about crew assignments, though. It seems to me that within each person's physical and intellectual limits the crew of a small cruiser ought ideally to be interchangeable. It encourages development of better habits, especially in beginners, if each crew member has a chance to handle each of the jobs aboard and appreciates more clearly what that position's regular occupant has to do. Revolving tasks also makes better-rounded sailors, and in a moment of real stress it's a tremendous advantage to be able to turn to any of the regular crew and assign them a job, confident that they can handle it.

At the same time, it's only realistic to acknowledge that some people are going to be better at certain jobs than will others: On a small overnighter, the best foredeck person may well be a teen-age girl—strong, light, and well-coordinated, she is likely to have the most suitable physique for the task. The most satisfactory helmsman will most likely be that person who has the best combination of concentration and eye-hand coordination.

By jobs, what are we talking about? You will have to make your own list, but here's a sample that will apply to a fair number of midrange cruisers. It deals with a tacking maneuver for a crew of three. We will call them *A*, *B*, and *C*.

Tacking

A on the helm; *B* at the sheet winch; *C* standing by the sheet winch on what will be the leeward side when the tack is accomplished. *A* handles the helm through the tack, keeps the mainsheet clear if necessary. *B* releases the old sheet and eases its run, then cranks for *C*, who takes in on the new sheet, makes the turns on the sheet winch, and tails.

As you can see, this is only a bare-bones description of what has to be done. It doesn't deal with how best to do it, a matter we'll get to in a bit. Of course, technique will be affected by the number of people available and by their skill levels, but in a small cruising yacht it's entirely possible to work up routines for crews ranging from a singlehander to half a dozen (and the latter setup is harder to do).

As a beginning list, maneuvers that require crew assignment might include: making sail; leaving slip or mooring; tacking; jibing; reefing; setting up spinnaker gear; raising spinnaker; jibing spinnaker; lowering spinnaker; lowering sail; docking; picking up a mooring. And that doesn't even include emergencies.

Both setting up and putting away a cruiser are jobs that tend to get done in a slapdash fashion, and for obvious reasons. At the same time, they are very important functions, and your safety depends on one, just as the condition and resale value of your boat depend on the other. The tendency in a small cruiser is for the skipper to do all the rigging and tidying, on the rational ground that he can do any part of either operation quicker and probably better than he can explain it. This has been my excuse for years, and it's a bad one. First off, the worker tends to go faster and faster, in time with the mental foot-tapping of the waiting crew, and the job doesn't get done better. Second, I'm convinced that it's best for all the crew to be involved with all aspects, fun and not-so-fun, of the boat's operation. Here is an area where it may pay to assign permanent jobs, according to the skills and temperaments of the people available.

Engine and instrument break-in

Engine break-in is something that's often slighted, yet it's as important to the long-term performance of the boat as was the breaking-in of cotton sails, in the days before artificial sail fabrics. With most powerplants, the break-in period is fairly short, and it can handily be combined with the moderately tedious job of calibrating the tachometer, speedo, and log. In most cases, breaking in the engine requires nothing more than an avoidance of full-throttle speeds or rapid changes of throttle, and perhaps in some outboards, a temporary, slightly higher oil-to-gasoline ratio.

This established, you can set out to calibrate your instruments, if you have any. First thing to locate, on your local charts, is a shoreline measured mile, if there's one available. If not, and if you have access to a pocket calculator (does anyone these days *not* have a calculator?), you can choose any pair of fixed aids to navigation at a convenient distance from each other and with a straight shot between them. It will make your work somewhat easier if the location is not swept by strong currents or unpredictable winds, and if you won't have to contend with heavy boat traffic.

Even if your boat is, in the salesman's appalling term, "pre-owned," it will be advisable to verify whatever speedo or tachometer tables the previous owner has given you. And it is not a bad idea to check your gauges against reality at least once a month during the sailing season, to see if overloading or bottom fouling is slowing you down badly.

For the owner of an inboard-powered yacht with a tachometer, establishing a table relating engine speed to boat speed is not difficult. The table that develops is, of course, not as accurate as the speedometer on a car, if only because it relates engine revolutions per minute (rpm) to boat speed through the water in a specific set of conditions. If you have the time and inclination, and especially if the tach is the only speed gauge you have, it will probably pay to work up a secondary table for engine rpm when there is a brisk wind and steep sea on the nose: The boat speed figures will be very different indeed.

Even if your boat has a speedo, it's a good idea to work up a tach table, as a cross-check. Marine instruments are notoriously temperamental, and the more independent sources of information you have, the more likely you are to know what's really happening.

Working up an approximate tach table is simplicity itself. Start by filling the boat's fuel tank right to the top: you might as well establish an approximate fuel consumption rate while you're under way. Locate your measured mile or range. If you're using a charted measured mile, you'll have a True course to convert to Magnetic; otherwise you'll have to plot the course yourself. (Needless to say, this operation will be easier if you have already compensated the yacht's compass, a process described in Chapter IV. If you've not adjusted the compass, and if it's grossly out of true, you'll have to employ a range whose opposite end is clearly visible when you begin your run, so you can hold a moderately straight line.)

Choose a day when the weather seems stable, and a time when the current, if any, will maintain its set and drift (speed and direction, respectively) during the entire operation—begin around the third hour of a six-hour cycle. The water tanks should be half-full, and the usual gear (or weights representing it) should be aboard. Lining up your course from well behind the first marker, establish your boat's engine rpm and speed through the water as you cross the start line. It may take a heavy boat with a small engine two hundred yards to get up to cruising speed, so allow plenty of space. For starters, choose what feels like a half- or three-quarter-throttle speed, on an even tachometer setting, say 2,000 rpm. Time the one-way run with a stopwatch, make a good, wide turn, pick up speed again, and retrace your course at the same speed.

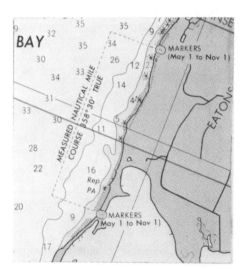

Measured mile: the shore marks are a pair of ranges, one at each end of the mile; the chart symbol gives the true course to steer when running the course one way, but for best accuracy, it should be run at the same rpm setting once in each direction and the speeds averaged. Some ranges, like this one, are seasonal; others are available all year.

Do the same for speeds at intervals of 100 rpm down to the kind of slow speed you'd use if you were picking your way homeward through a blinding rain or a thick fog (which is when you're most likely to need this table). In each case, make sure to run the course in both directions at the same speed, to cancel out any help from wind or current. When you have a complete table covering all the engine speeds (assuming you are not constrained by breaking-in considerations), head home and, on the way, top off your fuel tank, making a note of the total running time and calculating the amount of fuel consumed per hour. This is obviously not a precise figure, but it will give you a rough, average yardstick you can use for the time being.

To make your rpm table, average each pair of to-and-fro runs for time. Next, take a sheet of ordinary graph paper and mark off one axis for time and the other for rpm, as in the accompanying illustration. The dots indicating intersections of rpm and time will, when joined, make a curve that will suggest very clearly what is the boat's most economical speed—the shortest time for the lowest rpm. Unless your boat is very underpowered, the curve will be almost flat at the upper end of the tachometer scale, indicating that the boat has reached its effective hull speed, so that more power will just result in a bigger wake, more noise, and greater fuel consumption.

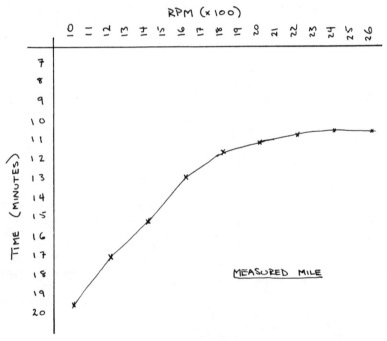

Sketch of speed curve showing speeds over a measured mile at various tachometer settings. It is clear that little or nothing is gained at engine speeds over about 2,000 rpm.

Now take your averaged times for the various runs and work out the actual speeds of the boat for different engine settings. The basic formula here is

$$\text{Speed in knots or mph} = \frac{60 \times \text{Distance in nautical or statute miles}}{\text{Time in minutes}}$$

(It should be obvious that if you employ distance in statute miles, your speed figure will be miles per hour, while if your distance is nautical miles, the result will be in knots, or nautical miles per hour.)

Thus, if you've used a measured mile, D will always equal 1, and you can work out speed by dividing 60 by the average course time in minutes. For instance, if you run the measured nautical mile in 10 min. 40 sec., that works out to:

$$\frac{60}{10.667} = 5.62 \text{ knots.}$$

(On most calculators, you must convert seconds to decimal parts of a minute by dividing the number of seconds by 60.)

If you use some fraction of a mile, the equation looks more difficult, but the simplest four-function calculator will devour it like popcorn. For instance, you measure the distance on the chart between the two aids to navigation that you've used as limits for your timed run, and come up with a distance of 1.15 nautical miles (we'll assume you're using a 1:20,000-scale harbor chart where this kind of precision is realistic). Your formula, for a run of 12 min. 32 sec., is thus

$$\frac{6 \times 1.15}{12.533} = 5.5 \text{ knots.}$$

Notice that as your boat approaches her hull speed—approximately 1.25 times the square root of the waterline length—the increases in speed per increase of 100 rpm become less and less. You can determine from the speed curve which you've already created an approximate rpm setting that should produce an even number of knots (or mph) in flat water. In moments of stress, it will assist your off-the-hip calculations if you don't have to deal with funny numbers like 5.62 knots.

Calibrating the speedometer and/or log involve somewhat different procedures, which will vary with the instrument. Most such devices are bench-calibrated before they leave the factory, and if you have a good installation in a proper area of the boat, with smooth waterflow over the transducer, the gauge should be reasonably close to the truth, even without calibration. As with the tachometer, the adjustment process normally requires timed runs over known distances, at steady speeds, after which the speed over the bottom is matched to the speedo's speed through the water. Follow the instrument manufacturer's instructions carefully, but don't expect that a speedo which registers to hundredths of a knot will actually be accurate to that kind of figure. If you can have speedometer readings correct to a tenth of a knot or even a quarter, you have every right to be satisfied.

As noted above, it will be a useful addition to your basic performance data (assuming your patience holds out) to compile a second time-speed curve and set of rpm settings for winds and seas on the nose. This information will make it easier to weigh the relative unpleasantnesses of beating home in a series of tacks or turning on the engine and bashing your way straight into it.

This procedure is all very well for the instrument-equipped yacht, but what about the outboard-powered cruiser or the boat with an inboard that has no tachometer (as more and more do not)? For the latter, my only answer is that a tach is not terribly costly nor difficult to install, and I would recommend the addition. The outboard skipper's problem is more difficult. He may, if he has a larger outboard, be able to install an auxiliary electronic tachometer. But chances are he will not have any gauges at all. And chances are it doesn't really matter: The standard outboard runs most efficiently only at speeds near the top end of its throttle scale and in fact often runs very badly at speeds below the "start" marking on the throttle, fouling plugs at a great rate. My recommendation here is to time and average runs at two speeds—full tilt and "start" —and settle for these readings. After you have some experience, you'll be able to tell by sound when the engine is running at or near full power, and you'll have a remarkably accurate appreciation, from the appearance of the wake, of how fast the boat is going.

One point to remember: Since the outboard's propeller is adjustable vertically and, to a certain extent, in the fore-and-aft dimension, it's very important that you ensure its complete immersion—the hull design alone will not necessarily do so. One outboard builder suggests that the cavitation plate—the horizontal fin just above the propeller, running all around the shaft—should be about two inches below the bottom of the transom for best performance, but this may not be possible. Do be alert to cavitation, whose symptoms are runaway engine acceleration coupled with loss of speed, often occurring in sharp turns. To oversimplify, cavitation simply means that your prop isn't getting a good bite of the water—you may be running too fast, or the wheel may not be adequately immersed. Outboards on small cruisers often cavitate when there's not enough weight aft—as when a heavy crew member goes forward to help in docking—and your crew assignments should reflect this fact.

Most skippers are too lazy to work out the exact fuel consumption of their engines at various speeds, and indeed in past years it really hasn't been necessary. Without fairly complex equipment, it's not possible to calculate fuel flow with real precision, and probably the most realistic program is to bring along a spare five-gallon container or two and work out the fuel figures by making one-hour runs at stated speeds, beginning with a topped-off tank and topping off again when the hour is up.

The average small diesel is not going to give you any great surprises in this area, except that you may find a fairly dramatic increase in fuel consumption, for little or no speed advantage, between running at three-quarters and at full throttle. British designer Ian Nicholson, in his *Boat Data Book* (see Bibliography), gives standard consumption rates of .37 pints of diesel per horsepower per hour, and .6 pints of gasoline per horsepower per hour. One must remember that a boat isn't normally using more than a fraction of its available horsepower to reach hull speed in flat water, so one approximate consumption figure related to speed and rpm can be meaningful to the cruising yacht that operates in areas where extended calms are common.

Improving basic skills

In cruising, the average sailor's tendency is to get the boat pointed in the right direction, more or less, trim the sails, and then just aim the vessel. As anyone who's ever raced is aware, skillful sailing doesn't work that way. The wind, which may seem to be from the same direction hour after hour, is in fact ever-variable, both in strength and direction. To get the most from a boat it's necessary to recognize that fact and sail her accordingly. This doesn't mean that the cruising skipper should emulate some of the Captain Blighs one finds on the race course, harassing their crews with endless sail changes. But I would venture that the sailor who sails his cruising yacht near her limits will have a lot more fun in the process, and when the weather gets difficult, as sooner or later it must, he and his crew will have far more soundly based confidence in themselves and their boat than will the crew who can only handle the basic maneuvers, and those haphazardly.

It is commonplace among cruising folk to speak scornfully of racers, and there's both reason and self-deception in that attitude. When it comes to general boating knowledge, or the ability to cope when shorthanded, many racers have become overspecialized. But it is also true that a racer learns routinely to handle his vessel in the maelstrom of a starting line, a place that any true cruiser finds terrifying. A good racer learns to sail the boat in the lightest of breezes, and he is—or ought to be—acutely aware of wind speed changes, because they often mean sail changes. Racers are also less likely to think of the boat's well-being, and the standard complaint about racing sailors is that they beat their boats unmercifully, a remark that's too often true.

While most cruising sailors go out on the water to escape from the kind of fevered competition that they imagine racing to be, it's also true that few cruising sailors can watch a boat of similar size pass them without trying—however covertly—to do something about it.

Personally, I have little time for the tactical, boat-against-boat aspect of racing, but I tip my hat to the sailing skills of many racers I know. And in no area of sailing, perhaps, is there more planning, thought, and work involved than in moving the boat to windward. This is reasonable, since all well-organized races involve a good dollop of windward work, and closed-course races may incorporate three close-hauled legs out of six legs all told. It is a commonplace of racing that one may lose a contest on the reaching or running leg, but one wins going to weather.

In those parts of the country where sailing is popular, light-air conditions are more common than heavy weather (with the exceptions of San Francisco and Buzzard's bays). For this reason, beating with full main and genoa is the standard of sailing for many skippers. In a masthead-forestay rig, the genoa is considerably larger than the main and exerts most of the drive going to weather. In a boat with the increasingly popular fractional rig, the situation is reversed. But in both cases, the skilled sailor makes use of the combination of sails.

The cruising yacht's genoa normally has an LP measurement of somewhere between 150 percent and 170 percent. This means that a line drawn from the sail's clew to intersect the luff at a 90-degree angle will be 150 percent to 170 percent as long as the boat's J measurement, the distance along the deck from the tack fitting to the base of the mast. In practical terms, this means that the genoa will overlap the mast by a healthy amount, and its clew, when sheeted home, will be nearly back to the cockpit.

As a rule, the genoa sheets through a lead block mounted either on a straight track that's bolted through the side deck between cabin and gunwale, or to a track that follows the gunwale's curve. In either case, the lead block can be shifted forward or aft, but seldom inboard or outboard except insofar as the track itself diverges from the centerline. The sail's shape, which conditions the type and amount of driving force it provides, is created by luff tension on the one hand and sheet lead on the other. Going to windward, most sailmakers agree, the genoa should form a smooth curve, with its maximum chord depth 35 to 40 percent abaft the luff.

What does that gobbledygook mean?

When one has a curved line of determinate length, a straight line joining the two ends of the curve is called the *chord*. The point of maximum chord depth is the point at which there's the greatest perpendicular distance between the chord line and the curve itself. A jib is designed by its sailmaker to have its greatest depth at a given point, in a given wind strength, for a particular halyard tension, and for a precise sheet lead angle off the clew. As you can imagine, the sailmaker has made a good many assumptions that you have to match in your trimming in order to arrive at the shape he had in mind. The chord he imagines is about halfway up the sail, looking down at its cross-sectional outline from directly above. On some jibs, to arrive at a better visual picture of the sail's curve, a sailmaker or skipper will attach a strip or strips of black tape from luff to leech, parallel with the foot.

To test your sail, you too may want to have such an indicator tape, but more useful sail-trimming tools will be a set of luff woolies. These can be real wool or strips of thin nylon, but they should be of a color that sharply contrasts with the sail, and should extend about six or eight inches on either side of it. (The easy way to install woolies is to pierce the sail—gently—with something like a knitting needle and then poke the wool through, knotting it closely on either side of the fabric.)

Three woolies should do the trick for your genoa, evenly spaced at a quarter, halfway and three-quarters of the distance up the luff, and between a foot and eighteen inches in from the edge, but not directly behind luff snaps. Many sailmakers provide a transparent window for the middle wooly, so you can see both parts of the pair even when the sun is behind you. In normal windward sailing, you employ the center wooly for trimming and use the other two to determine that the sheet lead is correct.

In average conditions—within the range for which the sail was designed—finding the proper sheet lead is partly trial and error. First raise the sail and sock down on the halyard until you get a slight tension line parallel to the luff, before the sail fills with wind. Now mentally divide evenly the angle formed by the intersection of foot and leech and lead the sheet as an extension of that imaginary line back to the lead block, which you have moved to accept it.

Head the boat off the wind till you're at approximately 45 degrees to the true wind and take in on the sheet, watching the luff woolies as you do so, until all three pairs of woolies stream straight back on either side of the sail. Now luff up slowly. If all three sets of woolies "break" at once, your lead is perfect, and that would be unusual in the extreme. It's far more likely that a lee-side wooly at the top or bottom of the sail will spin while the others stream: If it's the top wooly, then your sheet lead is too far aft; if the bottom wooly spins before the others, then the lead is too far forward. Look also for fluttering along the leech if the sheet lead is too far aft, or a loose foot if it's too far forward.

As a general rule, the shorter the sail's foot relative to its luff length, the farther forward the sheet lead should be, but as I say, only trial and error will establish the correct lead-block location, which should then be marked. Having done this, put the boat on the other tack and establish the best lead for the other side, which may not be quite the same as the first, although probably very close.

Assuming that you have carried out this exercise in average winds, you now have the proper leads for that wind strength. As the wind slackens, the draft tends to move forward, and this is countered in a headsail by easing the halyard slightly, which puts the draft back where it belongs. If your boat is equipped with a jib tack downhaul or cunningham, you would ease that as well, to even up the strain along the luff.

The opposite strategy is called for when the wind stiffens, and the maximum draft begins to go back toward the center of the sail: Take up on the halyard and cunningham to move the draft back forward. But if—as seems likely—your halyard is the only luff tension control you have, then hauling on it will raise the whole sail slightly (as easing it will lower the sail): The result, of course, is that the clew will come up (or down) and you may have to move the sheet lead aft (or forward) to preserve the proper trim.

The same procedure will be required for each headsail in the boat's inventory. If it's at all possible, try to set each sail in the wind range for which it was designed, as otherwise you may never be sure of what the proper trimming angle will be. This advice, while easy to give, may be a bit hard to follow, especially when it comes to storm headsails. Unfortunately, these little-considered sails are often bought and stowed, never having been set at all, until on some dreadful day they're trotted out and expected to set perfectly.

In any case, having fitted the genoas and working jib with woolies, and having worked out the proper trim points, do spend some time, even if the wind is inadequate, with the storm jib. Woolies are not so important here, as they will probably disappear fairly quickly in the conditions for which the sail was designed, but they are helpful in establishing the initial trim points. When setting up a storm jib, or any jib with a shorter-than-maximum luff, consider the possibility of a short tack pennant, to get the sail's foot up off the deck in bad weather. In the 1979 Marion (Mass.) to Bermuda race, many of the contestants suffered torn seams or ripped-off luff snaps when their deck-sweeping jibs were suddenly filled with wave tops during a gale. Chances are that your storm jib is specifically designed to be set with a tack pennant, and if there is not a permanent one affixed to the sail, check with your sailmaker. Obviously, if you have a tack pennant, its length will have to be taken into account when establishing the jib lead.

I've mentioned the idea of marking jib lead locations. The best and neatest way I know for doing this is with the adhesive-backed vinyl numbers sold in sets by yacht chandlers. They're useful in any application where a number of adjustments may need to be marked—for noting halyard tension, foot tension, and athwartships mainsheet setting, as well as the primary function of indicating the various settings for the headsail lead blocks. It will also help to keep, as a part of your log or workbook, a complete record of sails and sail combinations for different wind strengths and different headings, together with the appropriate lead block settings for each combination of main and headsail.

Even though you may use the same setting nineteen times out of twenty, there will be occasions when you'll want to refer to the book for a peculiar wind or sea condition, and if you loan your boat to a friend, having such a ready reference will help ensure that the proper sails get used and used properly.

Mainsail trim

The mainsail has even more possibilities than a jib when it comes to shape adjustments. It's easy to visualize how the sail's shape is changed by tensioning the halyard and outhaul, as well as the downhaul—if any—or cunningham. (You should, incidentally, insist that your boat's mainsail have either the one or the other. They do the same job, and in my opinion the downhaul gives an added degree of sail trimming flexibility, since one can not only tension the lower half of the luff with a gooseneck downhaul but also raise or lower the entire sail a foot or so on the mast, which may be a noticeable factor in balancing the boat as the wind strength changes.)

Because the mainsail acts in concert with the headsail, its maximum draft is normally built to be somewhat farther aft than the headsail's. The accepted figure is approximately 50 percent abaft the luff, at a point about halfway up the sail. As with the jib's, the mainsail's luff tension, achieved with halyard and downhaul/cunningham, controls the location of the maximum draft: Tighten the luff and the draft moves forward, ease off and it goes aft.

Besides this initial adjustment, there is also the question of the amount of draft. Whether or not you have a bendy mast, you can make the sail fuller or flatter. In the lower half of the sail, this is accomplished by foot tension, although for the average cruising yacht under thirty feet, one sets the foot tension while making sail and seldom fools with it thereafter. But easing the outhaul can make the sail considerably fuller, giving it more power in light winds.

The sail's leech line, a light cord that runs in a sleeve the length of the leech, can be used to change the amount of draft and to move the draft about. Normally, the leech line is used in jibs to remove annoying flutter from the trailing edge (although one must be careful not to overdo and cup the leech). Tightening the leech line in the mainsail, however, has the effect of putting a curve in the whole after part of the sail, thus both making the sail fuller and moving the draft aft. The leech line's effect is mitigated considerably by the direction and amount of the tension from the mainsheet, which is perhaps the most important sail-shaping device working on the mainsail.

In most of today's cruising sailboats, the mainsheet is set on a traveling car that rides at least partway across the boat on a track. The reason for having a mainsheet track at all is not to control the amount of mainsheet tension, but rather its direction, and also to control the angle of the entire mainsail relative to the wind. Let's examine the situation:

When the main boom is directly over the mainsail sheeting point, the pull on the boom is straight down. The effect of this position is generally to maintain a fair, even curve all the way up the sail, so that if one were to take cross-sections of mainsail near the foot, at the center, and near the head, each would cut into the wind at much the same angle. Now suppose the boat is headed off the wind somewhat, but the mainsheet block stays in the same place. In order to adjust the angle of the sail relative to the wind, you'll ease the sheet, but as the boom goes out, pressure of the wind in the sail also makes the boom rise slightly, and as it does so, the head of the sail falls off from its angle relative to the wind, and acquires what experts call *twist*.

While twist can be useful to depower an overloaded sail in heavy winds, it is normally not a very useful attribute. It is true that apparent wind direction changes slightly as one goes higher up the mast, but in small cruisers the change is not enough to make a sizable degree of twist useful. It's better to keep mainsail twist low—not to a minimum in most cases, however—and this can be done in several ways.

When going to windward, moving the mainsheet car so it's directly or nearly directly under the boom is the simplest and most obvious course. A certain amount of leech tension, supplied by the leech line, can also help, by keeping the battens from falling away. Be careful, however, not to tighten the leech so much that it cups, in which case the effective drive of the sail will be less forward and more to leeward. It is equally important to avoid both a tight and a loose leech, signaled by the line formed by the forward edge of the mainsail's battens. With a tight leech, the sail will hook to windward along the batten line, and with a leech that's too loose, the whole sail will fall away along the same line. (Sometimes a visible line along the inner ends of the battens can be caused simply by too wide a roach and battens that are consequently too long, or by battens that are too heavy, especially at the inner ends: Make sure your crew know that battens go in their pockets thin ends first.)

It may be that your cruiser doesn't have a mainsheet traveler, and in any case no traveler will be effective as a twist eliminator when sailing much off a close reach. In either situation, a boom vang is called for. On older cruising yachts, a boom vang often consists of a fabric strap that fits between the foot of the sail and the boom, and that has heavy rings sewn in its ends. These rings accept a snap shackle attached to a double block, connected to another double block with a built-in cam cleat and a snap shackle that makes fast to one of several pieces of deck hardware—toerail, padeye, or stanchion base, as the case may be. Such a vang can be moved around to provide a good downward lead from the boom, and the fabric strap helps spread the load on the spar (and may also serve with the halyard as a boom sling when the boat is put away during the week). It can also function as a mainsail preventer when the boat is running, simply by leading the block and tackle (sometimes called a handy-billy) to a deck fitting level with the forward lower shrouds: The mainsail is effectively prevented from an accidental jibe in most conditions, hence the name.

The problem with this kind of vang is that any significant change in sheet tension calls for a relocation of the vang base, to maintain the optimum downward pull. And of course it's impossible to tack or jibe without detaching the vang first—a point that many carefree skippers forget until halfway through the penultimate moment. As a response to the need for a multipurpose vang preventer, racing sailors dreamed up a different kind of vang. The tackle is the same, but the ends are permanently affixed to a ring in the underside of the boom and a similar fitting at the base of the mast. The vang need never be removed, and it can be tensioned or unloaded from the cockpit by the simple expedient of leading the bitter end of its line aft through a cam cleat. Such a vang will not of course serve as a preventer, unless the bottom fitting has a quick-release shackle, but it does make for much more efficient sail shaping, especially off the wind.

In fact, with a vang like this, there is only occasional need for the mainsheet track, since the sheet no longer serves to shape the sail. Only in light airs, when it's a good idea to position the main boom directly over the boat's centerline, will you need a mainsheet track so you can move the mainsheet car a bit to weather of the centerline. This smacks of racing extremism, however, and only the truly determined sailor will want to go this far.

Another main-shaping device, in boats with bendable masts (and usually with fractional rigs) is the backstay tensioner. Taking up on the backstay arcs the masthead aft. As this happens, the center of the spar bows forward slightly, pulling the mainsail luff forward and thus flattening the forward part of the sail; this in turn moves the draft aft. Mast bending can easily be overdone, especially in light air. On small cruising yachts, the standard mast-bending machinery consists of a backstay shaped like an inverted letter Y, with a pair of connected blocks riding the short legs of the Y. A tackle downhaul allows you to pull the linked blocks down, yanking the halves of the backstay toward each other, effectively shortening the whole wire. You normally flatten the sail going to windward and ease the backstay coming off the wind, to put more fullness in the mainsail for a run.

The final sail-shaping device, seldom seen on cruisers except when they happen to have a racing mainsail (or sailmaker), is a shallow flattening reef in the sail's foot.

With all these possibilities, you would think that a set of woolies in the mainsail would be de rigueur, yet they are less common than on jibs. If you're interested in really knowing what's happening up there, two sets of woolies are indicated. The first are single lengths sewn to the outer ends of the batten pockets. Their streaming will indicate that the air flow is coming smoothly off the leech, and if they hang limp you know that the trailing edge of the sail is too loose or too tight. A second set, designed to perform more like the woolies on a jib, are doubled lengths of wool or colored nylon, located at three approximately equidistant points down the center of the sail. The idea here is that they must be far enough aft to avoid the turbulence caused by the mast, and more or less where the maximum draft will usually be located.

Although they are not, in the normal course of things, considered sail-shaping controls, the three pieces of hardware that attach the head, tack, and clew of the mainsail are worth a moment's discussion. Most sails are built to have their corners take the neighboring edges out in a straight line to the terminal cringle. If, however, the tack shackle is too small, it will pull the corner of the sail into an untidy bunch at the tack, causing tension wrinkles to radiate upward in a fanlike pattern. If the shackle is too long, you will either have the foot of the sail pulled too far aft or a permanent tension crease along the luff.

In each corner of the sail, the wrong lead will have a rather dramatic effect in terms of a misshapen sail. Since sail hardware costs a good deal of money, it's worth enlisting your sailmaker to ensure that you have the proper shackles at each corner of the sail right from the start. If he doesn't recall which ones are specified, ask for an assortment, with the right to return the ones that don't fit (and make sure you have properly labeled spares for each one that does).

Here again, it pays to have a sailmaker located in the immediate vicinity, although you may also be able to get the same kind of satisfaction from your dealer or boatyard, especially if you explain the problem honestly right at the start.

II

~~~~~~~~~~~~~

Sailing Technique for the Cruiser

The casual sailor, no matter what size his or her boat, learns two things about maneuvering: how to make a tack, and that jibing can be dangerous. The cruising person is not generally known for maneuvering finesse, although frequently capable of executing without assistance maneuvers that require a full racing crew to handle well. By and large, cruising sailors let a perfectly understandable laziness master them, and instead of becoming skillful enough so boat handling is easy for them, they attempt to avoid it altogether.

As one of the laziest people alive, I enjoy relaxation as much as anyone, but I go out in sailboats in order to sail, and doing this in an artistic manner does occasionally require the crew to bestir themselves. The trick is to make maneuvering a delight rather than drudgery, and the only way to do that, in my opinion, is to give each member of the crew a spiritual stake in the planning and operation of the cruise, as we shall see in Chapter VI. A good way to start is to practice sail and boat handling until everyone large enough to do so is able to handle every job. Not equally well, but passably. In attaining this goal, the skipper may find some preconceptions going by the boards: My own thirteen-year-old is a ferociously attentive helmsman, although his attention span does not equal an adult's. Within his limits, however, he can tackle a surprising variety of jobs on the boat—and his limits expand each season.

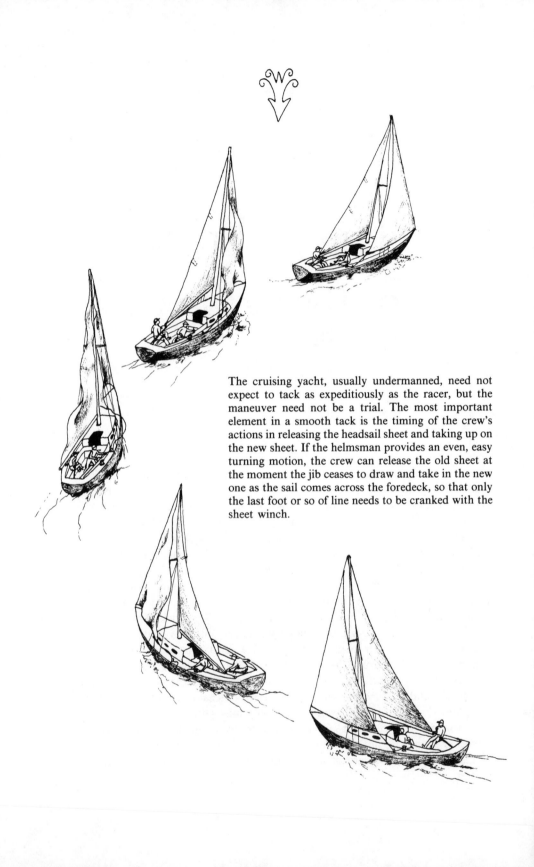

The cruising yacht, usually undermanned, need not expect to tack as expeditiously as the racer, but the maneuver need not be a trial. The most important element in a smooth tack is the timing of the crew's actions in releasing the headsail sheet and taking up on the new sheet. If the helmsman provides an even, easy turning motion, the crew can release the old sheet at the moment the jib ceases to draw and take in the new one as the sail comes across the foredeck, so that only the last foot or so of line needs to be cranked with the sheet winch.

Tacking

But back to tacking and jibing, those basic maneuvers we all learn, usually in a rather slipshod fashion. The modern cruising sailboat can be tacked by anyone with the intelligence to get the tiller from one side of the cockpit to the other, but doing it well and efficiently is another question. If you cruise in a catboat, of course, putting the helm over is almost all there is to coming about: A perfection of timing is the only thing that separates the experts from the beginners.

When you come right down to it, though, timing is all-important to skillful tacking, with or without a headsail. In extremes of weather, this fact is more obvious. Tacking in steep seas, for instance, the skillful helmsman learns to come about in a lull, timing the maneuver so the boat's bow swings through the critical part of its arc—the wind's eye—when it won't be slapped back by a sea. In light airs, the skilled crew knows how to head off slightly, pick up what speed is available, then come back up and through the wind without losing the small momentum that's been gained.

Watching a well-handled racer belt through a tack is informative. Although it appears that the boat has been slammed brutally over from one tack to the other, in fact it's not so: She carries her way right through the maneuver, but the speed with which the headsail goes from sheeted and drawing on one tack to the same position on the other gives an illusion of additional quickness to the whole thing. The small cruising yacht does not, of course, command the kind of crew that racers do. And even when a cruiser's deckhand becomes highly skilled, a small yacht's foredeck simply isn't big enough for someone to gallop around it pulling the genoa clew behind him.

Although the skipper may not have been navigating, he or she will normally determine when the tack takes place. The only exception is when some other crew member notices an emergency situation that calls for an immediate tack. No matter how relaxed the crew, you should always be ready to tack in no more than five seconds—all it takes is a casual agreement beforehand as to who's the tailer and who's the grinder, and the practiced knowledge of what each one does.

Anyway. Our skipper decides it's time to tack and announces that fact. Under ordinary circumstances, I prefer the old-fashioned "ready about," and I like my crews to construe it both as a preparatory command and a question; that is, I want them to get ready, and if there's any problem with getting ready, I want to hear about it—"Stand by, please," will do nicely. I also like all the crew who will be involved in the tack to acknowledge that they are in fact ready by saying so. Crew who will not be involved but who will be affected —someone in the head or galley, for instance—should obviously be warned if the maneuver will involved their being rocketed across the cabin, covered with hot gravy or something worse.

Hearing responses of "ready" from the crew, the skipper calls "Hard alee," or whatever equivalent pleases him or her. I find "Hard alee" a bit over-dramatic, especially since in a normal tack the helm is not put over hard, anyway. A good many beginners (and even some sailors who, in terms of time afloat, are well past the beginner stage) often experience a moment of blank panic just before tacking, forgetting which way to turn the damn boat. If the vessel has a tiller, "Hard alee" is a functional command, as one, of course, pushes the tiller to leeward in order to tack. With a wheel-equipped yacht, however, the command is no help at all.

The helm goes over. There is always the tendency to slam it, and unless you're sailing in boat-stopping seas this tendency should be resisted, as all it does is kill the boat's forward speed. At the same time, there is nothing to be gained by dawdling, as the boat is presumably already sailing at her most efficient close-hauled angle and any turn further into the wind will just cause the jib to stall. As the boat's bow comes through the eye of the wind, one crew member stands ready to run forward and free the jib clew if it catches on any fitting, but even if the decks are roomy enough, there's no reason to run the clew around, as is done aboard racers—on a small cruiser there's little to gain in speed, and the thumping of someone leaping about on the deck is likely to kill more speed than you could possibly pick up.

As the boat comes up into the wind, the sheet tailer takes up the slack on the new genoa sheet and stands ready. As soon as the boat is past the wind's eye and the jib appears to be moving across the foredeck without difficulty, the tailer begins to take in the sheet hand over hand. It's important, especially in light airs, not to get ahead of the sail, as you can easily backwind it because of overeagerness, leaving the boat in irons. Here is where repeated practice tacks will allow the skipper and sheet handlers to learn one another's rhythms, until the boat is coming about as fast as the sheet handler can gather in line, but no faster.

As the genoa begins to fill with wind, the tailer will find it harder to take in the sheet. The grinder should be standing by with the winch handle at this point, ready to pop it into the winch. If the breeze is light, the winch may really be unnecessary, or two turns around the drum will be adequate. In most cases, however, three turns of sheet are better, and sometimes four are required to allow the line to adequately grip the drum. Putting on these extra turns means that the tailer will have to stop tailing momentarily, just long enough to slip one or two more turns over the top of the drum. This takes perfect timing and coordination, and it is probably better to work into the maneuver by putting the turns on at a point that's recognizably too soon, rather than cutting back bit by bit: There cannot be too much strain on the sheet, or the line will back out and not allow enough slack to throw on the extra turns. At the same time, if the winch drum is still spinning free because there's no tension on the sheet, you're very likely to get an override, where a late turn winds up beneath a previous one.

Once the turns are on, the grinder slaps the handle into the socket atop the winch and grinds down the last few turns as the tailer hauls. Both people need to be braced to do their job properly, but the motions are different: The grinder needs to be braced at the knees in order to turn the crank, while the tailer needs to be braced right down through his feet, to get a straight-line pull of maximum power. If the timing has been right, the grinder should have to make fairly few turns to bring the jib in to optimum position, and it may help to premark the sheet to indicate that position (established, of course, during the sail-shaping sessions detailed earlier). Generally speaking, you will not want the jib right up against the spreaders, but it will take a little time to establish just how far off is best.

In any case, the proper amount of jib sheet as the boat comes out of the tack will not be the amount you'll want after she has picked up speed again: When the helmsman puts the rudder amidships on the new heading, the boat will necessarily have lost some speed, and the apparent wind will consequently have moved aft of its relative position on the previous tack. The jib thus should not be fully sheeted in but should have a little more to go, as the boat begins to pick up forward motion, until she is back at maximum speed and the jib can be sheeted to optimum flatness.

But why not sheet all the way in as the boat comes about, and take advantage of the few seconds of slow speed in order to point higher momentarily, then fall off as she picks up velocity? You can of course do this, and it does work reasonably well in brisk winds where seas are not too high. For the most part, though, you're best off having the power of a fairly full headsail until speed is up nearly to what it was before tacking.

As the tack is completed, the helmsman should find a hand free to adjust the mainsheet traveler, if that's necessary and if the sheet itself is accessible from the helm when the sheet trimmers are in the way. In day-to-day sailing, of course, no one is likely to bother with small mainsheet adjustments. Tacking from close-hauled on one tack to equally close-hauled on the other, the mainsheet traveler car will be set close to the centerline, except perhaps in very light airs, when it may be slightly to windward of the centerline, to allow the boom above it to center.

Tacking a cutter will, by and large, be the same operation as tacking a sloop, in that the cutter's small forestaysail is usually self-tending. In sailing the double headsail rig, the most common error is to sheet the staysail in too hard, attempting to get it clear of the airflow along the jib's or genoa's windward side. In a small cutter, there is little room between jib and staysail and between staysail and main, and usually the staysail spills air into the mainsail luff, backwinding it, and at the same time pulls the jib or genoa toward it, so that the jib leech nearly touches the staysail. Although it may seem much too free, the staysail sheet should generally be eased until the sail is out nearly as far as the jib or genoa, and the mainsail is undisturbed by wind off the other sails. Sometimes this condition is nearly impossible to achieve, and the trim is likely to be tricky. My own feeling is that if you insist on a double-head rig for a small cruiser—and then only for aesthetics, as there is little other reason for it—the best headsail combinations are, first, a masthead yankee (or high-clewed genoa) with or without a staysail, then a jib topsail (a working-size jib with a very high clew, often raised off the deck by a tack pennant) plus staysail, and for heavy weather, a staysail alone.

Clearly, tacking the double headsail rig chiefly involves getting the genoa or yankee quickly past the staysail stay. There is no magic way to accomplish this feat, and unless there is a persistent snag that needs to be padded or eliminated, the main requirement in a small yacht is patience.

As the cutter comes head-to-wind, wait for the genoa to work itself around the forestaysail stay. Trying to improve the moment by pulling on the new sheet will only result in backwinding the jib against the stay, delaying the tack or even killing it. With a jib topsail, on the other hand, there is relatively little overlap, and tacking can be nearly as fast as with a sloop.

Tacking small multihull cruisers can pose problems for those more accustomed to the behavior of monohull fin keelers. When a multihull's helm is put over hard, she will usually come up into the wind very quickly indeed, but she is generally so lightweight that she loses momentum equally fast, and she can easily stall out in light airs. In most situations, the best solution is to sail the boat right through the tack—fall off slightly to build up speed, then head up, trimming the headsail as you go, and even allowing the jib to backwind slightly as the boat's head comes through the eye of the wind. Then release the old sheet quickly and take in the new one fast, allowing the boat to pick up speed on a close reach before sheeting all the way in. Remember that with any multihull it seldom pays to imitate what monohulls are doing, and it nearly always pays to go for speed at the expense of close-windedness.

The small two-masted cruiser has some of the same problems close-hauled as does the small cutter, in that the sails tend to interfere with each other. In the case of small ketches and yawls, however, the mizzen is the problem child, as it usually lives in the wind shadow of its big brother, the main. On some large offshore boats, mizzens have been rigged on thwartships tracks to get them some clear air, but the small-cruiser owner will have to face the fact that when going to windward his mizzen is very likely more of a disadvantage than a help.

The late William Snaith, who owned a beautiful ocean-racing yawl named *Figaro,* certainly came to the conclusion that when she was going to windward it was often better to furl her mizzen if trying to point high. What happens is that the wind coming off the mainsail hits the mizzen luff at a narrower angle than does the apparent wind coming at the main luff. The result is that the mizzen always has to be trimmed slightly flatter than the main, and when the main is trimmed as flat as it will go, there's just no way to fly the mizzen efficiently. For a cruising sailor, perhaps the best light-air tactic is to sail a little low, until the mizzen draws properly; in heavy airs, sail high and strike the mizzen entirely.

Tacking, however, is no problem at all, as the mizzen is—or should be—wholly self-tending. Just be sure it's not strapped in too flat, or it may cause the boat to weathervane in light airs. Well-designed modern sloops with fin or semi-fin keels will do what their predecessors seldom could—tack easily from beam reach to beam reach. This is not an everyday maneuver, but it's something that comes in handy more often than you would think. Knowing the boat's capability in this regard is a piece of useful knowledge: Will she come clear about, sails luffing, or must she first be brought up to a proper close-hauled course with the sails drawing before she will make the tack?

Jibing

Most cruising sailors have a reluctance, however well-concealed, to jibe their boats. I suspect that this mental set originates in early sailing classes, probably when you spill a dinghy while jibing. It may later be reinforced by burning your hands on the sheet during an uncontrolled jibe, or damaging the boom or stays while jibing in heavy weather. I think it's important to get over the dislike of jibing, and the only way to do so is to use a jibe whenever it's indicated, even when the wind pipes up. Setting aside the spinnaker (which we'll talk about later), the sail that counts in a jibe is the main.

The most important thing in the maneuver is avoiding the sudden slam of the main boom from one side to the other, with the consequent lurch that throws the boat and her crew off stride and may do damage to the rig. Proper control of the mainsheet is the key, and *control* in this context means trimming and then easing the sheet from the beginning of the jibe to the end, in all but the lightest air. When the decision is made to jibe the boat, the hand on the mainsheet gets ready to take in the sheet rapidly. There is a conflict here, as you will need little or no mechanical advantage trimming the sheet in but will require some kind of help in taming its outward rush, once the boom is past the wind's eye. The usual four-to-one mainsheet system found in small yachts should be adequate, in that you're not required to pull in too many yards of line and you have enough mechanical advantage. The only thing to watch out for is accidentally pulling the mainsheet into the jaws of its cam cleat (if you have one) and locking it, just as it needs to go out in a controlled run.

Until your hands are in very good shape, it's difficult to control the sheet without gloves, since what you want is not a jerky, hand-over-hand motion but a smooth, even run that gradually slows the boom to a halt just short of the aft lower shroud. As the skipper says "Stand by to jibe," or whatever command suits the crew's taste, one sheet tender uncleats the mainsheet and makes sure it's free to run. As the skipper says "jibing," and puts the helm over smoothly (but not too fast), the mainsheet tender brings in the sheet just as fast as he can, trying to stay a bit ahead of the sail until it's through the wind's eye, when he eases what he has just gathered, keeping a strain on the line and gradually increasing it to bring the boom to a stop without a jolt.

The other sheet tender, if there is one, may move the jib across, if there's room in the cockpit to do so without inconveniencing the mainsheet tender, who is the star of this particular show. Blanketed by the main, the jib should be easy for one person to handle.

Jibing a ketch or yawl, the mizzen will usually go over ahead of the main,

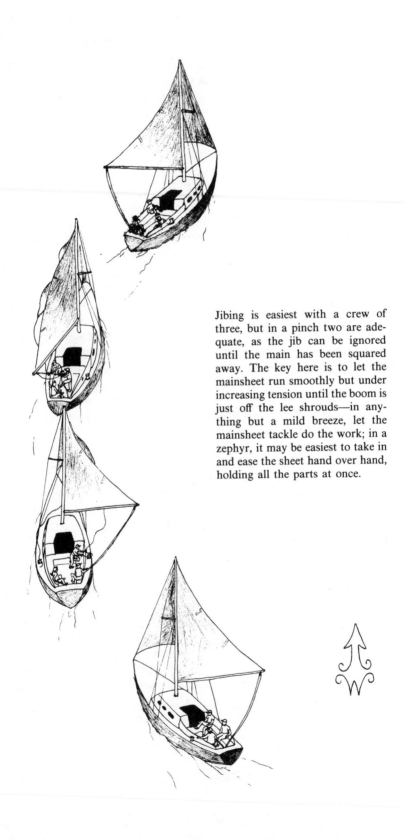

Jibing is easiest with a crew of three, but in a pinch two are adequate, as the jib can be ignored until the main has been squared away. The key here is to let the mainsheet run smoothly but under increasing tension until the boom is just off the lee shrouds—in anything but a mild breeze, let the mainsheet tackle do the work; in a zephyr, it may be easiest to take in and ease the sheet hand over hand, holding all the parts at once.

because it's never quite as far out when running as is the larger sail: Since a mizzen cannot, because of its location, have a standing backstay abaft the boom, its backstays normally run to the same chainplates as do the after lower mizzen shrouds, which are a little farther aft, in relation to the mizzen, than are the main lowers in relation to the main. The mizzen sheet is often inconvenient for a trimmer to reach, and it may help to reroute it forward under the mizzen boom to a cleat on the mast, just to make it more accessible for trimming.

Mizzen staysail and mule

While discussing mizzens, let me digress for a few paragraphs to talk about two sails peculiar to the mizzen mast. The more familiar one is of course the mizzen staysail, and the other, less well known than it ought to be, is the mule, or main backstaysail, set only in ketches.

The mizzen staysail, made of the same weight nylon as is the spinnaker, also sets flying—that is, its three sides are free and it is only constrained at head, tack, and clew. The standard, full-cut staysail is generally useful (depending on its shape) from close reaching to broad reaching, but racers can afford flat mizzen genoas that can be set close-hauled, or mizzen spinnakers for running. The cruising man will have a single, all-purpose mizzen staysail that will really come into its own on a beam reach and a couple of points either side of it.

The sail is, of course, hoisted to near the top of the mizzen, using a swiveling block mounted on the forward side of the mast. The halyard is double-ended, forming a loop that straddles the triatic stay. The staysail is generally sheeted through another block at the outer end of the mizzen boom, and it tacks to a padeye on the *windward* side deck, approximately level with the mainmast. The mizzen staysail can be trimmed with its own sheet, but it's most often adjusted with the mizzen sheet. Its halyard end is frequently led from the mizzen masthead down to a cleat on the windward quarter, to make a sort of additional backstay for the mizzen—something that will be needed in heavy weather, for the mizzen staysail is big, frequently as large as the main and sometimes larger. On a reach, in a brisk wind, the mizzen staysail can by itself justify the boat's second mast, in terms both of speed and of enjoyment. Moreover, it's perhaps the tamest sail aboard: Since it sets diagonally across the yacht, when you drop the staysail it falls into the boat, not into the water. The leverage provided by the mizzen boom makes it an easy sail to trim, and since it need not be drawing until it's fully raised, it is no trouble to hoist.

Although most ketch and yawl sailors swear by their mizzen staysails, a few seldom use them and don't understand them. While the staysail is—in my opinion—the only logical reason to have a twin-stick rig, it does have a couple of idiosyncrasies that you must accept. First, as noted above, it seldom sets acceptably on a run. I have a feeling that this confuses some sailors who expect it to behave like a spinnaker, since it's made from the same kind of cloth. In addition, a lot of sailors refuse to admit that it is only rarely possible to fly both the mizzen staysail and the mizzen itself. It's not at all the same relationship as between the main and the spinnaker, although there are resemblances, and in perhaps eight situations out of ten you must furl the mizzen in order to get the staysail to set properly. Sometimes it's possible to ease the mizzen staysail halyard and the sheet enough to get that sail clear of the mizzen itself, but far more often than not it's one sail or the other, and given the relative pulling powers of the two, the choice should be easy to make. (At the same time, I must confess, there is nothing in sailing more glorious than reaching along in a ketch with spinnaker, genoa, main, mizzen, and mizzen staysail all flying at once: easily worth going some miles out of your way just for the thrill.)

What about the mule? I first encountered it some years ago when I owned an undercanvased, thirty-foot ketch that needed every possible square inch of sail to make her go even respectably. What I required was more help getting to windward, and my sailmaker recommended that I try a mule. To visualize it, consider the ordinary ketch rig between the masts as a quadrilateral space, bounded by mainmast, main boom, and mizzen mast, with the masthead-to-masthead triatic stay forming the fourth side. The mainsail is a triangle taking up somewhat more than one-half the quadrilateral's area, while the mule occupies the rest: Its halyard block is on the aft side of the mainmast head, its tack is on the mizzen mast, just about level with the end of the main boom, and its sheet runs through the same block at the mizzen masthead that's used for the mizzen staysail halyard. To give it shape, the sail may have a single, long batten running at right angles from its clew to intersect its luff.

The mule can set flying, which will normally call for an extra winch on the mainmast to sock up the luff, or it can—as mine did—set on ordinary jib snaps attached to the main backstay (hence the sail's other name). On my small ketch, it was hard to get the main, mule, and mizzen to stay out of each other's way when close-hauled, but the mule seemed to add a knot, more or less, when on a close to beam reach. It's a fine light-air sail, as it picks up breezes well aloft, but I also found that by striking the mizzen, I could continue to carry jib, main, and mule in fairly heavy weather, without developing the ketch's traditional weather helm.

Unlike the mizzen staysail, which has to be lowered and reset when the boat is jibed, the mule is essentially self-tending, and needs little attention when tacking. Its useful range of apparent wind directions is rather narrow, but if you have a ketch with a substantial mizzen and an inverted-Y main backstay, the mule can make a significant addition to your boat's performance—and it certainly does attract people's attention, which may be half the fun of flying it.

Spinnaker handling

Like it or not, the spinnaker is certainly the queen of offwind sails, and the ability to set, jibe, and lower it has become one of the hallmarks of a skilled sailor. This observation is not intended to bully the confirmed, no-sweat cruising sailor into investing in a sail he mistrusts. On the other hand, I do feel it's a mistake to approach spinnakers with an attitude of built-in suspicion. They are just another category of sail, and while it's certainly true that they can be more troublesome than nearly all others in the modern wardrobe, it isn't necessarily the case that your chute needs to be a problem.

The conditions under which a racing sailor carries his spinnaker are likely to be considerably different from those that impel a cruising skipper to put his chute up. To begin with, when off the wind even a bit—close-reaching, that is—the hotshot racer will often try to fly a spinnaker (a starcut, if he has one), even though common sense may suggest that he'd have a smoother, more direct ride with a large genoa. The rationale, as explained by many able racers, is that with a fairly light boat (such as most racers are today), you can easily exceed hull speed, and while a genoa may yield hull speed, a spinnaker may promote surfing—in between broaches. Even with periodic broaching, a racer with a chute may well find he gets to the next mark more quickly than with a less taxing sail.

In addition, it's true that most racers carry at least two and often three spinnakers, individually suitable for running, reaching, and heavy weather. The range of wind directions in which they can put up a chute is thus considerably broader than it is for a cruising yacht with just one spinnaker.

Finally, there is the matter of crew. A proper racer will seldom have less than four people aboard, which makes handling a spinnaker a good deal easier than it is aboard a cruising yacht, where even if there are enough numbers, half are inexperienced and the other half lazy.

It remains a fact, though, that roaring downwind under a well-filled chute is one of the great exhilarations that sailing has to offer, and if you choose not to try it, you will have missed a considerable experience, as well as having lost a chance to widen your sailing skills. As a confirmed and purse-bound cruising sailor, I've spent less time under spinnaker than a lot of people, yet two of the times I had one up remain as vividly in my mind as when they happened. One was a variable run and reach from a harbor on Long Island to the Mystic River entrance across Long Island Sound, a distance of well over thirty miles. We flew the chute all the way, as planned, and halfway up the river as well, never in any kind of difficulty, and always moving well.

The other time I recall with affection was a half-day-long reach down the featureless sandbar that forms the barrier beach of Long Island. Our stubby, short-rigged little ketch had her spinnaker, #1 genoa, full main, mizzen, and mizzen staysail flying all at once, and for several hours the wind was at that absolutely perfect angle where none of the sails got in another's way. Because there were only two of us sailing the boat at the time, the takedown of this array was perhaps a little less smooth than it might have been—but we never broached, no harm was done, and we were both walking on air for the rest of the evening.

In recent years, sailmakers have rediscovered the single-luff spinnaker that dates back more than half a century. Bedecking it with names like Flasher and Shooter, they merchandise it as a perfect combination of the true parachute spinnaker's romance and the relative handling ease of a genoa job.

Well, yes and no.

The single-luff chute, with no pole and relatively little hardware, is definitely easier to use than the standard spinnaker, but it's still set flying and is a large enough piece of sailcloth to make a shambles of the foredeck when badly handled. As a sail, it is somewhat more versatile than any single regular-cut spinnaker, and for the shorthanded crew it has definite possibilities. But it's not a "real" spinnaker, in the modern sense of the term. We will talk about its handling a bit later on.

As suggested earlier, there are three quite distinct aspects of spinnaker handling—set, trim, and recovery. Among the several types of spinnakers, the tri-radial seems now to have emerged as the accepted compromise chute, adequately suited for both reaching and running, if not perfect for either. The tri-radial resembles the starcut, in that it is reinforced to all three corners, and it also has the full-cut upper body characteristic of the radial-head chute. A wide, horizontal band across its center, over the three-cornered "star," helps the observer to identify it at a distance.

Assuming you've never flown a chute before, it may be a good idea to crew with a friend who has experience with this sail, or invite him or her aboard your boat. Don't try to learn the complexities of a spinnaker during a race on someone else's craft, as the skipper won't have time to explain what's going on, and it may not happen according to plan, anyway. If you don't have an available sailing friend to explain the spinnaker's mysteries, that's no reason to give up. Wait for a relatively calm day, with a nice, steady breeze that's settled down to between 5 and 10 knots. With two or three crew, sail out to an area where you have at least a mile or two of deep water downwind and across the wind from your location, and set the chute there.

Before leaving the pier, you will have packed or otherwise arranged the spinnaker for hoisting. Although it's quite possible to set up a spinnaker in the main cabin of a small cruiser, it's easier, the first few times, to do it ashore. There are two basic strategies in readying the spinnaker for hoisting. The first, and more old-fashioned, calls for hoisting the sail to the masthead while it's contained in such a shape that it cannot fill with wind until you're ready for it to do so. The conventional method for achieving this state is to secure the sail in a tubular roll, from which it can be broken out once it's fully hoisted. The second method calls for packing the chute in a container (which, for obscure reasons, goes under the generic name of *turtle*), from which it can be hoisted flying, with its head to the masthead before the wind fills it. Both are acceptable methods, although the first is perhaps easier on the nerves of beginners.

The old method for presecuring a chute was to lay it out on the yacht club lawn and then gather the two long sides (called *leeches* until the sail is raised, whereupon one becomes the luff and the other remains *the* leech) toward the center. You don't, of course, roll the sail up like a rug, as it would then be impossible for it to break free except by unrolling. Having made a reasonably tidy linear bunch, you then proceeded to *stop* the sail: This involved tying short lengths of very light twine or heavy thread completely around the bunched sail at about two-foot intervals, save for the top ten feet or so, when the intervals were wider. The twine had to be strong enough to keep the tube intact until the sail was hoisted, yet weak enough to burst as the sail filled, after the bottom two or three lengths were snapped by pulling the leeches apart.

Obviously, it can be easy to misjudge the strength of even rather thin line. So string has largely gone out of fashion, to be replaced by rubber bands. Clever sailors have evolved a primitive but remarkably effective way of stopping a spinnaker that is well worth trying. Get a small plastic bucket, narrow enough in diameter so you can pull the bunched spinnaker through with a slight effort, after you've cut out the bucket's bottom. Now get a number of rubber bands—the cheapest you can find—and stretch them around the bucket's body. Bunch the spinnaker as described above, then pull it through the bucket, stopping every few feet to slide a rubber band stop off the bucket and around the sail.

One of the best aspects of this system is that you can store several settings' worth of rubber bands on the bucket at a time, and if you lower the chute and want to reset it, all you have to do is find the head—normally, the one corner with a swivel fastener, as opposed to an ordinary grommet—and pull it through, keeping the leeches running more or less straight so the sail doesn't get stopped in a twisted shape.

An effective variant of this system, and one that doesn't require you to waste rubber bands, is called the Spinnaker Sally. It consists of a number of plastic rings, held equidistant from each other by light lines. The spinnaker is bunched and stopped with the rings, which make fast at the head of the sail. Raise the sail, and as you pull the tack and clew apart, the rings ride up to the masthead, and the spinnaker blossoms. Better yet, you can release the spinnaker's sheet, pull down on the Sally's control lines, and smother the chute while it's still hoisted.

It's entirely possible to get a spinnaker hoisted without trouble and without one of these clever systems, however. All you need is some sort of container —a bag, a plastic laundry basket, a large bucket—suitable for the size of the sail. It should be possible to secure the container to a shroud or stanchion base, so you won't lose it as the sail goes up. Now take the ungathered spinnaker and find the head. From the head run the two leeches. Locate one of them and run your hand down it, flaking the sail back and forth as you go, and holding onto the flakes so that when you reach the clew, you have an orderly bunch comprising the entire edge of the sail. Now run down the other leech and do the same thing. Holding the three corners in one hand, stuff the rest of the sail into its container, making sure that the leeches don't get twisted around each

1. While one person holds one tack, the other flakes the sail from the second tack to the head, gathering and holding the flaked edge of the sail in one hand.

2. With one edge flaked and held, the other person does the same thing with the free luff, moving from the tack to the head. (After a little practice, both can flake at once without getting in each other's way.)

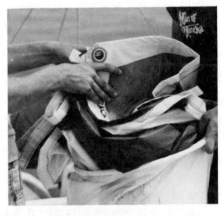

3. One person holds the tacks, head, and flaked luffs firmly while the other feeds the bunt of the sail into the bag or turtle.

4. The luffs and the head and tack grommets go in last, with the three grommets well separated, head between the two tacks. Made up this way, the spinnaker should be easy to attach to halyard and sheets and should come out of the bag without twisting.

other. Leave the three corners protruding, preferably as far from each other as the container will allow, again to prevent twist: This whole system relies upon the spinnaker emerging from its turtle in an orderly rush, with the leeches untwisted.

So far, so good. Let's assume that we have our spinnaker stopped or bagged. The next step, now that we're under way, is to rig the hardware and gear peculiar to the chute. Racers have to do this while approaching the windward mark, often short-tacking as they come. You don't. In fact, there's no reason that much of the spinnaker gear can't be set up before you leave the slip or mooring.

To begin with, you'll need the spinnaker's three control lines—the halyard, the sheet, and the guy. Remember, all the time you're setting up this gear, that the spinnaker sets flying *outside* every other piece of rigging on the boat. Probably the most common mistakes in spinnaker hoisting come from not getting one of the three control lines outside everything else.

In older boats, the spinnaker halyard goes to a swivel block made fast to a crane—a forward-facing protrusion at the masthead. Many racing boats have a pair of spinnaker halyards, each leading to its own crane-mounted block on the forward side of the masthead, above the jib halyard and the masthead forestay. Newer boats utilize a pair of jib halyards in the normal position, below and inside the headstay. This works well enough, so long as you remember that the spinnaker still must *set* outside the headstay. It may help to run the working end of the halyard, with its snap shackle, down to the bow pulpit and connect it there for the time being.

Now for the sheet and guy. If you're setting them up before you know on which side the chute will set, and thus which line will lead to the spinnaker pole, then it's customary to call both lines sheets. The bitter ends of these two lines should be secured toward the after end of the cockpit. If you're fortunate enough to have two sets of cockpit sheet winches, the spinnaker sheets can go to the secondary pair. From the winches, the sheets lead aft to the yacht's quarters—the corners of her transom—where there should be a pair of swivel blocks, either shackled to padeyes or otherwise rigged to have freedom of movement as the sheet or guy changes its direction of pull. The sheets lead through these blocks and then forward—*outside everything* on either side of the boat. Often there is a narrow space between the shrouds and the toerail in which the sheets may lie without falling overboard. After you have led the sheets all the way up the sides of the boat and snapped them to the bases of the foremost lifeline stanchions, check again that the lines are outside *everything,* and not twisted around any piece of running rigging.

The remaining control lines are associated with the spinnaker pole, designed to keep it in a horizontal plane regardless of the stresses trying to raise or lower its outer end. Although there are numerous possible arrangements, on most small cruising yachts the spinnaker pole will be rigged in one of two ways. The smallest boats will have a fixed ring on the forward side of the mast, at a height calculated to be the normal level for proper pole trim. The pole itself will usually have three lines running its full length. Two of the lines will have stainless steel rings inset at the central balance point. With the pole snapped into the mast eye, jaws facing up, the ring on one line is attached to the *pole topping lift,* the line that runs through a free-swiveling block normally located slightly below the spreaders. The pole lift runs back down the mast to a cleat, or sometimes down to the deck, through a lead block, and back to a cam cleat at the after end of the deckhouse.

The other pole control line is the *foreguy,* sometimes called the *pole downhaul.* It is made fast to the second ring-fitted line running the length of the spinnaker pole, runs down through a swivel block mounted more or less in the middle of the foredeck, and then back to a cleat at the after end of the deckhouse. As should be apparent, the pole lift keeps the spinnaker pole from drooping if the chute isn't filled with enough air to support the pole's weight (which will be much of the time), and the downhaul prevents the pole's outer end from skying, or rising uncontrollably, when the wind is so strong that it more than counterbalances the weight of the pole.

The third line running the length of the pole is made fast at each end to one of the spring-loaded pistons that close the pole jaws. Pull the line one way, anywhere along its length, and one jaw opens. Pull the other way, and the other jaw opens. This trigger line simply makes it possible to work the pole jaws from a distance, a handy thing to be able to do.

The rig for a larger boat may be slightly different. To begin with, the mast eye into which the inner end of the spinnaker pole is snapped may be mounted on a short section of track, with a spring-loaded or screw-in pin to allow you to set the eye at optimum height for best chute trim. While definitely important on racing yachts, this refinement probably isn't worth the extra money on a cruising yacht with no plans for racing, unless it is part of the spinnaker option package.

It's also possible that the spinnaker pole downhaul will run to a ring at the outer end of the pole, instead of to a bridle balance ring. If this is the case, the pole downhaul turning block will be well forward, more than likely at the tack fitting itself. The reason, which we will discuss in due course, has to do with a choice of methods for jibing the spinnaker.

Raising the chute

After you have familiarized yourself with all the spinnaker's hardware, set up its halyard, sheets, and downhaul (the last is normally rigged only when there is some prospect of using the spinnaker). The next decision has to do with which side you'll set the spinnaker from. To make things easy on yourself the first time out, put the boat on a broad reach, with the wind coming over the starboard quarter. The main boom is thus well out to port, and so is the genoa, just able to fill and draw on this heading.

Now bring up the spinnaker. Because it is slightly more demanding than setting from stops, let's say that we've decided to set the chute using a turtle. Set the turtle down by the port toerail, about midway between tack and shrouds, and secure it to a lifeline stanchion with a lanyard. (Make sure the lanyard doesn't impede the run of the sail from the turtle.)

Next, set up the spinnaker pole on the starboard side: Snap its inner end to the mast-mounted eye (jaw opening upward); hook on the lift and downhaul; now take up on the lift until the pole is approximately horizontal, and cleat the lift. The pole will be free to swing fore and aft, stopped at either end of its arc by the forestay and the starboard shrouds. Swing the pole aft until it's about midway in its arc, take up the slack in the pole downhaul, and cleat that line off. You will almost certainly have to readjust it later, but this will prevent the pole from skying when the chute is first opened. Since the boat is now heeled slightly to port, the pole will probably swing forward; let it.

Pick up the starboard spinnaker sheet from where it's lying next to the toerail. (You'll have to uncleat it at the cockpit first.) Put it into the outer jaws of the pole and let them close around it. That spinnaker sheet has now become the spinnaker guy, and it should be able to run easily back and forth through the pole jaws. Check to make absolutely sure that the guy is still clear outside all the boat's rigging, including the lifelines and stanchions.

Now go forward and unsnap the guy's shackle from where you'd fixed it, on the bow pulpit. Taking care not to lead the guy under or inside any rigging, pass it around the forestay, which will be something of a problem since the genoa is snapped to that length of wire. Reach under and behind the genoa and lead the guy between the sail and the lifeline, down to the basket-turtle, and snap the guy to the forward one of the two clew grommets. (Actually, of course, by snapping the guy to that grommet, you've just made that corner of the spinnaker into its nominal tack.)

Bring the halyard back, also between the leeward side of the genoa and the lifelines, and snap it to the chute's head swivel. Then unsnap the spinnaker sheet, which is already inside the toerail, pass it up, over, and down inside the lifelines, and attach it to the clew grommet. Make one final check to ensure that when you raise the spinnaker behind the genoa, all three of its control lines, as well as the sail itself, will be wholly outside the boat's rigging, once the sail has cleared the lifelines vertically. Some kinds of turtles are made to be suspended outside the boat, from the lifelines, which is fine if there's plenty of freeboard and if the sail is securely held in the turtle, so it cannot escape before you're ready. With a turtle like this, of course, you don't lead the sheet, guy, or halyard back inside the lifelines.

Now the sail is ready to hoist. Until you're used to handling a spinnaker, it really helps to have a crew of four. Later on, three or even two can do it perfectly well (at least in light airs). The skipper is at the helm, concentrating on maintaining a steady course. One hand is at the spinnaker halyard, one is ready to handle the spinnaker sheet, and the fourth is standing by the spinnaker guy. The skipper gives the word, and the halyard man raises the sail,

Raising the spinnaker

1. The sheets and halyard are made fast, with the head and tack emerging from the turtle as the crew begin to raise the chute. (Under normal conditions, the jib would be up, to allow the blanketed spinnaker to be fully raised without filling.)

2. Halfway up, with one person raising the sail, and the others hauling easily on sheet and guy.

3. Fully raised, the chute is catching the breeze. Note that both tack and clew have been extended, to prevent the sail hour-glassing around the forestay.

working as fast as he can. By hoisting behind the genoa, there is little or no chance the chute will fill prematurely. Take the sail up until there's about six inches between the head swivel and the halyard block, and cleat the halyard off.

As the sail is raised, the halyard tender calls out, "she's going up!" or the equivalent, and the sheet and guy hands take up on their control lines, pulling the tack and clew apart. The tack, of course, will not run through the spinnaker pole jaws—actually, its shackle won't fit through the opening—so as you pull the guy, the pole's outer end will swing aft until brought up at the end of the pole downhaul's slack. The sheet tender brings that line about halfway in, and both hands take a couple of turns on their winches, for purchase when load comes on the sail.

At this point, the spinnaker may be able to fill in spite of the genoa, but more than likely it will not. In any case, as the sheet and guy tender take up on their lines, the halyard man drops the genoa, which should fall in a relatively neat pile inside the lifelines, guided by the spinnaker, which should now fill of its own accord. Trim the guy and pole downhaul until the spinnaker pole is in a line with the main boom (but on the other side of the mast, of course). Now play the spinnaker sheet until the sail's luff—the side above the spinnaker pole —just begins to curl inward at the shoulder. Trim the sheet until the curl disappears. And there you have it. If the sail's tack and clew are level, the spinnaker is in good shape—a shade overtrimmed by racing standards, but safe and manageable. You may cleat the guy and the sheet, if you're on a long reach in steady winds, and let the helmsman steer the boat to suit the sail.

Raising a stopped spinnaker is considerably less demanding, and requires one crew member less right from the start (unless you're in a hurry). When the halyard man raises the sausage-shaped chute to within six inches of the masthead and cleats it off, he can then drop the genoa, which the other deckhand can help gather in and flake down on deck. The boat's speed will drop momentarily, but at this stage, don't worry about it. With the genoa secured, and a final check on the lead of sheet and guy, the deckhands go back to the cockpit. At the word of command, each gives a tug on his line, pulling the clew and tack apart until the wind gets in the sail. With a succession of *pops,* the stops let go and the sail blossoms; or if one is employing the Spinnaker Sally, the rings rattle up to the head of the sail as the chute opens. Trim the chute as before, and you're on your way.

There are lengthy, elaborate, and complex chapters written explaining the techniques of handling the spinnaker on runs, and on broad, beam, and close reaches. Much of this advice is excellent, but it can in principle be boiled down a good deal for the less than competitive sailor.

On a run, the spinnaker is essentially stalled, acting little more efficiently than a wall in blocking the wind and accepting its push. Therefore, the obvious tactic is to present the maximum sail area to the wind, at right angles to its thrust. You might think that this would entail pulling the tack and clew down as low as possible, but such usually isn't the case. It is generally more effective first to trim the spinnaker boom, as noted earlier, so it's both perpendicular to the mast and forming, when viewed from above, an extension of the main boom.

As with the mainsail on a run, the aim of spinnaker trim is to go for maximum fullness in the sail, which in turn means easing the sheet until the spinnaker luff is at the point of just curling slightly at the shoulder. It may also help, in anything but very light winds, to ease the halyard a little. This should allow a well-shaped spinnaker to pull forward away from the mast, not sag down, with consequent improvement in its set.

As the boat comes around toward a reach, ease the spinnaker pole forward as the main boom comes in. Trim the spinnaker sheet as well, flattening the sail. Many sailors hold that when reaching, the outer end of the spinnaker pole should be lowered, to lengthen and straighten the sail's luff. Sailmaker-author Wallace Ross says, in his authoritative book *Sail Power,* that this is a good tactic only for starcut chutes. With an ordinary spinnaker, he maintains, lowering the pole end will often cause the luff of the chute to fold back on itself to windward. It is better, at least with a conventional radial-head spinnaker, to raise the pole slightly, allowing the luff to fall away to leeward.

In very light airs, it may help on a reach to lower the pole as much as necessary to put a little tension on the spinnaker luff, which may otherwise sag out of shape. Unless you have an eager crew absorbed in the concentration of sail trim, you'll probably find that a little spinnaker work goes a long way, and that you are probably better off overtrimming the sail somewhat and accepting the consequent loss of speed (which will be less than apparent, anyway).

There will be occasions when you can carry both spinnaker and jib or genoa, or sometimes a spinnaker and a jib, tacked down to some point in the middle of the foredeck. This latter arrangement will seldom pay its own way, to my mind, except aboard the hard-charging racers where a quarter of a knot is something to cheer about. On the other hand, in light breezes to 10 knots or so, a thirty-footer can significantly increase her speed through the water with both spinnaker and genoa up and drawing.

You will, to begin with, be on a reach, more likely than not approaching the edge of the average spinnaker's usefulness. A fairly short-luffed headsail has the best chance of keeping clear of the spinnaker, and you may find it helpful to cock the outer end of the spinnaker pole upward somewhat. Don't trim the jib in, however, as it will just pull air from the spinnaker. Rather, let it set free, and take what you get. If a conflict between the sails does develop, you are almost always best advised to drop the genoa or jib and concentrate on the spinnaker.

On the other hand, you may well find yourself in situations where the apparent wind seems right for a spinnaker until you raise that sail. At this point, the increased boat speed moves the wind forward to where the spinnaker won't hold air anymore. You have the choice of dropping the chute and going back to the genoa or sailing off-course a point or so to carry the spinnaker. On the next page is a table showing the percentage of extra distance involved in sailing low on the course by various amounts. Of course, if all you really want is the fun of flying a chute, then efficient point-to-point navigation isn't your objective, anyway.

Extra distance sailed by heading off direct course

Angle	% Extra
5°	0.4
10°	1.5
15°	3.5
20°	6.4
25°	10.0
30°	15
35°	22
40°	31
45°	41

To my mind, many racing sailors become bewitched by spinnakers. Having convinced themselves that they're really sailing only when the chute is up, they tend to carry it far too long or in conditions where a genoa or other headsail would make much more sense. This is especially likely when reaching, because the drama created by the boat's heeling and her straining rigging as she crashes along under her spinnaker conceals the fact that she might be both faster and safer sailing upright under a smaller headsail. Likewise, if you're running or broad reaching in rising winds, and the boat swings uncontrollably up into the wind, the chute collapses and then fills with a bang—this should be all the warning you need that the vessel is overpowered and you should get the chute down.

Many modern yachts can generate far better speeds broad reaching under their spinnakers than they can running straight downwind. The table just mentioned will tell you what the tradeoffs are, but if you're interested in making time, consider tacking downwind. In terms of pure comfort, the boat may also be a lot more bearable reaching on a hot, light-air day than she will be while running, irrespective of where you're going.

The spinnaker jibe

Tacking downwind with a spinnaker is really jibing, of course. If the sea is choppy or you're not confident in yourself or your crew, you can drop the chute (we'll get to that below) and raise it on the other tack. But spinnaker jibing, when not done under conditions of stress (as in a race), is really no big problem, and it's something you ought to get used to if you're going to get the most out of the sail.

This maneuver entails going from a very broad reach on one side to the same relative heading on the other. There are, as I suggested earlier, two ways of

Jibing the spinnaker

1. The foredeck man takes the sheet in one hand as he prepares to pull the pole lanyard with the other, to release the inner pole fitting from the eye on the mast.

2. The pole is off the mast. The foredeck hand quickly places the sheet (which now becomes the guy) into the jaws and lets them close.

3. As he passes the pole across the foredeck, the cockpit crew tend the sheets and jibe the mainsail.

4. The foredeck man pulls the pole across, detaches the old guy from the jaws (it should leap free when the jaws are opened), and snaps the pole to the mast eye. During this operation, it will probably be necessary for the cockpit crew to ease the new guy and trim the new sheet.

doing it, although one of them is far simpler and more common on small cruisers. Let's assume for starters that your boat has a balanced pole, with the pole downhaul's turning block in the middle of the foredeck. Jibing under a spinnaker is most easily done with a crew of four—again, once you have the hang of it, you can reduce the numbers. The key person here is on the foredeck, and in a small boat the ideal crew member is light in weight, yet with a good reach; a teen-age girl basketball center would probably have the perfect physique. The point is that you want to avoid excess weight on the foredeck, but even on a small boat, the foredeck hand will need some muscle, good reflexes, and a long arm.

The helmsman calls the tune, as usual, and in this maneuver has the additional task of handling the mainsail (unless, of course, you have a five-person crew and a large enough cockpit to accommodate four of them). The sheet trimmers stand by spinnaker sheet and guy, and the foredeck hand stands with his back to the mast, facing forward. The most important concept for all hands to bear in mind throughout the operation is that the boat is being jibed while the spinnaker itself stays approximately immobile relative to the wind.

In a cruiser, you don't have to worry about maintaining the last quarter-knot of boat speed, so the emphasis should be on accomplishing the jibe in the smoothest possible way. With all hands in position and ready, the helmsman eases the boat around from a broad reach to a run, with the wind just about dead astern. Obviously, in conditions where the wind is shifting back and forth rapidly, the skipper will want to stay more on a reach, to prevent the possibility of an accidental jibe before the crew is ready for the real thing.

As the boat comes around to a run, bring in the mainsheet until the boom is approximately over the boat's quarter. The skipper will jibe the main one-handed, and it's important to avoid any more momentum in the main boom than necessary when the mainsail does go over. The mainsheet, of course, remains uncleated but with perhaps a half-turn around a cleat to make easing its run less demanding.

Now the skipper puts the helm over for the jibe. It should be a smooth, easy turn, just enough to swing the boat's stern through the eye of the wind. As he does so, announcing "Jibe-oh" as he makes his move, the foredeck hand reaches out and grabs the spinnaker sheet, pulling it inboard toward where he is standing alongside the mast. As the boat continues to swing through the wind, the cockpit hands ease the sheet and trim the guy to keep the spinnaker before the wind, while the boat is pivoting under the sail.

The foredeck hand meanwhile unsnaps the spinnaker pole from the mast ring and snaps the empty jaws around what has been (till this moment) the spinnaker sheet. At this point, the boat's stern should be passing through the eye of the wind, and the main boom should come across the cockpit, being eased out by the helmsman as the sheet and guy tenders continue trimming the spinnaker control lines.

The foredeck hand unsnaps the pole jaws from the old guy and pushes the pole out and forward along the new guy (to which it has just been snapped), until he has enough clearance to connect the free end of the pole to the mast eye. The hand tending the new guy may have to ease his line, to provide room for the pole to fit between the spinnaker tack and the mast. As soon as the foredeck hand signals that all connections are made, the sheet and guy tenders trim their lines back to the proper position for the point of sailing.

Since there is so much happening at once, this maneuver sounds much more spasmodic than it will be in the hands of a well-trained crew. It is good practice to jibe from one tack to the other, back and forth for a good hour, analyzing each maneuver immediately after it has been made, in order to establish the proper timing and rhythm among the crew. Most of jibing is in fact a matter of mutual timing, and the rest is self-confidence.

The end-for-end jibe is, as I have said, by far the simplest and most common type of spinnaker jibe, but there are other ways to accomplish the same thing. The only other one worth considering, to my mind, is the dip-pole jibe, and then only if for some reason your boat has its spinnaker pole so rigged that the downhaul is at the end of the pole and the pole downhaul turning block is up forward by the tack fitting.

Essentially, the dip-pole jibe is described by its name. The inboard pole end is never unhooked from the mast ring during the maneuver; instead, the pole lift is cast off as the jibe begins. The foredeck hand unsnaps the pole jaws from the spinnaker guy, slides the inner end of the pole to the top of the track, and drops the pole's outer end to near-deck level, allowing the pole end to pass inboard of the headstay, as the boat swings through the wind and the sheet and guy trimmers handle their lines to keep the spinnaker filled. Pull in the old sheet, snap on the pole, and the maneuver is essentially accomplished, save for taking up and cleating the pole lift. On larger boats, double sheets and guys are employed, and a description of the method involved is in most good offshore racing texts, such as Wallace Ross's *Sail Power*. But with the small cruiser, there really should be no need for anything but an end-for-end jibe.

Dropping the spinnaker

One of the things that has given the spinnaker its undeservedly fearsome reputation is the difficulty frequently encountered in getting it back down. I have had my share of these problems, but almost invariably they were caused either by waiting until past the last easy moment for lowering—as when one has just about run out of water—or by trying to undertake the operation while rounding a mark or engaging another boat in some kind of tactical horseplay. Even in quite strong winds, there should be no problem involved in dropping the chute—barring, of course, some mechanical difficulty, such as a jammed halyard.

Here is the sequence. Put the boat on a reach and, if convenient, raise the genoa or jib. (In some cases, as when coming into an anchorage, you may not want to hoist a headsail. Don't bother: It's not required.) More often than not, raising a headsail will steal enough wind from the spinnaker to tame it almost completely. With the jib secured and trimmed, trim the spinnaker sheet and ease out on the guy, while at least one member of the crew who is securely in the cockpit reaches out and firmly grasps not the sheet but a good handful of the reinforced spinnaker clew. If available, a second hand should stand by to help gather in the sail as the helmsman steers.

Now the foredeck hand goes to the bow and unsnaps the spinnaker guy from the sail's tack, as the cockpit hand tugs straight down on the clew. The sail's leech will suddenly become a more or less rigid leading edge, while the rest of the spinnaker streams away downwind like a banner. As the foredeck man eases off on the spinnaker halyard, the cockpit hands gather in the sail, making sure that none of it falls in the water. Allow the free luff to continue streaming and take it in last.

It may happen that the guy snap shackle jams when the foredeck hand attempts to unsnap it. In this case, one of the cockpit crew must cast off the spinnaker guy, which should run easily through the pole jaws and stream off downwind of the sail. It will have to be re-led later, but that is no big problem. When lowering the chute, the one thing to remember is that the sail must not be allowed to form a belly that can catch either air or water—always allow two of the three edges to stream free, even if it means casting a line off entirely.

This points up why you never put figure-eight knots in the ends of spinnaker sheets or halyards: It should always be possible to let the entire sail go—it will almost certainly float long enough to retrieve from the water. On the other hand, knotted sheets, when jammed in turning blocks, can cause a spinnaker to belly out like a giant sea anchor behind the boat, while a knotted halyard can cause the spinnaker to fly from the masthead, like a flag. Even if the worst happens, the most important thing is to keep your head. If you can ignore the flapping and thundering of the sail, and the boat's suddenly seeming to be out of control, it is almost always possible to figure out some way to get the chute back in hand—as long as you have sea room downwind.

So don't leave a spinnaker takedown until the last moment. It may look impressive to douse the chute even as you're sailing up to the mooring, but always consider what will happen if the spinnaker not only fails to come down as required but assumes a life of its own, taking over the boat.

Cruising spinnakers

Earlier in this chapter I referred to so-called cruising spinnakers, the new breed of single-luff sails created for cruising sailors who didn't want the expense or hassle of a full-fledged chute. Actually, the idea of the single-luff spinnaker is not new at all, but modern materials and trimming techniques have given it a wholly new lease on life. Much of the information that follows is adapted from literature describing the Flasher, which is the cruising spin-naker made and marketed by Charles Ulmer, Inc. The data will be more or less applicable to other cruising spinnakers.

In projected sail area, the Flasher lies between the standard spinnaker and a genoa. In the example cited by Ulmer, a 160-percent genoa is a shade over half the spinnaker's area, while a Flasher is over 80 percent of the spinnaker's size, or two-thirds again as large as the genoa. Like an orthodox spinnaker, the Flasher is made of nylon, usually ¾-oz., and it is cut rather like a slightly lopsided radial-head chute, with the leech somewhat shorter than the luff. These terms are not interchangeable, as they are with a spinnaker, because the luff is always the luff. The sail can be flown from a close reach to a run, and while it can employ a spinnaker pole (on a run), it doesn't require one for most headings. A short rope pennant is made fast to the sail's tack, as is a snap-hook, and a regular sheet leads from the Flasher's clew.

Because a Flasher is light and sets flying, you must first straighten out luff and leech before hoisting. Both sheet and tack pennant will warrant occasional adjustment under way, so you may want to lead the latter back through a snap-shackle snatch block made fast to the tack fitting, to a spare cleat at the aft end of the house or on the cockpit coaming.

Close reaching, the sail's tack should be low, not normally higher than the upper edge of the bow pulpit. As the wind moves aft from about 50 degrees apparent, gradually raise the tack and ease the sheet, allowing the Flasher to become fuller. According to Ulmer, the properly trimmed tack will be slightly lower than the clew and the luff will have a very slight curl.

As you approach a beam reach, at about 80 degrees apparent wind, ease the tack pennant slightly, until the tack is just about level with the clew. As the boat goes onto a broad reach, again ease the sheet to achieve the slight curl in the luff, and adjust the tack pennant to match tack and clew, both of which are now considerably higher than they were for close reaching. The Flasher may be somewhat unstable on a run, as it is almost certain to be partially blanketed by the main. If you have a spinnaker or whisker pole, it may well help to wing the sail out on the side opposite the main boom when running. Ulmer suggests first putting the boat on a broad reach on a course upwind of what you'll eventually want, setting up the Flasher on its pole behind the main, then jibing over to the proper course.

Dropping the Flasher is very similar to dousing a spinnaker, in that you free one corner of the sail to allow it to stream, while lowering the other edge under tension. In the case of the Flasher, however, you ease the sheet and pull down the luff, which should first be taken back from the headstay, to avoid wraps while lowering. If the wind seems too strong for this maneuver, head off onto a broad reach, cast off the tack snap hook and pennant, and bring the sail into the cockpit behind the mainsail, exactly as you would do with a spinnaker.

For reasons that are hard for me to understand, the Flasher and its single-luff relatives are largely banned from competitive sailing, except where a particular race or class may specifically allow them. This means that for most cruising people, operating with a limited budget, the choice will be between the single-luff chute and the regular variety. This is clearly a decision that no one can make for you, but it may help to point out a couple of factors. First, if you do plan to race, chances are you will want a spinnaker, and chances are even better that a single-luff chute will be of no use to you at all. On the other hand, if you consistently sail shorthanded or never race or have money enough for two light-air, off-the-wind sails, a Flasher type will certainly be useful, probably far more so than a drifter or reacher.

III

~~~~~~~~~~~~~~

Coastal Navigation:
The Equipment

A great many coastwise cruising yachtsmen do not navigate at all. They just aim their boats at a succession of objects, which they match to a vague memory or the chart. Any illusion about what they are doing is rapidly dispelled in a sudden fog, when they become almost completely helpless, or at night, when they can become hopelessly disoriented while surrounded by aids to navigation. At the same time, it is only fair to add that the requirement for navigation is seldom present for the weekend cruising yachtsman—indeed, he must often go out of his way to practice his skills, laying courses on paper for objectives he can see with perfect clarity right over the bow.

Compared to the big-boat navigator, the coastal pilot seemingly operates at considerable disadvantage: He nearly always has fewer, cruder instruments; his crew are limited in both numbers and skill; and his working area is often only borrowed from other users. Having made the shift from Spartan small cruiser to offshore yacht and back again, not once but as a matter of routine, I well know the delights of working on a full-size chart table, with instrument repeaters right at hand. By comparison, working a fix in the leaping cockpit of my own small overnighter is often a kind of soggy acrobatics, and the result is frequently far from precise. But the satisfaction, for me anyway, remains just as intense in a small yacht as in a large one, and if you are the sort of person who enjoys overcoming obstacles, your rewards as navigator of a small boat can be very satisfying.

The aim of the next three chapters is to set out a comprehensive outline of navigational practice, tailored for the small-boat cruising skipper. There are a number of excellent books that go into far more detail about techniques and equipment, but my own feeling is that the owner of a small yacht is best advised to master a few basic procedures appropriate to his vessel, and then—if he is really interested in navigation as an art form—to investigate the elaborate methods of position finding.

Charts

There are two basics of coastal navigation, the chart and the magnetic compass, and neither is complete without the other. A chart is, of course, a nautically specialized map, and a map has been defined as a picture of a portion of the earth's surface, drawn to scale. Because of the difficulties of rendering a three-dimensional curved surface on a two-dimensional flat sheet, there are some distortions in all maps, but in the types of chart we are discussing they are inconsiderable.

It is most important, first of all, to absorb the concept of scale on a chart. Essentially, a scale drawing reproduces the proportions of the original object, be it a chair or a harbor, while changing the size. On a chart, objects are represented either as scaled-down pictures or—when they would otherwise be too small to make out—as symbols. Chart scales vary according to the individual chart's purpose, and so do the symbols that are included. For instance, a small-scale *sailing chart* showing many hundreds of miles of shoreline may be on a scale of 500,000 or a million to one (shown on the chart as 500,000:1 or 1,000,000:1). This means that an object one inch long in its charted representation is half a million or a million inches long in reality. Charts of this scale are mostly used for general voyage planning or for extended offshore passages, and so they show only the most important and visible shoreline details—major seacoast lights, offshore buoys, important cities, and so forth.

A *harbor chart,* on the other hand, will most often be on a 1:20,000 scale. It will probably show detail right down to the outline shapes of large buildings or the presence of individual, navigationally useful trees. The area it covers is a tiny fraction of what the sailing chart shows, and it is specifically designed for close-quarters navigation.

The coastal cruising yachtsman will use only a few of the chart scales available. For our purposes, the 1:80,000 *coastal charts* which display, as a rule, about forty miles of coast per sheet, are the smallest scale required. (A small-scale chart, by the way, is one in which individual features are represented in a smaller size than on a large-scale chart. Obviously, a small-scale chart will cover more territory than a large-scale chart of the same sheet size; equally obviously, small and large scale are only relative terms.) It may well be helpful for the cruising navigator to have a single coastal chart of perhaps 1:200,000 scale for planning purposes, but most of your navigational plotting will be done on 1:40,000- or 1:20,000-scale sheets.

Besides showing the shape of the shore and islands and the depth of water (referenced to a common moment, Mean Lower Low Water), a chart has vast amounts of additional information on it. It shows the location, type, and color of government and private aids to navigation, bridge clearances, topography ashore, composition of the seabed, range of tides (if any), and literally dozens of other things. It has been said that a good chart is the equivalent of a 500- or 600-page book, and I do not doubt it.

The problem, for the cruising sailor, is that the damned things cost more and more, they become obsolete, and they take up valuable stowage space. For the skipper of a small cruiser, the real question is how to get away with the fewest possible charts for safety and convenience. In the United States, the federal government has historically been the preparer and publisher of charts (See Appendix 2, Publication Sources), and their product has to be designed to meet the needs of all users of the water. As a result, government charts, while excellent, frequently have more information on them than the yachtsman may require, and their cost reflects the extra work involved in assembling this data. It is, however, quite legal—at this writing—for private concerns to reproduce government charts and sell the result at a considerable break in price, and the development of first-class color offset printing has now brought the cost of these copied government charts down to reasonable levels, while at the same time keeping their quality very near that of the originals.

These reproduced charts normally appear in the form of large softcover books, containing both coastal and harbor charts for a whole cruising area— Chesapeake Bay, for instance, or the coast of southern California. Price is on the order of one-tenth what you would pay for the originals, if you bought them one at a time. For the small-yacht navigator, these chart books seem to me an absolute godsend, the foundation—and most of the structure—of your chart library.

At the same time, I usually carry a couple of government charts as well— one of my immediate area, on a 1:20,000 scale, on which I keep track of important local changes, and a small-scale coastal chart, for cruise planning. In addition, I will keep my chart book reasonably up to date by adding the regular corrections supplied—free—via the *Local Notice to Mariners,* an approximately weekly publication issued by local Coast Guard Districts. It lists changes in aids to navigation, both temporary and permanent, missing and defective aids, and unusual activity on the water—harbor dredging, say, or a major regatta. Making corrections from the *Local Notice* onto your charts is a fascinating off-season exercise, as well as excellent practice in plotting. Only a tiny fraction of the week's notices in any issue are likely to be pertinent to any individual yachtsman, and your yacht club or marina may already be on the subscription list—so don't add your own subscription if you can consult a public copy.

There are other sources of information you can employ to add more useful detail to your chart. Aeronautical charts, for instance, while generally useless to the sailor, do contain the frequencies and call signs for aeronautical radio-obeacons, many of which are just as useful for marine direction finding (see Chapter V) as they are for aircraft. Flyers' charts also list the heights of many major landmarks that aren't noted on nautical charts. Many new structures that make excellent landmarks don't get incorporated into charts for years, if ever. A telephone call to the proprietor can often reveal the height of a new building or its exact location. On the negative side, it is always a good idea to note when a charted landmark is destroyed or obscured, so that on another day, when you may be numbed by fatigue, you don't spend time looking for it. A chart, while a work of art, is not static. It is, rather, constantly evolving, and your own charts should reflect change.

Chart stowage and a plotting location aboard the small cruiser are two related problems that sometimes defy acceptable solution. Although more and more small cruisers today have some kind of horizontal surface on which to plot courses and positions, in any boat under about twenty-eight feet, this area is likely to be so small that it's functionally worthless. On overnighters at the bottom end of the size scale, one cannot really expect a chart table, or any table big enough to use. By working around the difficulties, however, it's usually possible to come up with a workable arrangement. For chart stowage on a small boat, you require a flat, dry space perhaps 24″ × 18″ as a minimum. This will accept chart books, or charts folded twice. (Don't fall for those overhead racks that hold rolled charts: They look neat, but a well-rolled chart is almost impossible to flatten in a small boat.) Anything bigger than 2′ × 1½′ is a bonus, and at the worst you can stow several folded charts under each berth mattress.

A place to do the actual chartwork may be harder to come by. In my previous book, *The Coastal Cruiser,* I examined the possibilities at some length. Proper chart table aside, they are dinette, folding table, icebox top, and galley counter, in approximately that order. None is ideal, and my own solution, when no other surface is available, is to create a portable chart board. Buy one of those oversize, heavy-gauge clear plastic covers designed to hold flat-folded charts or a chart book. Cut a piece of quarter-inch marine plywood to fit snugly inside it; then carefully round off the edges and corners and seal and varnish the wood. It should serve reasonably well and can be used on your lap just about anywhere you can sit down, above or below decks.

Other solutions include table-size plotting boards with plastic sheet surfaces and built-in drafting arms, such as the ones sold by Ritchie or Coast Navigation; or the self-contained plotter like the P-B-C, marketed by Davis Instruments. These devices combine plotting surface, chart protection, and protractor all in one unit, and while they are not cheap, they can serve well. It is important, before investing in one of them, to ensure that there is a dry, secure place to stow the board itself, as it can become an unpleasant missile if it breaks loose and begins to crash about the cabin.

Publications

Although charts are the basic publication you cannot do without, there are several others of varying degrees of usefulness. These days, the commercially produced annual cruising guides, usually in paperback, have replaced a number of larger, bulkier government publications for the coastal navigator intent on saving space. Examples of these cruising guides include the *Boating Almanac* series, the *Waterway Guides,* and the *Sea Guides,* all of which focus on providing detailed information about facilities—marinas, clubs, restaurants, and fuel stations—in the areas they cover, but which usually include tide, current, communications, and weather information as well. While some of these publications have a running text, most compress their information by the judicious use of tables and coded entries, with the individual facilities keyed to chartlets, so you can locate them from the water. The formats differ, and yet the real differences among the various guides seem to me very small. Perhaps the best way to decide which version will work best for you is to visit the book section of a large chandlery and sample a few, checking the listings that refer to your own harbor, so as to get an idea of style, completeness, and accuracy.

Besides the regional cruising guides, there are also annually published navigator's compendiums, notably *Reed's* and *Eldridge's,* which concentrate on general piloting data for an entire coast, and which do not have facilities information. My own feeling is that while the cruise guides and the navigation guides overlap considerably, there is still enough difference between them so that I like to carry one of each. Since the navigation guides are also annual paperbacks, they are not cripplingly expensive nor do they take up gross amounts of space. I usually keep last year's cruising guide at home, as a planning aid when laying out an itinerary.

In the good old days when every cruising yacht was presumed to have a sizable bookshelf below, the navigator was admonished to carry a full ration of government navigation publications. And while these highly specialized books and pamphlets do have a few attributes that aren't duplicated anywhere else, in most cases the small-boat cruising skipper can forego carrying them. Let me note, however, what each contains, so you can make up your own mind. (Sources are listed in Appendix 2.)

Special *Tide* and *Tidal Current Tables* are published annually in book form, covering the east and west coasts of North and South America. The information you need, however, should be contained in a commercial cruising guide, boiled down to eliminate irrelevant data. What you need to have is a tide table covering your boating season and your cruising area. Usually it will have two or three primary reference points, for which daily high and low tides are listed, plus another list of subordinate reference points, with the differences of time and height of tide referred back to the primary points. Your cruising guide should also contain the same kind of tabular information about tidal currents for your area, if they are of any consequence.

Whether they appear in official government publications or privately published cruising guides, tide and tidal current tables are laid out in much the same fashion, and their use is thus very similar. The essential premise in each case is that both tides and currents are predictable, and of course they are, since both are driven by the same forces, the gravitational pull primarily of the moon and secondarily of the sun. Because the sun's and moon's gravities sometimes partially cancel each other and sometimes—as at full and new moon—are additive, the heights of tides and the strengths of tidal currents change through the lunar month and through the year, being highest and strongest at the equinoxes. Tide predictions are based on an average water depth at the reference point—the *datum of soundings*—which is *Mean Low Water* on older charts, *Mean Lower Low* on new ones.

Using twenty-four-hour zone standard time, the table lists the two highs and two lows in each normal twenty-four-hour period, and the relative heights of water (first in feet, then in meters) that can be expected. A listing that reads, for instance,

1309   0.2   0.1   1924   7.5   2.3

means that on this day one low water is predicted for 1:09 P.M., standard time, and that it should be two-tenths of a foot (or 0.1 meter) above datum of soundings at the reference station; the following high tide is predicted for 7:24 P.M., with depths 7½ feet (or 2.3 meters) above datum at the station.

There are elaborate ways for calculating the height of tide at intermediate times, but for most small-yacht navigators they are more trouble than they are worth. An easy and normally reliable method is based on what might be called the rule of twelfths; that is, the rise or fall of water in a standard six-hour tidal cycle is divided into twelve parts, as follows: During the first hour, rise (or fall) is one-twelfth the total range; during the second hour, two-twelfths; during the third and fourth hours, three-twelfths in each hour; during the fifth hour, two-twelfths again, and during the sixth and final hour, a final twelfth. Purists may object that the cycle is actually about six and a half hours, but you may round off without hesitation.

In our example above, then, the total rise of tide between about 1:00 P.M. and 7:30 is predicted to be 7.3 feet. For arithmetical convenience, call it 7½. Say that we want to know the depth of water at the reference point at 3:00 P.M. on that day, two hours after low water. One-twelfth of 7.5 is 0.6; three-twelfths is about 1.9, which is added to the low-water reference of 0.2. Thus, the tide at 3:00 P.M. should be two feet above the charted depth.

It appears a lot more cumbersome on the page than it is in real life, especially once you have become used to the calculations. Predicting tidal heights at subordinate stations is a little more complex, but not inordinately so. For each of the subordinate stations that is referenced to a primary station the tide table lists four correction factors—time difference of high and low water between primary and subordinate, and height difference at high and low, expressed as a decimal fraction. Let us say that we want to find tidal height at a subordinate station referenced to our example above. The tide table of subordinate stations

JUNE

Day	Time h m	Height ft	m	Day	Time h m	Height ft	m
1	0114	0.1	0.0	• 16	0601	6.4	2.0
Tu	0721	6.4	2.0	W	1213	0.3	0.1
	1332	0.2	0.1		1829	7.2	2.2
	1945	7.0	2.1				
2	0209	-0.1	0.0	17	0057	0.1	0.0
W	0814	6.4	2.0	Th	0658	6.5	2.0
	1422	0.2	0.1		1309	0.2	0.1
	2032	7.2	2.2		1924	7.5	2.3
3	0259	-0.3	-0.1	18	0153	-0.3	-0.1
Th	0903	6.4	2.0	F	0756	6.6	2.0
	1507	0.2	0.1		1404	0.0	0.0
	2118	7.2	2.2		2017	7.7	2.3
4	0342	-0.4	-0.1	19	0248	-0.7	-0.2
F	0947	6.4	2.0	Sa	0852	6.7	2.0
	1550	0.2	0.1		1459	-0.3	-0.1
	2158	7.3	2.2		2113	8.0	2.4

Extract from the Tide Table: the times are Standard, in the 24-hour notation. Heights of tide, under "ft" and "m", are related to the datum of soundings on the chart. At 2:59 A.M. on Thursday, June 3rd, for example, the tide should be exceptionally low—four inches below the charted datum; six hours later it is predicted to be about six feet five inches above the charted datum.

notes that high water at the subordinate station is +0   28, or just about half an hour later than high at the primary reference. Low water at the subordinate is −0   02, two minutes earlier than at the primary. The range is given as 0.2 on high water and 0.0 on low—for practical purposes, just about the same range, since two-tenths of a foot isn't worth trying to calculate. By free-hand interpolation, we can calculate that at 6:30 P.M. on the day in question, the tide at our subordinate station should be about six and a half feet above the datum of soundings for that point.

The same rule of twelfths works for calculating tidal current, although the current table has a slightly different format. In practical terms, however, it is almost always easier to look up the appropriate hourly page in the tidal current chart (see below), find your location, and read off the current strength. And, in the appropriate months, add one hour for Daylight Time.

For areas where currents are a major factor, such as the country's major bays and sounds, the National Ocean Survey (NOS) has provided sets of current charts. These come in books of twelve, each chart providing a graphic representation of the local current at one hour in the cycle of ebb and flow. Most of the better cruising and navigation guides provide reduced-size reproductions of the official current charts, but if the guide covering your area does not, it's a good idea to invest in the government publication, which is not large and never goes out of date.

The NOS also publishes the government's own cruising guide, the venerable *Coast Pilot,* an oversize, annual paperback in many volumes. This publication, although certainly interesting, is written for the use of commercial interests, and its coverage of yacht facilities is limited, while its descriptions of harbors mostly contain information vital to skippers of larger vessels. The *Coast Pilot* does, however, present valuable statistical data on weather and the navigational background of larger cruising areas, and if you are planning a major cruise to a place that's new to you, the *Pilot* may be a useful tool in your planning phase, although it's not likely to be very helpful on board.

Besides the *Coast Pilot,* there are privately compiled cruising guidebooks to most boating areas. These are really travel books with a nautical flavor, as opposed to the directories discussed above. For a serious cruise, these books can be as useful as the *Pilot,* or more so, since they do concentrate on data for the yachtsman. Because they are quite expensive, you may want to sample one at the library before deciding whether you need it. Again, this kind of book is most helpful at the cruise-planning stage, although it can make interesting reading under way. Many of these books are classics and have been around for years, so it's a good idea to check the copyright page to make sure you have a recent version. With the rapid changes on today's waterfront, no guidebook over five years old is going to have very accurate detail.

Finally, there is one government publication that is unique. The *Light List* is an annually published tome that contains specifications for just about every aid to navigation (lighted or not) in U.S. waters. It is issued by the Coast Guard, which is responsible for American buoyage, and it amplifies the shorthand notations concerning buoys that appear on charts. While the *Light List* is certainly important to commercial shipping, or perhaps when making an extended cruise in strange waters, it has limited pertinence to most coastal cruisers.

Piloting equipment

In the last few years electronics have had such a vogue that a beginning skipper could be pardoned for thinking that there were no piloting tools that didn't flash or beep. Without even considering the magnetic compass, which appears in the next chapter, it's possible to list half a dozen implements that are basic to coastal navigation—and none of them is electronic.

Perhaps the most obvious is a course protractor, an instrument designed to measure angles and used to lay out courses or read bearings on a chart. For some reason, the idea of a course protractor appears to inspire a lot of navigators to invent their own versions, and the age of plastic instruments has made it relatively easy to get these devices into commercial production. The last time I looked, there were perhaps two dozen proprietary course protractors, each of which had at least something to recommend it.

In addition, there are the more traditional angle-measuring devices, parallel and rolling rules and navigator's triangles. The aim behind each of these gadgets remains the same, however different in appearance they may be. All of them exist only to enable a pilot to measure the angular direction of a course or bearing line, either against the chart's compass rose or against its parallels of latitude or meridians of longitude. Triangles and parallel or rolling rules require that a compass rose be visible on the segment of chart being used by the navigator, and given the constricted area available for chartwork on most small cruisers, they have been superseded by the patented rules and protractors, which in some manner contain their own compass roses, and which require only a parallel or meridian as a reference.

The problem here is that while a parallel rule can be used to read off a direction from the inner, magnetic rose, early course protractors would read only in true degrees, so the pilot then had the disagreeable chore of making the arithmetical conversion for magnetic direction, which is what his compass showed. Most of the popular protractors today, however, have integral dials that allow one to set them for any reasonable amount of magnetic variation, and for the casual pilot, I think that this attribute is a must. Beyond that, since nearly all patent course protractors are made of the same kind of clear plastic and operate according to the same rules, I think there is little to choose among them. Before buying any one, I would suggest reading the printed instructions that accompany it. Several protractors I've encountered were functionally marred by users' instructions that were virtually incomprehensible, although a set of instructions comprehensible to one navigator may be impenetrable to another.

Next, you will need a good pair of dividers. For the kind of rough work usually done aboard a small cruiser, I prefer the heavy, steel-tipped brass dividers designed to be used one-handed. The points are not particularly sharp, compared to the needles found on some others, but since sooner or later those points wind up stuck like a banderilla in some member of the crew, that may be just as well. And the one-handed operation, with practice, is definitely an asset. As you get more deeply into the complexities of navigation, you'll probably want to invest in a pair of compasses as well—not the magnetic kind, but the type that have two points—one metal and one lead-pencil. The cheap compasses sold to schoolchildren are quite adequate for drawing circles of position and marking limits of visibility of lights, and the cheap plastic ruler that often accompanies them can be quite useful itself.

Many sailors don't really think of binoculars as part of their navigational armory, but it's the navigator who uses them most, for identifying buoys and other aids to navigation. There are two schools of thought in buying binoculars for a boat. The first group feels that since conditions are so bad, one ought to get the best, preferably something waterproof and rubber-armored. The second holds that a heavily used item like binoculars will almost certainly be lost or smashed eventually, and it is best to minimize the blow in advance by getting something cheap. By and large I adhere to the second school, in part at least because I hate to part with the money now required for a good set of glasses. My 7 × 50 Bushnell Sportviews, while definitely a run-of-the-mill instrument, have been quite adequate for years. If they fell in the drink now, I would be sad, but not desolated.

One instrument that's hard to find but—in my opinion—a real treasure is a monocular with the sighting compass built into it. I bought one in England several years ago, and while its betalight illumination is fading and its compass fluid yellowing, it is still very useful indeed, serving the functions of sighting compass and binocular in one. From time to time a U.S. importer will bring a few of these devices into the country, and I commend it to your attention.

A regular hand-bearing compass is also mandatory. For years, these devices were designed with an absolute minimum of imagination: Atop an ordinary two-cell flashlight was mounted a liquid-damped compass; on one edge of the mounting was an adjustable prism, so that the user could sight through the prism's V-shaped notch, with the prism itself tilted to make visible the numbers on the compass card immediately below. The flashlight corroded overnight, the revolving prism broke, and the compasses themselves seemed very prone to losing fluid and developing annoying air bubbles.

While a number of these antique horrors are still available, often at heavily inflated prices, navigators who use hand-bearing compasses have almost universally gone over to the Mini, known affectionately to thousands of sailors as "the hockey puck." Shaped like a flattened cylinder, the Mini is protected by a black rubber guard around its perimeter, which makes it about the size and shape of a puck. It has a built-in, unmoving prism in its upper side, and to use the device you simply hold it up to your cheekbone and sight over it. A semipermanent betalight provides a greenish glow at night, and the whole thing will fit in your pocket. Similar small sighting compasses are made by the Finnish firm of Suunto, and they are also excellent, as is a development of the Mini called the Opti.

Another visually oriented instrument that comes and goes in the catalogs of mail-order houses is the range-finder, which may work according to either of two sets of principles. The first type operates like the split-image focus device common in many camera lenses, notably those made by Nikon: When the two halves of the image coincide, you read off the distance on an exterior dial. The second type of range-finder works like a simplified sextant, usually involving a sighting bar of some sort. Personally, I think neither is worth the problem of stowing yet another device, when you can instead buy an inexpensive plastic sextant and have done with it. Plastic sextants come in a variety of prices, according to the features they contain. I would insist on an instrument with a two- or three-power scope, a geared tangent screw, and several tinted shades in case you get ambitious and want to go on to sun sights. Why have a sextant at all? Well, it's not really necessary, but it's fun and impressive and it can be an excellent way of determining precise positions.

Finally, you will need an assortment of pencils—I prefer the reasonably soft #2 lead, which will normally not tear through even damp charts—a pocket-size pencil sharpener, and some red and yellow felt-tipped marking pens, of which more later. If you have no place in which this gear can regularly be stowed without its escaping, you can either invest in a commercially made wooden navigator's rack or make your own, out of scrap ¼" mahogany-faced plywood. I have found the latter course much more satisfactory, as the construction is childishly simple and the result is a rack exactly tailored to the navigation equipment you have.

Electronics

Electronic navigation gear is undoubtedly the glamour field of the last decade, and its popularity shows every sign of increasing. In *The Coastal Cruiser* I devoted a good deal of space to discussing today's marine electronics, and what appears here is both more compressed and more directed at technique than my other remarks.

There are perhaps six electronic devices that have some application to the type and size of boat we're talking about in this book. In order of usefulness to the cruising sailor, they are the speedometer/log, the depth sounder, the two-way radio, the radio direction finder, the loran, and the wind direction indicator/anemometer. Although not electronic, a good barometer is also a must, and so is an accurate, waterproof timepiece, preferably one that has an independently activated second hand, for timing lights. One of the new, inexpensive quartz crystal watches is ideal—I have a Casio, and endorse it heartily.

A speedometer and a log (which serves about the same purpose as a car's odometer) are quite different instruments, but they are frequently combined on a single dial readout and employ the same through-hull transducer. I would definitely insist on such a combined instrument, and I have found that most of the well-known commercial brands seem equally reliable. The paddlewheel transducer is almost universal now, and the level of accuracy is quite adequate for the sort of boat we are discussing, so there is little to be gained by spending money for a top-of-the-line instrument. It seems sensible to go with the inexpensive models from the lines of companies like Kenyon, Signet, or Brookes & Gatehouse that have established reputations. The old-fashioned patent log, consisting of a taffrail-mounted dial and a spinner trailed in one's wake, seems to me silly for a coastal yachtsman, as it is no cheaper, hard to read, and prone to fouling.

There are three types of indicators seen in today's depth sounders—flashing light, pointer, and digital readout—and the last is most costly by a good deal. I am one of those people whose brains were frozen before the advent of digital dials, so I find the flashing light just fine—of all three indicators, it alone will tell you something about the type of bottom you're over, according to the width of the light signal. Many depth sounders come with transducers that can be mounted inside an uncored fiber glass hull, and this seems to me a good way to go. Not only will such an installation reduce drag, but it avoids yet another damned hole in the boat, always a source of nervousness to me. Unless the waters in your area are uniformly shallow, I would choose a unit with at least a 200-foot range, some of which will be dissipated by an in-hull mount.

There are two ways to use a depth sounder; it can be a warning device to indicate when shoaling beneath your boat is becoming dangerous, or it can help to provide the navigator with a partial picture of what the bottom configuration and consistency are. Most sounders can perform either function, so the way you employ your sounder is up to you. If you set primary importance on the alarm function, then you must first determine that the general bottom contours are suitable; a seabottom that is gently shelving for the most part and largely devoid of abrupt reefs or rocks is best. When a bottom shelves very steeply, it's possible to be aground forward while the sounder head amidships is still reading 10 or 20 feet. And if you intend your sounder to provide a reminder warning, it's probably best to get a unit that has a built-in audible depth alarm. In general, these buzzing or ringing alarms are of two types. Either they are preset to a few selected depths—5, 10, and 20 feet, say—among which you can choose the one you want, or they have unlimited adjustability as to the depth that will trigger the sound signal, although this feature generally costs more.

The better navigator learns by practice how to use his depth sounder to give him an accurate idea of the bottom contour, which he can then relate more or less to the chart. For this kind of navigation to be successful, a bottom configuration with fairly dramatic rises and falls is useful. Even where the general trend of the bottom is flat, however, there will often be an abrupt elevation or a deep subsurface gully that will give you a valuable checkpoint for positioning. We shall examine a bit more detail on the use of the depth sounder in navigation in Chapter V.

Among beginning navigators, the radio direction finder (RDF) and its sophisticated sister, the automatic direction finder (ADF), still retain a good deal of their glamour, although some of the luster has transferred to the newer positioning devices, principally loran. The simplest RDF and the most complicated ADF rely on the same useful principle: When a directional antenna, which usually resembles an elongated rectangle, is at right angles to an incoming radio signal, reception is at maximum volume, and when the bar antenna is pointed directly at (or away from—it's the same thing) the signal, it's received at its weakest.

You've noticed this, of course, with the simplest portable AM radios, which can register significant increases and decreases of signal strength as they are rotated on a tabletop. The RDF and ADF just take this principle and design the radio around it. (In contrast, an automobile radio's antenna, or that of a VHF-FM, is largely nondirectional, designed to receive signals from all directions equally well.)

By using stations whose transmitting antennas are identified on the chart, it's possible to determine with some precision the magnetic bearing between your receiver and a given antenna. By crossing two or, better, three such bearings, you arrive at a position fix. Like many aspects of navigation, the principle is simple and the execution is less so. Problems arise at both ends of the system: A transmitter, to be useful in direction finding, must be located on or very near a relatively flat shoreline, and virtually all marine RDF beacons and many airport radiobeacons are so positioned. The difficulty often comes in using commercial AM stations, whose antennas may be well inshore and whose signals can be deflected by the coast. Commercial FM or VHF-FM stations can be employed in direction finding, but to do so requires special and very expensive equipment. The Coast Guard has it; you don't need it.

Aboard ship, the incoming signal may be skewed by large masses of ferrous metal, by other electronic devices, and, most especially, by wire standing rigging. It is very important, then, to establish a proper deviation table (see next chapter) for the RDF, and always to use the instrument in the same location below.

Most RDFs read out signal strength in two ways—audibly, often using a headset to screen out random noise, and on a meter. Different people have different reactions to these two methods, and I find them about equally workable. Because the human ear finds it easier to distinguish the relative strengths of two faint sounds than two loud ones, in direction finding you listen for a *null*, or lowest point, in the signal strength, rotating the bar antenna to find it. Under the antenna, which is located on the top of most sets, is a dummy compass rose, or *pelorus*, which also can be rotated. For direction finding, it is usually oriented to the ship's heading, so a signal direction can be read out in magnetic degrees rather than as a relative bearing. Many European and British RDFs use magnetic compasses built into the units and I have found this arrangement easier to work with, especially in a small boat where holding a straight course can be very difficult.

An ADF is essentially the same as an RDF, except that it automatically tracks the direction of the incoming signal and finds the null, either visible or audible, by itself. An ADF incorporates a small electric motor to turn the antenna, and it can consume a remarkable amount of power unless it is used judiciously. One of the best illustrations of the limitations of radio direction finding is the extent to which the ADF's motor-driven bar antenna "hunts" back and forth even after it has found a null. Few experienced navigators expect much more than $\pm 5°$ accuracy with either RDF or ADF, which means that the closer you are to a beacon or broadcast antenna, the better. Further, radio bearings become unreliable at dawn and dusk and are sometimes questionable through the night as well.

The standard RDF or ADF sold in the United States is a table- or desk-top model with a rotating antenna and pelorus. It has several bands, not all of them pertinent to the primary task—low-frequency beacon, which covers both marine and aircraft radio beacons; commercial AM; marine band, which is the old double-sideband AM band for nautical traffic; and commercial FM, which may include, if you are lucky, the marine FM band as well, along with the VHF-FM weather broadcasts of NOAA. The set cannot, of course, direction-find on FM frequencies, and there is little coastal traffic on the new single-sideband sets using the old marine band frequencies. As far as direction finding is concerned, then, you are pretty well restricted to beacon and broadcast.

At the same time, it may be convenient to have a monitoring receiver for marine VHF or weather, and it may be pleasant to be able to receive your favorite FM programs, so there's no reason, except possibly cost, to forego extra bands.

Do not, however, be wholly seduced by the number of bands alone. Your RDF or ADF should also have: (1) multiple power sources, preferably a 12-volt jack that can be wired to the boat's service batteries, internal dry-cell power (usually C or D cells), and 110-volt, for off-season use; (2) a sense antenna, which will enable you to determine whether a signal is coming from a given direction or its 180-degree opposite; (3) A VHF-FM antenna, to improve the line-of-sight reception of those frequencies; (4) an earphone, and a jack suitable for regular headphones, to screen out boat noise while trying to locate a faint station; (5) a visual null meter; (6) a visual battery condition indicator for the dry cells.

If you don't have a sizable flat surface for charting and fixing the RDF, you may be well advised to choose one of the hand-held portable direction finders. There are several models, but they all contain a compass, are battery-powered, and are built to be used on deck, away from magnetic or ferrous influences. I have one myself, and when fully charged it works quite well on either beacon or AM broadcast frequencies (it has no others). The kicker with this unit and —I have heard—with the others of its ilk is that their self-contained batteries are not very strong, and the sets must have some way of being recharged from the boat's power between uses.

Although the principle of radio direction finding is easy to understand, and the results, when arrived at by an expert, can be remarkably precise, for most people the device is a disappointment. And in nearly every case, it is their own fault. To become proficient with the RDF requires a considerable amount of time and practice under a variety of circumstances, and very few pleasure-boat navigators are prepared to spend the hours required to become confident about their bearings. The same thing, I ought to add, is true of virtually every aspect of navigation, and this is why I think it a good idea for the beginner to learn a few navigational basics thoroughly before attempting the frills.

If ever there was a frill—and a delightful one—it is the loran (acronym for **LO**ng **RA**nge **N**avigation), which at first sight promises to eliminate navigational effort entirely. The loran network consists of a master and several secondary stations (the latter used to be called slaves, but apparently this was politically distasteful). Master and secondaries transmit radio signals, and the incredibly tiny differences between the times of reception of these signals establish lines of position. These parabolic lines are numbered and plotted on special loran charts, and the numbers are also displayed on the loran set, so that all the navigator has to do is relate to the chart the numbers he reads on the display. Since the secondaries are well spaced, a line of position established by the master and one secondary, and then by the master and another, will usually give an adequate cut for a position, and in many places it's possible to get three such lines.

The process is idiotically simple, and on some sets it is made simpler still by having the unit internally translate the loran line numbers into latitude and longitude, often to an accuracy within a quarter of a mile. No wonder every offshore skipper wants one, and as quantity sales bring prices down, more and more coastwise boats will have them, too. To say anything negative about such a magical device seems like treason, and yet there are, I think, a few such points that must be made. To begin with, they are still expensive for the yachtsman on a budget—hovering around a thousand dollars minimum for some time now. They are not, in some areas, as accurate as expected (this seems to be a fault of the charted loran lines, rather than of the sets themselves, but the results are the same). They discourage any other form of navigation, because deriving a loran position is so damned easy. And eventually, being machines, they break. What happens then will depend on the boat's position and on the amount of true navigational skill available among the crew.

My own objection is that a device like the loran removes a lot of the sport from navigation, and since calculating the boat's position is for me one of the most satisfying aspects of cruising, I am interested in developing and refining skills, not extinguishing them. That said, I must admit that loran works, and if navigation doesn't turn you on, there's no reason to avoid loran—as long as someone aboard can get you home in an electrical emergency.

There are other kinds of navigational electronics, but I fail to see the utility of them aboard a small cruising yacht, especially in terms of the price. Most racing yachts have both anemometers and wind vanes reading from the same masthead-mounted senders. I don't see much point in an anemometer, as what's really important is the effect of the wind on the boat, and you don't need a dial to tell you that. A wind direction indicator, if it has an expanded-scale readout for the windward headings, can be useful for those who sail at night, when the jib luff woolies are invisible. You can, however, achieve much the same effect with a masthead windvane illuminated from below—the popular Windex has such an accessory available, but you can easily create it yourself.

And the list lengthens every season. Now there is satellite navigation (Sat-Nav), in which a satellite transmits a precise position to your receiver; recording depth sounders, which trace a bottom contour on special graph paper, have been a staple of the commercial fishermen for decades; an electronic compass is on the market, too. As a confirmed gadgeteer, I find myself strongly attracted by all these devices, especially the ones with lighted dials. As a small-boat sailor with limited electricity (and cash), I'm learning restraint. I don't, however, necessarily recommend that trait to you. Many very good sailors get their fun from watching dials, and you may be that kind of person. All I would suggest is that along with the electronics you have a reliable back-up which will, in the nature of these things, take some time to master. And by the time you understand the back-up, you may (like me) find it more rewarding than being admonished by a black box. (Yes, we now have electronics that talk.)

IV

~~~~~~~~~~~~~~~

Compass, Course,
and Bearing

It is possible, in writing a complete book about marine navigation, to assemble a tome running a thousand pages or more. On the other hand, it may be more helpful to reduce the essentials of coastal navigation to answers for two questions: "how to get your boat from here to there," and "how to pinpoint *here* when you're lost." This chapter, then, is a necessarily compressed introduction to a far-ranging art, aimed at arming the new cruising sailor with the bare essentials for setting a course and positioning his vessel. At the same time, I ought to reiterate that coastal navigation can be a delightful and challenging part of cruising, and I urge the reader to sample some of the books in the Bibliography, as a way of expanding basic skills.

Let me also reemphasize my belief that skill in any aspect of navigation is primarily the result of repeated practice. It's not like learning to ride a bicycle —you don't suddenly "get it." It's a matter, rather, of gradually eliminating first gross and then minor errors in technique and arithmetic until you can consistently come up with reliable answers, regardless of the distractions. Simply comprehending the information in this chapter won't do you much good until you make it work, over and over again. When at last you can find your boat's position in heavy fog or on a moonless night, when you can set a course that correctly allows for the vagaries of current and compass error, then you will, I think, feel a sense of accomplishment that makes all the work worthwhile.

Principles of the magnetic compass

As I said earlier, the chart and the compass are the two foundations of coastal navigation. Most of us have at least a second-hand acquaintance with charts, having dealt with land maps, their cousins. But a great many people today have little or no knowledge of how a compass works or how to use it. They may not even appreciate that our world has two norths—true and magnetic—which is a good place to begin this description.

The true north pole is the familiar point at the top of a map of the world. If you have a globe in your home or office, true north is the upper end of the axis around which the globe spins. True north is in one sense an arbitrary point, a convenience for mapmakers, but it has become a reality in people's minds. Magnetic north, which is a shifting, generalized area in northern Canada, is one focus of the earth's magnetic field. As such, it is the spot toward which one end of a bar magnet will point, if it is free to spin. If true north were in the same place as magnetic north, navigation would be a good deal simpler, but the magnetic compass, which is built around one or more linear magnets, orients toward magnetic north, unless it is distracted by some other nearby activity, usually electrical, or a piece of ferrous metal which can be as small as a can opener. Fortunately, however, magnetic north's attraction is strong, and it is near enough to true north so that by making an appropriate correction, the true north chart grid can be used in setting magnetic courses, all of which relate to north.

A modern mariner's compass is the sophisticated cousin of a hiker's pocket compass. In that primitive instrument you still have the essentials: a balanced, magnetized needle that is pivoted to swing freely and align toward magnetic north; a circular card whose surface is equally divided into 360 degrees or 32 compass points; and a protective casing with a transparent top. A sailor's compass has not one but a bundle of magnetized needles, for greater responsiveness to the earth's magnetic field; these needles are secured to the underside of the card, which is pivoted to revolve on a bearing. The card is often slightly dish-shaped, to improve the helmsman's line of sight to the numbers or letters that indicate direction, and the compass cavity is filled with fluid, to damp down the card's motion. Most compasses sold for marine use can be tilted off horizontal—a few degrees in the case of hand-held sighting compasses, or more than 30 degrees, in compasses designed for sailing craft. The hemispherical, transparent bowl is constructed so that it magnifies the numbers on the card, which are often illuminated for night use by a self-contained light.

A good marine compass is far more complicated than it appears, yet it remains an instrument of elegant simplicity. Choosing the right one for your boat is not hard, unless there's some peculiarity of cockpit design to consider. In many cases the style, if not the make, will be conditioned by where you plan to emplace it. There are several obvious locations, each with its advantages and drawbacks.

The steering compass has one primary function, to enable the helmsman to keep on course. It may also be possible to use the steering compass to take bearings, but this is a secondary function, an attribute you shouldn't count on. Every cruising boat should also have at least one back-up compass, which is usually the hand bearing compass. The steering compass is aligned so that the marks on its case, or inside its dome, line up with the yacht's fore-and-aft axis. This means that a person sighting over the compass can align a vertical needle on the compass card's pivot point with another mark on the forward side of

A. north pole   B. north magnetic pole

The relative locations of the north pole and the north *magnetic* pole cause the magnetic compass needle to point in a different direction from true north most of the time. The compass needle points toward the magnetic north pole, unless some deviation source —metal or electrical current in the boat—distorts its heading. When the magnetic pole (B in the drawing) is to the east of the true pole (A), the compass needle points to the east of true north, and is said to have an easterly variation. Only when true and magnetic north are in a line does the magnetic compass read out to true north.

the container—the "lubber line"—to determine the direction in which the boat is heading. The edge of the circular compass card is marked off in evenly spaced divisions, often in increments of five degrees. The degree mark adjacent to the lubber line indicates the boat's magnetic heading—its direction in relation to magnetic north. As the boat turns, the compass card appears to swing. Actually, of course, the compass case is turning and the card is remaining still —a fact that seems very difficult for beginning helmsmen to comprehend. After a while, however, most people are able to respond to the compass without thinking, making course adjustments automatically.

Obviously, for the helmsman to use the compass effectively, he must be able to see not only the forward side of the card but also the pivot needle and lubber-line mark. In larger craft, the compass is sited in a recess on top of the steering pedestal, so that someone standing behind the wheel is automatically in proper alignment with the sighting vanes. But relatively few small sailing cruisers have steering wheels, and in the ones that do, the helmsman frequently finds himself standing off to one side or the other, in order to see the luff of the headsail or traffic ahead.

Pedestal aside, the other locations for a cruiser's compass are in the thwartships cabin bulkhead, recessed in the bridge deck or coaming, in an instrument pod over the companionway, or mounted on a companionway hatch slide. Today's racing yachtsmen seem to favor twin compasses, recessed in the port and starboard bulkheads or the coamings. The advantage of this dual location is that the helmsman has a good line of sight to one instrument, no matter which side he is on. The disadvantages are that neither compass can be used for taking bearings; two compasses take up a lot of bulkhead space; and they are prone to impinge on something that will cause deviation (compass error from materials in the boat) in one or both instruments. A compass on the coaming, or mounted on the bridge deck, is vulnerable to feet, winch handles, and other hard bits of gear, but either site is handy for taking bearings. The compass in an instrument pod can be very convenient to see, but it is in a spot that's prone to magnetic disturbance from other instruments, while an instrument mounted on a companionway slide is inevitably in the way of anyone coming on deck or going below, and will also, like any removable, bracket-mounted compass, snag halyards and sheets.

In many cruising yachts the skipper has made a compromise by recessing a compass into the bulkhead on only one side of the companionway. This seems to me a poor arrangement, as it will make sighting the compass card almost impossible while beating to windward on one tack or the other. On my present boat, I've recessed the compass in the bridge deck, with a stainless steel (and thus nonmagnetic) guard over it, plus wooden braces either side, for the heels of the crew hiking out. It's not ideal, but it has been a serviceable set-up that allows me to take rough bearings from almost any place in the cockpit. The only thing I must remember is not to stow anything ferrous or magnetic on the shelf immediately under the bridge deck.

When you have decided where to put the compass, you have by extension also decided what model—bracket, flush mount, bulkhead mount—will be required. Most of the better compass manufacturers offer a complete range of styles, as well as a graduated—by size and price—range of models. In general, it seems to me, you want the largest size you can afford and for which there is room. The reasons are two: First, the helmsman and navigator of a small cruiser may find themselves operating from half a dozen different places, and the larger the compass card and its numerals, the farther away they can be read. Second, the larger and more expensive compasses are better built, by and large, and have more features that will be useful to you—red-tinted night lighting, built-in corrector magnets, card able to tilt to at least 30 degrees, extra sighting vanes at 45 degrees either side of the center line (so you can have a reference range while hiked out), built-in inclinometer, and choice of card styles to suit your taste. Of this last feature, let me say that I prefer the card divided into 5-degree increments, with numbered marks every 20 or 30 degrees, and letters—N, E, S, W—at the four cardinal points. Others feel cheated if every degree mark isn't on the card, but few if any small-boat helmsmen can hold a course within two or three degrees either side of a given mark, and having too many degree marks seems to cause some helmsmen to freeze on the compass, paying no attention to the set of the sails or to where they're going. This may be a splendid trait in the quartermaster of a battleship, but it has little place on an undermanned cruiser.

A good compass is surprisingly costly—surprisingly, that is, if you consider only its apparent simplicity and forget the careful workmanship that has gone into it. But since the compass is without question the most important single instrument on the boat, it seems to me that you ought to be prepared to pay as much for it as for, let's say, a depth sounder or a speedometer/log—yet you won't have to. For what it does, a good compass is not overpriced.

If your boat has a formal chart table, and if you're fascinated by navigation, you may want to have a second compass on the table. It's really useful only as a back-up or check on the helmsman, unless you have the kind of RDF with a pelorus, in which case you will find it much easier to check the pelorus card against the yacht's course without a lot of shouting up and down the companion. And even if you do have a second compass below, you'll still need a hand bearing compass. This instrument should be carried by whoever is in charge of navigation at the moment—skipper, navigator, or watch captain, depending on the crew structure. That's why one of the pocket-size modern units makes such sense—if it's in your pocket, you'll have it when you want it, and you'll take more bearings, the only way to become proficient. If the hand bearing compass is left lying about like a winch handle, the odds are no one will use it who isn't already a good navigator.

Deviation and compensation

Most good compasses are delivered with instructions on how to install them and check for deviation caused by wires, instruments, or masses of ferrous metal nearby. Danforth, which makes an excellent line of compasses, offers a free booklet, *Compasses and Compassing,* by R.D. Ogg (Danforth, 500 Riverside Industrial Parkway, Portland, Me. 04103), which deals in detail with both subjects, and which is applicable to any good compass. What follows is a somewhat abbreviated instruction, for the skipper whose steering compass, new or old, has already been installed.

The first step is to check the compass for deviation. If yours is a second-hand boat, the previous owner may have passed on a deviation table, indicating how much error there is on each of several headings. This can serve as a guide, but you will want to work up your own information, as deviation can change, whether because a given item has been relocated or because some new piece of gear has been added—or even because the boat's own magnetic field has changed, which happens occasionally.

Get an up-to-date chart of your harbor and locate on it half a dozen ranges, each composed of two fixed, charted objects that can be lined up visually from your boat. Ideally, these ranges should provide six pairs of compass bearings equally spaced around the 360 degrees of the card, but few harbors are so thoughtfully arranged. The best kind of range has the farther object higher than the one in the foreground, and enough deep water close around so that you can take time to line the moving boat up carefully. You may well have to settle for buoys as part of your range system, but these are not as good as fixed aids, because they swing around their anchors.

Now run each range, noting carefully the compass bearing as you head directly down on it and directly away from it. With two people—one sighting the range and one steering and sighting the compass—you may check even bulkhead-mounted compasses in this way. The biggest problem will be holding the boat steady, and you should be prepared to scrap a run and try again— even several times—if necessary. Run the courses approximating the four cardinal directions first, and check the compass readings against the actual magnetic bearings of the ranges. If on these headings you have no error, or even an error of up to two degrees, you can leave well enough alone: Your compass is sufficiently accurate for coastal work.

If you detect a compass error beyond these limits, however, you should take action. The first step is to examine the area around the compass for tools or devices that may have caused the observed deviation. It's not hard for relatively small pieces of ferrous metal—screwdrivers, beverage containers, even wristwatches—to find a temporary stowage place near the compass and then be forgotten. Even some presumably nonmagnetic items may turn out to have an effect on the compass—one reason that it's a good idea to check the parts of any installation you plan to make in the compass's vicinity *before* you do the work; simply passing your hand bearing compass within two or three inches of the components involved should flush out any ferrous parts. (Some but not all types of stainless steel, for example, are nonmagnetic.)

Electrically caused deviation can be harder to pinpoint, if only because it is likely to be periodic: On powerboats, a frequently significant cause of devia-

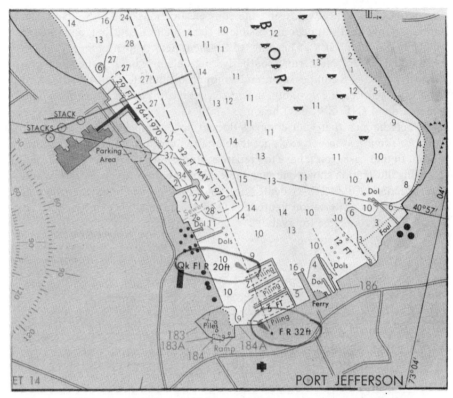

Natural and artificial ranges: Two of the three stacks at upper left in the chart segment form a natural range, while the quick-flashing red and the fixed red lights at the marina make an artificial range. Crossing the two ranges yields a nearly foolproof fix.

tion is a windshield wiper—or, rather, the small electric motor that drives the wiper. When the wiper is on, there can be considerable deviation, which stops the minute the wiper is turned off. Sailboats with binnacle-mounted compasses may have some ferrous metal within the binnacle, although the wheel and pedestal are nonmagnetic; bulkhead-mounted compasses can abut instruments or gear racks fixed to the inside of the bulkhead; and of course a compass recessed into the side or bridge deck can be affected by items stowed directly beneath.

If no source for the deviation turns up, or if it's not something that can be moved, you'll have to consider compensating the compass or making a deviation table. Nearly all worthwhile steering compasses today are equipped with internal compensating magnets, so compensation is only a chore, not a real problem. Set the boat on a range as close as possible to magnetic north and, as you run the range, use a nonmagnetic screwdriver to remove half the deviation on that heading, using the compensator marked "N-S." Now run another range that's as near as possible at right angles to the first, and remove half the deviation on that heading, using the other compensator, which will be marked "E-W." Next, run a southerly range, eliminating half the remaining error with the N-S compensator, and continue around the compass rose, until you have whittled the deviation down to a degree or two on the cardinal and intercardinal (NE, SW, etc.) headings.

It may happen that your compass doesn't have compensating magnets, or that for some reason you can't get the deviation down to an acceptable minimum. In that case, you'll have to prepare a simple deviation table: The accompanying illustration shows one such table, although there are many forms, and construction of it is self-evident, once you have the necessary information, which consists of deviation figures for headings around the compass rose, at about 15- or 20-degree intervals.

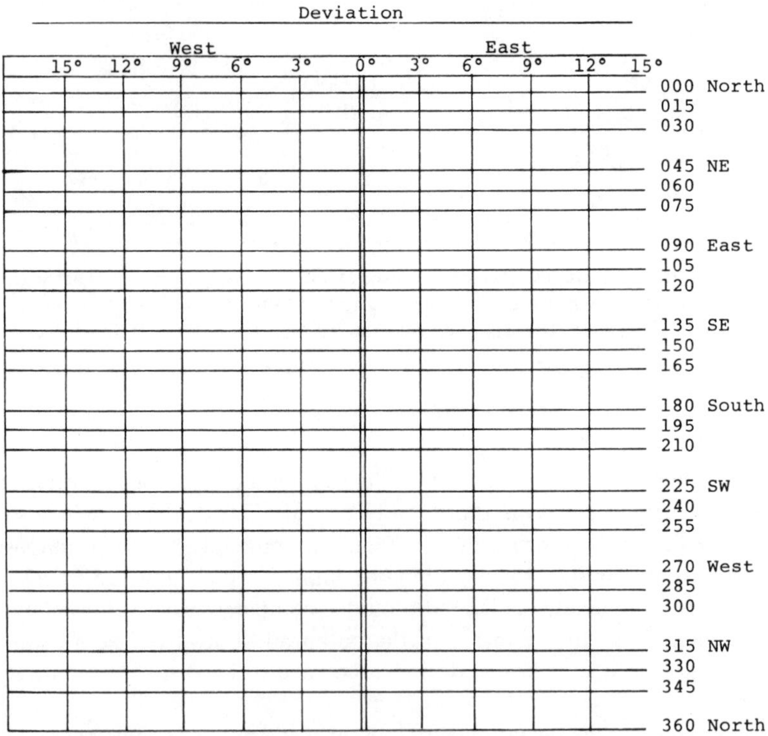

Simple deviation table, to be used with ranges that are at approximately 15-degree intervals. First, calculate the magnetic course in both directions on each range; then run the range in each direction, determining the deviation in each direction. Note the deviation, west or east, at the point on the table approximating the range's direction. (About 12 sets of ranges will be required for a complete table.) Connect the points with a smoothly curving line.

Laying a course

As I remarked in the previous chapter, each of the proprietary models of course protractor has its own system of use, often printed right on the plastic instrument. In what follows, therefore, I won't play favorites but will describe the process of laying a course on the chart using parallel rules, which are not trademarked and are still widely used. To use parallel rules, you'll need to fold the chart so that at least one compass rose is visible. This shouldn't be too much trouble, as these circles of direction appear frequently on every chart. The rose actually consists of two or three concentric circles made up of degree tick marks. The outside circle has its north-south axis aligned with the vertical meridians of longitude on the chart, and thus indicates true north. Inside it is a second circle, usually slightly skewed to the first. Its north is magnetic. There may, in addition, be a third, unnumbered inner circle of marks, which represent the 128 points of the traditional, prenumerical compass. This inner circle is of no use in plotting, and I only mention it to warn that you should avoid its tick marks.

At the center of the compass rose is a small inscription, around a cross. The center of the cross is, of course, the exact center of the rose, and the inscription will say something like VAR 12°30′W (1977) ANNUAL INCREASE 1′. "VAR" stands for variation, the angular difference in direction between true and magnetic north, and if you look at the north arrows of the two concentric circles in our example on the following page, you will see that the inner one is indeed just about 12½ degrees to the left, or west, of the outer one. (There are, of course, 60 angular minutes—60′—in a degree.) The date indicates the amount of variation at a definite time, but since the location of magnetic north changes, so does the amount of variation, and the annual prediction of that change is indicated. It is usually a very small amount, and unless you're using an extremely ancient chart, it shouldn't be worth bothering with.

Let us say you want to set a course between two buoys. With the help of a straightedge—probably the parallel rules themselves—pencil a line between the two buoy symbols. Now walk the rules toward the nearest compass rose, alternately putting pressure on the stationary arm while moving the other arm toward the rose, then reversing the pressure and moving the previously station-ary arm to catch up with the first. It takes a little practice to become used to moving the rules around the chart without their slipping or losing direction, but it's not a hard knack to acquire, and once you have it, you can handle any commercial course protractor easily.

Walk the rules until one of them lies directly across the rose, with one of its edges intersecting the center cross. Now read your magnetic course from the magnetic rose. Be careful to check the nearest numbered degrees and count in the right direction. This is probably the point at which most course-setting mistakes are made. The first few times you lay a course, you can check the accuracy of your rule walking by walking the parallel rules back to the course, to insure that they are still parallel with it. If not, start all over again. In fact,

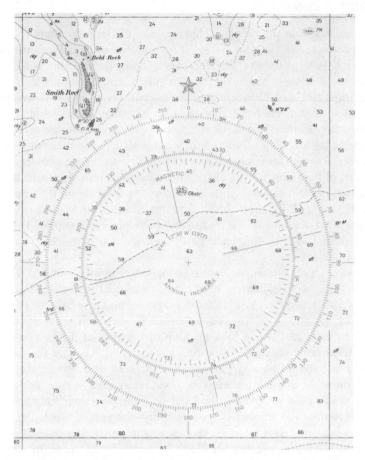

Compass rose: The outer circle of 360 degrees is oriented to the chart's latitude and longitude lines, and hence to true north; the inner, numbered degree circle shows a 12°30′ westerly variation and is oriented to magnetic north, as is the inmost circle, which is based on compass points.

if you have the time, you should probably plot each course line twice, both for practice and for certainty.

Now label the course line. I write three digits above the line, no matter what the actual magnetic course is—"020" for 20 degrees, for instance—and place the letter "M" after the digits, to indicate that it's a magnetic course. Some people add a small arrow to mark which direction the course is intended to show, but this should not be necessary. Under the course line, I put a second label indicating the distance of this particular leg, as an aid to my overall course planning.

There are two ways to measure distance on most charts. The most common type of chart today employs the Mercator Projection, in which the inevitable distortion caused by rendering a round earth on flat paper is relatively unimportant for the large-scale coastal charts. One useful aspect of Mercator charts is that the latitude scales, which normally appear on the sides of the chart (see next page), are marked off in nautical miles and decimal segments thereof. (One minute—1'—of latitude equals one nautical mile, which is 6,080 feet.) Using your dividers, then, you can measure off the distance of an individual course leg against the latitude scale, with a precision of one-tenth of a mile—600 feet—or better.

Charts also have standard distance scales printed on them, most often under the chart title. These scales express distances in nautical or land miles, yards or feet, and sometimes meters. They are accurate for the center of the chart, and while there will be some small distortion at the top and bottom of a Mercator projection, it will not be enough to matter on a coastal or harbor chart.

Course planning

In ordinary weekend cruising, a yacht can traverse long distances without ever requiring serious coastal navigation by her crew, and that's why so many coastwise sailors are so rusty when the need to pilot accurately suddenly arises. As I have said before, the only way to really absorb navigational technique is to do it. You may feel foolish solemnly calculating and plotting a course to a buoy you can easily see, but when you attempt to steer the course you've set, and find yourself 15 degrees off, it will point up your shortcomings dramatically. Even more revealing will be the first fix you attempt, using bearings on three objects: Instead of having the three bearing lines intersect in a tidy asterisk, you will almost certainly have a large, sloppy, and unnerving triangle, within which your boat just may be located.

As a novice, then, and in darkness or heavy weather, it always pays to set your courses from identifiable point to point, using landmarks and intermediate checkpoints to verify matters. First draw your light, penciled line between, say, two buoys. Now examine the course you propose to steer, checking on either side of it for depths too shallow for your boat's draft, for rocks or other obstacles, and for intermediate marks, which you can circle or underline as a memorandum to yourself. A checkpoint need not lie right across your intended course in order to be helpful. Indeed, at night a powerful light can be useful even if it's many miles away, as can a radio-beacon. In fog, even the rather generalized sound of a horn or bell on an aid to navigation can provide extra information—but only if you're prepared to use it.

If you, the navigator, plan to be available during the entire course leg you've

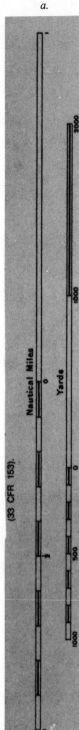

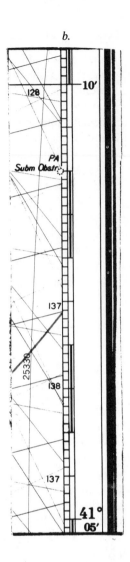

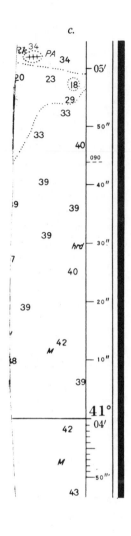

Distance scales: *a,* all charts have a scale in nautical or statute miles, and large-scale charts usually have a scale in yards as well; *b,* coastal charts divide the latitude scale (on the right- and left-hand margins) into tenths of a minute of latitude—a minute of charted latitude being equal to one nautical mile; *c,* large-scale harbor charts may show divisions of latitude in seconds—the distance from 41°04′ to 05′ is of course one nautical mile, and from 41°04′ to 41°04′10″ is one-sixth of a nautical mile, or about 900 feet.

plotted, then perhaps a few jotted notes on the chart will be adequate. But if you will be off watch, or cooking or working below, it may help the crew if you give them a quick briefing, with a written note or two as reminders. It needn't be formal: "Here we are at buoy 24, which you can see just ahead to starboard. From there, we change course to 315 degrees, heading for buoy 37, twelve miles away. About six miles along the way, you should pass lighted bell 1, the entrance to Middle Harbor, off to port about a quarter-mile. You can check the approximate position by turning on the depth sounder—the entrance channel to Middle Harbor is an extension of Middle River, which will show up as a narrow gully, about twenty feet deeper than the average bottom on either side. At ten miles, you'll pass over the edge of Sand Shoal. There's at least six feet of water under the keel, but the shoal will probably be marked by a tide rip, and it will be very noticeable on the depth sounder."

This description is rather elaborate, of course, and as the crew become more experienced, they can figure the data out for themselves. In the beginning, however, it is good practice for all hands to examine the course before sailing it, and for those on deck who are not at the helm to practice relating landmarks to their charted symbols.

As you doubtless noticed from the example, it is very helpful to know how fast your boat is going and how far she has gone, which is why I consider a speedometer/log a nearly essential combination instrument. (If you can only afford one part, the log is probably more important for a cruising yacht, but buy a transducer unit that will allow you to add the speedo later.)

Landlubbers are not too accustomed to formal speed-time-distance calculations, though all of us work a certain number of these problems in our heads every day. Aboard a cruising yacht, however, you want to be able to be fairly precise. The problem is that any sailboat's speed is infinitely variable and only partly controllable, and you can be reasonably sure that your speed of the moment isn't exactly what you'll be making five minutes from now. In many cases, changes in speed are relatively small and tend to average out over an hour or so. Unfortunately, relying on the helmsman for an accurate estimate of his average speed for the past hour can be a mistake. Most people seem to look at the speedometer only when the boat is on a surge, and so their estimates are consistently high. There are also some pessimists, and they tend to remember only the lows, with the inevitable results.

The arithmetic of speed-time-distance calculation rests on three related equations, which can be worked easily on the simplest calculator. Circular slide rules, made of plastic, are also available for the same purpose, and perhaps they are less prone to errors of input. Or you can just work the problem on a piece of scrap paper.

The basic formula is $D = S \times T$, where D is distance, S is speed and T is time. For example, if your boat has a speed of 5 knots and runs for 6 hours, you will have gone (other factors aside) 30 nautical miles. There are a couple of things to remember. First, the units of distance and speed must be compatible: If your distance is nautical miles, your speed will be knots (a knot is one nautical mile per hour); if your speed is in statute miles per hour, your distance must also be in statute miles of 5,280 feet each; if speed is in kilometers per hour, then distance will obviously be in kilometers, too.

It's obvious that most of the time the result of this formula will read out in hours and fractions. When calculating speed-time-distance on individual course legs, it can be more convenient to have the result in minutes, and to accomplish this, simply inject 60 into the equation in the appropriate place: to find time in minutes, when speed and distance are known—$60T = D \div S$; to find distance in miles, when speed and time in minutes are known—$D = S \times T \div 60$.

Whether planning courses or recording runs, it's important to bear in mind that this type of speed-time-distance calculation deals with a boat's speed through the water, either as predicted on the basis of past performance or as recorded on the speedo/log. But in reality, speed over the bottom is what counts, and only some of the more sophisticated loran units will register this information. Speed over the bottom differs from speed through the water because of a number of factors—instrument error, favoring or opposing currents, and heavy weather being perhaps the most significant. Because there are so many chances for error, it's a good idea to check your real progress between charted points, matching it against what your instruments tell you. If you discover a constant rate of error, you can make adjustments in your calculations.

Aids to navigation

The United States has the world's most elaborate system of government-installed and -maintained aids to navigation, amplified by hundreds of privately supervised aids. It sometimes seems that there are too many buoys and markers, but when a thick fog or cloudy night sets in, the average mariner will be grateful for anything he can identify. In this country, the Coast Guard is the agency in charge of aids to navigation and the two publications directly concerned with them—*The Light List* and *Notices to Mariners*. The system of aids to navigation is intended primarily as a service to commercial interests, and so most of the buoys and fixed lights are installed where they'll be useful to larger, deeper-draft vessels, using ports of commercial significance. As a result, the deep water marked by buoyage may be deeper than necessary for the average yacht, which can frequently take shortcuts or even avoid ship channels entirely. Given the increasing volume of commercial traffic around many of our ports, it's not a bad idea to stay out of the large vessels' path as much as possible—but in some areas the marked channels may represent the only available route for *any* type of vessel, and the cautious skipper takes shortcuts only when he knows they'll be safe. There are few things more embarrassing than to find yourself high and dry on a sandbar, in full view of

God and everybody for several hours, as the result of having tried to cut a half-mile off the trip back to anchorage.

In general, the buoyage system is set up to perform several different functions. It warns; it identifies; it directs; it informs. Sometimes a single aid may serve two or more purposes. From earliest times, aids to navigation have served as warnings—of reefs, rocks, wrecks, and many other dangers. Aids that serve as warnings may be isolated buoys, marking single rocks; they may be unlit daybeacons, stuck on the danger itself; they may be fixed lights indicating the seaward end of a reef system. There is no particular shape or color for a buoy whose purpose is to warn, but the function is usually clear from a quick look at the chart.

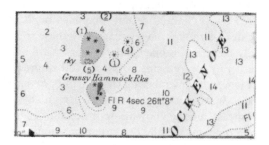

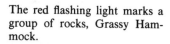
The red flashing light marks a group of rocks, Grassy Hammock.

Identifying aids may be buoys, but they are more frequently fixed lights. If a warning buoy repels, an identifier often attracts—at least to a degree—since it is likely to be located on or near a major traffic lane or a prominent land mass. The most familiar identifier aids are perhaps the primary seacoast lights and towers: Swiftsure, Nantucket Shoals, Ambrose, Fastnet—the list is long. While there is no distinctive form for these aids, they usually emit a light and/or Morse code radiobeacon pattern that will identify them.

Sea buoys, the offshore markers that indicate the existence of an inlet entrance several miles inshore of them, are other identifiers. They don't send radio signals and their light patterns are hardly unusual, but they stand out because of their isolation and because they often carry a letter identification instead of the numbering normal to buoys.

Aids to navigation that direct the mariner are most frequently organized into systems that mark a navigable channel. In coastal waters the system is fairly simple, although when a main channel branches, it can get complicated, as can a junction of two channels, each leading separately to the sea.

The principle of channel marking, as every beginning mariner learns, is "red-right-returning," a mnemonic that expresses the practice of setting red buoys on the right-hand side of channels when returning from the ocean, or when going from a larger body of water to a smaller one. On the other side of the channel from the red buoys are black [or, in the future, green] buoys, marking the left-hand verge of the channel from seaward. Beyond these basics, there are a few other characteristics of channel marking systems that are useful to know. As this is written, the Coast Guard is embarking on a massive changeover of buoy colors and light characteristics, to make the United States's system correspond more closely to other buoyage systems throughout the world. The changeover will not be completed until 1989, and I have accordingly given, in the following paragraphs, current buoyage colors and lights. Material in brackets indicates the new color and light patterns that will be going into effect between now and 1989. Until then, either old or new buoy colors and lights may be encountered.

Red buoys may be of any shape, but a majority of them are the unlighted, truncated cones called *nuns*. Lighted buoys of any size are usually shaped like midget oil derricks, with the light on top. Red buoys may have either white or red [red only] lights, and all red buoys, lighted or not, are even-numbered. Red buoys, lighted or not, may also be fitted with horns, whistles, bells, or gongs—although buoys that carry these sound-producing devices will generally be found in open water, where wave action can help produce the noise, either by compressing air to sound the horn or by swinging the bell's clappers. It is worth remembering that a bell buoy has four clappers acting on a single bell. Wave action produces an irregular ringing, all on a single note. By contrast, a gong buoy has four metal discs in a stack, and four clappers, each of a different length. The resultant sound is an irregular peal of four different notes, quite distinguishable from a bell.

Fixed aids to navigation may also be integrated into a channel marking system, in which case they will be numbered as part of the sequence. They will seldom, however, be painted the color appropriate to their station, but they will carry a square or triangular plaque of red or black [green] on which their numbers appear. A fixed aid's light also coincides with its nominal color.

Black [to become green] buoys may be cage-shaped if they are lighted or contain sound devices, but most often they are the familiar, cylindrical cans, carrying odd numbers. Lighted black [green] buoys display either white or green [green only] lights.

Sometimes, when a channel extends for a considerable distance with no sharp bends or clearly defined edges, it is cheaper for the Coast Guard to use a single midchannel marker, instead of paired red and black buoys. Midchannel buoys are black and white [red and white], striped vertically, and they never carry numbers, but may be lettered. If lighted, a midchannel mark repeatedly flashes a white light in a short-long pattern, sometimes described as "Mo A" on charts, short for international Morse "A"—dot-dash. The vertically striped midchannel buoys are also used to indicate the seaward entrances to inlets, being placed beyond the black "1" and red "2" that mark the beginning of the entrance channel.

The numbers on aids marking a channel run consecutively from seaward to the head of navigation or end of that channel—so that on rivers or long channels, you may see buoy numbers into the hundreds. Whenever a subsidiary channel branches off the main one, a new numbered channel begins, with

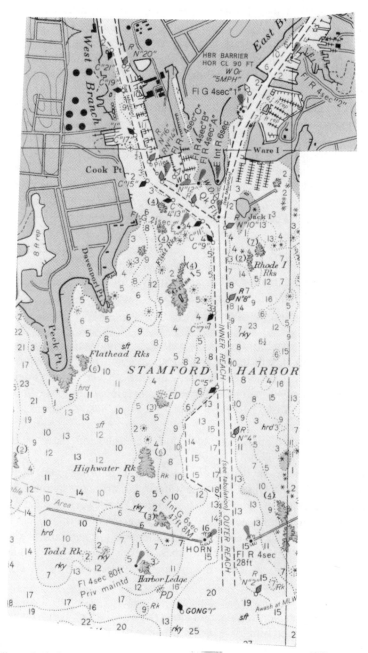

A well-marked channel; note that the numbering begins outside the breakwaters, with Gong 1. The straight channel is not marked with lighted buoys because the range at the north end—quick-flashing white and equal-interval red—is sufficient to indicate the proper course at night. The main channel is the West Branch; for the subsidiary East Branch, a new series of numbers is required. The bulkhead of the big marina on the West Branch is marked by three flashing red lights.

the junction marked by an unnumbered buoy striped horizontally red and black [red and green]. These junction buoys may be lighted, in which case the lens will be clear [red or green], but they can be of any shape—nun, can, or cage. The shape and the color of the top stripe are a clue to direction: If the top stripe is black [green] and the shape a can, the preferred or major channel (from seaward) is to the right. A red-topped nun indicates that the main channel from seaward is to its left. A glance at the chart will instantly show what's happening.

Junction buoys also serve to mark obstructions, either alone or as part of a channel system. The same rules apply, but the mariner is cautioned to pass well clear on either side.

Buoys, as well as fixed aids to navigation, have patterns for their light signals. The ordinary buoy, regardless of color, emits a single flash at 2.5- or 4-second intervals. (The chart notation will be "Fl 2.5 sec," or; for a red light, "Fl R 4 sec".) Because these two patterns are used over and over again, it can be very difficult at night to determine which buoy is which in a channel seen more or less end-on. In the new system, more patterns—one, two, or three flashes—will be available for red or green buoys. More important buoys may give a single flash at a different time interval, or may have a pattern composed of sixty or more flashes per minute, noted on the chart as "Qk Fl," for quick flash.

Junction and obstruction buoys, as well as aids marking abrupt direction changes in a channel, will have a special signal comprising a group of quick flashes followed by a period of darkness, listed as "I Qk Fl," or interrupted quick flash. [New signal will be red or green, corresponding to the buoy's top stripe, in a pattern of two flashes followed by a single flash—"Gp Fl (2 + 1)," for composite group flash.]

Fixed aids to navigation may have more complicated patterns of light flashes, often in two colors.

Although any aid to navigation can be said to be informational, the orange and white markers of the uniform state waterway marking system are particularly designed for this function. These can-shaped buoys warn of rocks or other obstructions, indicate the boundaries of swimming areas or other places forbidden to boats, and display speed limit and other operational data. It's usually necessary to come fairly close to one of these aids in order to read its message, but at the same time, you want to approach slowly, in case the information requires you to keep clear.

When setting up a course leg, especially for sailing at night, it's a sensible idea to pause at each aid to navigation along the way until you understand why it's there. If you're counting on seeing a particular fixed aid, you may want to note its light or sound characteristics in the instructions to the watch. Although it mars the chart somewhat, on a voyage to a new or demanding area, I usually mark the important aids to navigation with a yellow or red felt-tipped pen, so I can pick them out again more easily when I'm tired and confused. (If your chart table has a red night light, however, don't mark the chart—or anything else you'll want to read in the dark—in red, as the red reading light will cancel out the color.)

Besides aids to navigation, certain landmarks ashore can be identified by night or day. Most important bridges are lighted along the lengths of their supporting cables, not to mention the flashing red lights on their towers. A radio tower or even a high building will usually carry a flashing red aircraft warning light, while some industrial installations exhibit unmistakable strobe lights. It can be very helpful to learn the distinctive day and night appearances of both major fixed aids and landmarks in your area, so that after a while you won't need to check their identities on the chart.

Tides and currents

In the previous chapter, I discussed in principle the operation of tides and currents. Here, I want to examine how to allow for them in your course and trip planning. There is a wide variation in the range of tide and current around the coasts of the United States, even sometimes in two places quite close together. In Long Island Sound, for instance, the tidal range is about seven feet, while the current, in most of the Sound, is about a knot at maximum ebb or flood. Only a few miles away, in Great South Bay, the tide range is less than a foot, and the current about half the force of the Sound's. When sailing into new waters, examine the tide and current predictions rather than making a guess. In your own cruising area, you should be able to develop a feel not only for the tide range at various times during the lunar month, but also for the state of the tide at any given moment. If you train yourself by regular observation of pilings, prominent rocks that cover and uncover, or the clearance under bridges, you will soon have virtually instant recognition of the state of the local tide.

Estimates of current are somewhat more subtle. To determine the direction of the current's flow you normally need some fixed object—a buoy or piling —in relatively open water. If there is little or no wind, an anchored boat will serve as an indicator. (In breezy conditions, however, shoal-draft boats respond to the thrust of the wind, while deep-draft vessels normally align themselves with the current.) Trying to calculate the current's force by eye alone can be quite tricky. A buoy or other relatively small floating mark is the best gauge, but even then, you will need some experience of the current's action on that particular floating object in order to make an accurate estimate.

In course planning, tide and current are separate factors. The tide determines which shoals you may sail over and which form temporary barriers; sometimes, if a fixed bridge bars your path, you may be able to go under it at low tide, but not at high. Current, unless it is very strong, seldom creates an absolute obstruction. Instead, it may help or hinder you on your way, or merely set you off your chosen track. The degree to which this will happen is, of course, directly related to your boat's cruising speed: A 1-knot current on the bow, for instance, will slow a 4-knot boat down by a quarter of its total speed, while a 20-knot powerboat won't be affected enough to matter.

Aboard a vehicle as slow as a sailboat, it's a good idea to incorporate current predictions in your course planning. If, by adjusting your sailing schedule, you can have the current with you instead of against you, it can make a considerable difference in your forward progress. Instead of making 3 knots against a 1-knot current, for example, our boat with a speed of 4 knots through the water can make 5 knots over the bottom when the current is helping.

Remember, however, that the current has a cycle. It runs at maximum strength only during the two middle hours of its term (which is usually six hours and a quarter). During the first and last hours of the cycle, it may be inconsequential. And remember also that predictions of current strength, in the *Tidal Current Tables,* are just that—predictions. A strong wind blowing against a current can effectively retard it, as well as change the timing of current turn.

When the current is directly ahead or astern, as it often is on, say, a river, you should have few problems calculating its effects. But when the current is at right angles to your desired course, or at some other angle forward or abaft the beam, it can be difficult to set a course with real precision. Fortunately, that kind of accuracy is seldom required, but every navigator should have a reasonable idea of how to allow for current.

Although many of the new navigational calculators have elaborate programs to take current into account, it is simpler and no less accurate just to work out what is called a current vector diagram. This daunting term needn't scare you. To begin with, you need certain information: your boat's speed through the water; the course you want to make; the velocity of the current, called its drift; and the current's direction, called its set.

Using the mile scale on the chart, mark the course line to indicate an hour's expected run, A to B. (If you are under power, your speed through the water should be pretty predictable; if under sail, you should estimate conservatively.) Now, from the same starting point A, plot a second line, A to C, to show the effect of current for one hour. For example, let's say that our desired course from A to B is 090° magnetic, our boat's anticipated speed through the water is 4 knots, and there is a current on our starboard quarter whose set (direction) is 140° M. and whose drift (speed) is 1.5 knots. Our course line A–B, then, is 090° M., 4 scale miles in length. Our current vector, from A to C, is 140° M., 1.5 miles on the same scale. Now connect points B and C, and measure that line. Its direction, 073°M., indicates the course you should steer in order to make good the desired 090°. But with the current at least partially behind you, you'll be making more than 4 knots over the bottom, even allowing for the current set. Measure the line B–C in scale-mile units. You will find that it is about 3.5 nautical miles, and the length signifies that, thanks to the current, it will take you only as much time to go 3.5 miles as it would normally require to go 4.0. (In this case, $T = \dfrac{60D}{S}$, with D equal to 3.5—the distance between

B and C—and S the known speed through the water of 4 knots). In about 52 minutes, therefore, and heading about 075° M., you should have attained point B.

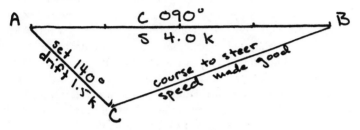

Current vector diagram.

This system works, but it does have several problems. First, it requires a new plot every hour, which is a nuisance, although a minor one; second, it does not read out in whole hours, which makes your computations with the tidal current tables that much trickier; and third, it reinforces the illusion that the current is exactly predictable. In answer to the first objection, if you really are in a situation where current is seriously affecting your boat's course, you should re-plot your position at least every hour; to answer the second, a simple hand calculator will resolve even the fractions with ease. As to the third difficulty, it will probably be best to work confidently with your plotted vector, even though you may have doubts about it—they can be resolved with your re-plot.

Take another current-plotting situation: Say you know there is a tidal current more or less across your bow, but you have no idea of its strength. Unless it is absolutely vital that you make a guess before setting out, it's best to plot your first course without taking current into account, but exercising great care to steer your desired heading and keeping track of your speed through the water. At the end of an hour, you find that instead of proceeding, as you had wanted to, from A to B, you have in fact wound up at C. You now have the information you need to construct a current vector for the next hour: Connect the points B and C, measure the distance and plot the direction, and that's the hourly vector. Just remember when establishing a course for the second hour to use C as your jumping-off point. Your correction may be slightly too great or too small—what you've established, after all, is the vector for the hour *past*, and the current is probably changing its force, if not its direction—but you should be back in the ball park.

Most of the time, however, the coastal cruiser doesn't bother with calculations like this. Familiar with the currents in his area, and with his boat's leeway on different headings, he lays off a rough, rule-of-thumb correction and finds it good enough. While that may be comforting most of the time, a feeling of confidence in working current vectors can be very helpful when, sooner or later, you have to execute a current correction on a rainy night or in thick fog.

In making a landfall when current has been a problem, there's one handy trick of the trade that has served many navigators well. Let us say you're heading for the narrow mouth of an inlet in an otherwise featureless beach (and there are more of these than you might think). There's a current whose general direction you know, but you've had nothing to measure its force against. Rather than make a freehand allowance, set your course for the desired objective. You won't, in all likelihood, come in on the inlet mouth, but at least you'll know which direction to turn when you sight the beach—which is more information than you'd have if you had guessed at a correction.

By reverse token, when approaching the same kind of isolated landmark and current is not a factor, it may be a good idea to plot a course that should give you a landfall well to one side of the object or entrance you're looking for. Once again, you'll at least know which direction to turn when you sight shore.

Establishing a fix

Many technically knowledgeable navigators are less than adept in real-life situations simply because they fail to take all the elements into account. Nowhere does this happen more often than in locating, or fixing, one's position. The traditional fix, which allows the pilot to say with confidence that his boat is in a particular place, usually relies on crossing two or more position lines. They may—most frequently will—be magnetic compass bearings on aids to navigation or charted landmarks, and with practice this is a very reliable and rapid method of getting a fix. But too many navigators forget that there are plenty of methods for establishing the necessary lines of position (LOPs).

Since this is not a treatise on navigation, I don't intend to present a complete list—and many of the techniques on such a list would be suitable only for experts. Even so, consider the potential sources of information that are usually available. First, of course, the presence of government or private aids to navigation. These are almost always the best assistance the pilot has, because professional care goes into their siting and their charting, and they are usually easily recognizable. When choosing aids (or anything else) for a fix, try to get the two sighted objects at right angles to each other. This will reduce the incidence of error. If you employ three objects—and you should, every chance you get—they will ideally be located at about 120-degree intervals, one from the next. Probably the smallest useful angle between two objects is 40 degrees or so; any angle shallower than that will create a large area of possible error, even for someone who is quite good with a sighting compass.

Next best after formal aids to navigation are unmistakable landmarks, preferably lone stacks, tanks, or bridges. Before relying on any such object, however, be sure to check the chart for possible twins. If you can see a tower or

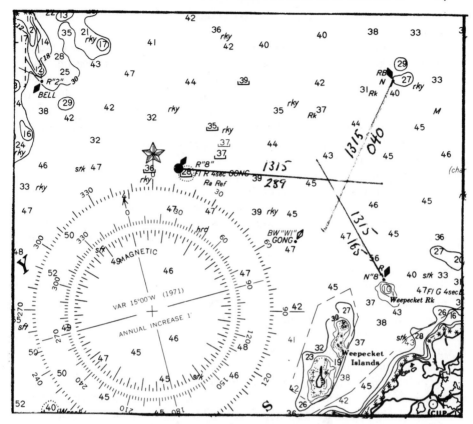

Three-point fix; above the line of each bearing is the approximate time it was made, and below is the bearing in degrees. Using the four-digit, 24-hour system for time and the three-digit, 360-degree system for the bearing avoids confusion as to which is which.

stack but cannot find its charted symbol, look further inland on the chart: It's amazing how often a vertical structure two or even three miles inshore can appear to be right behind the beach. Buildings can make very good landmarks, but they are seldom accurately or fully described on a chart. And abandoned lighthouses, at least from a distance, often look very functional indeed. Be suspicious of the high-rise that completely dominates the skyline—it may not yet be on the chart, just as the church whose spire was prominent enough to be charted a few years back has now disappeared behind a row of apartment towers.

Natural landmarks are useful, but the stranger must be cautious, especially in interpreting the sometimes whimsical names given on the chart. In my own harbor, the Sheep Rocks are as unlike sheep as you could imagine, but the nearby White Rocks stand out, courtesy of the gull colony, in sunny or cloudy weather.

Aside from visual lines of position, you may also use one or more radio LOPs—perhaps a commercial radio station and a marine radiobeacon. The seabottom irregularities detected by your depth sounder can sometimes provide a linear position indicator, and occasionally the range of visibility of a light will at least tell you in a general way how distant from it you are when it first appears on the horizon. Bear in mind that there is no rule against using one kind of LOP with another—crossing a radiobeacon line with a visual bearing, for instance.

Perhaps the most useful position-fixing aid of all is the charted range—not the seldom-available range established by the Coast Guard, employing two aids, one behind the other, but the natural range that occurs when two objects fall into line of sight. Such a range gives you an automatic and virtually foolproof LOP without the necessity of a compass bearing, and all you need is the alertness to notice it. You can give your powers of observation a jog in the right direction by scanning the chart in advance for possible ranges in useful positions: Especially when running along an unfamiliar shore, you are more likely to see something if you're already aware it exists. Sometimes it's possible to line up the steep side of an island or cliff with a stack or tower and create a range that way. This can be tricky, however, especially if the natural object has a curved shoreline. Two aids to navigation or an aid and a charted, manmade object are perhaps the most reliable sources for ranges.

On some dreary coasts, reliable landmarks are so few that two of them are seldom in sight at once. There are several techniques for making a single LOP do double duty, but one in particular is suitable for the beginner. The *running fix* sounds tricky, but once you have mastered it, it's immensely useful in all sorts of situations. Essentially, the running fix (or RFix, as it is abbreviated on the chart) consists in moving a line of position forward in space and time to a more convenient place, so that it can then intersect another LOP. Here's how it's done: Let us say that you're running along a relatively featureless stretch of coast, heading 270° M. at a steady 5 knots. In the next few miles, the chart shows only two identifiable aids to navigation, but they're spaced so far apart as to be invisible one from the other.

You pass the first buoy, and take a bearing on it of 170° M., marking the bearing and the time—1230—on the chart. (When it's necessary to indicate time in navigation, it's customary to use the twenty-four-hour system and always to write the time as four digits, so it cannot be confused with a three-digit course or bearing.) An hour and a half later, at 1400, the second charted object is in view on the bow, bearing 226° M. Because your course and speed have been approximately constant during the period, you know by simple arithmetic that you've come about 7.5 miles since the first sight, in the direction 090° M. Accordingly, you advance the 1230 bearing of 170°M. parallel to itself, and a distance of 7.5 miles. It now neatly intersects the 1400 bearing of 226°M., to give you your running fix.

Because the bearings in a running fix are not simultaneous, there is the possibility of error from a number of sources during the time between bearings: Your speed computation might have been wrong, there might have been a leeway factor you didn't know about, your helmsman might not have held a steady course. For these reasons, a running fix isn't considered as reliable as a standard fix, but in—and with—practice, it works out well. Be sure to label it properly, and to indicate how you advanced the first LOP. This is done by putting the time of actual bearing—1230, in this case—and the time to which the bearing was advanced: 1230–1400. There is no limit to the number of times a bearing may be advanced, but each time you do so, the cumulative possibilities of error become greater. If you need to employ a second running fix, it will probably be better practice to advance your 1400 LOP, rather than the one you took at 1230.

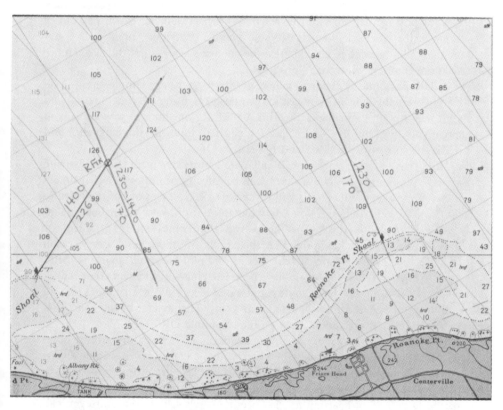

A running fix looks more complicated than it is. The first bearing (at right), of 170°, was made at 12:30 P.M. An hour and a half later the second bearing, of 226°, was taken. By walking the line of the first a distance equal to the distance run in one and a half hours, and in the same direction as the boat's course, the first line is "advanced" to cross the later bearing.

When your sole visible charted aid or landmark is very prominent, you can work a running fix using that single object alone. Take one bearing when the object is about 45 degrees off the bow, and another when it is in the same relative position off the quarter; advance the first to cross the second, and there you are. As long as you maintain a straight course and a steady, known speed between bearings, a running fix is remarkably reliable.

DR and EP

Sometimes, as when you are making a run of several hours out of sight of land, you won't have anything at all with which to make a fix at hourly intervals. Although there's nothing to prevent you from running blindly along your course, trusting to luck, it's generally a good procedure to work out a dead reckoning position, or DR, once an hour. For one thing, keeping track of your passage in this way sharpens your senses and helps you pay closer attention to what's happening. If you wander off course, or if your speed changes, you're more likely to notice the change sooner—and thus keep more accurate track of your boat's progress.

A DR position, by navigational convention, is a very simple thing. You simply extrapolate from your last known position, using the time interval and your boat's course and speed: Steering 357°M. for one hour at 5.25 knots, you move your position five and a quarter nautical miles north (magnetic) and mark the spot with the time and the letters DR.

Note that you don't attempt to calculate leeway or current when figuring a DR. Many times, in open water, it can be difficult or impossible to estimate these effects accurately, and it will be better to leave them out of the calculation. On the other hand, if you know the amount of leeway your boat makes on a given heading (the kind of knowledge that comes with experience), or have an accurate prediction for current set and drift, then there's every reason to write up the appropriate current vectors and plot the result, marking it EP, for *estimated position.* Since you have been working with elements that cannot be checked, you don't have anything as reliable as a fix or a running fix, but you do want to indicate to yourself and to any later reader of the chart that you've employed more data than go into a simple DR.

In essence, then, normal navigation generally involves nothing more complex than keeping track visually of where you are. Once you've become disoriented, even in waters you've sailed before, it can be extraordinarily difficult to pick up the thread again, while if you take the trouble to work positions regularly and shoot bearings as they occur, there's seldom reason to get lost.

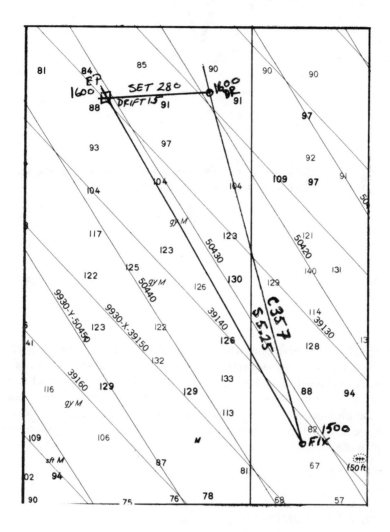

Dead reckoning (DR) vs. estimated position. The boat's course (357°M.), speed (5.25 knots) and 3:00 P.M. position are known. To find the dead reckoning position one hour later, simply advance the boat's position five and a quarter nautical miles on the course 357°. In this case, however, the navigator knows that there is a current with a speed (drift) of about 1½ knots setting approximately west. From the DR position, he plots a line whose length corresponds to the current's drift—1.5 miles—and whose set is the same as that of the current—280°. This estimated position (EP) consists of the DR position improved by a good estimate of current effect.

V

~~~~~~~~~~~

Tactical Navigation

So far, we've been examining the practice of elementary coastal navigation more or less in isolation—separate, that is, from the weather, the time of day, your boat's capabilities, and your own talents. What might be called tactical navigation involves the consideration of piloting techniques appropriate to particular circumstances. Let's consider the applied use of some familiar navigation tools, and then examine some special conditions of navigation you're bound to encounter sooner or later.

Chain of soundings

I have already mentioned the use of the depth sounder as an instrument of navigation, instead of just a warning system. Skilled coastal navigators are able to make considerable use of their depth sounders, and even a beginner can achieve significant results. Perhaps the most common piloting technique here is the use of a chain of soundings to create a position line. To work this trick, you require an accurately calibrated sounder, a general notion of where you are, a steady speed along a properly held course, and a bottom whose configuration can tell you something.

When delivered, a depth sounder is calibrated to read the distance between the seabottom and the transducer, usually located someplace forward at the bottom of the hull (not at the base of the keel). This means, of course, that there is an error of a few feet—the distance from transducer to waterline—

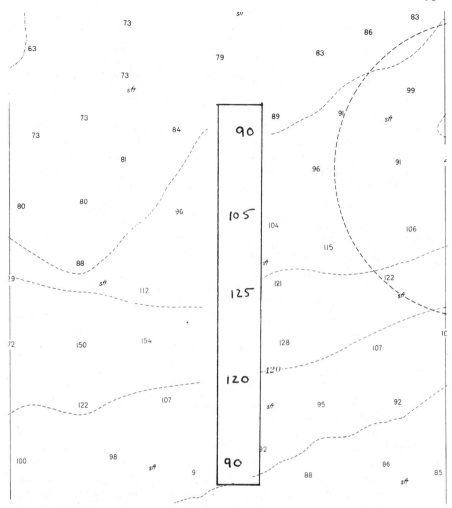

Chain of soundings. As described in the text, the navigator has noted his depth-sounder readings at intervals that correspond to the intervals of charted soundings. This line of five soundings closely matches only one area of the chart and gives a good indication of approximate position.

between the sounder's reading and the true depth at any point. Some sounders can be recalibrated to read either true depth or depth from keel to seabottom, but if yours cannot be adjusted, you will have to bear constantly in mind the amount of correction required on the depth sounder's reading.

An easy way of preserving the information is to punch it into one of those pressure-sensitive plastic tapes with adhesive backs, and then stick the message—"+2 ft. for true depth," or whatever—on the depth sounder dial.

Another correction that needs to be made when doing precise navigation in an area of considerable tidal rise and fall is the adjustment for present height of tide. As mentioned earlier, tide, like current, is generally amenable to the rule of twelfths, so if you know from the tide tables when the tidal cycle began and the tidal range, which is usually on the chart itself, you should be able to figure how much deeper or (rarely) shallower the water is at the moment than are the depth notations on the chart. For instance, if the range of tide is 6.5 feet in the general area where you're sailing, and high water was two hours ago, then you should add about 5 feet to the charted depths, based on Mean Low or Mean Lower Low Water: The first hour of tidal rise or fall is $^1\!/_{12}$ of the total, the second is $^2\!/_{12}$; so the present tide is $^3\!/_{12}$ *down* from high water —and, more to the point, $^9\!/_{12}$ or ¾ of tidal rise *up* from low water. Three-quarters of 6.5 is a shade under 5, but so close that the sounder will not make a distinction. The correction applies, of course, to all depth readings on the chart for the ensuing half-hour or so.

Presuming now that your boat is traversing an area where the bottom shows fairly marked changes of depth, you consult the chart to determine how far apart the soundings on it are. Let's say, for the sake of argument, that on this segment of your 1:40,000-scale chart, the soundings are about an inch apart. In real terms, then, the soundings would be 40,000 inches apart, or a little more than half a nautical mile. If your boat is moving at 4 knots on a steady course, she will cover half a nautical mile about every seven and a half minutes, which establishes the frequency with which you must record soundings. In practice, you should watch the sounder for fifteen consecutive seconds every seven and a half minutes, long enough to get a sense of the average depth. Take that figure and correct it according to the present state of the tide; if, for example, the tidal range is four feet from low to high, and if it is two hours after low water, then you subtract one foot from each depth sounder reading to correct the depth back to the datum of soundings. Write the result along the edge of a clean piece of paper, with the same one-inch intervals as between the soundings on the chart. With five or six corrected soundings in a row, you should now be able to match the line of soundings to your chart. Although in a slow boat this is a time-consuming and imprecise method, there are occasions when it may be all you have as a source of positioning information.

If yours is a flashing-light sounder, it may also be able to give you some ideas about the consistency of the seabottom beneath you. If the bottom is relatively flat and hard, each depth indication will be a single, thin line of light, but if the bottom is muddy, the light beam will be broad and fuzzy. Sharp, thin lines close together suggest an uneven, probably rocky bottom. Again, the evidence is not precise, but it can be better than nothing, and with practice, your observations can be remarkably accurate. Correlating the nature of the bottom with the line of soundings may give you a second chart clue, as many charts still include abbreviated notations of bottom composition, in italic type, among the soundings. (A list of abbreviations appears in the NOS booklet *Chart No. 1* and also as a part of the legend, or expanded label, on the chart itself.)

Understanding the RDF

The radio direction finder and automatic direction finder are perfect examples of instruments that can be trickier to use than you might expect. In each case, it's important to establish right away the amount of deviation that affects the instrument in its usual location. (If you employ a hand-held RDF, however, you want to find a spot on deck where magnetic interference will be near zero.) Chances are good that your fixed-location RDF or ADF will require a deviation table, if you want accurate readings. In order to work out deviation, you must first be able to see the transmitting antenna of a radiobeacon or, failing that, a commercial AM radio station.

Run the boat toward, away from and across the antenna on known magnetic headings, while taking radio and visual bearings. If the radio bearings, which are by their nature magnetic, correspond with the readings from the yacht's compass, you're in good shape. If you're off by 5 or 10 degrees, however, note the errors and the heading of the boat at the time, and then run as many more courses as possible. This procedure should provide an adequate deviation table, with readings every 10 or 15 degrees around the compass. Remember that the deviation is caused by forces within the boat, so it is the boat's heading, not the beacon's bearing, that determines the error. When making corrections, however, the magnetic bearing to the antenna ashore is what you apply the correction to.

For example, you've worked up your RDF deviation table, which tells you that on your present course of 275°M., deviation of the signal from a beacon, regardless of its direction from the boat, is 10°W. This means that the RDF "sees" the beacon antenna 10 degrees farther to the west than it actually is, and so to determine its real magnetic direction from the boat, you must subtract 10 degrees from the RDF bearing. If the deviation were east, you would add the error to the radio bearing to obtain the real magnetic direction of the antenna.

Plotting RDF or ADF bearings on the chart is simple enough. You presumably know the identity and position of the station on which you took the bearing. Using parallel rules and a convenient compass rose, take the bearing direction from the inner rose and walk it over to the antenna site. Extend a line back from the antenna in the direction of your boat's position. Plot a second radio bearing (or a bearing of another sort), cross the two bearings, and you have your boat's position.

Marine and aviation radiobeacons don't employ voice transmission, but use Morse code identifiers instead. This can be a bit daunting at first, but picking up the two or three letters of code is no great problem, and after a while you

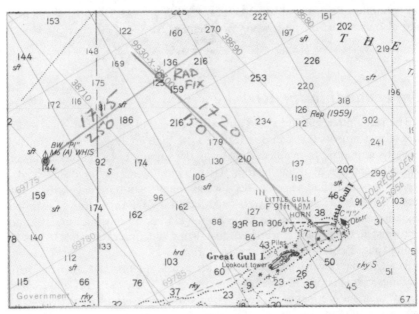

A fix employing one visual bearing and a radiobeacon. (Note that the Little Gull radiobeacon broadcasts on 306 kHz, transmitting a Morse code letter 'J' and, once a minute, a 10-second dash.)

will begin to recognize the characteristic signals of major radiobeacons in your area from their general patterns. Commercial radio stations only identify themselves occasionally, often on the hour or half-hour. If you use the same one or two stations regularly, however, you will soon be able to recognize the announcers' voices.

When taking a radio bearing, it often helps to use both the visual null meter and the headphones to determine the precise null. The RDF receives the station's inaudible carrier wave and homes on it, so you don't have to be receiving the actual dot-dash pattern in order to have a reading on the null meter. Your ear can hear only a signal, however, so most radiobeacons broadcast a ten-second dash every minute, to aid in aural direction finding. With a commercial station, of course, aural nulls are usually easier to obtain. When you are confident that you've captured the best available null, call out "Mark!" to the helmsman, who then reads the steering compass. Relate the boat's heading to your bearing, corrected for deviation if necessary, and that's all there is to it.

With a hand-held unit having a self-contained compass the process is, of course, simpler. Take the RDF on deck and determine your null by rotating the set itself. As soon as you're sure of the null, read the bearing from the self-contained compass. I find hand-held sets considerably easier to use, but this advantage is canceled by their relatively low battery power, which limits both the distance from which a signal can be received and the time you can use the set before recharging.

Keeping a log

Most cruising sailors are ambivalent about log keeping. That is, they know they ought to do so, and they fully intend to, but somehow the log seems to trail off after the first few entries. It seems to me that there are two possible causes (besides plain laziness, that is). First is the attempt, at first, to record too much data in the log. If you try to write down every possibly pertinent fact, you won't have time to sail the boat, or enjoy the water. The second difficulty is in the format of the logbook itself. I have used perhaps a dozen different styles of log over the years, and have even designed a couple of logbooks for publication, and I've yet to encounter a true all-purpose log. Perhaps the closest I've come to such an animal is the plain, spiral-bound school notebook, with lined pages and a soft cover, available in a number of different sizes at any stationery store. Its cheapness and simplicity are its best features—you can write any damn thing you want, unconstrained by columns or headings; make lists and tear them out without ruining a valuable volume.

The only real function of a log is to record and preserve information you might want to recall later. The type of information varies with the situation. For instance, on a daysail you notice that you're missing a couple of cotterpins in the standing rigging turnbuckles, and you replace them from your ditty bag, using all the spares in the process. If you're like me, you need a note to remind yourself to buy more, of the correct size: Measure them, write it down now, and it'll probably get done. Or maybe you don't need to replace a consumable part immediately but do want to record that your supply is dwindling: I keep a running "things to buy" list on the back page of my log, and every once in awhile I tear out that page and purchase what I need.

Say you notice that your crew have no way to brace themselves when the boat is well heeled on one tack. The log is a good place to record that deficiency, and a good place also in which to sketch possible solutions. A part of my log that grows through the season and shrinks over the winter is my "jobs to do" list. Some of the tasks are annual or seasonal, and it is good to keep last year's list, to check it against this year's chores.

Some people also record sail inventories and other lists of gear in the log, especially serial-numbered items. There's some point to this, but it seems to me more logical to keep such a list at home, since it is primarily a protection in case someone steals the boat.

All this omits the nominal purpose of a log, which is to record what the boat has done, where she's gone, and with whom aboard. It's obvious that someone setting out for an afternoon's sail isn't likely to make a log entry, but it can be an excellent idea periodically to put the boat through her paces and record the results, in terms of the accuracy of depth sounder, speedometer/log, compass, and other instruments. Last year's readings are interesting starting points but aren't necessarily valid this season.

On a more extended cruise, however, formal log keeping makes a good deal of sense. Generally speaking, there are three kinds of data you may want to record. The first is information pertaining to weather conditions. As most people are aware, local forecasting of weather isn't difficult, but it does depend on sustained observation. The best way to do that is to summarize, once an hour or so, the visible trends. These include barometric pressure and tendency (rising fast, falling slowly, or whatever the case may be); wind direction and speed; types of cloud cover and development. If you also have a source of professional weather forecasts, it's not a bad idea to jot down the essentials of these predictions in the morning, at midday, and before you go to bed. All this data will help you create your own forecasts for the immediate, local area, as well as picking up developing trends that may be more important in a day or two.

The second type of data to record is navigational. While you can keep a nearly adequate record of the yacht's progress on the chart itself, you can amplify that information by notes in the log. For example, if you have a log (the instrument, this time, not the book) to record distance traveled, it will be a good idea to enter the actual log readings at each change of watch, or other regular interval, and work the arithmetic right on the logbook page. Later, if you're in doubt about your figures, they are right at hand for checking. The same is true if you're applying deviation to correct your magnetic course. If a watchkeeper has the feeling that the boat may be making extraordinary leeway, the log is the place to enter that hunch—it may be valuable later.

A good deal of the log's navigational data can be anticipatory: If you expect an aid to navigation to become visible at a certain time, note down that expectation, together with the light's characteristics or the tower's appearance (both of which are specified in the *Light List*). If the weather is expected to change, the skipper can leave instructions for sail or course changes in the log —although on a small cruising yacht, either event is likely to be noisy enough to rouse all hands, and certainly the hyperattentive skipper.

The log is a good place to note the Morse code signal of a radiobeacon, and its frequency, to make things easier later when you will be listening for it. I always write such signals down in actual dots and dashes—the things I'll be hearing—rather than their letter equivalents. And if you can't locate an expected signal, make a note of that, as well, as something to check on later.

It will happen, especially in nighttime DR navigation, that expected runs don't materialize, that the course the skipper sets isn't what the boat seems to be making. Recording, preferably at short intervals, discrepancies between what you planned to happen and what is occurring will help the navigator and skipper figure out what went wrong and how best to correct it.

The final category of log headings consists of incidents along the way. These may be the names and addresses of pleasant people you run into, or dreadful marinas you want never to visit again. It may be the record, as nearly and vividly as you can reconstruct it, of an accident. It may be a sketch of a cove where the natural landmarks aren't charted. Your log's format should allow for all this data, too.

One final note: If your boat has a VHF-FM or SSB radio, you are required by FCC regulation to maintain a log pertaining to its operation and maintenance. The items that a yacht radio station must log are very few: Repairs or adjustments to the set made by an FCC-licensed technician, and distress or urgency traffic in which your station participates are about the only headings that are really necessary. If you keep a formal radio watch on VHF channel 16 or SSB 2182 kHz, you should record the hours of such a watch—although few pleasure craft stations bother to do so. A radio log can be a part of your regular log—many commercially published logbooks contain separate pages for radio data—or it may be a small pamphlet provided by the set's manufacturer, which I think is probably simpler.

Navigation under difficulties

The lucky beginning navigator will never encounter serious difficulties until he's mastered enough piloting to handle them with aplomb. Life doesn't always work out that way, however, and anytime you set out on the water, you should be prepared to face the unexpected. There are four main types of coastal navigation performed under duress—in fog, at night, in rough weather, and when you've allowed yourself to get lost. All four offer what can be serious problems, but a cool head and alertness to opportunity should allow you to get out of trouble without danger.

At first thought, navigation in fog and at night would seem to present the same kind of difficulty, but in fog you can see little or nothing, while at night you can see a considerable amount, often without being able to recognize much of it. Aside from your own inability to see in fog, there is also the unsettling realization, brought home by the sound of foghorns all around, that you may be surrounded by lots of other boats whose skippers are as blind as you. Fog also seems to distort the passage and volume of sound, so that fog signals, while welcome, are less than reliable as direction indicators. In no other setting, I think, is it easier for a beginner to become panicked than in a fog too thick for him to see much beyond the boat's bow.

Under some circumstances, you may be best advised to stay put. If you're at anchor when the fog rolls in, at least you know where you are to begin with. In most areas, a morning fog has a good chance of burning off or at least thinning considerably by noon, and if you're not in a hurry, consider rolling over and going back to sleep, if you're in a proper anchorage; if not, someone must be detailed to ring the fog bell for five seconds in every minute. Sometimes, however, there's no choice: Either you're already under way when the fog slips in or you've simply got to get moving to keep your schedule from collapsing. If that's the case, then there is every reason to proceed with caution.

The first rule of the coastal navigator under normal circumstances is to avoid losing track of his position, and that dictum applies even more strongly when fog has cut down or virtually eliminated the reference points along your course. Unless you're a very good navigator, and your boat has several meticulous helmsmen, you can't really count on finding small, single aids to navigation in the fog. You will need to rely on other aids that can be located without sight or at least without having to see more than the length of the boat.

Should your course be carrying you along the coast, a depth sounder can be a great help, allowing you to pick your way along shore at a particular depth, following a line of soundings. Most charts—especially large-scale ones —show two or three depth contours. The first, which may well be in waters too shallow or too rock-strewn for your boat, is often differentiated by tinting the shallowest water blue, leaving depths over six feet in white. This seems a reversal of logic, but you will get used to it, and the tint means that you don't have to examine the individual charted soundings—you know without looking that they're the minimum depth or less.

Unless the shoreline is very broken, you should have no great trouble following a line of soundings, but keep your boat's speed down and scan the chart ahead of your position for anything which might form a sudden obstruction or a landmark that could give you a fix. Larger fixed aids to navigation, such as those on the ends of harbor jetties, frequently have horns that emit distinctive sound patterns, specified in the *Light List* (but not on the chart). In diminished visibility, the accompanying lights will usually be functioning, too, and you should be alert for their diffused glow through the murk.

If possible, you should sail under just enough canvas to keep the boat moving under full control—say half your normal cruising speed. You may have to tack or jibe very quickly, so you should avoid fancy sail combinations that will require all-hands evolutions for a simple maneuver. Sail is better than power, because it allows your hearing full play, and you should have one crew member right up at the bow, ready to relay instantly any information he can perceive by sight or hearing. If he (or you) hears something unidentifiable, it's best to come up into the wind and lie in irons until you can figure out what's making the noise. I can remember sailing along the coast one foggy day and becoming aware of a regular, flat, slapping sound off to one side, like someone hitting the water with a board. It was almost too late by the time I suddenly realized I was hearing foot-high waves breaking on a hard beach, about twenty yards away and totally invisible.

All hands should also be aware that sight, too, can be distorted in fog. Often the fog bank will lie on the water, and only ten or twenty feet up, the air will be quite clear. In such a case, it may be worthwhile sending a lookout up the mast, to sit at the crosstrees. Conversely, the fog will occasionally hover a few feet above the surface of the water, and someone lying flat can see under it for a surprising distance. In each situation, you may see a part of some landmark or aid—the top or bottom—without being able to see the rest at all. Knowing what's available to be seen will make the job of recognition that much easier.

The lookout at the bow should keep his eyes moving back and forth in the effort to spot anything useful; never stare, in fog or at night; it's much more effective to swivel your gaze from side to side. At the same time, someone else should be assigned to the job of horn-blower. Nearly all small cruising boats now employ the ubiquitous aerosol-powered, hand-held horn for fog and right-of-way signals, and while it is certainly more effective than a mouth-powered signal, the freon-driven horn is only good for a couple of hours continuous sounding per can; carry at least one and preferably two extra cans of gas. The fog signal for sailing craft has recently (1981) been changed to one long and two short blasts, sounded at least once every two minutes. Sailing craft share this signal with tugs pulling a tow, vessels restricted in their ability to maneuver, and fishing vessels, while ordinary power craft (including sailing auxiliaries with the engine on) sound a single prolonged blast every two minutes. You may, for the next few years, occasionally hear one, two, or three long blasts. These are being sounded by old-timers in sailing craft, who haven't learned the new signals yet. They used to signify sailboats on starboard tack, port tack, and running free, respectively.

There is seldom much force to the wind in a fog, and quite often there's no wind at all. Not only may this force you to run under power, if you are to move at all, but it will also tend to flatten the swells and thus make the ringing of wave-induced floating aids—gongs and bells—more infrequent. If there is no wind or too little wind to allow you to sail under full control, it is a much better idea to turn on the engine than to sit slatting, like a target, on the open water.

Remember to give the proper fog signal, and try to set your speed through the water at a steady rate that will simplify your navigation calculations. You should, in any event, be able to stop your boat in half the distance of visibility, which will condition how fast you can go.

The direction finder is another tool worth having when visibility is low. If you are creeping alongshore, you may be able to pick up one of the very low-powered harbor entrance radiobeacons, whose nominal range is usually five or ten miles, but which are seldom audible to portable RDFs at more than a couple of miles. The trick of navigating in fog is to reach out for every aid, every clue you can get, because the evidence is so fragmentary.

Try to avoid extended runs, even straight ones, between checkpoints. The chance of error on a course multiplies tremendously with the distance of a leg, and you will have a far better chance of finding your target if you pick your way cautiously from buoy to buoy in a crooked line than if you strike out boldly across a wide harbor or bay. Making a landfall in fog is for me perhaps the least pleasant activity on the water. Try beforehand to visualize the appearance of the shore you're approaching. Will it be steep-to—a cliff, or high towers right on shore? If so, you may well see the tops of those landmarks before you can see the surf at their bases. You may also hear a surprisingly sharp echo from your foghorn bouncing off an abrupt shore. As you near shore—where you think shore is—keep an eye on the seas. As they become steeper and more inclined to break, it tells you that the water is shoaling. Listen for breakers, even to the point of stopping the engine every few minutes, if it is exceptionally noisy. Ready an anchor in the bow, rigged to drop at a second's notice. Above all, have confidence in your DR plot. Don't second-guess yourself except on the basis of compelling evidence. For every boat saved by a skipper's timely hunch, probably half a dozen have got into trouble by abandoning a workable plan. If a necessary landmark or aid doesn't materialize on time, stop the boat and hold her position while you go back and rework your plot. Chances are that some small error in arithmetic has thrown you off, but that the basic course is still sound and still retrievable.

Night navigation

Except when darkness is complicated by fog, night navigation is a problem only for the novice. Almost always there are plenty of visible aids to navigation, and even landmarks; it's just that they look very different at night. The essential thing, therefore, is to learn how to visualize what's out there, based on what you can see.

It is difficult to break the mind of its daytime habit of seeing only outlines. Perhaps the best way to go about this is to start from a known position and examine the chart to determine what you ought to be seeing when it's dark. From where you are you should be able to make out, let us say, a major fixed aid to navigation off to starboard, flashing a definite, identifiable pattern of two colors. Off to one side of it is a harbor entrance, with three lighted red buoys. All flash at 2.5- or 4-second intervals, and they may or may not be visible yet. To port is open water, and any lights should therefore represent shipping. Directly ahead at some distance is a city—below the horizon as yet, but you can expect to see a faint, steady glow against the sky.

Having determined what ought to be visible, go up on deck and take a look. You'll probably be able to spot the items you expected, and several others besides. If any of the mystery lights seem exceptionally powerful or have observable patterns, go below again and recheck the chart to see if you missed them the first time around. A quick bearing will be a great aid in location, but at night it may be a good idea to follow the bearing line farther inshore on the chart than you would in daytime. If there is one great sensory loss at night, it's depth perception, and only intensity, that misleading clue, suggests distance or nearness.

Having made certain that you have a couple of identifiable aids to navigation pinned down, and that you are where you thought you were, check next to see what the moving lights—other vessels—are up to. Until you're used to night navigation, it can be very difficult to be certain whether another ship is on a possible collision course with yours. If in any doubt, head away early and definitely. Do not hesitate to employ your VHF-FM on channel 16, calling the ship whose lights you see according to its approximate type, heading, and position: "Freighter headed southwest, one mile off Old Field Point," for instance. If your identification is even close, you'll get a response, because the other vessel is probably following your progress on radar. If there's no answer on channel 16, try channel 13, the frequency for intership navigational safety.

The key words in night navigation are *check* and *recheck*. Never assume that a flashing light is what you hope it to be. Go below to the chart table and make sure. Better still, keep a list of the prominent aids to navigation along your intended course. In timing the patterns of these lights, it may be handy to use a stopwatch. Remember that the interval given on the chart is the time required for the light to make a full cycle of its identifying pattern, which includes both lighted and dark periods. Thus, a light whose pattern is given as "Gp Occ. (3) 20 sec." will emit three periods of white light (always white, unless another color is specified), each one longer than the intervening periods

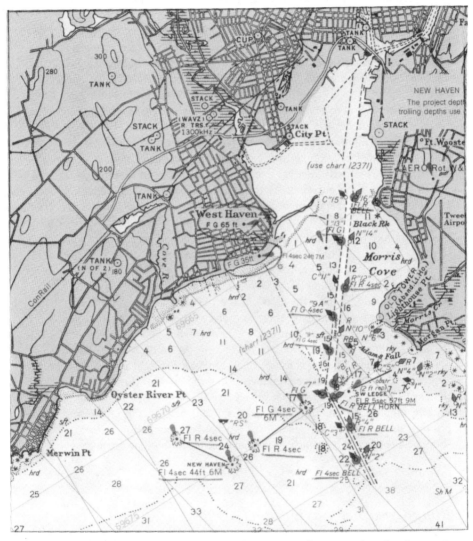

Before entering this harbor at night, it would be a good idea to review the chart and fix in mind the most important aids. Against the lights of the city, the major breakwater lights should be reasonably easy to pick out, as should the fixed green lights ashore of the West Haven range.

of darkness, the whole pattern to take 20 seconds before it begins again.

Although (as I noted earlier) red light blanks out red markings on a chart, I prefer to have my chart table illuminated by a red-tinted bulb, so I can retain at least some night vision when I'm below. At night, and especially in close quarters, the navigator is likely to be up and down the companionway many times in the course of a watch—checking the characteristics of a newly visible aid, taking yet another bearing and plotting it, checking the unfamiliar light pattern displayed by some vessel—and he shouldn't have to allow five minutes or so each time for his eyes to readjust to darkness. It will also make life easier for those on deck if they are not periodically assaulted by bright glare up the companionway. It's not unknown for even the most seasoned navigator simply to become disoriented in the dark, especially if he's tired or nervous. The quickest way to regain a sense of position—at least for me—is to check the compass first, to get a feel for the direction in which the boat is going, then find one major aid you can identify, take a bearing on it, and find your LOP on the chart. If you're reasonably skillful, the rest of the crew shouldn't even be aware of your lapse.

Landfalls at night are in one respect trickier than in daytime, but easier in another. Quite often, thanks to the distinctive patterns of major harbor aids to navigation, you will have an excellent general idea of where you are and which harbor you're entering. At the same time, your mind is likely to construct quite an erroneous picture of the harbor's shape, if only because the information presented to it is partial and in unfamiliar form. Many experienced navigators like to time their important approaches so that they can spot the harbor's approach lights at a distance, while they are still visible in full dark, and then make the actual entrance a little after dawn, when the land masses are apparent and traffic is light. If you can arrange your landfalls that way, it's fine (if a little hard on the crew). If, on the other hand, you have to make an approach at night, take extra precautions to be sure that what seems to be a line of buoys marking an entrance channel is what you think it is, and that the lights ashore are indeed aids to navigation. More than one tired mariner —myself included—has confidently closed in on a red light ashore that exhibited more or less the same characteristics as the one he wanted, only to find that, as he neared, its red letters resolved into the word "BEER," or something equally unnautical. But if you check each aid against the chart, and hold position until you're sure where the next aid to navigation is located, you should have no great problem entering even an unfamiliar harbor.

Rough-weather navigation

Perhaps the principal difference between cruising in ordinary as opposed to heavy weather is that under the latter condition, everything is just more difficult—getting around, reading, writing, or cooking. Most heavy weather is accompanied by decreased visibility, which of course restricts the number of bearings available, and often a high noise level down below makes working with an RDF very tedious. In addition, the navigator's tools, books, and charts are likely to be whizzing about, with the danger of damage to them and to the crew.

Before setting out in heavy weather, or before heavy weather sets in when you're already under way, it's important to work up as much of your navigational plan as possible. Part of this plan will be strategic—the what-if decisions discussed in Chapter VII: Heavy-Weather Seamanship. But even in conditions that promise to be nothing more than unpleasant, it's a good idea to get as much work done as possible before the chart table begins to leap about. You may be one of the lucky few who are relatively immune to seasickness, but even if you don't normally succumb, there are few situations more conducive to mal-de-mer than trying to read small print in bad light, while surrounded by smells, with the boat bouncing up and down.

Because fatigue occurs quickly in rough-water conditions, it's all the more important for crew members to take the time to work carefully, and to write down not only the results of their calculations but also the procedures by which they arrived at their answers. An unstructured logbook, whose pages can be used partly for record keeping and partly as scratch paper, makes this kind of work easier. A slate or notice-board in the cockpit, easily visible from the helm, can have written on it the course, next expected mark, and the ETA for that mark, as well as anything else the navigator or skipper would like to remind the helmsman about. Lacking a writing surface, you can use the cabin bulkhead: Gel-coat will easily take the ordinary grease pencil, and it can be edited or cleaned off easily, while being immune to erasure from casual splashes.

In heavy weather, with proper occasions for taking bearings relatively rare, it is especially important not to miss the few chances you'll get. The navigator should make sure that the people at the helm will call him whenever they see anything that looks as if it might be useful for positioning. This is often the case with aids to navigation that aren't the ones the deck watch were looking for. Any aid that's near enough to identify should be reported to the navigator—it may be his first clue that the boat is badly off course.

No one I know can work at an exacting task like coastal navigation if he must spend half his time grabbing at flying objects. The nav station, whether it be a formal chart table or a lap board, must be capable of being set up for heavy weather. At the well-equipped end of the spectrum, this means secure bins or slots into which the navigator may put pencils, dividers, and course protractors. It means some way of attaching the chart temporarily to the chart table surface—extra-long rubber bands will do, as will oversize metal banker's clips or even thumbtacks. It means easy access to electronics and the one or two really important publications.

Both electronics and paper react badly to prolonged dampness, and, unfortunately, on a small yacht there are few locations that will remain even partially dry in rough weather. The chart table is not one of them, as designers realize that the average navigator needs fresh air as much as or more than any other single thing. Some navigators make flexible plastic shields for the instruments and charts, but in my experience, spraying the machinery with one of the ignition-drying or -waterproofing aerosols is probably more practical. There are also liquid waterproofing compounds, available in yacht chandleries, with which you can paint a chart. These compounds, which are clear when dry and seem to cause no distortion of the page, often require overnight drying or more than one coat, so they must be applied well in advance of use. If you highlight your charts with colored felt-tip pens, you will want to waterproof the charts before marking them up, as the felt-tip ink will sometimes run.

The person with no formal chart table will need to set up some workplace for himself, out of traffic, where he can be as securely braced as possible. On a seven-day offshore voyage not long ago, in a boat with no nav station, I found that a plywood board, thin enough to fit under a berth mattress, served quite well as a work surface, to which the chart was secured with banker's clips. Dividers and pencils lived in my shirt's breast pocket while I was working, as did a small flashlight with a red bulb, for night plotting. Other publications had to be wedged in convenient corners of the berth on which I was sitting, but in many respects it was as comfortable a place to operate from as most formal nav stations.

Perhaps the most important procedure to learn, at least if you're as slapdash a person as I am, is the careful order of mind that always replaces a tool in the same spot, and that reduces every navigational task to a repeatable series of planned steps. If your piloting style is imperturbable, and if you train yourself to keep order in your part of the boat as well as in your work, your heavy-weather navigation is likely to be nearly as reliable as your calculations on a sunlit afternoon.

Reorienting yourself

Sooner or later, every navigator gets lost. Most often it's the result of not keeping track of the identifiable landmarks and aids that have been going by. Sometimes you get disoriented by exhaustion. Occasionally there just aren't enough clues from which to establish a position. The result in each case is the same.

If there's any danger of your running up on shore or heading into some other avoidable danger, the best immediate action is to stop the boat. Heave to, if you can, or even drop anchor. When you're not oppressed by the notion of heading blindly into danger, you can sometimes sort the situation out. If you can't, begin methodically to work forward from your last fix or your last solid DR position. At the least, you will then have an approximate position, although you may not want to dignify it by the name of DR.

From this dubious position, cast about you on the chart: What are the potential sources of information? What ought you to be able to see on deck? Can you get a series of soundings? At this point, you probably cannot expect to work up a refined position, nor do you need to. What you want is some approximation that you can put on the chart, as a new departure point. Chances are you will see or hear something that will suggest either a tentative position or perhaps a couple of possible positions.

Your next course should be set with the idea of providing yourself with a proper fix. An unmistakable lighthouse, a deep, narrow ridge along the bottom, a marker radiobeacon—any one of these can give you the necessary deciding clue, and it will usually be worthwhile to alter course in order to pass close enough to verify your guess.

Do not, however, hang your entire position on a single piece of evidence: Buoys are occasionally renumbered, radiobeacons fail or have their signal patterns changed, landmarks are transmuted by wishful thinking into other shapes. If you have not had a supporting clue, and you've become completely lost, the first recognizable aid or landmark should be treated with great caution.

If you have a transmitter, or even if you don't, you can ask a passing vessel for a position. There is no shame in being lost, and commercial craft especially keep a radar plot going continuously, so it is no difficulty for them to tell you your location. Do not, however, take what they tell you at absolute face value. You may mishear, or they may simply be a little off in their figures. For a commercial vessel proceeding at 15 knots, a plotted position only 45 minutes old can be relatively up-to-date, though useless to you. Be sure you know whether the position you're given is current. And if you can, find out diplomatically what it's based on. A fisherman's loran fix is probably both timely and accurate, while the estimate of another pleasure boat may be no better than your own ignorance.

VI

～～～～～～

Cruise Planning and Passage Making

All too often, the inexperienced yachtsman begins his cruising career with passages that would tax the endurance of Francis Chichester. When these end, as they inevitably do, in exhaustion and nervous tension all around, the frustrated novice begins to look sourly on the whole sport of coastal voyaging. Part of the problem is in the sailor himself—if he weren't a romantic, he wouldn't have taken up cruising in the first place—and part of it lies in the boatbuilders' ads that cater to unrealism.

The inescapable truth is that cruising, for all its delights, is a demanding activity that places its participants smack in the middle of a new world of constant motion, constriction, discomfort, and occasional danger. Despite the trend toward camouflaging boat interiors, making them look like kitchens or boudoirs or living rooms ashore, living on a small yacht is very different from living on land, and nearly everyone requires some time to adjust to the change. It is thus especially important at the start of your cruising life to avoid needless overdoing; there'll be plenty of time for that later, and plenty of unanticipated excitements during even the shortest cruise to wake up the old liver bile.

One of the most difficult adjustments to be made by people who are beginning to cruise is simply the choice of appropriate destinations—appropriate, that is, to the boat as well as the crew. I'm not talking here about matters of protection or water depth, which are discussed elsewhere, but rather the equally important aspect of selecting places that will be fun to get to and interesting to visit, and whose facilities will dovetail with the boat's requirements.

For a supposedly self-contained vehicle, the average cruising yacht is remarkably dependent upon help from shore at regular intervals. Water, ice, electricity, groceries, and entertainment must all be supplied or replenished, and they are not always available in the most scenic localities. Indeed, one might almost suggest that the presence of complete facilities occurs in inverse proportion to the physical beauty of a place. And while there are a few delightful shoreside towns where you can get absolutely anything you need within a few paces of the water, there are also grim dumps whose appalling ugliness is equaled only by their total lack of so much as an accessible hot-dog stand.

Perhaps more to the point, in planning a cruise you must bear in mind that you'll be arriving by boat and that you'll be more or less tied to your vehicle, save perhaps for sightseeing tours. Most towns, even those that cater especially to yachtsmen, are very different propositions when approached from the water than when reached by road. Sometimes this will work to the sailor's advantage: I know several places whose unmerited bad reputations derive from unattractive highway approaches, but which are quite pleasant when attained from the sea. On the other hand, the cruising sailor needs to receive with caution the praises heaped on a place by people who've never tried to sail there—usually they will have no notion of what's available in the way of moorings or slips, or how far you have to walk to get ice or a decent restaurant meal.

It seems to me that your first few cruises should probably be overnight or weekend affairs at the longest, where the consequences of mistakes in planning —and there are bound to be some—will result in amusing anecdotes, not horror stories. After you've reached a level of cruising skill where you can do the planning for a weekend voyage on the back of an envelope in a few minutes, then it's time to consider, if you want to, more ambitious cruises. There is, however, no urgent reason why you should ever embark on more than weekend cruises, if that's what you like best. I know of skillful and accomplished sailors who never make long voyages, simply because that's not their idea of fun. It's more than likely, though, that at some point you'll want to spread your nautical wings a bit—and there's nothing wrong in that, either. Just don't let someone else's attitudes define your amusements.

First cruises

The length of any cruise is conditioned by how long it takes you to reach your destination and—even more important—how long it will take you to sail home again. There are few more depressing ways to end a voyage than with a relentless, overextended beat home, arriving after dark with the boat still to be cleaned up. The strategy of scheduling the legs of a cruise can be debated almost infinitely—it is, in fact, one of the most interesting aspects of cruise planning, and there are a number of theories.

One school of thought holds that you should set out to windward, to get your beating over with early and to have the probability of a reach or a run home. This of course presupposes that you do your sailing, as most of us do, in an area where the prevailing wind direction is fairly dependable. My own feeling in this regard is that the destination is more important than the present wind direction—*except* in a case where the wind at departure time is strongly opposed to the prevailing direction. In that case, knowing the odds are heavy that it will soon change, you may care to gamble on the chance of having offwind legs both coming and going, a rare situation somewhat comparable to having cheated the almighty and got away with it. (You needn't feel unduly guilty, however; you'll pay for your good luck in time.)

A few principles of cruise planning have little or nothing to do with wind direction. In your early cruises, it will usually pay to set a short first day's leg, the kind of distance your boat can cover in three or four hours of sailing. Given the average speed of the small cruiser—3 or 4 knots under sail in normal breezes—you're talking about a distance of 10 or 15 miles. This seems like a short haul, and it is, but remember that the actual time from the moment you step aboard to the time the anchor is securely set is likely to be an hour or two over your sailing time. Although this fact is demonstrated to me a dozen times each season, it never really gets absorbed: I cannot truly believe that it's going to take at least a half-hour to get under way, and probably more than that to properly anchor or tie up in a visitor's slip. But it does.

In estimating the time for any day's cruise, remember to add the ragged ends of the voyage as well. There is a perfectly understandable tendency to measure your trip from harbor mouth to harbor mouth, forgetting the additional couple of miles at each end, under reduced canvas, which can easily add an unscheduled hour to your voyage.

There ought to be some formula that would allow you to predict the real additional time required for even the smallest detour from the basic cruise plan —stopping on the way out of the harbor to refill the fuel tank, for instance— but I have yet to see one. If you assume that it will take about twice as long as the most generous estimate, however, you will seldom be disappointed. For this reason, it's a good idea not to leave any errands until just before sailing time, and to perform as many of the normal presail chores as possible when you are actually under way, perhaps on that stretch from anchorage to harbor mouth.

Obviously, the boat must be in maneuvering condition before you slip the mooring or leave the pier, but she need not (I think) be totally shipshape. As a skipper, I want to be sure the engine is running smoothly or ready to start, the necessary sails are bent on or hoisted (according to whether you're leaving the harbor under power or sail), the boat hook and fenders are accessible (but the latter aren't trailing over the side), and the anchor is ready to let go swiftly

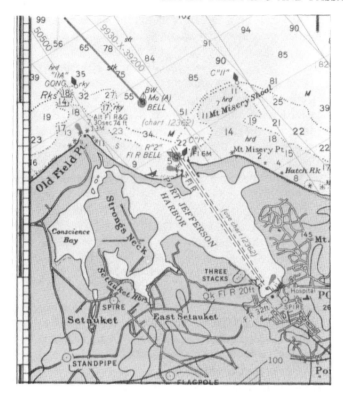

It is all too easy, on a small-scale planning chart, to plot one's course from entrance marker to entrance marker, as here. But there are several miles more to go before reaching the piers at the head of the harbor.

in an emergency. But unless we are leaving in a heavy wind, such jobs as stowing the clothes and food or making lunch can wait. As to crew requirements, if in a small cruiser there are two people topside attending to the boat, that should allow any remaining hands to get on with tasks below.

You will have planned your navigation strategy (see below) before leaving, and will have gotten a weather report as well. Before beginning a longer cruise, however, I usually keep an eye on the TV weather forecasts for three or four days preceding departure, as a trend in the weather will often become apparent after you've watched the frontal patterns for several days.

If you have a cruise routine aboard your boat (this subject is discussed more fully later), it can normally begin at sailing time, or at least on the exact hour nearest to departure. On even a short cruise, it helps establish an air of partnership if all hands discuss what the general plan will be. It's a fact of nature that some people like to dally and some are impatient; some are precise and some are slobs. And it is not unusual to have an assortment of all these characteristics and more among the average family crew. If your cruise is to be a success, it must offer something to everyone, and if you can't please all hands, then it will keep down rebellion if the troops are aware of the ship's cruising philosophy right from the start. By this I mean that everyone aboard should have a clear idea of the voyage's goals. It may be that getting to a given harbor is the point of the exercise. It may equally well be that just sailing in the general direction of that harbor is more important. While it's often a bad mistake to schedule a cruise too tightly, younger crew members especially want reassurance that they will actually arrive someplace in the (to them) foreseeable future, which often seems to have about a five-minute horizon. Thus, some kind of general itinerary can be handy, while at the same time it may be a good idea to establish early the possibility that you may have to deviate from or even abandon the timetable. Generally speaking, the more information the rest of the crew has, and the more they have participated in creating the cruise plan, the happier everyone will be.

As you become more practiced, you'll probably find yourself extending the range of your daily legs. This kind of thing can easily become a trap, where you keep trying for just a few more miles than logic tells you are possible. The result, almost every time, is a bored, resentful crew. Once you've got into the swing of a cruise—often about the third day out—you'll find that it may be a good idea to have a non-sailing day in some attractive spot, if necessary followed by a real thrash to make up lost time. This is where loose scheduling can come in handy: If you are not tightly pressed for time or distance, you can enjoy the real delights of exploring and sightseeing and just lying around in the cockpit. In planning an overall cruise schedule, it seems to me that two days with some sailing in them—anywhere from a couple of hours to the whole day—might well be followed by at least a day of no sailing at all. It will depend on you and your crew, on your boat, and on the locale.

In attempting to establish what are realistic daily runs for a coastal cruiser, perhaps the best beginning is recognizing honestly how fast your boat will go, on average, hour after hour. While it is technically possible to move along at hull speed (a speed in knots, you'll recall, equal to 1.25 times the square root of the waterline in feet), this is a ridiculous expectation for the average cruising yacht. A well-handled boat with good performance may be able to achieve a consistent speed equal in knots to the square root of her waterline length in feet. (That is, a boat with a sixteen-foot waterline will be capable of a steady 4 knots; a boat whose waterline is twenty-five feet may average 5 knots.) Even this is questionable for most cruising yachts. My current boat, a twenty-one-footer with a waterline of about seventeen feet, seems to be able to make 3 knots day after day, but we often sail her, rather than motoring, when winds are very light indeed. Another boat I've owned, a thirty-foot ketch with a twenty-five-foot waterline, would click off 4 knots as a cruise average, but we frequently turned on the powerful inboard in light airs, and hyped the average by temporarily increasing our speed to 6 knots. However you establish your own boat's average cruising speed, it's worthwhile making the calculation, and it will also be a good idea to estimate on the low side, both in terms of making more realistic plans and for the psychological effect of "beating" your own time.

As you gradually become familiar with your own cruising area, you'll want to visit ports that are farther away—but the chances are you'll have the same amount of time to do it in. This is where a trailerable boat can be a big asset:

An hour on the freeway and you can be fifty miles or more from your home port. Or you can do what other experienced cruising folk find useful: Begin your voyage in the evening, sailing all or most of the first night, and start true cruising the next day, well on your way. You can do the same thing at the end of a cruise, and you may have to, but my feeling is that a hectic finale makes returning to work even more difficult.

When you're selecting stopping places, either as destinations or potential harbors of refuge, there are several criteria to bear in mind. These will obviously vary according to the reason for the halt, and no one reference volume is likely to list all of them. As suggested in an earlier chapter, the almanac-type annual guides are best for determining what material facilities—fuel, ice, slips, hardware shops—are likely to be present. The more discursive cruising books, on the other hand, will be better for giving you a feel of the place before you've seen it. Even the chart can be helpful in presenting you with an idea of the physical size and layout of small harbor towns, as well as in showing the location of railroad lines and highways, in case you are changing part of your crew en route, or leaving the boat until the following weekend.

What to take along

Most novice cruising people find it very difficult to hit upon the proper list of gear to take with them—either they jam the boat with equipment, so that they have to spend half an hour shifting gear in order to sit down, or they set out (as I am prone to do) with a candy bar in one pocket and a toothbrush in the other, and leave the rest to luck. The amount of gear you really need on a short cruise has only a vague relationship to the amount of gear you may want to have available. There are several factors to bear in mind when deciding how much to carry. First and most limiting is the size and conformation of the boat. A decent thirty-footer can carry nearly all the bedding, clothing, dry stores, games, books and toys four people will need for a two-week cruise, as well as her normal running gear. Add perishables, some shore-going clothes, and money (never forget money), and you're ready to go. The only problem in owning a boat big enough to appear self-sufficient is that a certain amount of the "permanent" equipment seems somehow to evaporate; foul weather gear is worn home and fails to return; a half-eaten meal is put in the ship's best covered dish and removed ashore; someone halfway into one of the ship's books pockets it as he goes—everyone intends to bring the stuff back, but somehow it never seems to return, unless you make a point of it.

In a very small boat, on the other hand, you begin more or less from scratch for each cruise, and weigh every item, as there may not be room for spares. In our present boat, we've found it helpful to create separate carry-aboard bags for classes of gear: There is the dish bag, which also holds the silverware, cups, salt and pepper, napkins, dish towels, and the like; each crew member has his clothing bag, out of which he lives during the cruise (one item in it is a laundry bag, which swells as the clothes bag becomes thinner); the navigation bag contains the chart book, facilities almanac, tide and current tables, course protractor, and other small gear (it has pockets to hold each item). Most important of all is the ice chest: Like so many small cruisers, our twenty-one-footer has a fitted ice chest that is also removable. We pack it (having chilled it off first) directly from the refrigerator-freezer in the kitchen at home. Dry food other than condiments goes in yet another bag, and if we are making an exceptionally long cruise, we have an extra-large second ice chest that fits nicely at the head end of one of the quarter berths. (All ice chests sweat, so it's a good idea to move mattresses from under them if you employ this system.)

We start with a bare boat, except for foul-weather gear, daysailing nav gear, ground tackle, sails, and engine and safety equipment. We can take our bare boat out for an hour or the afternoon, and her interior remains clean and uncluttered. But when we set out on a formal cruise, whether it be overnight, weekend, or week-long, we know that everything else we'll need must be brought from shore, and much of it is more or less preassembled. By the same token, when we head home, we take back with us everything we brought. That way it gets properly cleaned, washed, and stored in a dry, mildew-free closet. True, it's somewhat more trouble than just opening a locker aboard, but there are fewer surprises and it works quite well.

Though everyone's list will be different, the following may give you an idea of categories of gear to consider in planning a cruise; it's based on our own packing for a week-long voyage in a twenty-one-footer:

CLOTHING:
Foul-weather gear—pants, jacket, boots, gloves (one set per crew member or guest)
    —is already aboard*
Shore clothing
Boat clothing,* such as swimming suits, sweatshirts, jeans, plus one set of
    "disposable" pants, shirt, and socks to wear under foul-weather gear
Extra hats or caps
Sunglasses

BEDDING:
Sleeping bag, with "stuff bag," for each guest/crew member
Sleeping bag sheet, for hot weather—one for each person
Pillows, as required (some people can use an old fender, some a small duffel, others
    require their very own pillow from home; be sure to check before you leave)

NAVIGATION GEAR:
Book of charts
Course protractor, dividers, pencils, colored pens
Hand bearing compass*
Boating Almanac
Eldridge Tide and Pilot Book *
Calculator, with instruction book
Logbook

GALLEY EQUIPMENT:

"Silver"—forks, knives, spoons

Cup, bowl, dish—one set per person

Cutting board and knife

(We use a one-burner gimbaled Mini-Galley by Forespar, with its own pot; a more
conventional two-burner stove would call for the following additional gear:
frying pan with spatula, small double boiler, coffee pot)

Plastic screw-top container for frozen concentrated juice

Can and bottle opener

Corkscrew

Ice pick

Portable grill

Dish towels, paper and cloth

MISCELLANEOUS:

Towels and washcloths

Toilet articles (in individual waterproof bags)

Portable radio with earphone

Camera, with lenses, filters, and film

Portable games, playing cards

Paperback books

Suntan oil*

All this materiel, plus (in our case) the filled ice chest and five-gallon watertank, comes aboard for the cruise. The remains go home at the end, except for the gear marked with an asterisk, which may stay aboard, depending on its condition and the next planned use of the boat. It sounds like a lot of work, but with the gear intelligently selected and packed in advance, it really isn't that much of a problem.

Even with the most rigorous cleanups after each use of the cruising yacht, gear does seem to accumulate aboard. It's a commonplace that, at the end of the boating season, the average sailor removes about twice as much stuff from his boat as he can remember putting on it—and about half again as much, when it is piled on the shore, as the boat could possibly have held. There is no way of winning this fight—a decent truce is the best you can hope for.

Meals and meal planning

Perhaps because of the fresh-air environment, and perhaps because there's relatively little else to do under way, meals and eating assume a special significance to the cruising yachtsman. On larger boats it's possible to fill a big icebox or even refrigerator with the kind of snack food you take for granted at home. On a smaller boat, there just isn't the room, especially for perishable between-meal nibble food. And while it is feasible on even the smallest boat to produce three nominal meals a day, plus necessary snacks between times, there's some question in my mind as to whether it is a good idea to do so.

As I have said elsewhere—and often—even the best small-yacht galley is no match for a third-rate apartment kitchen, either in efficiency or capability. Turning out a serious meal in a galley may be a labor of love, and the result a work of art, but it's not a vacation for the cook. Eating ashore frequently ought, I think, to be regarded as one of the pleasures of cruising, and the expense, which can be considerable, ought to be worked into the cruising budget in advance. At the same time, you may on occasion have to produce three meals a day aboard your boat, and you ought at least to have the techniques and the food available. Let's examine what's involved for each meal, in general terms.

Breakfast has always been a favorite of mine, and when at home I like to create a fairly elaborate weekend breakfast, whose dirty pans and dishes are washed (according to our house rule) by someone else. I've made a few fancy breakfasts on boats, too, but it seems to me that, by and large, such meals should be saved for special events—the morning after a harrowing storm, for example. Normally, you can produce a perfectly adequate breakfast from boxes and tins. When cruising *en famille,* we have often invested in a couple of those multiple packs containing ten or a dozen individual servings of five or seven different types of dry cereal. Not only does this allow the younger (and usually pickier) members to choose their own sugar-laden, drug-preserved junk, but it also helps keep the contents from becoming limp as quickly as will the cereal in a large, previously-opened box. The drawback, aside from the extra garbage involved, is the residue of unselected cereals too loathsome even for subteen-agers to consider. Don't save them; they will not improve.

Coffee cake is the big breakfast treat on many small cruisers; it lasts longer under sea conditions than most other baked goods do, has no particular shape to be smashed out of, and tastes enough like dessert so anyone will eat it. The plain, boxed items are best, we have found: The more elaborate, frozen variety will thaw in the reheating tin, and condensation will often make the bottom layer mushy and distasteful.

For years, we've drunk frozen concentrated juice, but it often reacts badly when reconstituted with the contents of a plastic freshwater tank. The last year or so, we've switched to half-gallon containers of orange juice instead, and while they take up more room in the ice chest, the consensus seems to be that they taste better. The absolute consumption of space in the boat is of course the same, but the question is whether you can spare the cubic inches in the icebox.

Instant coffee and cocoa (in cold weather) are other staples. It pays to get the smallest containers of coffee and individual envelopes of cocoa, to ward off staleness. I am not crazy about tea anyway, but tea fanciers tell me that it is another beverage requiring really good water, which is seldom found aboard ship. Coffee, on the other hand, can survive quite amazingly bad water, especially when the drink is liberally treated with sugar and condensed milk (the old army cure-all for recipes gone awry). If you use sugar aboard, it's best to get a bunch of those little envelopes containing one-teaspoon servings. Like salt, sugar in quantity tends to set up into cement under damp conditions, but the paper envelopes found in so many restaurants are quite resistent to anything but a direct soaking.

The same is true, perhaps even more so, for salt. There are several patented salt and pepper shakers available for marine use, with tight-fitting lids to prevent moisture getting in. My own feeling is that nothing beats the little individual containers served on aircraft, but it can get expensive to fly commercially just for the condiments.

On very cold mornings, nothing beats hot oatmeal or grits, dishes that are easy to prepare on one burner. Scrambled eggs are not too difficult but almost require bacon or ham as an accompaniment, and that can be a problem. Very thin slices of Spam or similar canned meat fry more neatly, without so much smoke and spattering, and if you can stand the taste, they are quite filling.

Boat lunches are nearly always based upon the sandwich. This seems to me inevitable, if boring. We used to cruise occasionally with a talented Finnish lady who could be relied upon to come aboard with the makings for marvelous Scandinavian open-faced sandwiches for all hands. We ate them with rapture, although none of us ever had the slightest inclination to duplicate our friend's feat. On the other hand, by using more tasty bread or rolls, you can produce much better sandwiches using the same old fillings. And rolls keep a lot better than bread does. Plain French or Italian bread and fancy cheese can make a splendid variation on the sandwich, but you will have to cope with a fair number of crumbs in the cockpit afterward.

While scurvy is no longer a problem at sea, it is probably sensible to serve fresh, raw vegetables and fruit with lunch—the remaining veggies can be resurrected, with a dip, at cocktail time. Lunch should not be a fancy meal, however, and since you will usually be either under way or ashore exploring or involved in some other activity, the loss will hardly be noticed, except subliminally.

It has long been a truism in the restaurant business that no eating establishment makes much on the food—it's the booze that earns the profit. If you take this saying to heart, you can probably afford to eat decent meals ashore more often than you might have thought possible, and only the restaurateur will be inconvenienced. The means, of course, is the cocktail hour aboard, furnishing your own bottle and taking the keen edge off your hunger with some kind of simple snack. Although many people enjoy preparing quite elaborate appetizers, I've never felt the need to do so. What does seem to hit the spot is freshness or crispness or both. On short cruises and with small crews, the only way to avoid soggy, stale food is to purchase small quantities and use the leftovers almost immediately. There's so much moisture in the air that trying to preserve already-opened containers of things like crackers or peanuts is close to impossible, and food storage can be a formidable problem. The only sure-fire answer I've come across is purchasing as many items as possible in single-serving, hermetically sealed containers.

As the reader will have gathered by now, I'm not much in favor of having the main meal of the day on board. At the same time, I must confess that there are times when it can be great fun to sit down below in a crowded, companionable cabin—no matter what's being served. And supper in the cockpit can be very pleasant too, for just about everyone except the person who has to prepare it and the person who must clean up afterwards.

If there is a standard fault with main meals aboard small boats, it's that they tend to be too ambitious. The cook or skipper seems to feel that dinner must include not only a main dish and two vegetables, but salad, rolls, dessert, and coffee, too. The result, unless you have a very large galley and lots of time, is a shambles of half- or overcooked food, dirty plates and pots, and spilled dishes.

The best seagoing meals I've had over the years have almost always involved one combinative main course—a stew or hash, often canned but always improved with extra garlic, onion, and spice, and often mellowed with wine, both in and accompanying it. While relatively bland food is undoubtedly best for tender stomachs the first night or so, most people I've sailed with have preferred rather incendiary meals when they had a choice. (Curiously enough, the same people often prefer very ordinary and unspiced food ashore.)

Any number of main dishes are now available either canned or frozen, and while nearly all of them are far too mild, they can be assisted by the cook. In choosing between frozen and canned foods, my feeling is that the former seem to preserve the tastes of the ingredients better, while some of the latter have more interesting collective tastes—as well as being easier to stow, and for longer. Early in the voyage, frozen meals in the typical plastic pouch offer the twin bonuses of keeping adjacent foods chilled and of being cookable without dirtying a pan—indeed, the water in which they boil can and should go for coffee or dishwashing. I won't have anything to do with boxed or packaged foods if I can help it, as the nonwaterproof containers are so vulnerable to accidents—I can still remember the smell of a packaged macaroni and cheese dinner that had reconstituted itself in a leaky locker six days before we were able to figure out what had happened. Freeze-dried foods have generally good taste, but their appearance and cost are against them, and they must remain *absolutely* dry until they are reconstituted.

Since many foods, especially crackers, cereals, and snacks, come in cardboard boxes, it will be a good investment to buy an assortment of screw-top or snap-top plastic containers of various sizes, not just for leftovers but for original storage. If the containers are to go in the ice chest or in crowded lockers, more or less cube-shaped boxes will save an extraordinary amount of valuable space over cylindrical containers. The best plastic food storage boxes I know are those made by Tupperware; I've used them on various boats for years and have seldom found them to be anything but superior.

One main-meal trick that cooks on small yachts soon learn is to prepare main dishes ashore, well in advance of the cruise, and bring them aboard either frozen or partially thawed, depending on how soon you'll want to eat them. Again, stews and hashes, which have no intrinsic shape, are much easier to package than, say, fowl or steaks, and many items like spaghetti dishes, which are too much trouble to cook aboard, reconstitute amazingly well, sauce and all.

Whatever your meal plans for your cruise, always carry the preserved ingredients for one complete meal on board, in case you fail to make port, or you find that the town's only restaurant just burned down. Since canned food ordinarily requires little care, the ship's emergency rations usually include such staples as canned corned beef hash or beef stew—and these will do very well when the crew are hungry and cold. Stews and hashes almost always contain large amounts of potato in them, so a side dish of potato chips is not such a great idea. If you can manage a sliced tomato or some lettuce and salad dressing, that should reduce the monotonous nature of the meal. Bear in mind, however, that cans don't last forever: You should examine them periodically for excessive rust, and if a can shows any sign whatever of swelling or deforming, get rid of it immediately. If cans are to be stowed in the bilge—or in a damp locker, for that matter—remove the manufacturer's glued-on label and write the name of the contents in grease pencil on each end.

While you can plan your cruise meals down to the last carrot stick, you will soon find that this isn't practical. For one thing, the crew will constantly be nibbling between formal meals, and for another, the delightful tuna fish salad that seemed like such an inspiration when it was 85 degrees in the shade will look at lot less appealing when everyone is cold and wet. In my experience, it's better to establish a general policy about breakfast and lunch, so that the ingredients are more or less the same from meal to meal, and carry a reasonable assortment of mutually compatible main dishes for the dinners you plan to eat aboard. My strong feeling is that the smaller the boat, the more meals you should have ashore: where a thirty-footer's galley can be expected to turn out dinners two nights in three without a major dislocation, the twenty-five-footer ought to reverse the proportion, and have the crew eat off the boat two nights out of three. By the third or fourth day, they'll be ready for shore anyway.

If formal meals in a restaurant are too expensive, or require too much dressing up, consider picnics on the beach. These can be great fun for all hands, require a minimum of cleaning up afterwards, and present a good excuse to lower the claustrophobia index. All you need is some charcoal and a beach—or even an open-air cooking fireplace, such as is found at many yacht clubs or municipal beaches. Make sure in advance that no one objects to your using this sort of facility; as long as you ask, most people are very generous, and if you're careful about rubbish, the owners will continue to welcome other cruising people.

Although what follows isn't intended to be a hard-and-fast prescription, it is the kind of realistic meal planning that should work for a summer coastal cruise for four people in a small yacht. The assumption is that the boat has a two-burner stove, but no oven; a portable charcoal grill; and a reasonably large icebox. The menu is fairly flexible, so that an exceptionally cold or warm day can be matched with a suitable meal.

FIRST DAY

Lunch (under way): Take-out meal from shoreside fast-food restaurant; fresh fruit; soft drinks.

Cocktails (at anchor): Raw vegetables with ranch house (or other) packaged dip.

Dinner (at anchor): Frozen and reheated chicken curry; salad; rolls and butter; beer, milk, or coffee; cake.

SECOND DAY

Breakfast: Orange juice; choice of cereals or coffee cake; milk or coffee.

Lunch (under way): Tuna fish salad sandwiches; potato chips; fresh fruit; soft drinks.

Cocktails (at anchor): Tinned nuts.

Dinner: Charcoal-broiled steaks; salad; red wine or beer; milk or coffee; coffee cake.

THIRD DAY

Breakfast: Juice; cereal with sliced fruit; milk or coffee.

Lunch: Leftover steak on rolls; hard-boiled eggs; raw vegetables; soft drinks.

[Afternoon shopping ashore for ice, milk, cheese and crackers, coffee cake, frozen dinner.]

Cocktails: Cheese and crackers; nuts.

Dinner ashore.

FOURTH DAY

Breakfast: Juice; coffee cake or cereal; milk or coffee.

Lunch: Cold cuts sandwiches (bologna, salami, cheese, ham); fresh fruit; soft drinks.

Cocktails: Omitted, because of overnight passage to come.

Dinner (under way): Beef stew; hot rolls and butter; salad; beer or wine; coffee.

Snacks for the watch: Cocoa, coffee, soft drinks, candy, chewing gum, cookies.

FIFTH DAY

Brunch (at anchor): Juice; scrambled eggs; fried Canadian bacon; rolls and butter; milk or coffee.

Lunch ashore [visit deli].

Cocktails: Crackers and cheese.

Dinner: Cold sliced ham and roast beef; potato salad (from deli); bread and butter; beer or wine; cookies; coffee.

SIXTH DAY

Breakfast: juice; choice of cereals; milk or coffee.

Lunch: Canned ravioli with cheese; fresh fruit; coffee or cocoa.

Cocktails: Rum punch, hot or cold; crackers and cheese.

Dinner ashore.

SEVENTH DAY

Breakfast: Juice; cereal; milk or coffee.

Lunch: Ham and cheese or roast beef sandwiches; salad; soft drinks.

Dinner (if required): Canned corned beef hash; canned vegetable; wine or beer; milk or coffee.

There are several points that might be made about this menu. To begin with, it presupposes that the cook and the navigator are in each other's confidence (if they are not the same person). The cook must have an accurate idea of when the yacht will stop at a port where additional supplies may be purchased, and the navigator must be aware when particular supplies are beginning to run short. At the same time, the cook will need to be flexible enough in the matter of buying provisions so that if an opportunity offers, the menu can be altered to suit. The basic menu allows for one unseasonably hot day, when the main meal aboard is cold cuts and potato salad; and one cold and wet day, when a hot lunch is served, and when even the cocktail hour can be warmed up with a punch. (Rum punch is one of the world's easiest drinks to make, since it really doesn't matter a great deal what you include, and no two recipes are the same.)

Dinner under way ought to be a one-dish meal; if necessary, the salad can easily be omitted, and the cocktail hour has been erased. One glass of wine or a beer with dinner does not seem to me too overwhelming an alcoholic consumption when under way, but this is an area where the skipper must know his crew, the coming night's demands, and his boat. Almost more important than dinner will be a constant supply of snacks for the watch on deck, and even in midsummer hot coffee or cocoa is likely to be appreciated along about four in the morning. If you have teak decks or cockpit trim, do not serve greasy snacks in the dark.

For crews not used to overnight passages—and most of us are not—the following dawn is likely to present a pretty grim sight below. Breakfast at the usual hour is probably not necessary, but it may be a useful thing to serve all hands a fairly substantial brunch in midmorning, to get them back on the same track.

Meals on the last day of any cruise are likely to be bizarre combinations of leftovers; I have allowed for a dinner, but as the reader can see, it comes out of the ship's iron rations, and the thoughtful (or lucky) skipper will not have to eat aboard at all.

Cruise routine

A great deal has been written about the many ways a yacht's crew can be divided for watch standing on long-distance cruises, but this is a problem that only occasionally arises in a coastal cruising boat. Unless there is an all-night passage or some special need to stand an anchor watch (as in case of a severe storm), the crew's lives at sea will pretty much parallel their timetables ashore. Even so, it seems to me important that the skipper set up, where possible, an informal watch system in which certain members of the crew are in charge (under the skipper's overall responsibility, of course) of performing particular duties at stated times. For one thing, such a watch system will prevent one person's being stuck with all the dirty work, and it will also get the younger element of the crew used to taking the helm for (in their terms) extended periods.

One way of accomplishing these goals is to revolve all the jobs on the boat each day, as much as possible. That is, on a given day one crew member will be skipper, another navigator, another cook, and all will take turns at the dozens of other jobs that aren't dignified by a title. This approach requires some redefinition of certain jobs, especially skipper, since there are usually limits to the competence of a cruising crew. Still, the nominal skipper-of-the-day can establish the sailing goal, assign helm watches, and be in charge of general sailing tactics—when to shorten or increase sail, when to go over to engine power, when to refuel, and the like. While the regular skipper may be surprised (and even faintly chagrined) at how easily some of his crew can take over, a little tactful coaching will also be necessary from time to time, and all hands must realize that in a crisis the regular skipper may change a plan, veto a maneuver, or reassume charge.

The daily routine in a family cruising yacht might go something like this on a typical cruising day: The cook gets up first, at a time agreed upon the night before, when the next day's plan was established. He has first crack at the head; as he begins breakfast, another member of the crew washes up and goes on deck to secure the anchor light, check the anchor, and mop off the dew. The navigator gets up and tunes in the morning's weather forecast, making sure that the expected weather suits with the day's sailing goal. If he has not done so the previous night, the navigator writes up whatever instructions may be necessary for the first watch under way.

By this time, everyone should be up and ready for breakfast. Those whose bunks are also the dining area will have to roll up and stow their sleeping bags immediately, but my feeling is that other bedding can benefit by airing out for an hour before being stowed. We have usually found that breakfast is a good meal to eat in the cockpit, and in any case, everyone who's not involved in cooking should stay out of the galley as much as possible during meal preparation.

After breakfast, someone other than the cook cleans up the residue of the meal, while the bosun and the skipper check that the yacht is ready to depart, and the rest of the crew tidies and stows down below. If the weather promises to be rugged, it's best to securely stow as much gear as possible and only leave loose what you'll really need under way. Also, if it promises to be rough outside the anchorage, it's a good idea to have some hot or cold drinks prepared in advance, and for everyone to put on foul-weather gear before leaving. This unpopular decision may have to be gently enforced by the skipper, especially for the younger members of the crew. Before leaving, the bosun may ask for a garbage dropoff or a refueling or watering stop, according to the state of the boat, and the skipper will establish the rig under which you'll set out. Frequently, it will be the same sails as were used the day before, but if you're thinking of a spinnaker run, it will be easier to rig the extra lines before leaving the anchorage.

When everything is ready, it's the skipper's job to assign stations for getting under way. This sounds terribly formal, I know, and on most small cruising boats it can be done in a matter of half a dozen words, but the concept is worth preserving: Getting under way and docking or anchoring are moments when the most public screwups are the most likely, the times at which a predetermined plan is most helpful.

You may, aboard an anchored, middle-sized cruiser with a dinghy in tow, want to have two people on the foredeck—one to haul the rode, the other to feed it down the hawsepipe into the rope locker; one aft to keep track of the dinghy; one at the helm; and one or two to make sail. Run out of crew? It's not surprising. But a well-thought-out plan can make it possible for one person to handle two or even three jobs: You may bring the dinghy up on a shortened painter and let it fend for itself, or the skipper may also be the helmsman during the maneuver, or you may just raise the anchor and leave the rode on deck for the moment, getting under way on the engine or under mainsail alone.

To prevent a lot of untidy and sometimes embarrassing shouting back and forth between cockpit and foredeck, you may want to set up a few standard hand signals. All you really need are signals indicating *steer to starboard; steer to port; straight ahead; reverse; cut the engine; anchor broken free;* and *anchor snagged.* Coming to rest, you'll require the foregoing signals, plus one indicating *let go the anchor.*

Whether raising the anchor or leaving a pier, the skipper should go over his plan with the crew beforehand, so everyone knows what's supposed to be happening and what his job is.

Once properly under way, with the departure entry made in the log, the dinghy painter streamed out to towing length, and the anchor and rode stowed, the only people with continuing jobs will normally be the helmsman and possibly a lookout, depending on how much can be seen from the helm. Obviously the navigator will have intermittent duties, except in thick weather, when he may be working all day, but everyone else will normally be free. On most boats, the skipper hogs the helm until he gets bored, at which point he inflicts it on someone who has already lost interest in steering. My feeling is that time at the wheel is one duty that should be formally apportioned, to the extent that the crew have stated hours on the helm, crises aside. The duration of a watch can and probably should vary according to the individual crew member's attention span. Few young children are good for more than an hour at a time, although it seems to me that you ought to aim at no less than an hour per trick. Some people are able to steer adequately well for several hours at a time, and enjoy doing so.

At some point in midmorning, people will begin to think about lunch. If there's to be a choice—of sandwich fillings, say—the cook can take orders. He should check with the watch captain and the skipper and navigator as to the best time at which to serve the meal; there are few things more irritating than the skipper who decides, for wholly mysterious reasons, on a sail change just as the food is coming up the companionway. Lunch is normally the kind of one-handed meal that everyone, even the helmsman, can eat at once. But there is an order of priorities here, and everyone should be aware of it: The boat comes first, and helmsman and lookout may have to wait their turn at the food if conditions make it impossible to do their jobs properly while eating.

On the high seas, it has for centuries been customary to mark local noon with an elaborate position check, and while this procedure isn't necessary in coastal voyaging, midday is a good time to take stock of where you are in the day's run, recheck the weather forecast, and change your goal for the day if that seems advisable. At the same time, the debris of lunch can be cleared away.

When the marina or anchorage that marks the end of the day's run is clearly in sight, the skipper can call all hands—or as many as he thinks he'll need, if he has a surplus—to get the yacht ready. As I have suggested elsewhere, it may well be proper to take a spin through the selected anchorage or past the piers in order to plan a final approach. In some areas, it may be necessary to radio to a harbormaster or marina dockmaster to obtain a berth or anchoring assignment. In any case, now is the time to shorten down to maneuvering canvas or to strike the sails entirely and turn on the engine, depending on what the situation seems to call for. Whatever you do, you should know exactly what kind of power—engine or sail—you'll be using for the final approach, and how much it will help or handicap the yacht's maneuverability.

Once the skipper has decided on his approach plan, he can spread the crew about as required. This is a situation when you'll probably need every hand you have; if nothing else, a crew member can stand by with a fender. Once the boat has come to rest and the anchor is securely down (or the guest mooring picked up, or the yacht safely in her berth), the first order of business is usually getting the yacht shipshape. People new to boats often wonder at the seemingly endless amount of stowing and tidying required, but it soon becomes second nature, and it is essential: In a moment of stress such as will happen aboard even the best-run yacht, it can be vital to know where every bit of gear lives, and it can be equally vital that a crew member sprinting forward with a fender isn't tripped up by a carelessly abandoned bucket.

There may also be immediate errands to do ashore. My brother-in-law, an experienced family cruising skipper, has perfected a drill that absolutely baffles onlookers at marinas. As the yacht pulls into her slip, some members of the crew dash off to the showers, soap and towels in hand, others dart away to offload the ship's garbage, while another will head for the marina laundromat, toting a sack of dirty clothes and a handful of quarters. It's a remarkable performance, but the effort behind it ensures that all hands have more time for fun, with the chores nailed down right away.

In an anchorage, there are different priorities, but the overriding concern, as always, is that the boat must be secured before the crew attend to their needs. Someone should sum up the day's run in the log, noting the amounts of fuel and water consumed; as soon as the powerplant is shut down, someone should check the oil level of the engine and the water in the fresh-water cooling system. Other maintenance chores (see Chapter XIV) can also be taken care of while there is still daylight and before the crew begin the serious business of relaxation.

Cocktail hour and dinner follow the course they would ashore, except that if you leave the boat at anchor, you should consult the yacht's "want" list and turn on the anchor light before you go ashore. This latter chore applies even —perhaps especially—in a crowded anchorage, where it's not done to prevent collision but to enable you to pick out your boat from a hundred others without anchor lights. Before bedding down for the night, the crew should decide on a general plan for next day, and the navigator and skipper should obtain a late weather forecast. The last thing before retiring, the skipper should check the anchor or mooring rode, or the docklines, and the anchor light. If there's any weather at all, I usually find myself aware of it, and may even poke my head up the companionway hatch once or twice during the night, just to make sure that everything's in order.

If your schedule has brought you to an exceptionally delightful place, and you plan to spend all day or even overnight ashore, you'll want to take special care about how you leave your boat. It may help people with poor memories (like me) to have a checklist written up in the log. It might contain the following list of things to do before going ashore. First and most important is keeping the boat in place. In a well-run marina, you can rely on the employees keeping something of an eye on your boat, but don't expect the kind of care you'd lavish on her yourself. If the help seem reliable, you might ask a particular attendant to check the boat's lines and fenders periodically (be sure to tip for any extra service). But the responsibility is inescapably yours, and you should tie her up as if there would be no one to watch her at all. At a mooring or at anchor, be sure her swinging circle won't impinge on other boats, and check the chafing gear. If there's any chance of your being away till after dark, it may not be a bad idea to leave a cabin light on as well as the anchor light. All hatches should be closed and locked, as well as any ports within arm's reach of valuables inside. On the other hand, it will provide good ventilation to leave open ports in the head and any other place where a sudden shower won't soak something that could be damaged.

If you have an automatic bilge pump, set it in that mode, and check the bilges before you leave. Also make absolutely sure that the stove and any kerosene lamps are out, and that the seacocks are closed. If you're in any doubt about the weather, leave an extra dockline accessible, in case someone else has to add a spring. Finally, tie off your halyards so they won't clatter against the mast—it's a noise that can drive some people mad.

Diversions

A cruising boat, unlike a racer, is normally an easygoing vehicle. The sails, once trimmed, tend to be ignored except when a course change or wind shift forces the crew to uncleat a sheet. In many ways this is unfortunate, since the lazy sailor not only fails to appreciate the full potential of his boat, but he also misses much of the fun of skillful sailing. Be that as it may, however, on many cruising boats the skipper can disturb his crew's rest only so often without risking mutiny.

Not that the crew are engaged in life-or-death activities themselves, as a rule; it's just that they're not interested in working under direction. Quite frequently, in fact, the same crew members who resent being ordered around on ship's work are also the first to complain of boredom when left to themselves.

Sometimes it seems the skipper cannot win. The point, I guess, is that only a rare family enjoys cruising equally, and even they are likely to prefer one aspect to another. Children are especially difficult on a small boat, since they usually fail to find being cold, wet, and cooped up for long periods a substitute for television. The key to enjoyment aboard a cruising yacht under way or at anchor is to provide plenty of diversions for the crew off watch. These may take the form of excursions off the boat or activities on the vessel, and they may involve participation by all hands or be solo amusements.

The most obvious entertainment is simply watching what's going by, whether it be shore or other boats. To enhance your enjoyment of this sedentary activity you need a few simple tools. Most important, perhaps, is a decent pair of binoculars—not the navigator's, unless he is very tolerant or the boat is very small—inexpensive 7×35s are quite good enough, but of course 7×50s are better. One of the least formal popular games on our boats has been identifying other craft as they go by. We used to carry a *Lloyd's Register* to help us spot the larger yachts but of course that handy publication is no longer in existence, and the last issues are becoming less and less useful. Lacking *Lloyd's*—and it did take up an awful lot of bookshelf space—you can still have a great deal of fun picking out stock boats. As a field guide, so to speak, you can use either the annual *Sail Directory* (published by *Sail* magazine) or *Boatwatch*, by Max W. Averitt, a book published specifically for boat spotters.

Many adults and some children enjoy reading under way, and most have their favorite books to bring along, some of which will inevitably find their way into the yacht's own library. Unfortunately, the really good ones tend to disappear, and the boat is left with the indigestible long shots. On a vessel of any size, I have always found it a good idea to assemble a basic library of paperbacks that live aboard. Since choosing books is almost as personal a decision as choosing a mate, my list may well have no relevance for most people, but I offer it anyway. One basic component is a decent group of guides. We carry a guide to water birds, one to fish, and even one to shells and tidal flora. A good paperback dictionary and thesaurus will be helpful to the crossword puzzle addict. One book that gets a good deal of use is an illustrated guide to knots and ropework, and we even have a paperback cookbook of the "I-hate-to-cook" variety. For real reading, I always like to have two or three collections of short stories, some mysteries, and a book of light—i.e., nonintellectual—verse. Contrary to popular legend, very few people I know care to attempt really double-dome reading while on a boat, and in most cases your reading time comes in short bursts, so that diplomatic history or advanced fiction can be hard to follow. If you have nonsailing guests aboard, a good instructional sailing book will help them figure out what you're up to, and you won't have to try to explain your actions while you're in the middle of them. Beyond the basics, idiosyncrasy takes over. For years, our most-read volumes aboard (and ashore, too) were Tolkien's *Lord of the Rings;* we wore out two whole sets of the trilogy. And we have always preferred British mysteries to any others. Somehow, one category that doesn't seem too popular on our boats has been nautical fiction. Perhaps it doesn't flourish next to nautical fact.

As for games, playing cards still seem to be the most reliable amusement. They are reasonably durable, easily portable, and inexpensive. If you lose an ace, you can afford to throw out the rest of the deck and replace it. Games involving small, loose pieces seldom seem to work well under way, and the counters often seem designed specifically to clog bilge pumps. If you are devoted chess or Scrabble players, invest in a form of the game that has magnetic or pegged pieces, and even then you can count on losing a few.

Small children prefer to bring their own toys, of course, but few of these are suitable for use at sea. Most kids like to draw, and it's an activity we've always encouraged. The youngest may prefer to crayon the bulkhead of their sleeping area, but you can get washable crayons that come off painted wood or polished plastic surfaces quite easily. Older children can spend hours drawing at the dinette table, and it is amazing how many crayons can disappear from a box without making it useless.

You will probably wind up with a good many small, wheeled vehicles made of metal. On a fiddled tabletop, they respond well to the yacht's motion, and they are often too large to find their way easily into the bilge. They also sink, which can be a blessing. In the early days, our boys enjoyed towing model boats along behind the one in which they were riding, and if you are prepared to come about quickly and go back after one when its towline snaps, this can be a pleasant way to pass the time. The models must be simple and tough, because they will lead a brutal life. The ticky-tacky wood models found in gift shops of resort areas will seldom serve.

One traditional amusement for all hands is music. We have always carried a guitar aboard (a battered, sacrificial model) and have been amazed at how enjoyable it can be for everyone. A harmonica is probably more practical, but it means the player can't sing, which seems unfair. If you do bring a musical instrument, invest in a couple of those paperbound collections of old favorite songs as well, so you'll have some idea of what comes after the first verse.

Cruising in company

One way that many cruising people have found to widen the variety of their coastal voyaging is to make passages in company with other vessels. Cruising in company can involve a simple one-day leg alongside a chance-met yacht from the night before, or it may consist of a carefully structured fleet action comprising a dozen or more boats sailing together for a week or two. Perhaps the largest difference between collective cruising and the one-yacht voyage is at the level of planning. Given a seaworthy, well-found boat, a single skipper and crew need to plan on only a very basic, day-to-day level, but once two or more craft are involved, the level of logistical complexity goes up geometrically.

To begin with, there are the speed differentials within any fleet. Even if the boats all come from the same mold, some will be markedly faster than others, and when you consider the very small speeds we're talking about, it's amazing how much time spread there can be, over the course of a single day's sail, between first boat and last in. By and large, a cruise in company will be easiest to arrange if most of the boats have approximately the same speed potential. For those who are not mathematically inclined, the Performance Handicap Rating Formula (PHRF) (see Chapter XII) provides for most stock cruising yachts a good rule of thumb for potential speed. A boat that is faster than the others can either leave later in the morning or press on ahead, with the assigned task of securing the next night's accommodation. A yacht that is very much slower than the rest may have to set out earlier each morning, but it is only fair to say that being the slowest boat in a group can be a very wearing experience for the crew, who might do better to find a flotilla they can keep up with.

Next there is the matter of mooring space. These days it can be very difficult to find slip space at the same facility for a group of any size, unless you and your friends are willing to plan quite far in advance. Ensemble voyages to popular places are often set up during the winter previous to the planned passage, and this is probably none too early.

The alternative is rafting up at anchor, which can be a delightful or horrendous exercise, depending on the amount of thoughtfulness that goes into the rafting exercise. The anchorage itself is the first important element of a proper raft. You absolutely require first-rate holding ground, excellent protection from waves or surge, and good shelter from wind. Swinging room is not so necessary, simply because a raft of more than about three yachts (with one anchor, that is) cannot swing. Instead, you require reasonable assurance that wind and current will continue from the same direction through the night.

It's possible to create this situation, up to a point, by anchoring near the mouth of a river, where the current's force may wax and wane but its direction will be constant. Or choose a virtually landlocked pool, where the only current is likely to be gently circular. The wind will be harder to arrange, at least in most areas. Where there is a prevailing breeze that happens to be onshore, the otherwise normal offshore breeze of evening may be weak or nonexistent.

The best practice, in terms of safety, is to plan on breaking the raft at twilight or even slightly earlier, to allow boats to find their own anchoring spots. Whether the skippers in your raft plan on sticking together through the night or not, however, the raft itself should be well constructed from the beginning, or it may not last through the first wake. The initial member of the group should be one of its larger boats, using oversize ground tackle. It should anchor in the normal way, but with a scope of ten to one if possible. Ready all the yacht's fenders (three oversized fenders are a minimum) and a couple of docklines, and allow the second boat to come alongside.

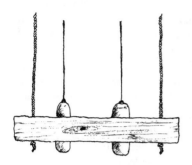

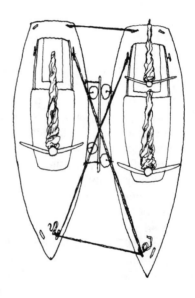

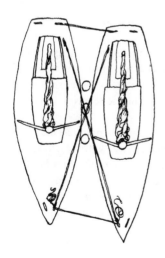

When rafting two boats of different sizes or different hull shapes, a fenderboard is most useful, as it provides a flat surface against which each yacht may lie. Of the four lines involved, the bow and stern springs are the most important. Make sure that the boats do not lie so that their spreaders can tangle if they begin to roll—this may mean aligning the yachts so that their hulls don't exactly match, but don't worry about it.

While it will be easier if both boats are more or less the same length and hull type, it's best if their rigs don't exactly match: That is, the masts should not be adjacent to each other: One of the biggest problems in rafting, should the boats begin to roll, is locked spreaders. Even if it results in slightly misaligned hulls, make sure that the masts are as far apart as possible. One obvious way to accomplish this is simply to raft the boats alternating bows and sterns, but such an arrangement kills half the fun of the raft, by making it impossible to socialize from cockpit to cockpit at arms' length.

Most of the time, large fenders will allow boats to lie comfortably side by side. On occasion, however, and most often when the fleet consists of pinched-end racers designed for the International Offshore Rule, it will be necessary to create an intermediate flat surface against which each vessel can lie. Do this by using a fenderboard, a piece of 2″ × 6″ or 2″ × 8″ timber drilled to accept lanyards at each end. Each yacht puts out fenders in the normal way, and the fenderboard lies between the two sets of fenders, acting like a solid, if abbreviated, bulkhead.

The boats in a raft are, of course, lashed bow to bow and stern to stern, but the really important lines are the springs, running from one boat's bow to the other's stern, and vice versa. The idea is to make an X of the spring lines, which are then taken up tightly, as are the bow and stern lines, causing the two boats to ride more or less as a single unit. Given the stretchiness of nylon, you may well have to tighten the springs after about an hour at anchor.

Since most of today's cruising boats have bow and quarter cleats that are too small, it may be difficult to get all the required lines on the few cleats available. In some cases you can put a snatch block in a convenient place and lead the fall of the spring line back to another cleat, or use a cockpit sheet winch to lead a line. Just make sure that these improvised set-ups provide adequate support in the plane for which each device was designed. Don't, for instance, pull upward on a winch, unless you're positive it's securely backed up beneath the deck. And be careful that a snatch block receives the line so the pull goes around the sheave, not across it.

In calm waters it can be safe to secure—temporarily—as many as five yachts to the same anchor, but beyond that it will be necessary to run out more anchors, in a more or less balanced pattern on either side of the first hook. As long as wind and current are in approximately the same direction, there should be no problem, but a raft with more than one anchor out cannot change its orientation easily, and if it does swing more than about forty-five degrees, you may need to reset the anchors.

While it's easier for a boat to peel off the outer end of a raft, it's not impossible to dislodge a yacht that's somewhere in the middle, if all hands are reasonably alert and if it's not too choppy or windy. Let the departing boat drop back out of line, carrying her fenders with her, until she is hanging by her bow line. The remaining boats close ranks and secure their lines and fenders, while the yacht that is leaving has time to clean up her decks and make sail before casting off.

If it should become necessary to break a raft in the middle of the night, however, it is far better practice to begin at the ends and work toward the middle, with the crew in safety harnesses. This kind of maneuver lends itself to confusion, and someone can easily fall between boats.

Communications between boats are an essential of group cruising. Assuming the vessels involved are of approximately equal potential speed, any of the ordinary types of ship-to-ship radio should work perfectly well. Given the horde of voices on the airwaves, however, you will find it easier to send messages back and forth if you establish in advance a common working frequency on which to initiate calls, and avoid the standard calling and distress channels if at all possible. A calling timetable will also be helpful: If each skipper knows that the others will be listening at, say, quarter-past each hour, fewer messages will be missed. If all the boats don't have one type of communication in common, then you'll have to try to find one that can bridge the gap —carrying both VHF-FM and CB, for instance—to act as a radio link.

If the collective voyage will cover any great distance, you can expect at least some of the boats to be out of sight of the others for part of the time. In this case, you may want to set up a more formal communications net, with regular check-ins and one or more craft maintaining a listening watch at all times. Having sailed in a fleet that conducted this sort of net for over five hundred miles, I can say that it works well. For more information on radiotelephone procedure, see Appendix 3.

One of the best ways to make time pass happily when in a group of yachts heading the same way is to organize an informal passage race. Unless all the boats are nearly identical, you'll have to work out a handicap system, probably using the PHRF's figures, but you won't want to make too much of a production out of it. In some groups, there are likely to be boats that cannot be handicapped effectively at all. These are likely to be either very old, very undercanvased or very poorly sailed—and of course occasionally you'll encounter a boat that's all three.

To make such a boat less unequal, you may want to add an engine allowance, under which one or all of the boats can use auxiliary power for a certain period, at a time of her skipper's choice. Since many boats that are short on sail area have oversized engines, this can be a surprisingly effective handicap arrangement. Passage racing can be a great deal of fun, and is nearly unavoidable in any case, as I have yet to see two cruising boats sailing side by side without surreptitious efforts by both skippers to move their vessels just a shade faster —usually while pretending to ignore the yacht alongside.

Your planning should insure that the race is not too demanding for the slower boats, and that everyone gets in in time for the cocktail hour. And when arranging the race, be sure to set up a definite finish mark, with the first boat to cross taking her own time and then anchoring to form one end of a finish line. The start line may work the same way, with the temporary "committee boat" setting out at a preestablished time—say five minutes—after the rest of the fleet. Trading crews with other boats or having someone other than the skipper in charge is another good way of increasing the amusement while decreasing the pressure.

VII

~~~~~~~~~~

Heavy-Weather Seamanship

To many yachtsmen, the Fastnet Race tragedy of 1979 brought home for the first time the potential strength of the sea in fury. Judging by the response to that storm, cruising sailors even more than racers took the lessons seriously and made sincere attempts to ensure that the same fate never befell them. This kind of concern is certainly to be applauded, but at the same time it's important to remember that storms are not alike, and a given tempest far at sea may be very different when later it strikes the coast. In terms of both strategy and tactics, the coastwise skipper must consider that he or she is probably facing different requirements from those encountered by someone on the open ocean. It's not a question of better or worse seamanship or preparation or seaworthiness. Just different.

High-seas vs. coastal storms

To set the stage, then, consider first some ways in which the open-ocean storm differs from one encountered near shore. Time is frequently, but not always, a significant factor. In coastal voyaging, the prudent American mariner has access to literally endless weather forecasts, both government and commercial, and the approach of extended bad weather is almost always signaled well in advance—or at least far enough ahead to make seeking shelter a serious possibility. Those who remember the Fastnet storm will also recall that the speed and unexpectedness of its arrival were major factors in its impact, but it was approaching the land from a relatively deserted sea area, and the boats that got hammered were ones that had deliberately isolated themselves from the protection of the coast. It is, of course, foolish to suggest that another storm of similar speed, intensity, and duration could not hit any shore without adequate warning. Anything is possible. But it's extremely unlikely. Far more common is the three-day storm that approaches slowly and builds gradually to a climax. By the time its weather has become serious, most skippers will have had time to get to shelter, if indeed they had set out in the teeth of the weather forecasts. Books on cruising seamanship seem inevitably to become involved with determining the navigable semicircle of a tropical hurricane, and to be sure anyone in a small vessel on the high seas may eventually have some use for that information. For most coastal sailors, though, tropical storms are if anything too well heralded these days, to the point that normally weatherwise skippers become bored with forecasters crying wolf, and neglect to take obvious precautions. Even so, only spectacularly foolhardy or obtuse coastal yachtsmen will find themselves afloat in such a tempest.

More dangerous to most of us is the relatively sudden storm, nearly always of short duration, that is too localized for general weather warnings or too fast-moving for radio forecasters to keep up with. I am thinking, in this connection, of the kind of hot-weather thunderstorm whose towering clouds are veiled in haze until the last minute, or the line squall racing ahead of a cold front. These storms are no joke, and they may carry winds as strong as those in a hurricane, but usually they pass as quickly as they arrive. As a rule the weather conditions that cause such storms are distinctive, and someone who wants to be sure he isn't caught out can nearly always avoid them—at the risk, admittedly, of passing up some good sailing. Even if you make a mistake and get nailed, there is the consolation that it will soon be over. The second important difference between high-seas storms and coastal bad weather is a matter of the relative intensity of the two types. The two dangers of a storm on the water are, of course, winds and seas. On the open ocean, the wind is able to build to the full potential of the weather system, unhindered by geography or by the friction of terrain. The result is that the same storm will usually generate considerably stronger winds at sea than it can when it has been braked by land. On the other hand, the coastal sailor may find himself pinned against a lee shore by the full force of storm winds that have been created far at sea, but for most longshore sailors, it is possible at least half the time to use geography as shelter, to minimize the wind when it becomes too strong to use simply by interposing an element of shore. This is an asset the deep-water sailor cannot call upon, just as the long-distance voyager seldom has to worry about rocks under his lee. Shelter from the wind can be a tricky matter, though, as certain kinds of geography funnel and intensify existing winds, to the point where you may find that conditions out in open water are considerably milder than in what appears to be a sheltered harbor.

Much the same considerations apply to wave formation on the ocean and inshore. This is reasonable when you consider that air and water are both fluids and, despite the great disparity in their densities, operate under the same natural laws. The majestic storm waves of the open sea, which a coastal sailor may never encounter in a lifetime of cruising, march across the ocean, pushed by the wind and unhindered by land masses. This allows them to build to the maximum height consistent with wind strength and duration—the factors that, together with distance, condition the size of a wave. Many immense open-ocean waves are relatively harmless and become dangerous only as they approach shallow water and begin to trip on the shelving sea bottom. And while coastal waves seldom if ever reach the size of their high-seas counter- parts, they may be far more threatening to small cruising yachts because they are far more likely to be breaking.

The ocean cruiser must take the waves as they come, and virtually his only area of choice is the aspect of his yacht that he presents to the seas. The coastal cruiser, on the other hand, must often deal with waves in combination with the effects on them of land and tidal current. He may be able to use land features as shelter, but that shelter may be illusory. And if there is a major wind shift, the shelter of a few hours ago may become a present danger.

While the other differences between open-sea heavy weather and coastal storms are important, the presence of land is the essential variable. Deep-water sailors often have a developed mistrust of shore. By and large, they would prefer to take their chances in the open. With faith in their craft and their skill, they see the coast as a mass of deceptive hazards, more dangerous than the winds and seas. Given a true ocean cruising yacht such thinking is probably correct. Certainly the decisions are fewer and simpler—not a small matter when you are tired and afraid. Speaking personally, I find that the inevitability of an approaching storm far from land is often easier to confront than the many dubious choices caused by impending bad weather along a hostile coast. Inex- perienced yachtsmen, by contrast, flee irrationally toward land. It is perhaps the natural reaction of land-oriented creatures, but in many cases it may not be the most sensible decision. Your decisions must take into account a great many factors, and it is the purpose of this chapter to suggest, first, what ought to go into establishing a storm strategy, and second, what tactics to employ in carrying it out.

Setting storm strategy

If you're afloat when a storm approaches, the basic choice is between run- ning for shelter or making for open water. Because of the slow speeds of most cruising auxiliaries, this decision may have to be made fairly quickly, and there are several elements involved in it. Briefly, these involve the nature of the storm, the seaworthiness and seakindliness of your boat, the abilities and endurance of your crew, and, perhaps most important, the nature and proximity of available shelter.

Take the last first. It may help to divide shelter into four general types, each of which has its advantages and drawbacks. The most obvious, with a storm in the offing, is a formal harbor, whether it be natural or manmade. By and large, a place becomes used as a harbor because it offers shelter from the prevailing winds and seas. It is generally easy to locate—and this may well be a vital factor if you are faced with finding it once visibility has deteriorated. In appraising the usefulness of a harbor, then, a major concern will be spotting it: Are there radio beacons, or at least commercial AM radio stations along the shore, with which you can employ an RDF? Are there good landmarks, visible in the dark? Is the entrance channel well buoyed and easy to distinguish, even for a stranger?

Ease of entry is equally important, and it may well depend on whether you are beating up to the harbor or flying downwind toward it. Given the choice, and given a seaworthy boat, I would usually prefer the upwind approach. For one thing, the winds and seas will generally ease the closer you get to shelter, so as your endurance ebbs, so does the difficulty of the task. For another, you can—within limits—regulate the speed of approach when beating or close reaching, whereas when running, you may not be able to stop in case of uncertainty or danger. Elements to consider in appraising the ease of entry are off-lying hazards; jetties and breakwaters that may be submerged in heavy weather; tidal currents that may set against the wind and whip up a dangerous, short sea right at the harbor mouth; or currents that may set across the harbor entrance.

Then there is the value of shelter once achieved. A commercial port can be downright unfriendly for a small boat in a storm. Not only are there relatively few places of suitable size for a yacht to tie up, but the harbor may be packed with shipping, some of it in motion, some of it anchored. Consider in your appraisal what will become of the shelter if the wind turns, as it frequently will in the course of a major storm: Try and find a spot within the harbor that will still be protected, more or less, should the wind clock 180 degrees.

One thing that probably will be available is assistance. Even if you arrive in desperate condition, there will be someone to help you. Consult a detailed cruising guide first, to determine what kinds of help are accessible, and how best to reach them with the communications you have aboard. In a bad storm, you may be limited to VHF-FM, CB, or even a flashing light, and you will want to position yourself to get the best advantage from these devices. You may also find yourself among a great flock of moored vessels of approximately your own boat's size. This can at first be very comforting, and it suggests that the holding ground at least is adequate. But it can also mean that you will spend the ensuing hours or even days fending off other craft as they break loose and come down on you.

Another type of shelter is a cove, which I'll define only as an undeveloped harbor. Most of the same considerations apply as in deciding on the approach to a commercial harbor, but there will be fewer aids to navigation, less chance of finding formal assistance—Coast Guard or marine police—available. On the other hand, there may well be fewer dangerous nuisances, such as other vessels, to consider or to dodge. Assuming that a cove offers good natural protection from seas and winds, at least for the immediately foreseeable future, and that approach to it seems reasonably simple, the next question is holding ground, since there will presumably be no piers, or at least none that are reliable. If the area is used as an anchorage, there may be vacant moorings, but unless you're directed to one by a harbor master or a knowledgeable native who knows the boat that normally uses it, a strange mooring is a chancy bet. If your boat is properly equipped, your own storm anchor is probably more reliable.

If you have time to send a dinghy ashore, it's not a bad idea to establish contact with local residents, especially if they seem water-oriented themselves. They may be able to suggest what usually happens to their cove in a severe storm like the one you're expecting—where the best holding ground lies, whether the wind is funneled over hills or through gaps, and other useful information.

Consider, in choosing where you anchor, what will happen if the wind veers. Ideally, you would want protection against seas coming from any direction and a flat, soft shore under your lee if worst came to worst. Obviously this will not often be possible, but do determine that your swinging circle at anchor doesn't impinge on any natural obstacle and that you're a couple of hundred yards off any bulkheading or bluffs that can bounce waves back at you, should the wind turn. An area where other boats are moored is tempting, but they will probably be using chain and heavy mushroom anchors, with considerably less scope than you will have, and thus a smaller swinging circle. If you have a choice, perhaps the best type of sheltering shore has a gentle slope and is heavily wooded. Trees break the wind nicely, and if a few of them go down, it won't matter. The foot of a steep hill or the mouth of a gully can, as noted earlier, be a very unpleasant spot when the wind blows strongly, even if the seas cannot develop.

A landlocked cove should either be reasonably large or so small that you can take lines ashore in at least three directions. In the latter situation, you must have the place to yourself, and you will gamble that it won't be necessary to get out—because you probably won't be able to. In the former, you want a spot that will allow you some room to maneuver if your anchor drags, another boat comes down on you, or some other factor makes it necessary for you to get under way.

Really well-protected coves are few, and they're usually full of local boats. When you're seeking protection from a storm, don't overlook the apparently open spot where a barely submerged reef or sandbar can effectively take the legs from under quite sizable seas. To be sure, you still have the wind to consider, but in most situations short of a full gale, it's the surge and the breakers that do the damage. Until you've experienced it, you cannot realize the extent to which a reef six inches or a foot below the surface can flatten oncoming seas, so that a boat anchored in its lee can be quite comfortable. The only things to be wary of are, first, that there is some protection on your windward side, in case the wind clocks, and, second, that extra-high tide or wind-driven water won't submerge your sheltering bar so deeply that it loses its effect. But in anything less than a hurricane, you're not likely to see so unpredictable a rise of water, and you can probably assume that if the bar is just covered at full-moon high water, you're in a good spot.

Perhaps the most dubious route to hoped-for safety, running ahead of an oncoming storm, is through an inlet. Having grown up sailing in the shifting

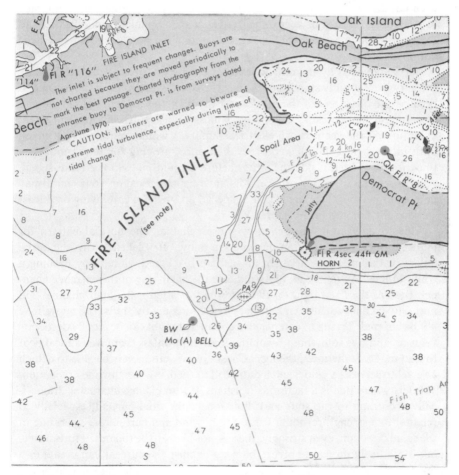

It is often impossible to chart a shifting inlet, like this one. Approached from the east or even from the south, the inlet's mouth might be screened from view. Note that charted buoyage begins with can 9, suggesting that there are at least a few buoys in the inlet itself. Note also the tidal current arrows indicating the direction and strength of ebb and flood.

inlets of a barrier beach, I have considerable respect for the savage bodies of water they can become, and there have been several occasions—and not in storms, either—when I've chosen the open sea to an unfamiliar inlet.

When considering an inlet as a possible refuge, there are several matters to worry about. First is locating it, especially in deteriorating weather or poor visibility. While many inlets are wide and obvious, carefully marked with major, fixed aids to navigation, lots of them are relatively narrow—that, after all, is what makes them inlets, not harbors. Along a coastline that has a *littoral drift*—a prevailing, alongshore movement of sand-carrying current—the standard conformation of unstabilized inlets has one arm of the barrier beach overlapping the other, so that the inlet channel actually runs diagonal to or even parallel with the shore, and the entrance may be screened from one side or dead ahead. It can be very difficult to spot such an inlet from offshore, and frequently you must take the boat almost among the shoals in order to see the entrance.

Inlets stabilized by man-made jetties are somewhat easier to find, because the jetty itself usually stands out against the contrasting color of the beach and because the outer end of the breakwater often carries a fixed, lighted aid and sometimes a marker radiobeacon, too. Unless your boat has an excellent RDF, operating off the yacht's own electrical supply, I would hesitate to put much faith in marker radiobeacons; more than once, groping for inlet mouths in thick fog, I've been inside the jetties before I could pick up the RDF signal. A local AM radio station ashore, if its antenna is marked on your chart, may be a better bet, but there are of course special problems in employing broadcast stations for homing (see Chapter V).

Aids to navigation are generally more reliable. The normal pattern for marking inlets consists of an offshore sea buoy, often labeled with the initial letters of the inlet's name; then an inshore black-and-white buoy flashing a white Morse "A" (short-long), to indicate the beginning of the entrance channel. Besides the fixed light on the outer end of a jetty, the inlet channel will normally be buoyed, although if that channel frequently shifts, the buoys may not be charted. Trying to enter such a channel at night can be a truly desperate venture, and it is something I would not attempt unless there was a local boat to lead me in. Sometimes, the local Coast Guard station may be able to detach a vessel to serve as a guide, and a radio call to them is a worthwhile precaution.

Inlets where tide is a factor, as it usually is, can change character dramatically according to the state and direction of the tidal current, especially in relation to a strong prevailing wind. When wind and current are operating in the same direction, even strongly, there is not likely to be too much turbulence, but a relatively moderate breeze blowing against the current can create in a few minutes a surprisingly high, steep sea. Thus, in considering whether or not to attempt an inlet, you want first to know the direction the current runs and when it changes. Although tides and currents are more fully considered in Chapter V, it may be worth emphasizing here that current prediction requires the *Tidal Current Tables:* Turn of tide seldom coincides with turn of tidal current. In a gathering storm, running an inlet requires wind and current in the same direction, preferably offshore; failing that, if you are truly determined to get in, time your approach for the half-hour either side of slack water.

And as if all that were not bad enough, be sure to check the chart to make sure that you won't simply be entering a cul-de-sac: Many inlets have quite low drawbridges near their mouths, and while these ought to be manned at all times, bridgetending seems increasingly to be an area where local governments are prone to make economies. These days, many bridges have ship-to-shore VHF-FM communications on channel 13 (the frequencies for each bridge are—or ought to be—listed in the applicable *Coast Pilot*). If you cannot raise the bridgetender on VHF, ask the Coast Guard to do it by shore telephone, emphasizing that it is a matter concerning the safety of your vessel (assuming, indeed, that it is). But do not count on any bridge's being manned, or on its being capable of opening, even in an emergency, in under an hour.

All in all, as you have probably decided, I'm less than sanguine about entering inlets in storm or approaching storm conditions, and I would put this type of possible shelter in the "very dicey" category.

Setting storm tactics

The nature of the storm and of the coastline are two elements that are beyond your control. But there are two other areas where you can exercise a certain amount of influence, both well before and just before bad weather. The first of these is your boat and the second, your crew.

Fairly early on—perhaps from the moment you first considered buying her —you should have devoted some thought to how well your boat could handle bad weather, and what kind of heavy-weather tactics would be indicated. Among the other things you'd want to know, perhaps the most important (at least to my mind) is how well she can go to windward as the weather worsens. In coastal storms, as opposed to deep-sea tempests, a yacht's windward ability, or the lack of it, will often decide her fate.

More specifically, you should have a good idea of your boat's ability to get to windward through various kinds of seas and wind strengths, how she handles under reduced sail, or when motorsailing, and her endurance while beating. Take an example from my own experience. My little AMF 2100, a lightweight twenty-one-footer designed for day-racing and occasional weekending, is quite typical of the new breed of high-sided, fractional-rig boats whose shape and performance derive from dinghies. As delivered, she had a 150 percent genoa, a lapper, and a mainsail with a single set of reef points. Going to windward, the genoa is good to about 10 knots of true wind, and then there is a fairly rapid set of changes: The genoa and reefed main seem about equal to working jib and full main and either arrangement can go to about 15 knots true, when lapper and reefed main are called for. At about 20, things get really uncomfortable, and if it's still necessary to work to windward, we usually drop back to the working jib alone or the reefed main alone. With each reduction in sail area, there is an increase in the amount of leeway and a decrease in pointing ability that have to be taken into consideration when calculating destinations. In spite of these problems, the boat will continue to bash along at or near hull speed.

One of our problems usually relates to crew weight: Like other boats of her type, the 2100 responds radically to shifts in her live ballast and, in heavy winds, she really requires the weight of four average adults—say 650 to 750 pounds—on the windward rail. Our normal crew total more like 350 pounds, and the deficiency is very evident in the boat's heeling angle; like any dinghy type, she is happiest when sailed nearly flat.

Another problem we have to live with is that motorsailing in any kind of chop is out of the question. Not only does the boat heel so much that the outboard, mounted on the port side of the transom, has its prop immersed only on starboard tack, but the engine itself is too small, at 3.5 horsepower, to be much help. (We opted for this size to save weight and money.)

The foregoing paragraphs are not intended to reflect badly on the 2100. In what is, for her, heavy weather, she usually does very well for her size, and the only boats that can operate more comfortably are either considerably bigger or of very heavy displacement. My point, rather, is that when we are faced with a heavy-weather beat, we must adjust the boat's performance characteristics accordingly, grin and bear it. One thing we're reasonably sure of, and that's that the boat's endurance almost certainly exceeds her crew's, barring some piece of bad seamanship or an unforeseeable accident.

Off the wind

Generally speaking, in heavy weather any sailboat is happiest reaching, but you should determine what sort of reach your boat prefers when the weather disintegrates. For most small cruisers, keeping the apparent wind a bit abaft the beam will usually produce the fastest, safest, and most comfortable ride. And every once in a while, that may even be the heading you'd like to make. Even if it isn't, as the weather deteriorates, you may have to settle for a broad reach.

On the face of it, running might seem to be the most comfortable heading in heavy winds, and it certainly reduces the apparent wind force dramatically. But if there are sizable seas running, and if those seas are at a slight angle to the wind, you may well have a problem holding the boat on course and avoiding an accidental and possibly serious jibe. Again, the decision whether to run or tack downwind will be easier to make if you have a knowledge of how your boat behaves on this heading. Running in heavy winds is where the old-fashioned, long keel is said to have an advantage over the fin-and-spade underbody. In one respect this is true: A long-keeled boat will usually track straighter than will a boat with substantial chunks of her underwater shape erased. On the other hand, a detached, high-aspect-ratio rudder will usually yield far quicker and more positive steering. Probably it's fair to say that most experienced helmsmen can handle either variety of boat easily, while a less than seasoned hand at the tiller is likely to have a slightly easier time with a full-keel hull, especially if he keeps adequate sail up forward of the mast.

Reefing considerations

The question of shortening sail breaks into two subquestions, *when* and *what*. The answers will depend on a number of factors—the yacht's heading, the sail wardrobe available, the crew, and how the boat handles under various combinations. Going to windward, it is usually sensible to keep up a larger jib, if possible, even at the expense of the main. This is especially likely to be good strategy in masthead-rigged boats, where a generation of skippers has learned to reef the main before shifting down from genoa to working jib. On the fractionally rigged boat, the same practice may or may not be advisable; as noted above, the genoa-and-reefed main combination may have almost the same windward potential as the working jib with full mainsail. The objective is a well-balanced boat, with just a slight weather and no lee helm, and that goal probably should condition your decision.

There is also the question, when the weather is obviously deteriorating, of what to do after the first sail reduction. If you suspect that you'll have to shorten sail further in the next hour or so, then it will pay to change to a smaller headsail now, if your boat's main is reasonably easy to reef. The reason is that as the weather worsens and the crew gets more fatigued you'll want to keep them in the cockpit and off the foredeck.

The ancient wisdom of sailing holds that you should reef as soon as you find yourself wondering if it's a good idea, and certainly for a cruising boat this seems to me sound. (The reverse—that you should add sail as soon as the thought occurs to you—is probably a better prescription for racers than cruisers.) That doesn't mean that you should have your crew on deck instantly. Take time to plan what you're going to do, even with a crew you're used to. This is not a case when seconds count, at least not as much as the hours that will follow. Especially if the crew is already tired or sleepy, the skipper will do well to make sure they know what they're to do, and that the proper safety equipment is rigged (see below) before sending anyone forward.

The crew

Although in fact it seldom works out that way, racing sailors aim at putting to sea with nothing but trained, physically fit crews who are familiar with their craft and capable of getting the most out of her in any circumstances. The cruising yachtsman has somewhat different criteria when choosing his crew, if indeed he is able to make choices at all. By and large, the people who cruise are selected, first, because they're available and, second, because they're pleasant company. It is a lucky owner who can specify something approaching competence as well.

On the other hand, since most cruising complements are families, they presumably know each other's general strengths and weaknesses already. And if some or all of them come aboard as complete beginners, there is the opportunity to train them up properly, right from scratch.

Once heavy weather approaches, however, the skipper must make do with what he has, and he should have taken pains to know his crew's capabilities in three areas—endurance, skill, and courage. It would be hard to say which is more important, and to some extent they are interconnected: Endurance is at least partly conditioned by courage, and skill can stretch one's physical endurance, if only by making a given job easier to accomplish. The person confident of his or her skill is likely to have more heart to face unpleasant weather, is more likely to remember that all storms end sooner or later.

The skipper must keep track mentally of how much energy each crew member is expending, and how much each probably has left. He must assign jobs, both below and on deck, that are within the particular crew member's capacities at the time. He should, when possible, buoy the crew's spirits by keeping them informed of what's going on. As an example of what I mean, let's presume a typical family crew—father, mother, teen-age daughter, sub-teen-age son, all of whom know the boat reasonably well. In terms of physical power, the adult male is likely to be ahead, at least at first, and it is important that his reservoir of muscle not be expended sooner than necessary. If, as is likely, he is also the skipper, then there is all the more reason to husband his strength. Early on in a storm, the kids can probably handle the helm and the reefing chores, while the adults work up their storm plan and alternatives. Once the seas get really nasty, however, it can be actively hazardous to go forward. Children especially should be given something else to do—lookout or radio watch is both a necessary and a time-consuming job within their capabilities.

Always keep an eye out for approaching seasickness, as it can weaken even a strong crew member amazingly. Everyone has his own remedy for this problem, but in every case I know of, early action is vital. Staying dry and warm—or as dry and warm as possible—is especially important, as is absorbing at least some nourishment. It is vital that the mate, usually the wife and mother, be kept up to date as to what is happening, and have a sound idea of what to do if unpleasant weather should suddenly be compounded by an emergency. It is a fine distinction, perhaps, but one of the skipper's jobs is to communicate real urgencies without incurring panic.

Heavy-weather tactics: the "unannounced" storm

As suggested earlier, there are few really unforecast storms in coastal waters. But there are many forecasts that go unheard, many weather signs that are unheeded. The cruising skipper and crew must acquire both the habit of listening regularly to whatever professional forecasts are available and the skill to prepare their own local forecasts, using tools on board. These techniques are often in the navigator's department, and I have dealt with them in the sections on navigation, but it would be excellent practice if more skipper/navigators encouraged the development of weather forecasting skills in the other members of their crew.

Generally speaking, there are two types of storms that arrive with relatively little warning. One is the line squall, often associated with a fast-moving front, and the other is the relatively local thunderstorm veiled, as often happens, in late-afternoon overcast. This muggy haze of summer should be a warning in itself, and a keen observer can sometimes make out the vague outlines of thunderheads, if there are any. Conventional AM radios—but not commercial FM or VHF-FM sets —are prone to heavy static when there are electrical storms making up in the vicinity.

Make a habit of getting a local radio weather forecast from the NOAA VHF-FM network three times a day—before you set out in the morning, early in the afternoon, and then just before bedtime. You will need a special receiver to get the NOAA stations, which are spaced at approximately thirty- to forty-mile intervals, and which broadcast on three frequencies just above the commercial FM band. Most VHF-FM transceivers have at least two of the weather frequencies, probably labeled WX-1 and WX-2, and your yacht's radio, with its masthead antenna, is the best receiver.

The sudden storm is almost certainly a short-lived one, and while its intensity may be startling, its duration is seldom more than half an hour. Your manner of readying the boat can reflect this fact. As it becomes likely that a squall will hit—and if it is visible, you should presume some chance of being involved, even if it seems to be moving away at the moment—you should make sure that your engine, if any, is ready for use; that loose gear above and below is not just stowed but chocked, so it cannot shift if the boat heels; and that the crew is aware of the potential problem. Gear necessary for reefing or shortening sail should be got ready now.

While the crew are handling this part, the skipper and navigator should take time to appraise the situation carefully. If a squall hits, it may involve hail or blinding sheets of rain, as well as winds to 50 knots or more. Can you head up or off, as the situation requires, without danger of running into something?

If you must head off at hull speed, how long can you run without approaching an obstacle? What vessels are near, and what do they seem to be doing?

As the storm gets quite near, the next step is for the skipper to check the crew's preparations, and for all hands to put on foul-weather gear and lifejackets—or, if it is very hot, at least the latter. It seems to me unrealistic to expect a crew to wear lifejackets except in the presence of danger (although nonswimmers on deck aboard my boat must wear a life vest at all times), but it should be a standing rule that when the skipper calls for lifejackets, there is no discussion. My own preference is toward the fitted vest that utilizes slabs of foam for flotation and is closed by a plastic zipper. Each member of my crew has his or her own fitted vest, with the boat's and the individual's names prominently and indelibly printed on. I've also added large squares of retroreflective material (made by 3M), for nighttime visibility. The vests themselves are by Stearns, and I have found them generally satisfactory, though not cheap. Guests will probably have to use the inexpensive but CG-approved kapok-filled vests, although I always encourage a weekend guest to bring his or her own vest. Any vest should have a whistle attached, and if possible a light. Crew who will be working on deck should at this point also put on safety harnesses, and if there are not enough firm attachment points on deck, a jackline should be rigged from cockpit to bow pulpit.

Shorten sail now, and if you're in doubt as to the storm's strength or the boat's seaworthiness, reduce sail drastically, but leave enough of a balanced sailplan to permit maneuvering. Assign jobs: helm, sheets, radio watch, and on-deck lookout. Whoever gets the last task should try to memorize the positions of nearby boats as the weather closes in.

During the storm, it can be important to keep a reasonable track of the boat's position, especially if you're moving fast. Someone below can probably do this better than can a person on deck who is distracted by wind, rain, hail, and noise. The navigator will of course need to know the boat's course and speed, as well as some estimate of the leeway she is making, and should keep his plot going on a chart.

The lookout's primary responsibility, if the boat isn't closing the shore fast, is to keep track of other boats in the squall. Normally, all anyone wants to do is keep clear, but should another yacht be knocked down or dismasted or even appear to be out of control, you will have to attempt to remain nearby, so you can help as soon as the squall eases.

With fancy maneuvering out of the question, the sheet tender's job is simply to ensure that your own boat isn't overwhelmed by a sudden gust, keeping the sheets neatly coiled and ready to run. It's advisable for the sheet tender to wear some kind of gloves, both to enhance his grip and to protect his palms. The helmsman, meanwhile, will presumably hold course unless the boat is taking too much of a beating or is running out of sea room. Be sure to give navigator, sheet tender, and all hands below adequate warning of a tack or major course change: Not only does any maneuver take longer to set up in heavy weather, but it can be quite alarming for those in the cabin if you tack or jibe suddenly while they are disoriented by the noise and buffeting of a squall.

As soon as the main force of the storm has passed, check the rigging and sails to make sure that there's been no unseen damage, and take a quick census of the boats in the vicinity. If another vessel seems to require help, don't hesitate to offer it, but don't hurl yourself into assistance without the other crew's assent—unless, of course, the need is so obvious that no conversation is required.

Caught offshore

Sooner or later you're likely to find yourself in an exposed position along the coast, several hours from the nearest good harbor, with the weather deteriorating. Sometimes the realization will result from a changed forecast, sometimes from your own observations, but one way or another, it becomes clear that there's a strong chance of nasty weather. The first thing to do, when your suspicions are aroused, is tune in the NOAA VHF station in the area, to see if an updated forecast is available. As a general rule, the VHF-FM network's forecasts are updated to reflect any serious weather change. Local AM or FM commercial stations may have weather updates as well, often at the hourly news breaks. The Coast Guard, too, issues weather warnings, announced on VHF-FM channel 16 and then broadcast on the CG's own channel 22A (which every VHF-FM set should carry). Few cruising sailors keep channel 16 on the air while they sail—I certainly don't—so you're not likely to have picked up such a warning broadcast. If you're isolated and the weather looks really terrible, try calling the local CG station on channel 16 (see radio procedures, Appendix 3) to see if a weather warning has been broadcast.

If you keep an hourly position plot for the log, a thing very few cruising sailors do, you ought also to have an hourly barometer reading recorded. Using a book called the *Sager Weathercaster*, a compilation of coded short-range forecasts keyed to wind direction and barometric tendency, you can produce a surprisingly reliable local forecast for the next twelve hours or so. The *Weathercaster*, which has been around in one form or another for a couple of decades, is available from most large mail-order chandleries and is well worth carrying aboard.

With whatever information you've been able to collect, you must now appraise your situation and make some decisions. The primary, obvious one has to do with heading for shore or staying out. I've already noted some of the dangers involved in approaching the coast as the weather deteriorates, but if there is a good harbor nearby, you may well decide to make for it. Consider the time and distance involved, and if you choose to go for shelter, don't dither: Motorsailing is probably fastest, and this is not a time for sportsmanship.

As you proceed, whether seeking harbor or not, you should ready the boat in case the storm does catch you. While maintaining speed, charge up your yacht's main and auxiliary batteries, and if any of your self-powered electronics—depth sounder or RDF, in particular—can be recharged off the engine, then do so. Clean up loose gear and stow it carefully below, break out the storm sails, if you have them, and set up the proper sheets and leads. Rig jacklines and assemble the crew's safety equipment—life vests, harnesses, whistles, lights. Flares should be located where they can be got at if necessary, and you should check the running lights, man-overboard lights, and flashlights.

Make certain the ground tackle is set up and ready to use. It's not at all unusual in a storm to have to lower an anchor in a hurry. If you can handle the storm anchor easily and if it can be safely chocked on deck, then that is probably the one to have ready, but use the working anchor if the larger hook cannot be safely secured topside.

If you carry a sea anchor—many boats do not—you should probably get it out, check its set-up, and move it near to where you will want it later on, either forward or aft. Generally speaking, you would only consider a sea anchor if the storm was likely to blow you offshore; in an onshore wind, unless you're actively seeking shelter, you will probably need a far more positive course of action to keep clear of the coast.

If you carry weather cloths to protect the cockpit and its occupants, now is the time to rig them—in cold climates, lightweight Dacron cloths can make it much more comfortable to sail in early spring and late fall. Conversely, it will probably be a good idea to considering furling and lashing the cockpit dodger, if you have one. This should only take a minute or two, and can wait until the weather is quite bad, but few dodgers are made to handle really strong winds, and if you should take green water over the cabin top, the last thing the helmsman needs is a dodger that's come adrift.

While taking care of the boat, you should not neglect your crew. If the storm seems likely to be of long duration, make sure that those prone to seasickness have taken whatever medication they require. You may not be able to cook later, so serve a bland, warm meal now, and prepare or set out some quick-energy snacks for later. If you have a Thermos bottle or jug, hot cocoa, coffee with milk and sugar, or soup, according to taste and availability, is very heartening. Bedding and dry clothing should if possible be sealed in plastic garbage bags.

The navigator should take special pains to establish the yacht's position and should set up chart and log so that a plot can be determined and written up when things get rough. Aboard a small boat, nearly everything gets sodden in a storm, so try to protect the working chart with clear plastic or protective spray coating. It would not be amiss at this point to make certain that your radio is in working order and that the Coast Guard knows where you are and what your plans are.

Once the work is done, those crew members who have nothing more to do should rest as much as possible. When the storm seems imminent, or when the weather has slowly deteriorated to the point where it is actively unpleasant, it will be time to take the final preparatory steps. Set the storm canvas, or whatever you have that will serve that function, and strike the other bagged sails below. Don't be misled into leaving them on deck lashed to the rail—they can all too easily become unwanted sea anchors.

Loose spars—spinnaker and whisker poles, boat hooks and awning poles— should be carefully stowed or firmly lashed down. Dog down all the ports and hatches, except the main hatch, and if you carry wood covers for the ports, now is the time to rig them. Remove nondorade vents and cap them.

Down below, close the seacocks for the head and sinks, and if you have softwood plugs, make sure these are tied off near the seacocks. A portable bilge pump must be easily accessible and in working order. Pump the bilges dry and record that fact, with the time, so you can have some idea later of how much water the yacht is taking aboard. Unless you're actually approaching or making port, it's probably time to shut down the engine.

During the storm

Once bad weather has arrived and you're still out in open water, good preparation and planning should make it possible to carry on until you reach port or the weather moderates. The skipper's most important job is to stay on top of things, and not wear himself out by doing everything personally. He must stay rested and calm and keep the crew informed of what's going on.

The navigator—who may, in a small yacht, also be the skipper—has three important functions. Keeping an accurate plot of the boat's position is vital, but he should also keep track of the weather forecast, monitoring the NOAA VHF-FM station as well as Coast Guard emergency forecasts. At the same time, since the yacht's radio will already be tuned to channel 16, it's a good idea to stand by for any distress traffic on that frequency, since yours may be the boat nearest to an accident. The foregoing suggests why, if possible, skipper and navigator should not be the same person, or why someone other than the skipper should be qualified as back-up navigator (and back-up skipper, for that matter).

The cook should have little to do in really bad weather, as all the cooking will have been done beforehand. It is most important to keep the prepared and snack food set aside for the crew out of the regular galley stowage, where everything should be chocked in as tightly as possible. No other part of a small yacht can create as complete a shambles as a galley run amok. The cook can make sure that off-watch crew take some nourishment if they can handle it, that hot drinks are available for the watch on deck. About the only practical utensils in a storm are mugs, deep bowls, and tablespoons, since everything will be bouncing around and people will have to eat while braced against seatbacks.

Few small boats have a crew member officially entitled bosun, but the functions are necessary and can be listed under that heading. The bosun, known in a previous time as the ship's husband, is primarily responsible for keeping the yacht's fabric in working order. He should monitor the rig, being alert for chafed lines, incipient tears in sails, and shackles starting to back off. If the engine is in use, he should check the instrument panel regularly, since the boat is likely to be heeled and few engines function well in those circumstances. He should also keep track of fuel consumption, advising the skipper how many running hours remain. The bosun must watch out for gear breaking loose from its lashings, leaks that threaten to soak down unwrapped clothing or food, and the like. Finally, he should be responsible for periodically checking the bilges and pumping them if necessary. Any serious problem should be reported to the skipper immediately, as soon as the bosun has an accurate idea of what's happening. Sometimes, in the noise and confusion of a storm, the real cause is not instantly apparent; I remember vividly a sudden leak that seemed large enough to sink the boat I was on, yet with no sign of where it was coming from. Only after several minutes of pumping did someone have the wit to taste the water, at which point we knew that a freshwater tank must have cracked a seam but that the boat itself wasn't leaking.

On deck, there should if possible be a helmsman *and* a lookout, both in the cockpit. While these crew members should stay as warm and dry as they can, they must also tend to the yacht's comfort ahead of their own. Especially if the shore is near, the lookout may be the most important person aboard. Anything he sees should be reported to the skipper and/or the navigator, even if what he sees makes no apparent sense. Anything that looks like a distress signal is even more vital: Take a bearing on it instantly (the lookout's primary piece of equipment should be a hand bearing compass), as it may be the only flare you'll see.

The helmsman's job is largely self-explanatory, but in a storm, his focus closes down to the yacht and a few feet beyond. His only aim should be keeping the boat moving and easing her motion as much as possible. During really bad weather, these two goals may be mutually exclusive, at which point it will be up to the skipper to decide which is more important.

It may be necessary, especially when running before steep, breaking seas, to shut the companionway hatch and secure it. You don't want to take this step any earlier than necessary, both because of the disorientation and lack of ventilation it entails for the people down below, and the psychological strain it imposes on everyone. At the same time, if there seems to be any danger of the yacht being pooped or rolled, the hatch should be closed and bolted and the companionway slides locked in place as well. You may want to remove the dorade vent cowls and cap their openings, and shut the seacock on the engine exhaust, too.

It is now that sound planning will show. The crew's fatigue and probable discomfort are very likely to evidence themselves as lethargy, or a nearly uncontrollable desire to chuck it all and retire to one's bunk. This may be the best thing for those who are very ill, for small children, and for crew off watch, but for the others, it is absolutely necessary to follow through with the plan you adopted before conditions got bad. At the same time, it's obviously foolish to beat the boat and crew unnecessarily, and if the weather changes, you should be prepared to change your tactics. (You should, in fact, have considered the possibility of a weather change in your first planning, and developed an alternate strategy.) Remember that even a minor change of heading or shortening of sail may produce a major increase in crew comfort, and if the storm seems likely to last, it may well be best to sacrifice a little distance in order to give the crew some rest.

With an offshore wind, heaving to or lying a-hull may be viable alternatives. Making a judgment in this area will depend on how your boat behaves, and if possible you should know in advance. Lying a-hull simply means dropping and securing all sail, lashing the tiller, and leaving the boat to handle herself. She will probably lie more or less at right angles to the seas, headreaching slowly but making a good deal of leeway. If she is high-sided, as so many small, modern cruisers are, she is likely to be well heeled. In many lightweight boats, steep seas are both too uncomfortable and too dangerous to make lying a-hull worthwhile.

Heaving to is somewhat the same, but the boat will usually be under more control and will adopt a more seakindly position vis-à-vis the seas. There are almost as many ways to heave to as there are hull shapes and rigging plans, but the commonest are as follows: In a ketch or yawl, drop all sail but the mizzen, which should be tightly sheeted. Lash the tiller or wheel hard over, so that the boat heads up and falls off. She should ride like this, with relatively little wear and tear on the mizzen, and with reasonable comfort for the crew. In a sloop or cutter, it's usually necessary to back a small headsail and sheet it that way, while lashing the tiller so that the boat attempts to round up and then falls off under the influence of the backed jib. In some cases it may work better to strap the mainsail down amidships, so that it works against the headsail. In any case, the single-masted boat will probably assume a position nearly at right angles to the wind, sliding ahead and to leeward. If she has a full-length keel, however, she may well point up to sixty or seventy degrees off the true wind while working her way almost at right angles to the wind, and the same behavior is likely to be characteristic of a twin-sticker, regardless of underbody shape.

Heaving to or lying a-hull buys time, and if the boat is heavy enough to lie gently, rather than being tossed wildly about, you may be able to get a little rest, or at least prevent yourself and your crew from getting even more fatigued than you already are. If at all possible, one person should remain on deck to act as lookout even when hove to, to watch out for other vessels.

Some craft, especially those with extremely cut-away underbodies, may not heave to or lie a-hull effectively. In this case, if you have plenty of room under your lee, the best tactic may be simply to run before the wind under bare poles. If the wind is severe, its force in the rigging should give you steerage way, and you may in fact find the boat moving quite swiftly. Presumably you will be moving away from shore and the wind, in consequence, will be increasing. If the seas are steep and beginning to break, and if your boat begins to surf, you

The only way to determine how (or even if) your boat heaves to is to try it, preferably in a brisk wind. A sloop will generally —but not always—heave to best with the reefed main amidships, the jib sheeted to one side, and the tiller lashed to the other. A ketch or a yawl, if her mizzen is large enough, will probably heave to with the tiller lashed to one side and the mizzen sheeted over hard to the other. If the mizzen sheets to a single point on the transom, as many do, you may have to rig a preventer to keep the sail backed.

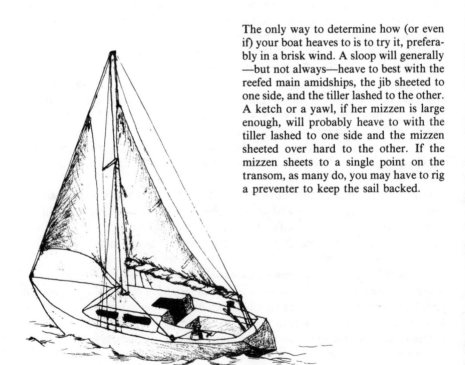

will probably be well advised to slow her down, perhaps by trailing doubled lines, with the ends made fast to your boat's quarters. A sea anchor will probably not take such punishment for long, and if it does, your deck fittings may give up instead. What you want, when the weather has reached this stage, is a drag that will slow the boat without bringing her to a jolting halt.

Here again is where planning ahead will be invaluable. A spare anchor line in a bight is probably a good beginning as a drag, but you need more friction-creating bulk. High-seas voyagers always seem to have a couple of old automobile tires handy for this situation, and yet I've never seen a coastal cruiser that carried them. One possible solution is to put one sailbag—empty—inside another, and then load the doubled bag with spare anchor, chain, sleeping bags, and the like. You want enough weight to keep the load from skipping over the seas, and the most bulk obtainable. Sling the doubled sailbags from the bight of the streamed rode, and it should slow you down considerably.

Suppose, however, that after an extended struggle you reach a harbor. You must then decide whether, with the storm in full force, it is worth the risk of entering. As noted earlier, if the wind is off the shore, chances are that you can get into shelter and that it will be worth doing. With the wind at your back, however, it's another thing. Take time to sort out your boat and your crew; make sure you know exactly where you are and what's happening at the harbor entrance—breaking waves seen from seaward, especially in dubious light, hardly appear as impressive as they do to someone ashore. And while it's possible to surf a cruising sailboat into a narrow harbor entrance, it's not something that anyone in his right mind would do casually.

If you decide that you'll attempt the entrance, try to raise the nearest Coast Guard station to tell them what you're up to. If conditions aren't too bad, they may be able to send someone to guide you in, or at least to stand by just inside the entrance and pick up the pieces. Your entire crew, even the seasick ones, should be on deck, dressed as warmly as possible under foul-weather gear, and with lifejackets on. If possible, they should also have waterproof lights, or the little hand-held personal flares, and whistles. Even a waterproof flashlight is better than nothing. If the crew are secured to the boat, they should be able to release themselves if she capsizes. Running a harbor entrance in a severe storm is one of the very few times when I'd be inclined to relax the almost invariable dictum to stick with the boat at all costs, but you would only want to separate if the shore under your lee was something a swimmer could land on—sand or mud, that is, not rocks or coral. In the latter two cases, it would be better to ride the boat in until she hit, if you could do so.

All this sounds dreadfully apocalyptic, and I hasten to emphasize that very few coastal cruisers will ever be faced with even a slight need for considering this kind of action. Well-prepared sailors in particular will find that nine times out of ten their care will make heavy weather something that's experienced in a safe harbor.

Major storm in harbor

Sailors who cruise the East and Gulf Coasts of the United States become accustomed, along about August, to keeping one ear on the radio's hurricane warnings, and while several seasons may go by without so much as a near-miss, it's well to know what steps to take in case a tropical hurricane homes in on your harbor. In other parts of the country the incidence of tropical storms may be low, but there is always the chance of a major tempest, and some of the same precautions will apply.

The salient points of this kind of storm are, first, that there's time to get ready and, second, that the boat is likely to face the storm unattended—and unreachable. It's a hard thing to leave a beloved boat to face a storm by herself, and there are some cruising skippers who cold-bloodedly choose to camp aboard during the heaviest weather. This is one of those decisions that no one can make for you, and I have considerable sympathy for either point of view. My only feeling is that if you do choose to fight it out aboard your boat, you shouldn't count on any help from the authorities, who will have plenty to do without getting you out of a situation you created for yourself.

As the storm season approaches, you will want to pay extra attention to weather forecasts. Hurricanes don't sneak up the coast the way they used to, but they remain as unpredictable as ever, and only when a storm is completely past your area can you put it out of your mind. Chances are you'll have several days of general awareness of a tropical storm before it gets near enough so that you have to do some coherent planning. Obviously, you don't want to set off on an extended cruise to an unfamiliar area when there's a storm in the offing, no matter how far away it may be. At the same time, a hurricane presently threatening the Windward Islands is no reason for a Connecticut sailor to postpone a weekend voyage.

Perhaps your first decision, and one that can be weighed long before a storm even exists, is whether hauling the boat is a viable possiblity. If you sail in an area where hurricanes are relatively frequent—a couple of good scares per year, at a minimum—check with your marina or club about the chances of getting out of the water fast. And if you are hauled, where will your boat go? If your marina or club is on low ground, you may be better off afloat. Ask what has happened in the past, and be guided by that experience. On the other hand, if yours is a trailerable cruiser, you may be able to have her taken well away from shore, perhaps to your home. Make sure that if this is the case, the trailer frame is braced by cinderblocks at the corners and the boat is lashed onto the trailer to keep it from shifting. Try to pick a spot where falling trees won't be a hazard.

If you decide to leave the boat in the water, there are a number of possibilities, depending on where she will be lying. Whatever you do, it will probably be worth a couple of hours' work to remove and/or strike below much of the gear. Any portable electronics should be taken home, and the nonremovable instruments covered as well as possible: It is sometimes hard to believe the amount of moisture that can get below when pushed by storm-force winds. Bedding and clothing, all food that isn't canned, your on-board library—all these items might as well go home with you.

On deck, you'll want to reduce the windage as much as possible—and in a serious storm, the slightest protrusion can represent serious windage. This means not only obvious things like dodgers, boathooks, and spinnaker poles, but even booms and the sails on them. The sails can be struck below, but it would be as well to take the spars home—if someone needs to get aboard quickly, perhaps to stem a leak, it will be a lot easier to work down below if the interior isn't hopelessly cluttered.

It may be quite possible to remove a small cruiser's mast, boom, and standing rigging, and I would recommend this course of action if there's time and if the storm is likely to be Force 10 or worse. It is not unknown for truly severe winds to capsize a boat at anchor just from pressure on the rig, and during severe storms, boats in adjoining marina slips sometimes roll badly enough to lock each other's spreaders.

By contrast, some items of gear should not only be on board but should be visible and accessible: extra lines, beyond those used to tie up the boat, and extra fenders; if you have no extra fenders, they are a small investment when set against the cost of refinishing a hull. Even if you have all the fenders you think will be necessary, it won't hurt to have available some kapok-filled seat cushions or cheap life vests, which can serve as adequate padding in an emergency. If you don't plan to use your anchors and you're at a mooring, it would be well to have them lashed down on deck with the rode below ready to go. The boat herself should be sealed as tightly as possible—not only ports and hatches, but also seacocks, ventilator hoods, and chain pipes.

There are essentially two places for a boat to ride out a major storm unattended—on a mooring or anchor, and in a slip or alongside a pier. In the first instance, the plan is to stay well away from shore; in the second, the vital element is to keep the shore a fender's width away at least. My own feeling is that a conventional slip, with a bulkhead or float at one end and a pair of pilings at the other, is perhaps the most dangerous place in which to ride out a major storm. Not only are the pilings themselves especially vulnerable to collisions and simple pressure from the tethered boats, but in extra-high seas, the ends of pilings have been known to punch holes in the hulls of boats tied to them. In addition, a boat in a slip is immobilized, a sitting target for other boats and floating debris that may break free. Unlike a boat at anchor, she cannot give with the blows of a colliding object.

If the harbor is well protected and the slip system itself is in good repair, though, you are probably safe enough. You will want to adjust your lines for the unusual conditions of a serious storm, during which the water level may rise by several feet above full-moon high. If possible, try to move your boat to a slip vacated by a larger yacht. This will at least give your vessel more room to surge about. Tie the boat so that she lies well away from a solid bulkhead, which will pose more danger than will isolated pilings. Use crossed lines at bow and stern, and double them; and rig spring lines from the pilings to that end of the boat nearest the pier. Pad the lines with chafing gear, rags, or fenders wherever they may rub the hull or cabin, and try to visualize where the lines will strike the boat with the water extremely high or low. In a severe storm with heavy surge, fenders will not be very useful when the boat is in a slip, unless there's someone on board to tend them. As noted before, I don't particularly advocate staying aboard in a storm, but I have done it myself, and feel more comfortable sharing the boat's travail. If you do decide to ride it out aboard, try to ensure that your boat is on the shore side of a marina that has a sea wall. Boats just inside the outer bulkhead may well become unreachable as seas break over the wall.

A boat alongside a pier will have more freedom to move, but she may well ride more easily, as long as the pier can take the stress. A floating pier will simplify the problem of tying up, as you won't have to take into account rising and falling water height, but it may not be as strong as a fixed structure. Again, it may be a good idea to ask old-timers how well the floats have made out in past storms. And beware if a tender-hearted harbor master allows the piers to be overloaded with doubled-up craft. The requirements for lying alongside a pier are much the same as for being in a slip, except that in the former case, fenders must be rigged. I would think that a minimum of three fenders for the smallest cruiser and up to six for a thirty-footer would be called for. If the bulkhead is faced with pilings, a fenderboard is absolutely vital: You cannot otherwise make sure that the fendered part of the boat will strike the pilings as the surge increases.

Riding out a storm at anchor or at a mooring is likely to be easiest on a boat —but paradoxically, if there is any damage at all, it will probably be serious. Not only is the boat inaccessible when things begin to go wrong, but the most obvious cause of disaster—breaking free from the mooring—often leads to a total loss on the beach immediately afterward. One of the more important secondary factors in boats being lost from or damaged at moorings is simply the time of year: In the East and South, major storms tend to come at the end of the boating season, when your own gear and that of other skippers has had several months' unremitting use. For this reason, the sailor who leaves his yacht in an anchorage to ride out a storm must be concerned not only with the integrity of his own ground tackle but with the state of moorings to windward of him.

If there is time before a storm's arrival, you or one of your crew ought seriously to consider putting on mask and fins and diving on your own mooring and on those nearby. Check especially the connectors—shackles and swivels —as these are often the weakest elements in the system. My own feeling is that a mooring hook-up ought to impose no strain on the buoy itself, and that the load should go straight from the boat to the anchor.

Having reassured yourself about the soundness of what's under the water, the next step is to double the lines that lead from your boat to the terminal chain shackle. If your boat, like so many, has paired chocks on either side of the forestay, doubling the lines and putting one through each chock will definitely reduce the boat's tendency to dance around her mooring, itself a cause of needless chafe and load on the anchor. Now double up the chafing gear on the mooring line or anchor rode. Make sure that antichafe protection covers not only the obvious length of line going through the chocks but also any other part of the rode that could rub against a fitting. While you're at it, take this time to make sure that the mooring cleat and chocks are through-bolted. The former should have a sizable backup plate, ideally stainless steel or fiber glass, but acceptably plywood, which is bedded in epoxy compound or, better still, chopped glass and resin, to even the load on the probably uneven underside of the deck.

While the chocks generally receive only a shearing, or horizontal, load, if the boat starts to pitch wildly, they may have to accept a brief upward pull as well, so through-bolting is advisable. Just as important is ensuring that the rode doesn't jump the chocks when the boat begins to pitch. The best way to do this is to use a bulky chafe gear material that fills out the entire chock—the best I know of for this application is the leather strip, prepunched along its two long edges, that you sew tightly onto the rode. It is of course a semipermanent rig, but it is almost immune from slippage and wears like iron. Next best, in my opinion, is the slitted rubber tubing with overlapping edges that goes by the commercial name of Chafe-Gard. The overlap will deter the line from escaping (unless the rode takes a sharp bend where it is chafe-guarded), and a pair of leather thongs, one at each end, can be woven through or tied tightly around the rode, to prevent the gear from riding out of the chocks. On my own boats, I use the leather chafe gear on the mooring line and the Chafe-Gard on my anchor rodes, where a different scope will probably be used each time.

Riding out a storm at anchor instead of at a mooring, with no one aboard, is a judicious compromise between the procedure described above, and the tactics for storm anchoring set out in Chapter IX. Placement of the anchors and the maximum amount of scope are as important as snugging down the boat and rigging the chafing gear, but with a good, long rode and a hefty storm anchor, you should be secure.

With the decks cleared, sails and booms struck, and the boat sealed tight, you are nearly ready to face the storm. If possible (and if you are not going to stay aboard), remove the tiller and rudder, too. Steering gear takes a tremendous beating on a boat at anchor in a storm, and if you have a transom-hung rudder, there should be no reason you cannot stow it out of harm's way. But if you can't remove the steering gear, then lash the tiller or lock the wheel, as may be appropriate. It is best to lash the tiller with something moderately flexible—a number of strands of ultra-thick shock cord, for instance—in order that it may yield a couple of inches as the boat yaws wildly from side to side in the puffs.

In facing heavy weather, either in open water or at anchor, preparation is almost always far more important than the action you take during the storm itself. If your boat is sound and your planning sensible, there is no reason you should get into serious trouble in a storm—in fact, there's every reason for you to be able to avoid all but the occasional, suddenly-occurring summer thunder-squall.

VIII

~~~~~~~~~~~

Close-Quarters Handling

Just about anyone can handle even a large cruising yacht out in open water, with no distractions and plenty of time to plan the next move. But when it comes to maneuvering under sail or power, with boats bearing down on you from all sides and the wind made puffy by nearby structures, then there's a visible difference between the summer sailor and the real seaman. Skippers having the skill to handle a sailing cruiser around piers and moored boats have become surprisingly rare in recent years, to the point where many marinas forbid sailing within their confines. And they're probably right, given the capacities of the average client. But even if you have no intention of sailing into and out of your slip, there are excellent reasons why you should be able to do so if the need arises—and even if it doesn't. The obvious rationale is the fact that your boat's engine won't always function when you need it. Murphy's Law being what it is, you'll probably be entering the harbor at 5:00 P.M. on a busy Sunday afternoon when the powerplant succumbs, presenting you with the choice between an ignominious tow and a safe if mildly hairy arrival under your own sail.

Beyond need, though, it seems to me that you're not truly master of an auxiliary yacht if you cannot make it behave with or without the engine. Skill begets confidence, and confidence leads to the kind of deep satisfaction that is difficult to explain but eminently worth achieving. When you know you can bring your boat through a tight spot without her engine, you can make better choices as to when you really have to use power. You also have a wider spectrum of maneuvers available. But in the end, being able to cope without power is a self-test that is worth preparing for.

Until you have real faith in your own skills, you may be well advised to have the engine turning over in neutral as you practice the operations detailed below. It's a little like having a pacifier—after a while you'll decide of your own volition that you don't need the engine. In some situations, however, you may always want the safety factor of an available engine: My home harbor, some years ago, was a truly tight spot, with rows of boats moored bow and stern, facing into the prevailing wind. One could not sail across the rows even when the moorings were vacant, as the spaces between mooring buoys were filled by permanent, floating pick-up lines. I always had the engine on, but the shift in neutral, as I sailed down the outside row of yachts, ready to come sharply up into the wind and pick up my own mooring. I wasn't even sure why I felt better with the engine running until one afternoon, without warning, a swimmer appeared between the moored boats just ahead, saw me, and froze. As luck would have it, the rows of boats sagged toward each other at this juncture, and there was no room on either side to pass the swimmer.

I jammed the engine into reverse and slowed the boat enough for the swimmer to come to himself and get out of my way.

There are things you cannot do under sail, and in achieving what is possible, you should also learn what is not. Another example will suggest what I mean: In that same harbor, moored a few boats upwind in the same string as my own, was a small cruiser whose owner was determined to sail to his mooring. Each time, he would run down to the leeward end of the mooring area and attempt to pinch his way up between the rows of moored yachts to his own buoy. He never made it, but even if he'd had a couple of world champion sailors in the boat with him, he would still have fallen short, because the operation was patently impossible. While giving him top marks for determination, after the first five tries the rest of us had to give him an "F" for brains.

Picking up a mooring buoy is perhaps the basic under-sail maneuver, yet as harbors fill up with moorings and more boats are kept permanently at marinas, this skill is less frequently used than it once was. There are several factors involved in the operation, of which the only predictable one is the boat herself; one of the things every skipper should know from experience is how his yacht behaves when turning and how far she will shoot up into the wind, the current, or both. This knowledge is achieved only by practice, and when you get a new boat it is a good idea to set up a practice buoy in open water and spend a couple of hours making passes at it from every conceivable direction, until you have engraved on your reflexes the amount of room you need for your approaches. A boat's momentum, or carry, will, of course, vary not only with the way you execute a maneuver but also with the force of wind and current at work, not to mention the boat herself—although this last will be a constant except in the case of an ultra-light cruiser that can exhibit quite different characteristics according to how heavily loaded she is. But the manner of handling is controllable, and you can come to use it to your advantage. Take coming about onto your final approach: If you slam the boat through the tack, with the helm hard over, you will brake the yacht's speed considerably, whereas if you sail the boat easily through the tack, you can add quite a bit to her fetch—to the amount she will carry into the wind with the sails luffing. After you get a good handle on this kind of thing, you'll find that skillful last-minute adjustments can retrieve even a badly bungled maneuver.

Before getting into the details of approaches and landings, let us first talk about sailing under control in constricted or crowded areas. Clearly, you need to maintain enough speed to tack or jibe, as the case may be, without losing steerage way or falling into irons. At the same time, you don't want the boat to be going too fast for safety, nor do you want so much sail-handling complexity that your crew are fully occupied tending sheets when you need them for fending off or picking up a buoy. And, finally, you want the decks as clear as possible, consistent with the need to maintain a reasonably balanced amount of sail for reliable maneuvering.

It can be a real problem to attain this ideal, especially in those yachts with very small mainsails and big working jibs. Such vessels really require some sail forward of the mast in order to be reliably maneuverable, because you can easily delude yourself, running down under main alone, that everything's in hand, only to find (when you miss the first shot at the mooring buoy) that the boat refuses to tack without a headsail. Again, only open-water practice will tell you which sail combinations work under various conditions.

Sailing to a buoy

Very light boats, such as multihulls, often require to be driven right up to their objective, whether under sail or power, because their lack of displacement, their shoal draft, and their high freeboard cause them to lose way and sag off very quickly. This behavior can take a good deal of getting used to, especially if your previous sailing has been done in a heavy boat with lots of fetch. By the same token, switching from a lightweight to a solid, old-fashioned type of hull can result in even more dangerous moments, caused by keeping the boat powered for too long and then not having the room to sheer away.

The ideal approach to a mooring is on a close reach, with the current, if any, also on the bow. By having a bit of potential sail trim still in hand, so to speak, you can always harden up a little without pinching, if you have to, but you can also head off and let the headsail stall, then round up suddenly, with the sails luffing, to bring the boat to a halt within a boathook's reach of the buoy. Relatively few crowded harbors will permit an unobstructed approach of any kind, however, and you may have to settle for a beam reach and then a quick hook up into the wind, which also will work for most boats. If your maneuver-

Sailing up to a mooring buoy is a good deal simpler if your boat is adequately maneuverable under mainsail alone, so that you can lower and bag the jib beforehand, leaving the foredeck clear. If the boat undershoots the mooring, she can fall off to port or starboard equally well, but if she overshoots, the skipper had better have a more precise plan in mind—falling off to starboard looks like the better bet here. Once the mooring rode is hooked on, the helmsman should tend the mainsheet so that it runs freely, to prevent the sail's catching wind and the boat's sailing off before the mooring line is cleated.

ing space near the buoy is very limited, consider slowing the boat by backing both the headsail and main—holding them out by hand so they act as air brakes. It will require a larger crew, but it can take the momentum off a boat to a remarkable extent. Coming in on a close reach, the helmsman will want to carry the buoy close aboard on his windward side, especially if the jib is still up and drawing. The reason is that the headsail will be down to leeward, and the foredeck hand, with the boathook, will have more of the windward side of the deck unobstructed. A few simple hand signals for close-quarters handling (similar to those used in anchoring) will probably be enough for most situations. But the person at the wheel or tiller won't be able to see the buoy during the last few yards of the approach, and will have to develop a feel for where it is.

As soon as the final approach is begun, and the boat is committed, you will probably want to slack sheets except if you're aboard an extremely lightweight boat in a brisk wind. Don't cast off the sheets entirely, as you may want to harden up under control very quickly indeed, if the foredeck hand misses the buoy; that crew member should be aware that if you miss, you will head off under sail, and he must take his own precautions to keep from being involved with the headsail in case of a tack. In most cases, the best place to be in an average size cruiser is right in the bow pulpit, which should certainly be strong enough to support the weight of one person. In a very small boat, however, or a very light one, the weight of a full-grown adult right in the eyes of the yacht may have dramatic effects on her ability to come about, and you should know in advance if you can tack with this much weight so far forward.

It's nearly always a mistake for a second crew member aft to try to grab a missed buoy: The last thing you need is for your boat to be hung from a mooring by the stern, with the mainsail still up and a crew member at full stretch halfway out of the cockpit. If you miss the pickup, bear away and try again—and be sure your crew knows that this will be the standard operating procedure. Better still—assuming you are the helmsman—have in mind a plan for bearing off in case you *do* miss. Look far enough ahead of the boat so you're aware which will be the clearest channel to open water, where you can regroup for another try. Everyone misses a shot at a mooring once in a while, but the good skipper is the one whose miss looks like a dry run, so smooth is his recovery.

Part of success or failure in picking up a mooring is, of course, the gear with which you attack the problem. An extra-long boathook can make even a sloppy helmsman into a hero, and the best kind of hook I know is the telescoping aluminum style that can extend from 3½ to 8 feet or, for larger boats, from 4½ to 12 feet. The only caveat is that in order to keep the telescoping mechanism working, the hook must be hosed down regularly with fresh water, and it should not be stowed on the deck along the scuppers. Pick-up gear on the buoy is also important. Unless the mooring line itself is polypropylene, which floats, the rode will sink out of sight. Secure the pick-up loop to a float or to a small buoy, with a fiber glass wand sticking up three or four feet above the water, so you can grab it with or without a boathook.

Where a harbor has bow-and-stern moorings, normal practice is for each buoy, and thus each anchor, to hold the bow of one boat and the stern of the next ahead. A quarter-inch pick-up line runs between the buoys, made accessible by plastic floats every few feet. Hooking this line at any point along its length means you've got the buoys, and it's only a matter of hauling the boat forward until you reach the actual mooring loop, to which the pick-up line is spliced.

Coming up to a rig like this requires somewhat different tactics, as the perfect approach will leave the boat dead in the water, her bow just short of the windward buoy, and her stern a little ahead of the after buoy; it is really more like landing alongside a pier than anything else. Unlike a pier, the pick-up line will not bruise the hull; also unlike a pier, the line can foul your prop, whether it's turning or not, and then disappear under the boat. In today's harbors, bow-and-stern moorings are usually resorted to because of extreme crowding, and there is seldom much room around them. If the moorings are in lines, close together, the only ones accessible to sailing approaches will be those across the leeward end of the area, as well as the moorings in the outside lines on either side of the area. Be sure before attempting to sail up to an outside buoy that there's enough water around it to maneuver; harbors are now filled literally to the edges of deep water, and while there may be room to edge up along the outside of a line of moorings, there may well not be space to tack or jibe. This is especially likely on the lee side of a slightly misoriented line, where the boats have sagged down under pressure of the wind.

Away from a buoy or anchor

Sailing away from a mooring may be easier or more difficult than approaching it, depending on the layout of the anchorage. The important thing to remember here is that after you let go the mooring, your boat will nearly always sag off to leeward before picking up forward speed. As a plus, it is far easier for a foredeck hand to cast off a mooring than to pick one up, and there's no reason you cannot have full sail raised before cutting the umbilical. If space permits, probably the most effective way to leave a mooring is to have the foredeck hand cast off, then back the headsail on the side *away* from the direction in which you wish to head. The boat may make momentary sternway, but her head will quickly fall away from the wind; as soon as it does, the foredeck hand should come aft, as you trim first the main and then the jib, and bear off on a reach. If there is no room to reach or even beat from the mooring, you may have to run off it. The simplest way to accomplish this is to end-for-end the mooring line, till the boat is swinging by her stern. Then raise a headsail, cast off, sheet in, and sail down to where there's room to round up long enough to raise the main.

Dropping anchor under sail is largely a special case of picking up a mooring. You have somewhat more flexibility, as a rule, because there is seldom a precise spot where you've got to let go the anchor. You can and should wait until the boat has completely lost her forward momentum, something that you can only judge in relation to the shore or already-anchored vessels. Even if you think the boat's stopped moving, you will probably find that she is in fact still inching forward over the bottom. The helmsman can wait until the yacht begins to helplessly fall off from the wind, at which point her headway is well and truly killed. There is a great deal more to anchoring than the sailing part of it, and

The important thing to remember, when sailing off a mooring, is that a sailboat will sag off to leeward for a bit before picking up any forward speed. After dropping the mooring pennant, the crew backs the jib slightly, while the mainsail luffs; the boat will fall off to the side opposite that on which the jib is backed. Once the bow lookout assures you that the boat's bow is clear, sheet in the main and jib and sail off. It is always safer, in the confines of a harbor, to sail below an anchored boat than to try and pinch your way above it.

the principles are in Chapter IX. For the moment, bear in mind that in this situation it is extremely important that the foredeck be clear of sails. The headsail should if possible be both down and off the forestay as you come up to drop the anchor. But always keep maneuverability available, even if it does mean a muddy sail or an occasional rip from an anchor fluke. Unless your boat picks up leeway from windage very quickly, or unless the bottom of the anchorage is unusually soft, you will probably want to set the anchor by reversing the engine. This is one case where you're right to rely on the power-plant, as here it can do something that the sails normally cannot.

Sailing an anchor out of the bottom can be almost the most difficult maneuver in the modern sailor's repertoire. Its success will depend a lot on how deeply the hook is buried, and in what, not to mention the amount of sailing room available and the wind strength and direction. What's required to sail the anchor out is, first, a good scope on the rode—say 10 to 1—and enough room to leeward and on either side of the anchor to use that scope. You also need a boat that can turn on a dime, and ideally one that can do it without having her jib up. Here's how the maneuver works: Begin by dropping about halfway back on the rode and raising the mainsail (assuming your boat will handle under that sail alone). Station an agile and preferably lightweight crew member forward, and have him slack off the rode while the helmsman puts the tiller over to one side or the other, with the main strapped in. As soon as the boat picks up adequate way on one tack, come about, while the foredeck hand begins taking in rode; at this point, there should be as little strain on the rode as possible. Tack at least once again to bring the boat up near enough to the anchor so that the next tack will bring you right over the buried hook. Continue to take in rode, but without putting the line under tension. As you come about on this next-to-last tack, snub the rode so that when the boat comes to the end of the line—literally—the jerk will bring her about and, you hope, break the anchor free of the bottom. As you sail over the anchor on the final tack, take in line quickly until you are just over the hook, then snub it off once again. This time the anchor should come up easily, and you can close-reach off while the foredeck hand gets the ground tackle on deck, cleans it off, and stows it. Your boat may not be nimble enough to tack without a headsail, in which case you'll be best advised to use the working jib. If the boat is large enough, a second hand forward can help coil down or stow the rode while the first is taking it in, to keep the deck as clear as possible.

It may well happen that the anchor won't come up the first time, and the boat will come to a shuddering halt with the rode taut as a bowstring. Go back to the beginning and run the same series of moves again, but this time snub the line on the other tack—that is, coming from 90 degrees in the opposite direction. Also, wait for the final snubbing until you are past the anchor, so as to capsize it if possible. If this doesn't work, chances are the anchor is hooked under some underwater obstruction, very likely an old cable or heavy piece of gear. You may as well switch on the engine at this point, and try running a tight circle around the anchor, with tension on the rode, to try and work it free from whatever the flukes have caught. After that, assuming you're in shoal enough water, about the only step left is sending down a swimmer (one reason why a mask and fins are always useful aboard a cruiser).

In tight spots

Sailing in narrow channels imposes an extra burden of watchfulness and even second sight on the skipper of a cruising sailboat. Even if the channel in question is well marked, your requirements in terms of draft may still be a mystery to powerboat owners, who as a class have virtually no idea what sailboat skippers are up to. Your first obligation is to be aware of the rules of the road (see Appendix 4). In inland waters sailing craft have the right of way over most powerboats, but not if those powered vessels are engaged in commercial fishing, unable to maneuver, or constrained by their draft to stay within the channel. Nor do sailing craft have the right of way over any vessel, sail or power, that they are in the process of overtaking. If the wind direction forces you to beat up a crowded channel, you'll be a pain in the neck to most other boats bound either way, as it will be difficult for most of them—sailboats excluded—to guess when you are going to tack next (or why). Although it appears to contradict what I've said before, I am inclined to think it a poor idea to beat up narrow channels when they are crowded with other traffic (assuming you do have an engine); if nothing else, it's damned inconsiderate. If the water depth allows, or if you can do so by raising your centerboard, it may be far better to sail just outside the channel and parallel to it, out of people's way.

In any case, you should employ your boat's most easily handled sail combination, considering the breeze and the direction in which you're going. Unless the channel is wide or deserted, a spinnaker cripples you and is just asking for trouble. You may decide to have your engine turning over in neutral, and this is certainly a reasonable course of action. But bear in mind that it can get you into additional difficulties, if your exhaust is visible to another boat. His natural assumption will be that you're under both sail and power, which according to the rules of the road makes you a powerboat pure and simple. The best tactic here is to avoid right-of-way situations entirely—give way early and obviously.

If a potentially dangerous situation does seem to be developing, and you cannot get out of it, sound the danger signal—five or more short blasts on the horn. Sailboats don't sound right-of-way horn signals as powerboats do, but the danger signal is definitely allowed, and it should attract the attention of everyone within hearing. Assuming that you do have to maneuver—take a short tack across the channel, say—be sure to check traffic both ahead and astern of you. Don't ever tack across a powerboat's bows if you can help it, even if you know she'll pass clear ahead before you pick up speed; her skipper may panic and turn right into you. And don't sail too close to the stern of a large vessel; her prop wash can literally pick up a small yacht and spin it through a couple of jibes.

Keep a sharp eye out for fishermen. The ones who drift, troll, or cast while in the channel are not given any special protection by the rules of the road—they are not entitled to a commercial fisherman's right of way—but they can be a problem in that it's very easy to snag a line and let yourself in for a barrage of unwelcome vituperation. It passes my understanding that a person can deliberately seek out a fishing line that will be invisible to fish and then be surprised when it's also invisible to humans. About the only way to avoid lines like this is to keep a very close watch on anything that looks like a fishing pole and try to calculate where a line running from it would lie. Beyond that, there isn't much that can be done.

Running or beating down a channel, especially in a light breeze, you can be nearly swamped by large powerboats passing you close aboard at speed. There is, to be honest, no real remedy for this. Many planing cruisers leave a far more damaging wake when they considerately slow down and come down off plane into the displacement mode. It can sometimes be hard to wave a "thank you" to someone who's pulled this one, but he means well. Probably. There are, to be sure, some powerboat skippers so sunk in imbecility that they simply have no idea of the wake they leave behind. The law makes them responsible for the damage they may do, but trying to enforce it could be a lifetime job. You may have some success waving them down, especially if you don't assume too belligerent an attitude. But the most effective trick was pulled, entirely on impulse, by a lady of my acquaintance. While running down an extremely narrow channel, with her husband at the helm of their small cruiser, she looked up through the companionway to see not one but three immense power cruisers bearing down from behind, throwing great sheets of wake to either side. Without even thinking, she seized a pillow from the bunk, stuffed it under her sweatshirt, and ascended the ladder to the cockpit. Seeing a woman apparently eight months pregnant, all three powerboat skippers dropped their boats to a crawl and inched past. It was a stroke of brilliance, but I wonder how often it would work.

Gauging tide, current, and wind

If you sail in tidal waters, it can be extremely important to play both the tides and tidal currents when sailing in narrow channels, especially in light airs. Be wary of abrupt turns in the buoyed axis of a channel, as the current may sweep in a straight line, carrying you into shoal water despite your best efforts. We have largely got out of the habit of using soundings as they were intended in shoal waters, and we seldom make the most of the rise and fall of tide. Entering a harbor, it can be a good idea to take a sounding at a known point, and compare the result with the chart—it will at least suggest the state of the tide, if there is no other evidence available. But there should be. The alert navigator uses all the clues furnished by nature, from watermarks on rocks to the tilt of tide-riding ramps; from the color of the water over a shoal to the size and force of wavelets pressing against a buoy. Much of this information is difficult to reduce to digits, but it all helps to create a general—and surprisingly accurate—picture of what's happening in the harbor.

Entering a brand-new harbor is especially tricky, because you don't have available the benchmarks provided by repeated observation, as you do in home waters. There are, however, many clues and the wary skipper will seldom find himself in a dangerous or embarrassing position. The first thing to do, before entering at all, is of course to consult charts, and tide and tidal current tables. The latter two publications, more fully explained in Chapter V, will tell you the predicted state of the tide and current; "predicted" is the operative word here, because these tables are compiled a full year or more before the day you consult them, and their information is based on averages, including prevailing winds. Unusual weather conditions can throw them off considerably. Try to enter on a rising tide, if you have the option.

The information on the chart is more static and predictable. For entering harbors, you'll want the largest-scale chart available, preferably 1:20,000 and never smaller than 1:40,000. If your chart shows a large harbor with a narrow entrance, particularly an entrance channeled and stabilized by jetties, it's a good bet that currents will run strongly in and out. If the harbor entrance has high ground on either side, the odds are that the wind will blow straight in or straight out, but that you'll seldom have a reach, no matter what's happening elsewhere. High ground is generally indicated on a chart by contour lines, the same as on a topographical map.

If there are areas of the harbor marked "anchorage," you may or may not find them occupied by large commercial vessels, but if you see a "special anchorage" notation on the chart, you can be dead sure that it will be absolutely jammed with moored pleasure craft, at least during the boating season. This can be important if the special anchorage is a cul-de-sac and you're planning to enter under sail and downwind. You may very well find yourself in a funnel, with literally no place to turn around. As a general rule of sailing into small harbors, always check the chart for a way out before committing yourself, even if it means sending the dinghy in to scout ahead.

Wind patterns close to shore can be extremely tricky, as tall buildings and even high wharves can bend the breeze sharply, or channel it. By the same token, large areas of asphalt ashore may heat up so much that they cause a localized onshore breeze, frequently unpredictable from a yacht. Even if the harbor seems tranquil, try to avoid putting your boat needlessly at risk by sailing unnecessarily close to shoreside installations, especially large ones. Also stay clear of piers, particularly older wooden ones that do not appear to be in use. Piers collapse slowly, and there are frequently ancient snags of pilings just under the surface near them. Be careful as well to stay clear of moored or tied-up commercial ships. The current runs strongly past them, and you may be becalmed in their lee and carried into the hulls. If a freighter's huge prop is turning over, no matter how slowly, sail well clear of it. And don't sail across the bows of anchored barges, when the current is running down on them: You can be pinned under those overhangs like a butterfly on a card.

Check the chart for bridge and overhead cable clearances before entering, and if a bridge will have to open to admit your yacht, it will probably not do so unless you are under power. If in doubt, one long whistle blast, followed by one short will usually do the trick, but do not expect too much: Bridgetenders are not appointed to their jobs on account of their initiative, and while many of them are hard-working and helpful people, there is a surprising number who appear to be drunk, mad, or homicidal. It is, by the way, a very inconsiderate thing to attempt to beat through a busy drawbridge against even a slight current. You will almost certainly miss the first tack, because the current will be stronger than you expect, and you will create havoc considerably out of proportion to your boat's size. Use the engine if you can or, if you must sail, wait for other traffic to come through first.

Sailing up to piers

The two salient differences between sailing up to a mooring and sailing up to a pier are, first, that the buoy has a lot more give to it than do pilings, and second, that you can (at least in theory) approach a buoy from any direction relative to the existing wind, while with a pier you have much less choice. This much said, it still seems to me that in most cases the difficulties of landing under sail are often magnified out of proportion. After all, small-boat sailors routinely sail up to floats and docks, and the principle (if not the potential for disaster) is the same.

First pick your pier. There are two things to take into account—the structure itself and the possible lines of approach, considering wind direction and water depth. The ideal pier, from the sailor's point of view, would be approximately gunwale-high to your boat at the main shrouds. It would be flat-sided, not faced with pilings, padded with a heavy rubber guard, and fitted with large, firmly attached cleats at about ten-foot intervals. Best of all it would be unoccupied. The ideal approach would allow you to make your landing on a side that was parallel to the channel, with deep water at either end, and with the wind and current running down the side, so that your boat could nose into both as she came alongside. In real life, of course, things seldom work out this way. The pier is either a good deal higher than your gunwale or is a float with a mere six inches of freeboard. Often its face is studded with pilings, close enough together so the yacht's side cannot find a free stretch in which to nestle. Moreover, both the pilings and the wood facing are decorated with protruding spikes, in a random pattern; or perhaps there is what appears to be an adequate amount of rubber padding, but it has been secured by the tried and true method of driving a nail in halfway, then bending it over to leave a sharp scraper concealed, like a cat's sheathed claw, in the fendering. If the pier has cleats, they are either impossibly large or absurdly small, and placed in the least convenient spots. This kind of thing is a cruiser's nightmare, and the normal state of affairs is something between best and worst. The best way to gauge the situation is to make a practice pass before each landing, until a given pier or float becomes completely familiar (and *then* watch out!). This dry run should be made under the same reduced-sail combination you plan to employ in the actual landing (preferably main alone, if the boat is reliable under that rig). Size up the force of the current, if any, and the distance you'll need, when luffing, to kill the boat's forward speed (if she's your own boat, you should have a pretty accurate feel for this already). Having appraised the situation, head away into open water before you lose all forward speed and take a wide swing while you get ready for the approach. Your fenders should already be hung

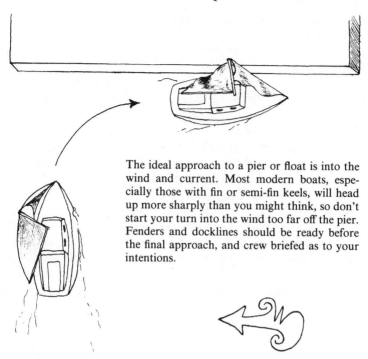

The ideal approach to a pier or float is into the wind and current. Most modern boats, especially those with fin or semi-fin keels, will head up more sharply than you might think, so don't start your turn into the wind too far off the pier. Fenders and docklines should be ready before the final approach, and crew briefed as to your intentions.

out, needing only a height adjustment to correspond to the pier. Under normal circumstances, you'll want fenders just forward of the main shrouds, just abaft them, and about level with the end of the deckhouse. Secure them to the toerail or the upper lifeline, not the grabrail on top of the cabin, where they'll impede the crew's passage fore and aft. Your docklines should be ready, too—four for a thirty-footer, two each at bow and stern, each at least as long as the boat.

If the size of your crew allows, you should have line handlers fore and aft and a third person ready to move the fenders in case the landing is a little harder than you've planned. A good inflatable fender jammed quickly between gunwale and pier can make up for a lot of misjudgment at the helm. If the pier is faced with pilings, you'll have to rig your fenderboard, as described earlier, in the section on rafting.

Your crew should have as precise an idea as possible of what you intend; here is a sample of what the skipper might say to a crew whom he trusted but whom he didn't know too well. "I'm coming in port side to the pier, close-hauled on starboard tack, with just the main up. I'll shoot up into the wind when the boat's level with the downstream end of the pier, and we should luff to a stop about the middle. Foredeck hand takes the first line ashore, to a cleat forward of the bow. After-deck hand gets the stern line over next, and the fender handler drops the main as soon as the two lines are secured, but not until. If we miss the approach or have to sheer off, I'll call out 'tacking.'

Foredeck hand, keep an eye out for any boats or dinghies coming out from behind anchored boats off the pier: If you see one, sing out—don't assume I see it, or that the people in the dink see us." It should be needless to say that in the foregoing maneuver the skipper will handle the mainsheet, if any handling is required. When a crew has sailed together for a season or so, the drill should be nearly mechanical—but it will be up to the skipper to foresee any point at which something different might be required.

With a smaller crew, the action can get a little more hectic. Let's take the normal husband-wife team. It doesn't matter which of them is at the helm, since there should be no call for large amounts of muscle in the operation. Indeed, trying to fend off a 9,000-pound cruiser with main strength is a sucker's play—that's what fenders are for.

Besides the helmsman, there is the combination bow line—fender handler. This crew member should station himself at the shrouds, with the bow line led from the forward cleat, through the chocks, and back outside the lifelines. Rig one fender at the height of the pier edge and just level with the shrouds, and stand by with another (not made fast), in case something goes wrong with the approach. If everything works according to plan, the boat should luff to a halt, with the fixed fender just kissing the pier. The line handler steps ashore and secures the bow line, while the helmsman, having cast off the mainsheet, makes the stern line fast.

The solo sailor will have to rig all the fenders and lead his bow line from the bow cleat, through the bow chocks, and along the waterway just inside the toerail, outboard of the lifeline stanchions, with the terminal loop to hand just at the cockpit. Luffing up to the pier, cast off the mainsheet and step quickly ashore with the dockline, taking it a little ahead of the boat to secure. Make sure the line is fast to the bow cleat before you leave the boat, however, or you could be in serious difficulty. Also be sure that the mainsheet is free to run or it may kink, jam, and cause the boat to sail off by herself. With the bow line secure, drop the main and then make fast the stern line.

There will frequently be lines permanently attached to the cleats on the pier, especially at gas docks. And often there will be dockboys or spectators eager to lend a hand. It's rather a put-down of these people not to let them help, but I have to say that I feel much more secure handling the landing with my own lines and my own crew or, if it comes to that, by myself. What I do appreciate, if the wind is strong, is the helpful person who stands by, clearly available, but who doesn't do anything until asked. My own admittedly snobbish rule of thumb for would-be helpers might be called Gibbs's Law of Hats: The person wearing no hat, or a wool watch cap in winter, is probably reliable as a line handler. But the person wearing one of those "captain" hats with scrambled eggs on the visor should be avoided like poison. He will grab a thrown line, brace his feet, and give a needless great pull, slamming the bow into the pier and ruining what would probably have been a perfect landing.

Sometimes it's not possible to come into the wind with the boat's side along a pier. Then you have to decide whether to attempt a broadside landing from

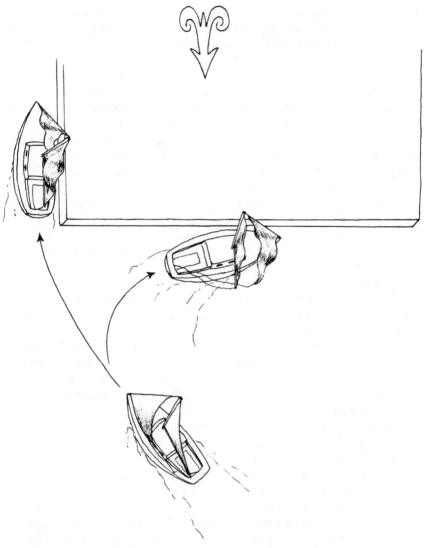

When the breeze is directly off a pier, you sometimes have two choices. If there is enough water along the pier's sides, you may be able to sail in on a close-hauled course and then luff up, as shown on the left. More often, however, the pier's sides will be too short or the water alongside too shoal, and you will have to make a buttonhook approach, letting main and jib sheets run fully and early. If the main boom cannot run all the way out because of the aft lower shrouds, you will have to compensate by heading a little off parallel to the pier face. Quick line handling at bow and stern is a must in this sort of landing.

a reach or luff up inartistically with the bow to the pier. The answer will depend on three things—how much carry your boat has (that is, how long she carries her way after you begin to luff the sails), where the wind is (a beam reach approach is different from a close reach), and how long (and empty) the pier is.

Coming in to a pier on a close reach is not terribly demanding. Make your actual approach close-hauled, to keep the boat's speed down, then let the sheet or sheets run as you head off slightly, to bring the hull parallel to the pier for the actual landing. The sails should luff easily and hold no wind, and you should come to an easy near-stop—but don't be afraid to head off if you have any doubts about the speed at which the boat is moving.

Trying to land from a beam reach is something else again. To make a controlled approach, the boat will have to be pinching a bit, so she is at about 45 degrees to the pier, assuming you are under main alone. When you head off to bring the hull parallel to the pier, she is likely to pick up speed, no matter how rapidly you let the mainsheet run; it may be wise, if you have a friction-bound, multipart mainsheet, for a crew member to force the boom out to leeward just before you turn. Depending on your boat's characteristics, you may require a foredeck hand with a bow line, a hand at the shrouds ready to step ashore with an after bow spring, or a hand at the stern ready to drop a stern line on a cleat. The after bow spring, of course, leads from the bow cleat aft. Like the stern line, it is a brake. Putting tension on it will also bring the bow in and make the boat pivot around the turn of the hull just forward of the shrouds, so you should rig two fenders—one at the shrouds, the other a little forward—as well as having a free fender for emergencies. If you stop the boat with the stern line, you should have a large fender rigged right at the quarter, which will be dragged into the pier as the line takes up, and a bow line handler reader to leap ashore and make fast before the bow swings out.

You may feel that it will be easier simply to pinch up slowly to the pier, luffing at the last minute, as you put a man ashore from the bow, after which you can toss a stern line to the pier. Depending on the clearance from the bow to the pier, this may work quite well. Its success will also depend on how well you can control the boat's inching forward the last few feet, and how nimble your bow man is. One trick that will make such a landing considerably more artistic is to rig an extra-long stern line and lead it forward, outside of everything. The bow man takes both lines ashore, makes the bow line fast first, then leads the stern line to a suitable cleat and lets the crew warp the boat up to the pier.

A downwind landing under sail is probably the real test of a skipper and crew. If the wind is light, you can drop all sail on the approach and simply blow down on the pier, using the rudder to ensure a beam-on landing, with a number of fenders to cushion it. Just bear in mind that virtually no boat will drift straight downwind—even with no sail up, a properly designed hull will headreach slightly, a matter of concern if you are in danger of running out of space. In this situation, you may be better off using one of the other sides of the pier, so you can lay the boat's side against the pier on a dead-slow run, with no sail up, stopping her with a spring line or stern line as described above. If the water all around is deep and the boat nimble, you may be able to land alongside one of these faces of the pier by reaching toward it and hooking up into the wind at the last moment.

If there is no maneuvering room or a brisk wind blowing onto the face of the pier, pocket your pride and use the engine. If you're determined to sail, however, then probably the best tactic is a so-called *Mediterranean moor:* Bring the boat up into the wind fifty or a hundred feet off the pier and drop

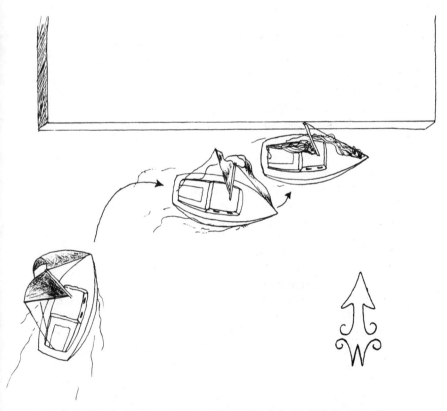

Landing directly downwind under sail is only advisable if the boat and breeze are both light. The trick here is to wind up dead in the water, sails luffing, with the boat parallel to and slightly off the pier face. She will drift down onto the pier, but bear in mind that she will forereach a bit as well, so leave a little room ahead. Many boats with high bows and/or low sterns won't blow down exactly sideways; their bows, having more windage and less grip on the water, will move more than their sterns. In this case, come to a dead stop with the bow a bit farther from the pier face than the stern is. Obviously, only practice will tell you how your boat handles in situations like this.

the anchor. Ease back, keeping the sail (or sails) luffing, using combinations of backed sail and rudder to keep the boat stern-to. About thirty feet from the pier, check the hold of the anchor, and if it seems to be firmly into the bottom, drop and furl sail, then ease back to the pier. Depending on the circumstances, you may want to ride with just the transom toward the pier, about a yard off, or you may wish to allow the boat to swing around and present her side to the wharf. In the first instance, make sure the anchor is well set; if in doubt, take the storm anchor out in a dinghy. In the second, if there is likelihood of the wind staying onshore, leave the anchor in place and allow the rode to sink to the bottom to keep it from being cut by passing boats.

Leaving a pier under sail

For some reason, watching a sailboat leave a pier under sail instead of under power seems to have a peculiarly galvanic effect on other yachtsmen, especially the proprietors of powerboats. Yet under most circumstances, I find it easier to sail off than to sail on. If you are superbly fortunate, the same wind that was right on your boat's bows as you landed will in the interval have switched 90 degrees so that it's now blowing you off the pier. Single up the lines until the boat is held at bow and stern only. After checking that there's no traffic approaching to screw up your maneuver, raise the jib, allowing it to stream as you do so. With all hands ready, cast off the bow line and as soon as the bow has begun to swing clear of the pier, let go the stern line as well. When the average cruising sailboat lies broadside to the wind, her bow will swing away to leeward faster than her stern, although cockpit awnings or canvas spray dodgers can change the center of effort of the hull-cabin-rigging combination. Once the boat is well clear of the pier, sheet in the jib and head off on a reach until you've arrived in water open enough to luff up and raise the mainsail. In this connection, it's a good idea, before you leave the pier, to plan *where* you will head up into the wind to raise the main, or at least where you'll reach open water. If your boat is aimed in the wrong direction and the harbor is too crowded to make a safe tack under jib alone, don't be too proud to swing her end for end by hand before you leave. Until you're thoroughly familiar with your boat's behavior in tight spots, always give yourself the best possible odds in any maneuver, and you should never, never begin an operation without (a) a good idea of how it will turn out and (b) a plan for when the whole maneuver comes unglued.

Suppose, as is more likely, that you made your initial landing directly into the wind, which has stayed in the same quarter. In this case, you will simply peel the boat off the pier, a maneuver that is both pleasantly dramatic to see and easy to accomplish. Before raising sail, reduce your mooring lines to two, a bow line and an after spring, leading from the stern cleat forward to a cleat on the pier about amidships. This after line should be doubled: That is, it

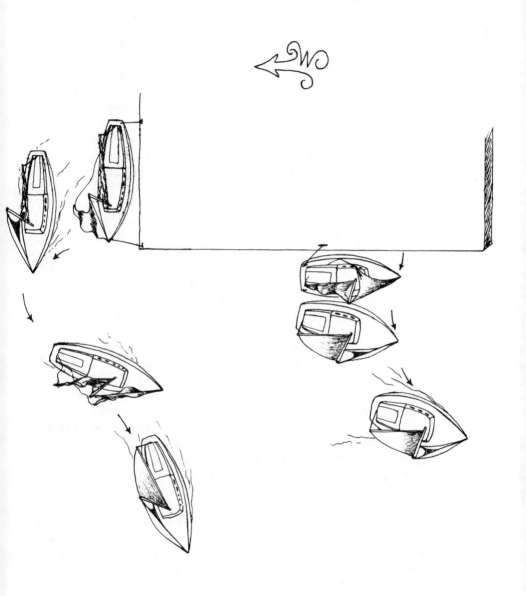

When your boat is lying alongside a pier, head to wind, sailing her off is very simple. Single up the lines until the boat is held by bow and stern lines; make sail, allowing the sails to luff freely. Now let go the bow line and the bow should fall away from the pier, although it may be necessary to back the jib. If the pier is not padded—or even if it is—a fender between the boat's quarter and the pier will prevent scratches. The stern line should be doubled around the dock cleat, so that you can release one end and haul it in without help from ashore. If the wind is blowing your boat away from the pier, it is probably simplest to raise only the headsail, drop bow and stern lines, and move off under that reduced sail. Once you are in clear water, head up, raise the mainsail quickly—before the boat loses her forward way—and sail off.

should lead from the stern cleat around the dock fitting without being hitched, and then back to the stern cleat whence it originated, at which point it can be hitched. Rig one of your largest fenders about level with the stern cleat.

Now hoist both main and jib, but don't sheet them in. With hands standing by the jib and mainsheets, have a crew member cast off the bow line and come quickly aft, boarding the boat at the stern. By this time, the bow may be paying off from the pier, if there is any offshore component to the breeze. If not, the jib sheet tender may back the jib slightly, taking up on the shoreside jib sheet enough to give the bow a slight push off—only a little will be required, and the sheet tender can release the line almost immediately and stand by the other jib sheet.

The bow will continue to swing away from the pier, while the stern is held in by the spring line and protected by the fender. As soon as the boat has swung about 45 or 50 degrees off the pier, sheet in the jib and main. As the boat begins to move, cast off one end of the after spring, allowing it to run freely around the dockside cleat, and retrieve it briskly, as the sails sheet home and you head easily out into the stream. About the only thing that can go wrong here is if the after spring line snags on something as it runs out, in which case you will have to cast it off the stern cleat very quickly indeed, sail off, and come back to get it.

At some point in your sailing career, you will find yourself pinned onto the pier by the wind. If it's not too strong, you can use the engine to get off, as described below. But if you've become a purist or if your engine isn't available, you should have a plan for getting the boat clear. If the wind was onshore when you landed, and you took the precaution of setting an anchor offshore when you came in, you can now take advantage of that foresight. Pull yourself off about thirty feet from the pier, make sail, and then sail her out. Chances are the hook will not have been too deeply imbedded, and it should break out easily. It may in fact come out *very* easily, so you should not dawdle while making sail. If it doesn't, pull up until you're on short scope, then ease off, let the boat take a sheer, and sail the anchor out as described earlier.

But one of the problems with dropping an anchor close to a pier, or in any heavily trafficked area, is that there is likely to be all sorts of heavy junk on the bottom. It is definitely wise to buoy the anchor with a trip line, as described in the next chapter. Then, if the anchor snags, you can simply cast off the bitter end of the rode and sail off, as if from a mooring. Swing back under sail and pick up the tripline buoy, with which you can pull the anchor out backwards —and still wind up looking like a hero.

Sailing into and out of slips

Slips are the habitat for more and more marina-bound cruising yachts. Unless the wind strength and direction are suitable, there are very few ways

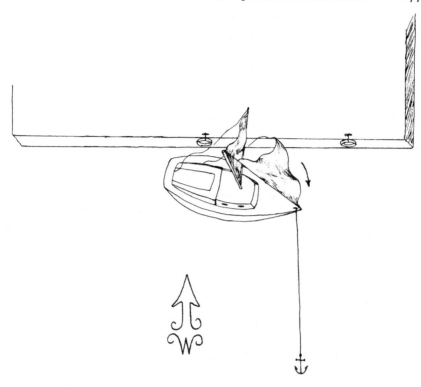

When the wind is blowing directly onto the pier or float, there's no graceful way to sail off. Probably the safest method, although it's not the easiest, is to run an anchor well out to windward, make sail, and then pull yourself out to the hook until it breaks free by itself, at which point you can sail clear. If the anchor snags something on the bottom, however, you will either have to buoy and temporarily abandon it or send a diver down while still anchored. Powering off is a better choice—if you have a choice.

of looking good trying to sail into or out of a slip. Before we deal with the various scenarios, let's define our slip. The one I normally visualize consists of a pier or float with a row of pilings parallel to it and far enough apart and away from the pier so a boat can occupy the space between two pilings and the pier, with her stern normally lying aft nearly against the pier for crew access. In some posh marinas, there will be a finger pier on one or both sides of the boat, so she lies alongside on one or both sides, and the main pier is at bow or stern and at right angles to the hull. Usually there will be a single piling between each two finger piers, and the boats occupying adjacent slips will secure their bows or sterns on one side to the same piling.

In most parts of the United States, there are fairly reliable prevailing winds, and it is normal marina-construction practice to build slips so that they face into the wind. Since the marina pier starts out T-shaped, this means that half the slips can be sailed into (under prevailing wind conditions) and half cannot. Merely securing a slip is hard enough in many parts of the country without being picky about which side of the pier it's on, but if you have the choice, opt for a space where the main pier is at the windward end of your slip. In such a set-up, you will moor bow-in to the main pier or float, and you'll be able to sail in. When you practice, do so initially on a day of zephyrlike breezes, and keep the engine running in neutral. Given the more constricted circumstances of a marina, although timing is critical the docking maneuver is nominally no more difficult than coming up to a mooring, and in one sense it's simpler, since you can hardly miss the slip. The two problems are undershooting, in which case the bow will fall away, leaving you in a truly tight spot, or overshooting, in which case there will be a more or less startling impact. In the first case, your best bet is instantly to jibe right around and sail out of the slip area, get your ducks in a row, and try again. (Unless, of course, you have fallen off facing out of the slip area, in which case you can simply reach clear.) Overshooting is more of a problem. One important thing *not* to do is attempt to stop any but the smallest cruiser by main physical strength; all you're going to get is a broken limb or a flattened hand. The best emergency tactic is to snag the piling or a cleat on the finger pier, or both, with a dockline led around a sheet winch drum, and drag the boat to a halt. If your docklines are strategically placed in your slip, hooking one or both should present no insuperable problem, and you can have them sized in advance so that at full length they will still prevent the bow from striking the main axis of the pier.

To sail out of such a slip, merely drop back until you're secured to the outer piling by a bow line and a slack stern spring. Raise the sails while the bow line is taking the strain, then cast it off and take up rapidly on the spring line to slingshot the boat off onto a reaching heading where her sails will draw. If your boat has a windward slip, however, there is not much that can be done to sail clear without it's being more trouble than it could conceivably be worth. Use the engine and be grateful you have one. If the wind is very light, however, you may still be able to sail downwind into the slip without any difficulty. The trick of timing here requires that you get all sail down and under control—roughly furled—before you turn into the final approach. The boat should be barely moving as you line up on the pier—she may pick up a slight amount of speed as she noses in, but chances are it will still be an easy and painless landing.

To do any of this requires, of course, that you be intimately knowledgeable about the air currents in your marina. While it is generally far calmer within the confines of a slip area than outside, the reverse can be the case, especially if there are large buildings or high piers to funnel winds. For this reason, it's not normally a good idea to sail into a strange slip unless you've been able to stand off for a bit and get a complete understanding of what the air is doing. When you're first assigned a slip, spend an afternoon watching other people make landings and approaches to adjacent slips. It can be both entertaining and very informative.

Docking under power

Because a cruising sailboat's natural mode of locomotion is her sailing rig, there can be a kind of ponderous inevitability about docking her under power, and when things start to go wrong, the ensuing disaster is a slow-motion nightmare; you can usually see the shambles approaching, but there's not much you can do to avert it. The trick, of course, is to plan the entire maneuver to avoid the bad dream.

The average auxiliary cruiser today is high-sided, underpowered for nimbleness, and afflicted with a rather small propeller for greater efficiency under sail. Its weight makes it slow to gain or lose speed, and it's usually a mistake to try to fend it off by hand or foot in moments of crisis. The boat's limited maneuverability is ordinarily controlled by the propeller-driven flow of water over the rudder. In the case of an outboard-powered boat, there is additional —and sometimes quite useful—maneuverability to be gained by swiveling the engine as well as using the rudder. Because the outboard steers as well as propels, it's a little like having two rudders.

Most skippers are vaguely aware that all boat props are either right- or left-handed. This means that when viewed from astern, with the engine in forward, the propeller turns respectively clockwise or counterclockwise. A

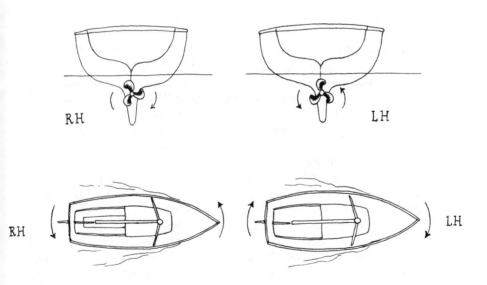

Viewed from astern, a right-handed propeller turns clockwise, and a left-handed prop turns counterclockwise, when the engine is in forward. The clockwise-turning propeller pulls the boat's stern to starboard as she moves ahead, an effect that is most pronounced when starting up from a dead stop. As the boat's stern works to starboard, she pivots somewhere amidships, and her bow moves to port. The effect is reversed with a left-handed prop.

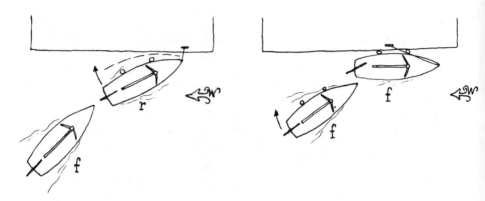

When a boat is suddenly put into reverse, the propeller's sideways creep is usually the first noticeable effect. Once you know how it works, you can use it when docking. At the left, a right-handed prop is reversed as the boat approaches the pier (fenders out) at about a thirty-degree angle. The boat stops, but before she begins to move astern, her stern swings to port, bringing her neatly alongside. (Had the skipper approached starboard-side-to, the same effect would have left him nose-on to the pier.) At left, a boat with a left-handed propeller will tend to edge her stern toward the pier as she approaches portside-to. She can be held to the pier easily—cushioned by fenders, of course—with a bow spring line and the engine just turning over in forward.

boat with a right-handed wheel tends, when moving ahead, to "walk" its stern to starboard. If the stern goes right, the bow must necessarily go left (most boats pivot, under power, at about the same midships point they do under sail). In some cases, boats will have their props slightly offset to counter this tendency, and in any case it is not great when going ahead, easily correctible with a slight angle on the rudder, or by angling and locking the outboard motor.

The tendency becomes serious, however, when you back down. Sailing cruisers are notorious for backing irresistibly to port or starboard no matter where the rudder is, and this attribute is no asset. It happens because, in reverse, the prop-driven water doesn't flow past the rudder. There are, however, other aspects of the same habit you can use when approaching a pier. It's also important to remember that when you put a boat into gear, either forward or reverse, the vessel's first response will be to turn, in response to propeller "walk," and only then to move ahead or astern. It is sometimes possible to turn a vessel virtually in her own length with alternate bursts of forward and reverse, if the boat has a tendency to ignore her rudder when going astern. But it's important to know which way your boat's propeller turns, and what effect this has on her helm in both forward and reverse.

Most gasoline inboards have right-handed props that will normally pull the stern sharply to port when reversing. As noted earlier, outboards (which are of course all gasoline-powered and right-handed) can easily be set in their steering brackets to provide any angle you like. Most small diesels—but not all of them—have left-handed props. These pull the stern to port when going ahead and the stern to starboard in reverse. It is sad but true that some boats have a helplessly neutral helm in reverse, refusing to turn either way, while others are virtually unpredictable. But the majority will obey the dictates of their turning props.

It takes little thought to see that a boat with a right-handed propeller will have a smaller turning circle going ahead to port than to starboard, while a boat with a left-handed wheel will be able, going ahead, to make a sharper turn to starboard. The difference can be dramatic, and can determine on which side you make an approach, when given a choice. Most boats with left-handed wheels will find it more convenient to approach a pier or float starboard-side to, so that when you back the engine to stop the boat's forward way, the reversed prop also pull the stern into the pier.

Many small cruisers have their auxiliary outboards offset to one side or the other to keep clear of a transom-hung rudder. This can be taken to extremes in the case of catboats, and the offset makes a tremendous difference in such a boat's turning circle. On my old cat, for instance, the three-horsepower Evinrude was hung on a bracket way over on the port side of the transom, to keep it away from the barn-door rudder. With the engine and rudder aligned fore-and-aft, the boat's bow would fall off to starboard, and I normally locked a small offset into the outboard's alignment. Even so, with the engine set to drive the boat straight ahead, she would turn far more easily to starboard, with the engine in effect levering the boat around the corner, than she would to port. It is worth remembering—and experimenting with.

Even if a pier is one you're well acquainted with, it doesn't hurt to make one initial pass before your final approach. You can thus assess the force and

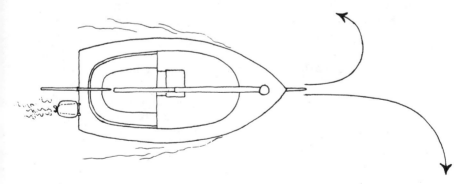

Outboard-powered auxiliaries with transom-hung rudders have the engine offset to one side or the other—markedly so in some cases. When maneuvering in close quarters, it is worth remembering that such a boat will turn much more tightly away from its engine than toward the side on which the outboard is hung.

effect of currents, decide where to place your fenders, and explain the maneuvering plan to the crew. Now is also the time to bring the dinghy, if you're towing one, up on short scope to keep the towline clear of the prop.

As with sailing to a pier, making your approach into wind and current and nearly parallel with the pier is ideal. If you have a left-hand prop, come in starboard side-to, at about a 10-degree angle off parallel, and put her into reverse a few yards off. This should, if your timing is right, pull the stern in and the bow slightly out, and lay her alongside dead parallel to the pier. The first line to go ashore is a bow spring (from the foredeck cleat to a dock cleat about amidships). With the engine turning over slow ahead and the rudder heading the boat *away* from the pier, this line should hold her in position while you get other lines ashore. Make sure you have a fender ready at the point of impact, normally about level with the forward shrouds. This same strategy should work with the wind off the pier, but come in at a slightly sharper angle, say 15 degrees.

If you are coming in with the wind blowing strongly down on the pier, the best tactic is probably to stop the boat dead in the water, as close to the pier as you can, and let her drift down, with the fender party standing by to place the fenders as required. If possible, lay the boat dead in the water with her bow slightly farther out than her stern, as the bow will blow in a bit quicker than the stern in most cases.

Leaving is normally no problem if the wind is off the pier, and if it's on the nose you can peel the boat clear as you did sailing her off. With the breeze directly onshore, however, getting off may be harder, especially if you're wedged in by neighbors fore and aft. If the wind is not too strong, you can probably spring the stern out: Set up a bow spring line and cast off all other docklines. Make sure there is a large fender forward at the shrouds, turn the helm toward the pier, and put the engine in slow speed forward. The boat will slowly pivot around the turn of the hull, putting her nose into the pier and sticking her stern out into the stream. When you've got her stern as far out as possible, straighten the helm, cast off the bow spring and quickly back clear —fending off the docked boat under your lee. In most boats with a left-handed wheel, this maneuver will work best with the port side to the pier. With an outboard, you can have the additional steerage afforded by turning the engine and backing out.

Remember when coming up to a pier or into a slip that a sailboat engine's reverse (especially in boats with folding propellers) can be a feeble thing. Don't put too much faith in it until you've accumulated a good deal of experience. In nearly all circumstances, dead slow speed and lots of fenders are the best precautions.

IX

~~~~~~~~~~~~~~~~

Tying Up
and Anchoring

Under most conditions, tying up a small cruising yacht is really quite simple, so it's surprising how many people consistently make a hash of the operation. You need to know only a few simple knots (see Chapter X), and the gear involved is basic. The two parts of the objective are to keep the boat in place at the pier, float, or slip, while at the same time preventing her from scarring her own topsides and those of other boats.

Alongside pier or float

The easiest type of tying up is for a relatively short period alongside a pier or float, where rise and fall of tide will not be a factor. Except for the smallest yachts, three or at most four lines are required. You need bow and stern lines led to fittings on the pier from the boat's bow and stern cleats, and you will probably want spring lines as well. These lead from the same cleats on the boat to a pier fitting more or less amidships. Some skippers find it more convenient to have, instead of two short springs, a single utility line about twice as long as any dockline. It can be taken from a cleat at bow or stern, hitched to a midships dock cleat, and then led back to the deck cleat at the opposite end of the boat from where you began, forming bow and stern springs. This same line can also serve as an emergency towline, where you'll need something longer than the ordinary dockline. (The latter should, in any case, be at least as long as the boat, and never less than twenty-five feet.) Regardless of the strains to be imposed, there seems to me little point in a dockline less than ⅜" in diameter, as anything smaller can chafe through very quickly.

In this form of side-to tying up, a small cruiser will as a general rule require two fenders and a larger one, three. My own favorites are the inflatable cylinders made by any of several suppliers; they aren't cheap, but they seem to last a long time in the most difficult service. Hang the fenders vertically, so they are just clear of the water—if they're too high, the action of the boat rolling against the pier can force them up and out, leaving the hull unprotected. Don't expect a fender to stay put, protecting a precise spot on the boat's side. With any harbor surge at all, the fender will move back and forth a bit. If you require to bolster one particular area—from a protruding pier fitting, for example—set up a fenderboard to take the wear and tear. And speaking of wear and tear, don't forget to set up chafe protection for the docklines, at points where they pass through chocks or over the gunwale, and also anywhere a line may rub against a deckhouse or deck fitting in its transit across the boat. Remember that nylon docklines stretch a good deal under load, so the tubular chafe protection should be fixed with most of itself on the inboard side of the offending fitting.

This type of set-up—short bow and stern lines, and springs fore and aft— is adequate if tying up to a float or to a fixed pier when there is little or no tidal rise to contend with. When tide is a factor, however, you will want to run the bow and stern lines well ahead and astern on the pier, and you may well want to run the springs to dock cleats at bow and stern, thus making each spring as long as the yacht itself. This allows the boat to rise and fall, while preventing it from surging forward and aft along the pier. If you're in doubt about how long a given dockline should be, check the permanent tie-ups of locally based craft at adjacent slips. Whether there is tide or not, try to avoid docklines that lead more or less vertically from the pier down to the boat. This places a pulling rather than a shearing stress on the boat's fittings and may just yank them out of the deck.

Tying up in a slip where there's a considerable range of tide can be a real problem. While it's not hard, given a large enough slip, to prevent the boat hitting the pier, she may at low tide wind up so far off that you cannot leap safely back aboard. The best rig for an ordinary slip—two pilings out by the bow and a pier astern, at right angles to the boat's centerline—requires no fewer than six lines. First, there are two short lines from the pilings to the bow, to keep it from moving side to side. From the same pilings, two long lines run aft toward the pier. They should be just long enough to reach the stern cleats and keep the boat's stern away from the pier at high water. The final pair of lines are also connected to the boat's stern cleats and lead to fittings on the pier—but these lines are crossed abaft the transom to allow the boat to move away from the pier and thus ease the tension at low water.

Precise adjustment of all these lines can be tricky, and if you are setting up a seasonal rig in your own slip, take the time to observe the boat's movement through a complete tidal cycle (ideally at tidal springs) to make sure you've got a set-up that will work at both high and low water. At this point, you can seize the rope ends for a semipermanent, properly sized arrangement. Unless your budget is exceptionally tight, the convenience of picking up premeasured, attached docklines as you come in will more than outweigh the cost of carrying another set on the boat for temporary tying up.

In the previous chapter, we dealt with the stern-to Mediterranean moor, wherein a boat lies to an anchor, with her stern abutting the pier. To my mind this is a set-up that works well enough for large yachts using all-chain rode, in very stable harbors, but it's definitely a last choice, especially for a boat with a transom-hung outboard or rudder. Remember that the nylon anchor line, at least fifty or seventy-five feet long, will have nearly twice the stretch of a normal dockline, aside from the possibilities of the anchor's dragging or snagging. Use crossed docklines at the stern and, if the boat's transom is shaped for it, a couple of large fenders and even a fender board. You can make the stretch in the anchor rode work for you, if you set up the rig so the boat rides six or eight feet off the pier with the anchor line at normal tension. A couple of reasonably muscular crew members should be able to pull hard enough to bring the boat within stepping range.

Anchoring

For many American yachtsmen, anchoring has become something of a lost art. According to the proprietors of Caribbean bareboat charter firms, the biggest deficiency they note in their American clients is an inability to anchor a boat reliably. Although it can sometimes be difficult, anchoring is a skill that can be absolutely indispensable; it's also an area where a little practice will compound success. Perhaps half the anchoring battle is arranging to do it on your own terms, and that means, for the most part, care in choosing your anchorage. In the popular sailing centers of today's world, that prescription is easier given than followed, and all too often you will have to take a less-than-ideal spot among crowds or see your perfect anchorage at three in the afternoon become a nautical parking lot by sundown. Even so, here are some thoughts on choosing a proper anchorage. Essentially, what you're seeking is protection from half a dozen different things, and by careful attention to the chart's details, plus a little local knowledge and common sense, you should have a reasonable chance of avoiding most if not all of them.

In terms of safety, the most vital requirement is good holding ground; without it, no skipper save a careless fool can sleep soundly. The chart often notes the composition of the bottom, especially in anchorages, but don't count on the listing's being accurate. Check if you can, either visually or with an old-fashioned sounding lead—the kind with a hollow in the base. To get a sample of the sea bottom, fill the hollow with waterpump grease and lower the lead briskly. The best holding ground I know is reasonably hard sand; it may require sharp flukes and several tries to get an anchor dug into tide-scoured sand, but when you do, it will hold like grim death. Next best is a combination of mud and sand, or firm mud. Clay is not bad, either, as long as it's not overgrown with duckweed or some other vegetation through which flukes cannot bite. Really soft mud can offer very little holding power.

Of the bad types of holding ground, gravel is, I think, the worst. Depending on the size of its components, gravel will cause anchors to skate over its surface, plow through it, or (and especially in the case of the Danforth) pick up chunks that will jam between stock and flukes and destroy the anchor's holding power. A rocky bottom can be all right if you have an old-fashioned yachtsman or kedge style of anchor, which can hook into the clefts, but it's easy to break an anchor out of rock by accident, while at the same time anchors are prone to jamming under larger rocks—always buoy the anchor in a rocky bottom. A thick surfacing of weed on any bottom, or free-floating kelp between bottom and surface, can load up nearly any style of anchor with vegetable matter and make it useless as ground tackle. Finally, a coral reef will hold like steel, but as with a rocky bottom, your anchor is likely to fall free when tension comes off the rode, and it is essential to have most of the rode composed of chain, to protect against chafe.

A good anchorage also offers protection against *surge*—not breaking seas (although you hardly need those) so much as the constant up-and-down of swells, converted when at anchor into rolling, pitching, or a corkscrewing combination of the two that is synergistically worse than their sum. It is often difficult to predict whether a cove or bay will be free from surge, especially during the day, when so much disturbance is likely to be man-made. In choosing an anchorage, try to avoid dips in the shoreline which are close to the end of an island or peninsula past whose tip seas roll unimpeded. A surprising number of waves will bend around that apparently protective corner and nail you, especially when there is even a slight change in the direction of the wind. The more landlocked a harbor is, the more protected it will be, and a flat beach will absorb seas whereas a steep shore or bulkheading will bounce them back at you.

Sometimes, in areas where there is an offshore breeze, the water along shore can be flat indeed. Bear in mind that as the land heats up in the morning, the breeze is likely to turn onshore. And it may do so in any case, regardless of the time of day, leaving you on a lee shore. This can be a peculiarly uncomfortable and exposed spot at three in the morning with the wind rising: While any shore can become a lee shore, try to select your anchorage so that if the wind does shift, it won't have a straight shot at you with a long fetch (that is, an extended distance of water over which to build up seas).

Gusty areas are also to be avoided where possible, and by *gusty* I mean only those places where winds are caused or exacerbated by the shape of the neighboring shore. While low hills will offer protection, steep, high bluffs will frequently funnel winds down their slopes, increasing their speed remarkably. An anchorage at the foot of abrupt hills or mountains can often become a maelstrom of wind in a few minutes—and with little warning. This should not be too dangerous, assuming your ground tackle is sturdy and your anchor well dug in, but it can certainly be nerve-wracking and is hardly conducive to a sound night's sleep.

When possible, you'll want to anchor your boat well away from high-traffic areas, such as primary channels or even the entrances to large marinas. Remember that anyplace with a high concentration of commercial or charter fishing boats will be extremely noisy very early in the morning. Look on the chart for obvious traffic patterns and avoid them. Although the boats in it may not be moving, a permanent anchorage can itself be a very noisy and disturbing place. When people don't sleep on their anchored or moored boats, they have no pressing need to suppress the clanking of wire and rope halyards against hollow aluminum masts. Many people find this racket, even aboard a fairly distant boat, quite insupportable. Permanent anchorages are also bad places in which to drop a transient hook, as the bottom has over the years become a mass of old ground tackle, much of it unconnected with any buoy and well barnacled in the bargain. Be especially careful to note chart markings that indicate submarine cables: It's not hard to hook one of these things, and it can be the very devil to release from anchor flukes.

The next-to-last category of things to be avoided includes noise and lights from ashore. The source for these can range from a waterside nightclub to a bridge with a grillwork roadbed, over which every passing car whines in a slightly different key. Commercial fishing depots often involve lots of cracked ice being loaded well before dawn, to the accompaniment of shouts and cries. An airport may or may not be a problem, depending on its size and complexity; most small airports cease operations at dusk and don't get much traffic until midmorning, but major commercial installations run well into the night and begin at the crack of dawn.

Finally, try to locate a place where you'll be reasonably free of insects. Bugs are a frequent problem because many otherwise ideal anchorages—free from surge and excess wind—are also near relatively low and swampy shore, from which the bugs will mount like the Luftwaffe attacking Britain, just about at dusk. It's amazing to me how far so unairworthy a creature as a mosquito can fly—and close-hauled, at that—when there is human flesh in the offing. Only a really stiff wind can deter no-see-ums, black flies, and horseflies, and it is probably a good idea in any anchorage close to damp ground to rig your insect screens in advance. When the bugs arrive, it's likely to be all at once.

Having said all this, I really ought to qualify it by adding that once you've found a proper anchorage you may have considerable difficulty forcing yourself to leave. The extended search makes the final discovery that much sweeter, and if there is any part of cruising more delightful than relaxing in the cockpit while anchored in a well-earned harbor, I don't know what it may be. Even a less-than-perfect anchorage, after a good, hard sail (or a bad, hard sail, for that matter), becomes a true haven, one of the reasons to go cruising in the first place.

Anchoring procedure

So we have selected our anchorage, using the chart and perhaps a reliable cruising guide (see chapter 3), and we're now approaching it. As with any other demanding maneuver, anchoring is twice as easy if you prepare for it. Unless we've been in this particular cove or harbor often, it will probably be a good idea to plan on taking one exploratory swoop through before actually dropping the hook. At the same time, the ground tackle should be rigged and ready to go as soon as a likely spot presents itself.

If possible, the boat's foredeck should be cleared for action. This means that the headsail or sails should be lowered and bagged (or rolled up, as the case may be). It's usually possible to bag most of a headsail while its luff snaps are still fixed to the forestay, then rest the bag on top of the pulpit, largely out of the way. Don't strike the headsail, however, unless you have confidence in the boat's ability to maneuver in close quarters under main alone. In making any unfamiliar approach, try to retain the ability to turn and get the hell out if necessary.

The anchor, chain, and line should be rigged and ready to run. Assuming you have a bare foredeck, this means flaking down a little more rode than you plan to use. If, for instance, the chart suggests a high-tide depth of 15 feet, and your boat has four feet of freeboard forward, then you'll want to plan on letting go just about 100 feet of rode (counting the chain); this breaks down to a scope of just over five to one. (*Scope,* the ratio of anchor rode length to water depth, is an important concept. Most authorities calculate scope using as the vertical element of the equation the total distance from deck to water level to bottom at high water, rather than just the present water depth. Five-to-one scope is usually about right, given a reasonably sheltered anchorage and ground tackle of the proper size. In an exposed anchorage and unquiet conditions ten-to-one scope may be called for.)

An experienced cruising friend always sails with 100 feet of anchor line flaked in long coils on deck and stopped with twine to the lifeline stanchions. This seems to me extreme, as long as you do have the ability to get the anchor over the side quickly. Laying the line out on deck is just a guarantee that when you need it, it'll run easily without a kink's jamming in the hawsepipe. Get the anchor out of whatever chocks you carry it in, ready to lower over the side at the proper moment. (Of course, the rode's bitter end is secured to a ring or eye in the anchor locker.)

If your preliminary reading of the chart suggests that this anchorage has the kind of bottom that may require the anchor to be buoyed with a tripline, a light line and a float should be rigged in advance and the tripline itself coiled on deck and ready to run. You will need only as much line as will allow the buoy to float at the surface at high water, but make sure the tripline has a proper lead and won't tangle as it runs. If the size of the foredeck permits, a second deck hand to tend the tripline isn't a bad idea, and this job can usefully be performed by even young members of the crew. If your boat is equipped with a depth sounder, it should of course be going as you enter the harbor. You will have calculated the state of the tide before entering, and you'll know how much to add to the sounder's readings to estimate high water depth, and how much to subtract to estimate depth at low tide. Although many sounders these days are capable of precision to a foot or less, you needn't expect the soundings on the chart to correspond exactly, even when corrected. If you don't have a depth sounder, a simple leadline works fine. It can be swung by the foredeck hand, as he or she will have plenty of time to set it aside before dropping the hook. Using a leadline with ease requires some practice, but it's a knack that can come in handy. Without a leadline, you can still use a sounding pole—a boathook marked off at one-foot intervals will serve well in depths from eight to ten feet.

The person at the helm should be alert, as you ease into the anchorage, to the strength and direction of the local wind, and to any change between these

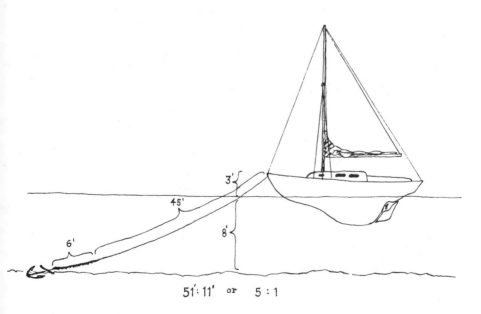

Scope is not an absolute length, but a ratio—the ratio of anchor rode to water depth. In measuring the first, include the chain leader and count the length of rode from bow chocks to anchor; for scope measurement, the vertical depth is from the gunwale at the bow to the sea bottom.

conditions and what's happening outside. If other boats are present, whether anchored or permanently moored, remember that by virtue of being there first they have rights over you, and you must set your anchor to avoid them. There is always the temptation to anchor close to other boats, perhaps on the grounds that they may know something you don't. A good deal of the time, they have no better information than you do, and you gain nothing by getting in their path except possible trouble later.

If circumstances permit, anchor in the approximate neighborhood of boats that are more or less the same size and type as your own. Chances are that they will react similarly to the forces of wind and current, so that you'll all swing in the same direction at the same time. Even so, try to allow enough room so you and your neighbors can swing in complete circles without colliding. Your boat's swinging circle will have a diameter equal to twice the amount of line out plus twice the boat's length. In many harbors you won't have anything like this much room, and for your own safety you'll have to rely on the nearby boats behaving in more or less the same way yours does. It's fortunate that the most likely circumstance under which this will *not* happen is when there's no wind and no current, and all anchored craft will revolve more or less aimlessly. A collision under such conditions, while embarrassing, is hardly a federal case.

Having made a complete assessment of the situation—it will take less time to do than to read about, once you've become used to the process—you're ready to anchor. As you make the final close-hauled approach, let the sail luff to lose speed, then head up. Wait until the boat has definitely lost all forward motion—sight the shore or fixed objects, not the water alongside—and then give the signal to the foredeck hand to lower the anchor. "Lower" is the word, too. Let the anchor go over the bow hand-over-hand until you feel it touch bottom, something that should be apparent in even the softest mud. If your anchor rode is marked for depth you will have an accurate idea of the true depth at the moment. Call the information back to the skipper: It is not only useful in itself, but a convenient check on the depth sounder's accuracy.

As the boat gathers sternway, pay out anchor rode. Keep just a slight tension on the line. When you've let go as much line as planned, take a hitch on the foredeck cleat. The boat should bring up into the wind, from which she will have fallen off slightly, with the sail luffing. The anchor should hold with this light load on it. Now lower the mainsail and furl it. The five minutes or so that this requires will allow the anchor to dig its way slowly into the bottom. When the sail is furled, turn on the engine and put it into reverse, at dead slow. The rode should take up until it's visibly taut, and perhaps drag the anchor a few feet before the boat comes up sharply.

All this is fine if—as is usually the case—the anchor sets without a struggle. Sometimes, however, you will drop the hook and let it sit, only to find when you apply reverse that it hasn't taken hold at all. If you have more rode (and room) available, ease out another fifty feet of line as the boat drops back with the engine in neutral, then snub the line and reverse again. If this doesn't work, raise the anchor. You may have fouled a stone or bunch of seaweed that's preventing the flukes from digging in. If this is the case, clear the hook and try again. But you may simply have to move to another place, or use a different style of anchor. Depending on the bottom, the one you're using may not be right.

Once the anchor has set to the point that you're satisfied—which, for my money, is solidly enough to resist half-throttle in reverse without dragging—check your depth sounder, lead, or sounding pole if you dragged a significant distance before the anchor set. Let out your five-to-one scope, unless you're in an exposed spot or there's a Small Craft Advisory or Gale Warning. In either of those cases it's a good idea to use as much rode as possible, while leaving fifty feet for insurance in the rope locker. (The reason for leaving some extra is that if the anchor drags in the night, your first line of defense is to let out more line and try to reset the hook.) Now make a visual check of the boat's swinging circle. Be alert for natural obstacles and also for boats that may swing into you. In many crowded weekend anchorages, you can be as alert as you like, but if the wind or current turn materially, there are going to be boats butting each other all night. That's civilization. And that's why it's handy to have a small, shoal-draft cruiser that can edge up into the corners of harbors.

With the rode set, rig your chafing gear. Remember that if a wind comes up and puts a strain on the rode, it'll stretch—even the small length between the bow chocks and the foredeck cleat. Rig your chafing gear so it'll still ride in the chock if the rode stretches. Before you check out for the night, be sure to turn on your anchor light. There are two standard types—one is the fixed, masthead white light that shines 360 degrees around the horizon, drawing its power from the ship's 12-volt system. The other has the same all-around arc but is self-powered, usually by a 6-volt dry cell. It is hung from the forestay, at about the height of the spreaders, with a light line downhaul to a foredeck fitting, to keep it from swinging wildly as the boat pitches. Some of these self-contained lights have automatic sensing switches that turn them off at dawn, which is nice but a bit rich for my blood.

I've always been torn between the self-powered and the ship's-battery-powered anchor lights, and have usually opted at last for the former. There are two reasons: First, a reasonably powerful anchor light (and that's what you want) will appreciably flatten a small 12-volt system overnight; and if you have a tall spar, your masthead light may not be noticed by careless drivers of small boats. By contrast, a light halfway down (or up) the forestay is more likely to be seen by the people whose attention you want to attract—skippers and lookouts aboard vessels of your own general type and smaller. (This argument doesn't hold true for running lights: The optional masthead white-red-and-green is good because it does impinge on the field of view of commercial vessels' lookouts—but they won't be tooling around small-craft anchorages.) Moreover, a self-contained light is no drain on the yacht's system, and being detachable it can also serve as an auxiliary cabin light or worklight at need. The only drawback is that it will speedily kill its own battery in a couple of nights. If you have a six-volt battery charger, that's great. If not, carry an extra dry cell.

If bad weather is forecast during the night, or if you can't find holding ground you trust, there are a couple of precautions you can take. First, get the bitter end of the rode up on deck and tied to a pickup buoy, unless the anchor itself is already buoyed. The point here is that you want to be able to cast off your anchor in a hurry, while being able to find it again later. Consider rigging a drag alarm. This consists of a light line weighted and dropped to the bottom (a leadline is perfect) with a little extra to allow for the boat's swing. Tie the line inboard to an empty bottle, large can, or other object that will make a noise if it falls. Set the object on a thwart or table in such a way that if the boat drags a significant distance, the "alarm" will be pulled off the table or thwart, to awaken you with its crash. Frankly, I think this sounds a little Rube Goldberg, but there are many who swear by it.

At anchor in heavy weather

If you do any substantial amount of cruising, you will sooner or later find yourself in a windswept anchorage facing a thoroughly bad weather forecast, with nothing to do but sit it out. There are several useful steps to take. First, get the boat squared away: Strike and stow all unnecessary gear, and stow it well: The last thing you need to hear in a moment of storm-created stress is an unidentifiable crash from down below. Clean up on deck, too. Get boat hooks and spinnaker poles chocked, and the latter lashed down (you may need the boathook in a hurry, so if you do lash it, make sure you can get it free).

If you have a dinghy, bring it on deck and lash it upside-down, or if it's an inflatable, deflate it and stow it below if you can, rolled and lashed on deck if you must. Furl the sails and stop them carefully. You may need them if you have to move in a hurry, but the furling should be tight and neat so the wind can't break them free. If your boat will handle under reefed main alone, it might be a good idea to reef the sail in advance of need. Make sure the storm jib is available, but don't clutter the foredeck with it yet.

Have fenders ready in case you need to cushion the blow of another boat dragging into you. Set out flashlights, life jackets and safety harness for the hands you've decided will work on deck. Make sure the working party all have sharp knives and, if possible, sailing gloves. Charge up the batteries and get a good, hot meal into everyone, setting aside some coffee or cocoa in a Thermos.

Get as many weather forecasts—*marine* weather forecasts—as you can. Don't depend solely on either the government's VHF-FM predictions or on those from civilian sources, but get them all and write down the salient data —predicted wind speeds and directions, probable times of wind shifts, wave heights and temperatures anticipated, probable visibility limits, and expected precipitation. Check your barometer against the current reading at the station nearest to you, and note the difference in the log.

If you have good reason, based on the forecasts, to believe that the wind direction will be substantially unchanged during the night, then you are probably best off, in my opinion, setting out two anchors from the bow. They should be on at least ten-to-one scope and be set in such a way that they form about a 30-degree angle, with the boat at the apex. The two rodes should *not* be the same length, so as to minimize the chance of the hooks fouling each other if they drag into line. If you can suspend a heavy weight from the rode of the light, working anchor, it will flatten the direction of pull and increase the anchor's holding power. But don't tie a knot in the rode, as this will materially decrease the line's strength. Make absolutely certain that you have plenty of chafing gear on the rodes.

If the forecasts lead you to believe that the wind direction will change substantially during the blow, then I think you would be advised to set only one anchor, your heaviest, with maximum scope and a buoy on the bitter end of the rode. Have the working anchor on the foredeck with its rode flaked down and stopped with twine, out of the way. Try to locate a couple of substantial landmarks that you'll be able to see during the storm. Fixed, lighted aids to navigation are probably best, but don't ignore towers ashore or whatever's available. Try to get three or even four that are on the chart, and take a series of very careful bearings until you can plot your position precisely. You may have to draw a quick sketch of a portion of the chart to accommodate the large scale you'll need. Write the bearings down. These will be your checkpoints during the storm.

Set up anchor watches of perhaps two hours apiece. The person on watch will have to sit in the companionway where he or she can see what's happening, but the watchstander should not go on deck without making certain another crew member is awake and up.

With all your preparations made, there's nothing to do but hit the bunk and get what rest you can. Chances are your precautions will have been unnecessary, but I've never felt particularly foolish about overdoing it—at any rate, not nearly as foolish as having to realize that damage to my boat was caused by *not* planning ahead.

X

~~~~~~~~~~~

Marlinspike Seamanship

Among the consistent pleasures of being a sailor are the repeated opportunities to indulge in what is still usually called marlinspike seamanship, even though the marlinspike is largely symbolic. What we're talking about is the art of working with rope (a term that includes both fiber and wire line)—knotting, splicing and protecting. It helps to know something about the materials themselves—what they're good for, where they fail—and so the best beginning is, perhaps, a brief look at what's available in line today.

Types of rope

It seems likely that three kinds of rope—nylon, dacron, and stainless steel wire—will continue to dominate the average cruising sailor's horizon for the foreseeable future. Other types of line exist, and have their devotees, but tend to be either experimental or expensive or narrowly limited in their applications.

NYLON

Of the three, nylon rope is certainly the universal marine line in this half of the century. It has three valuable characteristics, one of which has its flip-side drawback. To begin with, nylon—an artificial fiber—is immensely strong, compared to the natural-fiber ropes that have gone before, and to many other artificial-fiber lines as well. Its second salient characteristic is its stretchiness: Nylon line will often stretch as much as 20 percent when stressed, an attribute which can be very useful in some applications and absolutely exasperating in others. When put under extreme load, close to its breaking strength, nylon may be irretrievably damaged, although apparently still intact. Finally, nylon is technically rot-free. It will not support the growth of weakening spores that can destroy natural-fiber line, and this is a big plus, since it means that nylon can be stowed while still damp, and drying line is often a virtual impossibility on a pleasure boat. On the other hand, nylon can mildew, with the consequent unpleasant odor and the spread of mildew to other surfaces, so that some ventilation is really necessary for rope lockers where nylon rode is stored. And while nylon does not rot in the conventional sense, it—like other artificial-fiber lines—does deteriorate when exposed to strong, direct sunlight for extended periods. In most parts of the country, this poses a relatively minor maintenance problem, but in the south or the tropics it can be a very important factor in both safety and running costs.

As you might imagine, nylon is at its best when employed where its great strength and stretchiness are assets, which is to say that nylon is ideal for dock lines and anchor rodes, two applications where stretch not only reduces the shock load but also makes life a bit more comfortable for the humans aboard. The longer a nylon anchor rode, the greater its potential stretchiness, and being at the end of ten-to-one scope is a little like hanging from a gigantic rubber band. Robert Ogg, inventor of the Danforth lightweight anchor, has said that it's important to choose a nylon anchor rode thin enough so that it will respond to load by stretching; at the same time, the thinner a line, the easier it is to chafe through, so you must make the decision about diameter carefully. (It is, by the way, a good point to remember that, strength aside, a rope which is going to be handled frequently should be of a diameter comfortable to the users' hands. I find a perceptible difference in my ability to grip rope of ⅜″ diameter, as opposed to 5⁄16″, the next thinner size.

Both anchor rodes and docklines frequently require permanent loops in one or both ends, and because nylon generally has a relatively slippery surface (at least when it's new), most ropework experts recommend an extra two series of tucks—five instead of three—in eye splices (see below), and security taping of stressed, unattended knots. Another characteristic of artificial as opposed to natural-fiber lines is that the latter have a "memory" of the shape that has been twisted into them under stress, while the former do not; as we shall see, this can be a factor in ropework.

DACRON

In most respects, dacron line is much the same as nylon. It, too, is very strong, will not rot (but will deteriorate under sunlight), and has no memory of its constructed shape. In one important respect, however, it is very different from nylon: Dacron does not stretch anywhere near as much, and when it has been treated by a process called "prestretching," so little elasticity remains that it can be and is used in applications formerly reserved for wire. Such applications, of course, are mainly as halyards and sheets, uses where a line, once tensioned, is expected to remain at a constant length even when the subsequent stress may vary in intensity. In the past, halyards in even quite small yachts were made up half of dacron and half of wire, most commonly with a splice to join them. The idea was that the rope tail would be used to raise the sail by hand nearly all the way, at which point the end of the wire would come down to the base of the mast, to be wrapped around the halyard winch drum three or four times, after which you could put tension on the halyard with the winch. This was fine when nearly all sail luffs were themselves strengthened by a wire, and extreme tension was necessary to keep the luff from scalloping under load. Now, however, a slight amount of stretch in a wire-less luff is seen as a positive requirement in many cases, and prestretched dacron has so little remaining elasticity that it can serve by itself for all halyards in quite large cruising (if not racing) yachts.

WIRE

Stainless steel wire is characterized by great strength—far greater than that of fiber rope—relative to diameter, and nearly nonexistent stretch. It has some corresponding defects: Although nominally stainless, most wire will eventually rust somewhat, especially (and most dangerously) inside the terminals that are usually pressed (or *swaged*) over its raw ends; wire rope has different degrees of flexibility, depending on its construction, but even at best it cannot coil as conveniently as fiber rope, and it is prone to kinking, which may put permanent crimps in it or break some of its component wires; it is very difficult to splice (although there are often ways around splicing situations, if necessary); it is very heavy for its diameter; finally, it is both thin and slippery, unsuited to human grip—it must be tensioned by a winch or lever of some sort. These qualities of wire determine its uses. Although wire cable has been employed for anchor rodes, it must be spooled on a reel to avoid kinking, and so is irrelevant to most yachts. On larger racing craft, such as Twelve Meters, wire sheets are common, but they have no place on small cruising boats. Which leaves halyards, and even here wire has largely been superseded by low-stretch fiber rope in boats under thirty feet or so.

You occasionally see an all-wire main halyard, with the wire running to a reel winch on which it is permanently stored. While an all-wire halyard has some advantages, the reel winch has just about none, and is generally considered a major safety hazard, because it can, under certain circumstances, spin backward, turning the handle into an uncontrolled weapon. By and large, therefore, when wire is found on a modern cruising yacht, it is either as standing rigging, lifelines (when it is covered with white vinyl), or, in combination with rope, as halyards. A problem with the rope-to-wire combination halyard is the connection between the two materials. As noted above, the spliced connection is difficult for amateurs and costs at least twenty-five dollars when done by a professional. Even if well executed, it remains a weak point in the overall structure, and it is also prone to developing *meat hooks*—individual strands of wire that work loose from the splice to gouge the sailor's hands, scratch the varnish, and abrade fiber glass.

An alternative to the rope-to-wire splice is a swaged eye at the wire end of the halyard, through which the bitter end of the rope tail is passed and then eye-spliced. This form of connection is quite strong and allows the rope (which is likely to wear out first) to be replaced; the swaged loop will not, however, pass through a halyard sheave, and a rope-to-wire splice will.

Wire line normally occurs in one of three cross-sectional structures, according to the wire's intended use. Where line need not take abrupt bends or run through blocks, as in lifelines and standing rigging, it is usually made up of 19 separate strands, wound around each other in a conformation called 1 × 19. For halyards and lifts, which require some flexibility, two slightly weaker arrangements are employed—7 × 19 and 7 × 7. In each case, the main cable is made up of 7 individual bundles of strands—7 strands in the one case and 19 in the other.

Other types of line

Among racing sailors, an artificial material called Kevlar is increasingly in the spotlight for both sails and line. It combines great tensile strength—far greater than nylon or dacron—minimal stretch, and (alas) savagely high cost. For the relatively small demands of the cruising yacht, the cost and the side defects of Kevlar (as yet not fully explored) outmatch its advantages.

Polypropylene line, sometimes referred to simply as propylene, is easily recognizable because of its slick, slippery texture. It is often, but not always, seen in bright colors. Polypropylene is weaker than other artificial-fiber lines, and more prone to ultraviolet deterioration from sunlight, but it has one unique, positive attribute: It floats. Fishermen use it where they need a floating line, and some yachtsmen employ it for mooring pick-up lines that will take little strain, or for the towlines of dinghies, but aside from such specialized functions, it has little application aboard pleasure craft. When utilized, polypropylene should be knotted or spliced with extreme care, as its slippery surface makes it very prone to untying and even to unsplicing itself.

Manila line, which for several centuries dominated the world of fiber rope, is still available commercially, usually in hardware stores or discount marine outlets. Its price remains well below that of artificial fiber line, but it is far weaker, rots easily if stored wet in a dark place, and is generally suitable only for temporary or sacrificial applications—such as tiedowns for winter covers. A recently developed drawback of manila line is that it has become more difficult to tell what grade of line you're buying—and there are many grades of natural-fiber line, of which true manila, made from hemp, is perhaps the best. Now that sophisticated buyers no longer seek out the best manila for marine use, the substance has become one of half a dozen natural-fiber lines sold more or less indiscriminately by less than knowledgeable dealers. One good use for manila is as a practice line when learning knots and splices, as it has the natural fiber's tendency to remain in the conformation into which it was forcibly twisted during the rope-making process, so that you can, for example, use the same three unlaid strands to make two or three successive splices, without the ends turning into mops.

Structures of fiber rope

Most landlubbers, when they think of rope, summon up a mental picture of the old-fashioned type of line composed of three strands, each made up of several yarns, and each of *them* containing a number of fibers. In manufacturing this traditional line, the vegetable fibers—which are of random length—are twisted, or *laid up* in one direction to produce the yarns; the yarns are laid up in the opposite direction to form strands; and the strands, usually three, are laid up, once again, in reverse order to form the finished rope. Thanks to the opposed stresses of the different stages of laying up, and the natural "memory" of vegetable fiber, an assembled rope tends to maintain its structure. Today's *laid line* uses many of the same construction techniques, but since artificial fibers, which run the length of the rope, have no memory, the line itself must be carefully handled, especially at the ends, to avoid having it become nothing more than a mass of tangled fibers.

Although laid line has been largely superseded by braided line (see below) for sheets and halyards, it remains widely used for rodes and docklines. Most sailors feel that it is significantly easier to splice laid line, and many also believe that laid line offers a better grip when it is being pulled hand over hand; by contrast, the smooth surface of braid is generally considered to be easier on the palms when a line must run through your hands. There is now no significant difference in strength or cost between the two, and I have found it convenient to use braid for halyards and sheets and three-strand laid for rodes and docklines. If nothing else, using the two constructions for definitely different purposes makes it easy to tell, in a cockpit full of loose line, which one to pick up in a given situation. (It may also help to buy braid with different-colored flecks, to color-code sheets or halyards.)

There are several conformations of braided line, but the general construction is likely to be the same, except in the very smallest diameters. By and large, braid consists of two parts—an inner core and an outside skin. The former may have some structure or it may be just a bundle of strands, but the skin is nearly always carefully constructed so its strands form a protective casing over the core.

A third type of line construction is usually seen with the polypropylene types of rope whose slipperiness makes them difficult to assemble in the conventional rope shapes. *Plaited* line is related in structure to the skin of braid, but the plaiting does not cover a core. Since the number of plaits making up a rope varies with the manufacturer, splicing is likely to be equally idiosyncratic. It is usually possible, however, to examine a plaited line and figure out some way of splicing it with reasonable success, if you really have to.

Cutting and sealing rope ends

Because modern artificial-fiber lines seem sometimes to have a positive desire to disassemble themselves, it is especially important to arrest this tendency where it is most likely to start—at the bitter ends. There must be a dozen methods for treating rope ends to prevent their unraveling, according to the desires of the line's owner, or his convenience, or his skill. Before dealing permanently with the rope's end, however, it is as well to begin by creating a neat cut. Too many sailors carry knives suited only for haggling through warm butter, with the result that when they are faced with the need to cut a rope, they simply hack and saw their way through, pulling the line out of shape and winding up with a rope's end that strongly resembles a cow's tail. The best way to cut artificial-fiber line is with a so-called hot knife, which is usually just a heated wire in a frame that looks like a jigsaw's. As it melts its way through the dacron or nylon, the hot knife automatically seals the edges of the cut, providing a temporary finish. But a hot knife is an expensive toy for the average sailor, and he can get nearly as good results with a conventional knife, as long as its blade is kept razor sharp. To prevent the rope on either side of the cut from unraveling, put tight turns of masking tape about half an inch apart, and slice between them, putting minimal pulling stress on the line while you're cutting. The sliced end may then be sealed with a match, unless you're planning to splice it immediately. An ordinary heat seal, with an open flame held under the line until it catches fire and then removed, will usually make a safe, permanent, and only slightly knoblike end for a line. It is a lot better than waterproof tape, which many lazy sailors rely on simply because that's how the line arrived from the chandlery. Taped line may endure for years, but when at last the tape comes off, you're guaranteed to have an instant mess.

Finally, I ought to mention that there are a number of proprietary fittings —usually some form of collar—that you may apply to the end of a line to seal it. If you follow the directions, these work quite well, but I have to confess that for me at least they spoil the fun.

Basic splice

If a knot is a temporary connection or loop, a splice does the same job permanently. This is the most obvious difference between them, but perhaps more important is the established fact that a proper splice is the best way of retaining most of a rope's original strength. Most knots work by creating friction through pinching one or more parts of the rope, and this pinching will, when overstressed, tend to break individual fibers of line. A knot will usually reduce a line's breaking strength by anywhere from 20 to 40 percent, and sometimes more. On the other hand, a splice achieves its goal by duplicating the friction in a rope's own structure, so that a well-executed splice with five tucks should retain more than 90 percent of the line's original strength.

My own rule is that I employ a splice whenever I can, both because it looks better and because it's stronger, and I leave knots for uses where I know I'll want to untie the end for another application later, as with fender lines. My docklines have an eye spliced into one of their ends, and my anchor rode has an eye spliced around a metal thimble, to protect against chafe. I do, however, keep one long line aboard for emergencies, and since I don't know how it will next be employed, I leave the ends well whipped, but otherwise virgin.

In the illustrations on the next two pages, I have attempted to show clearly how to make the one essential splice, to put a permanent eye in the end of a rope. I can't say how long it will take you to perfect your splicing, or indeed if you will ever learn, but I can say that once you've done it, you'll be possessed of a skill that can offer you many hours of pleasure.

Basic knots

I remember reading someplace that in the latter days of commercial and military sail a truly able seaman might master literally hundreds of specialized knots during his career. A great many knots, hitches, and bends still exist, in that we know how to tie them and what they were used for. But a very few knots will serve for most purposes, even if they make the purist wince. I'd go so far as to say that you could get by on the water knowing how to tie only one knot—the bowline—although you'd have a rather messy boat. I have included in this basic section five knots and variations on three of them. You don't have to know all of them, but you'll find that each has a definite place in modern sailing.

Eye Splice in laid line

1. Unlay the end of the line about six inches. Tape the bitter ends of the three strands to keep them from unraveling. With whipping twine, tie a square knot around the point beyond which you do not want the line to unlay.

2. Form a loop of the desired size and lay the three strands over the line. Using a fid (the Swedish fid shown is an excellent model), open up the rope. Push through the middle of the three unlaid strands and draw it up, but not too tightly.

3. Now open up the rope again, at the strand just to the left of the original opening. Push through the free strand to the left of the first one.

4. This is the key point, at which most beginners go wrong. Turn the splice over. There is now one free strand and, if you inspect the main part of the line carefully, only one place where it may be pushed through without lying alongside one of the two other free strands that have already been inserted.

(continued overleaf)

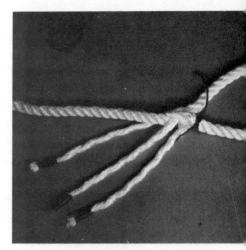

5. Insert the last strand, being sure to lead it in the same direction as the first two.

6. Draw all three strands up tight, pulling on them alternately. Make a second series of tucks; you should have no difficulty from here on in determining which strand goes where. Draw all three strands tight again.

7. When you have made five series of tucks, with each set drawn up as it is completed, the splice is finished.

8. Cut off the ends of the spliced strands about one-quarter of an inch from the main part of the line. Heat-seal them if you like. Remove the whipping twine. Roll the completed splice underfoot a couple of times—this will even out its appearance. Although I have used nylon line here, manila line is easier to practice with, as it holds its shape better.

The **bowline**, sometimes called the king of knots, is of course employed to make a secure temporary loop. It has two of the three important attributes of a good knot—once tied, it will stay put; at the same time, it is easy to undo if necessary. But it's not an easy knot to learn, and baffles some people completely. There are several ways of tying a bowline, and the most common is illustrated, but it doesn't matter how you do it as long as you can repeat the process every time, even in the dark.

The **square knot** isn't in itself very useful, since it is prone to jam, especially when wet or under severe strain. But in the variation also shown here, with one end slipped, or looped, it is very handy for tying in reef points and similar work. The single slipped loop—only one is really required—makes it easy to undo the knot.

The **clove hitch** is, in skilled hands, the quickest method for putting a line around a piling. Unfortunately, in its plain form it can work free, especially if the line is subjected to a series of sharp tugs. For that reason, if you're going to leave a clove hitch unattended it's a good idea to tie one or two hitches, as shown, around the standing part of the line. Another variant, the **rolling hitch**, is also more secure than the original knot.

Better than the square knot for joining two lines, the **sheet bend** is related to the bowline, and won't jam. It is also handy on those occasions when the lines to be joined are of perceptibly different diameters, as illustrated. For additional security, the crossed loop may be doubled.

The **figure eight** is a stopper knot, tied into the end of a line to prevent its running through a sheave or other narrow opening, It also serves as an emergency measure to keep a fraying end from becoming worse. There are stoppers that make a larger knob, but the figure eight is quick and easy, and it will not jam except under extreme, prolonged stress.

Although it is not, strictly speaking, a knot, the proper way to **cleat a line** is something not every sailor knows. The splendid thing about a classical cleat is that its shape allows you to release a cleated line that's under tension, while absorbing the load with a turn around the cleat's base. Thus, the hitch around one of the cleat's horns is never under direct stress. Beginning sailors in small boats are often told never to cleat a sheet, but while this may well make sense aboard a Sunfish in a squall, it's not realistic aboard a cruising yacht. The point of the warning—that you should always be able to release a sheet quickly—applies equally to halyards, and *proper* cleating is the answer.

Coiling line

Finally, coiling a line is a vital ropework skill that is too often used by self-styled experts to intimidate new crew members. There is no single, right way to coil a line, and the only requirement is that the coil retain its shape, so the line can be put to use without the need for untangling it first. The type of

Bowline

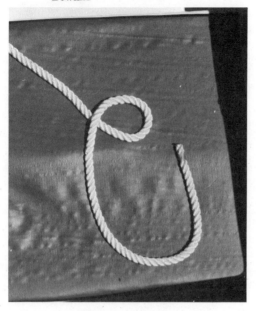

1. Form an eye in the line, as shown.

2. Lead the bitter end up through the eye, entering from underneath the loop and emerging in front.

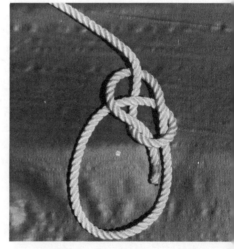

3. Take the bitter end around behind the standing part.

4. Lead the bitter end down through the eye. Draw the knot up tight by pulling simultaneously on the standing part and the bitter end.

Square knot

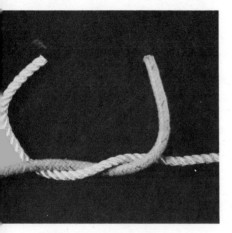

1. Make an overhand knot.

2. Repeat it, but in reverse. Note that the result must be two interwoven loops, as shown.

3. Draw up tight. When wet, this knot will be very difficult to untie.

4. By "slipping" one end of the second overhand knot, as shown, you can make a knot that's just as secure and a cinch to untie. If both ends of the second overhand knot are slipped, you've tied a shoelace.

Clove hitch

1. Make a full turn around a post or stanchion, leading the free end up and across the secured end. Now make a second turn, leading the free end under the crossover, and draw tight.

2. One or two half-hitches around the standing part of the line will keep it from working free.

3. A clove hitch with an extra turn in the middle is called a rolling hitch, and is considerably more secure.

Sheet bend

1. Form a loop or bight in one line (the larger, if lines of different diameters are being joined). Lead the other line as shown.

2. Draw up slowly and carefully.

3. A double sheet bend is more secure.

Figure eight

1. Formed.

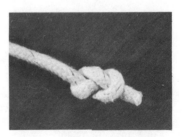

2. Drawn up.

Cleating

1. Take a turn around the base of the cleat.

2. Lead the bitter end up and diagonally across the top of the cleat.

3. Under the other horn and back across the top, crossing the first turn.

4. Hitch the line over the horn. The bitter end should lie parallel with the first turn over the horn. You can now uncleat the line slowly, with its friction on the cleat taking any strain that may be on the working end.

Coiling

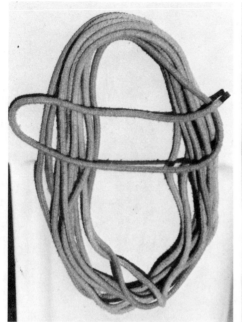

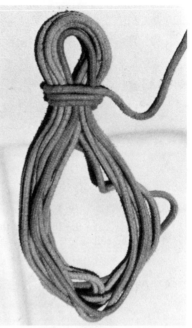

1. Make up the coil with about two feet of the bitter end to spare.

2. Take three or four turns around one end of the coil.

3. Pull the last turn through the coil to form a loop.

(continued overleaf)

4. Take the loop over the top of the coil.

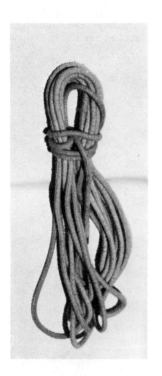

5. Pull up tight with the bitter end. The coil can be stowed flat or hung by the smaller loop.

coil shown is for free—that is, unattached—lines. The use of a small tie is an even simpler way of making a coil, if you have a hook from which to hang it.

Other useful ropework

Specialized knots doubtless evolved in part because they performed a single common function better than any other knot, and partly because they satisfied the skilled sailor's sense of professional artistry. Although you can get along forever without the bits of marlinspike seamanship that follow, I for one have found them amusing and helpful.

From time to time, you'll find it necessary to take the strain off a stressed line that cannot itself be untied—as, for instance, a sheet that's jammed in a winch override. The **rolling hitch**, shown on page 206 with its parent, the clove hitch, is a specialized knot that will allow you to make a second line fast to the first without slipping. The problem, of course, is that the application arises seldom, and so you're not likely to remember the knot when you need it.

Looking through an old manual of knots, I ran across the **topsail sheet bend**. It is, of course, just a clove hitch around the standing part of a line, to form a loop that may be snugged up tight (as the loop of a bowline cannot). Now I use it regularly on all my headsail sheets (and some halyards), because it minimizes the likelihood of a knotted sheet snagging on the standing rigging as the boat is tacked, and it also allows a deck-sweeping genoa to be sheeted right down to its trimming block.

The **fisherman's bend** is another loop that can be snugged up tight. The advantage of the doubled round turn at the beginning is that it retards chafe; the fisherman's bend is most frequently used as a temporary connection to an anchor ring or a shackle, since it won't chafe as much as a bowline will. For security, tape the end to the standing part.

I have not dealt here with purely decorative ropework, although that can be a genuine pleasure aboard a cruising yacht, both to do and to see. There are plenty of good books on the subject, and several are listed in the bibliography.

Topsail sheet bend

1. Essentially, this knot is a clove hitch made with the bitter end of a line around its own standing part. Because it makes a loop that can be drawn up snug, it is a good attachment for headsail sheets or halyards. After leading the line through the head or clew grommet, make one round turn.

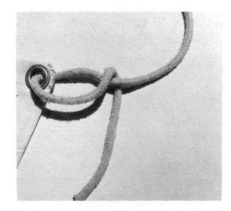

2. Complete the clove hitch, as shown. The second, securing part of the hitch is nearer the grommet; this prevents the knot from flogging loose.

3. Draw it up tight around the standing part.

4. Complete by snugging the loop.

5. Even doubled sheets make a tidy pair of knots.

Fisherman's bend

1. and 2. Lead the rode once through the anchor chain shackle, then double the loop.

3. Pass the bitter end around behind the standing part, then through the doubled loop.

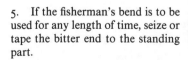

4. Draw the loop up tight and make a half-hitch around the standing part.

5. If the fisherman's bend is to be used for any length of time, seize or tape the bitter end to the standing part.

XI

~~~~~~~~~~~~~

Maintenance

In the halcyon days of yachting—not so very long ago—most skippers prided themselves on being able to jury-rig their boats in almost any emergency, but the normal, dreary procedures of routine maintenance they left to their boat-yard. Today, the situation is almost reversed: Boats have become so complex and their construction so sophisticated that expert repair is almost mandatory, while farming out the maintenance chores—scrubbing, waxing, bottom paint-ing—has become so costly and the work (thanks to modern products) so simple that more and more owners are doing their own upkeep work. To a certain extent, of course, maintenance does involve repair, but with a rigorous program of preventive maintenance, the only repair work you should encoun-ter will be that caused by accidents; you can expect to minimize or even eliminate repairs necessitated by neglect. This is, anyway, the case in every category except electronics, since water and electricity remain uneasy neigh-bors and, despite your best efforts, your boat's electrical system may succumb to a variety of mysterious ailments.

The place where you keep your boat, be it yacht club, marina, or old-fashioned boatyard, will determine how much of the work you will be able to take on yourself. While no place I know of objects to an owner cleaning his yacht, when it comes to repair work you may run into objections. In part such difficulties will stem from the yard's, club's or marina's natural desire to keep their own staff employed, but other owners often complain about having to pick their way among greasy engine parts strewn on the pier, or about finding that your varnishing work has caused their boat to be speckled with airborne droplets. So as soon as you decide what level of maintenance you're competent to undertake, check with your slip neighbors and the management as to how much of your boat's work they will allow you to handle.

Hull above the waterline

It's fair to say that the great majority of today's cruising sailboats are made of fiber glass; in fact, the imbalance is so large that this chapter will proceed on the assumption that all the boats under discussion are fiber glass. (For the same reason, I'm assuming that your spars are aluminum and your sails dacron and nylon.)

In the early years of fiber glass boats, prospective buyers used to hear fiber glass-reinforced plastic (the true name) described as "the no-maintenance material." In time, reality overtook enthusiasm, and owners now realize that while fiber glass can survive great periods of neglect, if it is to endure in presentable condition owners have to take some care of it. We have lately, in fact, gone slightly overboard in debunking the low-maintenance aspect of fiber glass, forgetting, perhaps, just how much trouble the classic carvel-planked wood hull was, or how critical is the proper maintenance of an aluminum or steel vessel. Be that as it may, while maintenance of a fiber glass hull does require tedious work, the tasks involved are not complicated. In most parts of the country, a fiber glass hull in good condition, used in salt water, should have something like the following maintenance program:

Before launching. Scrub the hull thoroughly with one of the new fiber glass cleaning compounds, making sure you remove all traces of salt, dirt, oil, and tar. Follow carefully the directions of the particular compound you use—most of them specify cleaning a small area of hull at a time, and then wiping or hosing the work area down immediately. When the hull is as clean as you can get it, give it a good coat of wax or silicone polish (I have used the latter for two seasons, with excellent results), buffed up to a high shine. When you're done, sight carefully along the hull to pick out spots you've missed; chances are you will find several. Remember that this wax coat is not only cosmetic but is also your hull's first line of defense, so apply it with care.

Between the waterline and the topsides proper there is frequently a strip of contrasting color called the boot-topping. On most modern boats it is simply a vinyl tape laid on over the gel-coat (the ultra-smooth outer layer of fiber glass), and it is thus prone to fading and chipping. It, too, should be waxed, and perhaps treated with a vinyl cleaner to bring back as much of its color as possible. If your boat rides at anchor in an open harbor, you may find that constant spray wetting the hull just above the waterline has allowed marine growth to establish itself in this intermediate zone. You have three choices: Scrub the area once a week or so, which isn't too good for the gel-coat or the boot-topping; cover the boot-topping in antifouling paint; or raise the water-line, and thus the level of antifouling paint, to a point above which wetting doesn't continually occur (you may have to apply a new taped boot-top above the new waterline). This problem is more common in a small cruiser which has been trimmed so the waterline is level when the crew is in the cockpit, and which consequently adopts a slightly bows-down attitude on the mooring, when the crew weight is removed. You may be able to remedy it by removing or restowing some of the major weights, or at least getting all of them out of the anchor locker, but chances are that antifouling the boot-top will be the most satisfactory solution in the long run. Obviously, if you elect to go this route, you won't apply wax or silicone over the antifouling.

During the season. Boat wax (or car wax, which is just as good) is very tough indeed, but you ought periodically to check your wax job. Especially in areas where you've had to scrub away stains or where a solvent, such as gasoline or diesel oil, has run down the boat's side, the wax may have perished. Consider a second complete wax job on some calm, cloudy day in midseason, or at least touching up the spots where the wax seems dim. Stains of any sort are best removed as soon as possible after they occur, and the removal process will probably call for rewaxing the area around the spot.

Haulout time. When the boating year is over, allow time to carefully inspect the entire hull. You will almost certainly find a number of previously unsuspected scars and dings in the smooth surface. Very slight gouges you can and probably should ignore, but if they pierce the gel-coat so that you can see the fiber glass cloth below, you should patch them. Perhaps the best material for this work is any one of the proprietary brands of epoxy filler, although automobile body compound will work quite well, too. For general marine applications requiring a puttylike compound that can be molded to complex shapes and then sanded after it hardens, I have found that a substance called Marine-Tex is quite satisfactory. After it hardens, a patch kit of gel-coat should disguise the scar beyond casual discovery. Of course, a colored gel-coat will be far harder to match than white, especially if the hull has been in service long enough for the color to fade slightly. (That alone is a good argument for white hulls.)

Deeper gashes that penetrate one or more of the boat's structural layers are more serious, although they may not be more difficult to cover up. If you can, try to inspect the fiber glass on the inside of the hull, opposite the damage: You should be able to tell if the wound is superficial or if the hull is cracked through. In the latter case, you may have to grind off the paint on the inside and put a fiber glass patch in place, to prevent leaks and to strengthen the hull at the critical point. Bear in mind that you must remove all paint or other surface treatment completely before trying to apply fiber glass to the surface —scrimping the paint removal, tempting as it may be, will just mean a failed job. Also remember that unsealed gashes through all or part of a fiber glass hull may allow moisture to leach into the hull and eventually to delaminate it. The same problem is even more pressing in the case of cored hulls or decks —that is, constructs involving a sandwich whose filler is either wood (ply or balsa) or an inert plastic foam, between two layers of fiber glass. Wood cores are especially prone to damage, and even rot, if penetrated by water. And if between-layers water freezes, it will expand and, perhaps, cause serious delamination.

Wood trim

Even the least expensive boats have some wood trim, and it does seem that a natural material like wood is necessary to warm up the chilly surface of fiber glass. There are differences of opinion as to how much wood a fiber glass boat needs, and of course the answers tend to be very personal. In most areas of the country, however, I would have to say that the practical answer is as little exterior wood as you can bear. While fiber glass requires a certain amount of scrubbing and waxing, wood necessitates much more close-in work if it's to retain its attractiveness—and shabby woodwork is guaranteed to make a shabby-looking boat, irrespective of how the rest of the vessel is cared for.

Exterior woodwork on today's boats is nearly always teak, with mahogany a distant second (on cheap craft the trim may be plywood, faced with the expensive wood on one or both surfaces.) Treatment of the two woods is quite different. Mahogany, which is generally richly red or red-brown when newly sanded, needs to be varnished to preserve its luster. Let nobody kid you about varnishing on a boat: It is a delicate, difficult, time-consuming job that must be done at least once and usually twice each year, depending on the climate, and the varnished surface must be taken back down to bare wood every three years or so. That's what makes teak so popular. Not only do you not have to varnish it, but you probably shouldn't even if you want to. The reason is that most teakwood is heavily impregnated with natural oil which not only makes it resistant to rot and deterioration but also makes it resist proper adhesion by paint or varnish. When teak *is* varnished after having been thoroughly dried out, it can present an eye-popping beauty; but if your boat's teak was oiled or "natural" (surface-bleached) when she was delivered, you would be well advised to leave it that way. The best oil for teak is something called tung oil. It's very expensive, but there are numerous commercial compounds containing some tung oil (they are often labeled as "teak oil" or "teak preservative"), and they will serve well.

Oiled exterior teak must be reoiled from time to time. The time span between oilings depends on the climate and on the amount of airborne pollution. For example, when I owned a Cheoy Lee thirty-footer with teak veneer cabin sides (oiled) and a laid deck of bleached teak planks, I at first kept her in Long Island Sound, about a quarter-mile downwind from a municipal powerplant. The filthy grit from the stacks assaulted both decks and cabin sides, turning the latter a dingy brownish-black, with particles of soot clinging to the oiled surface and coming off on clothes and skin. The bleached teak decks could be scrubbed and hosed relatively clean, but they, too, would turn gray after a couple of weeks. The result was that I had to scrub the oiled surfaces with a strong bleaching compound about every three weeks, to remove both surface oil and dirt, and reapply another coat of teak oil to restore the protective luster that also kept the teak from shrinking in the summer heat. At the same time, I would bleach and scrub the decks, but it was a considerable struggle to keep the teak oil off the newly-whitened decks, and eventually I wound up doing the job in two separate stages—cabin sides first, decks afterwards.

Somewhat later, I moved the boat about thirty miles away, where the breeze came in clean, directly off the ocean. I found that two months would pass before I even thought about the necessity for doing the wood surfaces, and a good oiling and bleaching would serve for three months at a stretch. The same is true in most places, except that the strong sun of the tropics will tend to dry and shrink teak veneer surfaces more quickly. In many parts of California, where the climate is both exceptionally warm and very smoggy, wood-trimmed boats live under elaborate cloth covers when they're not actually in use.

My present boat has, I think, reduced exterior wood to a minimum. The tiller, rudder head, and part of the outboard motor bracket are varnished oak —not, in my opinion, a terribly attractive wood, but strong and durable. One (removable) seat and the companionway hatch slide are teak-faced plywood, and the support member of the mainsheet track, about eighteen inches long, is varnished mahogany. Maintenance is simple, and the boat doesn't look too sterile. What's more, all the wood is functional, as opposed to those purely cosmetic teak strips and slabs set into the fiber glass on some boats.

Interior wood offers few maintenance problems. Generally speaking, it is oiled teak, although some boats are now appearing with bulkheads of varnished ash or pine—light-colored woods that brighten a dark cabin. Varnished wood should last almost indefinitely below, and even oiled wood needs only to be waxed twice a year. I use commercial furniture polish, because it works well and because its smell is less oppressive than that of teak oil.

Deck and deck fittings

Virtually all yachts today have some sort of nonskid surface where the crew will put their feet. As a rule, this consists of a textured gel-coat, although in some cases builders rely on paint with a nonskid additive, such as ground cork, mixed in. While good nonskid is certainly vital to the safety of all aboard, it's a surface that by its design is bound to trap small particles of dirt and grit, which are then very difficult to hose out of the thousands of indentations. There are perhaps two keys to keeping your nonskid clean; first, sluice the decks frequently with fresh water from a high-pressure hose, and second, don't let the remaining residue set—go after it with a stiff-bristled brush and cleanser as soon as it becomes visible. For my money, cleaning a nonskid deck on a boat that's kept downwind of a coal-burning powerplant is perhaps the most arduous maintenance chore in today's yachting, bottom painting not excepted. But if you don't do it faithfully and energetically, the boat will look terrible.

Deck fittings, too, come in for deposits of salt and dirt. To keep gear working easily and well, it's important to combat the kind of build-up that can freeze sheaves and rust stainless steel. Vinyl surfaces, such as ventilators and lifelines, are easy to clean with just about any mild scouring powder and fresh water, and this is definitely the kind of job that can be turned over to the kids—the work is not hard and the results are pleasantly dramatic.

Nonmoving metal parts, such as lifeline stanchions and pulpits, may be stainless steel, but they tend to acquire rust streaks, especially in hard-to-reach corners. Marine metal cleaners designated for use on stainless steel will work well, but after using them and hosing down the cleaned surface with fresh water, consider waxing the fittings as you did the hull—it will protect them to a degree and will make the next cleaning easier. Electrical fittings on deck, such as running lights and the dials of your speedo/log, depth sounder, and wind gauges, should not be hosed too vigorously or too long: While most of them start out waterproof, running lights especially can be drowned by repeated wetting, and they will get quite wet enough in the normal course of things. It is good practice to disassemble each running light once a season and inspect the interior to ensure it hasn't become damp. At the same time, check the sizes and part numbers of the running light bulbs and get spares for your tool kit, and replace the light's gasket if necessary.

The moving parts on the deck of a sailboat—winches and blocks and traveler cars, for the most part—are designed to function adequately even when not freshly cleaned or lubricated. Obviously, they work a good deal more smoothly if properly maintained. Blocks and traveler cars should be hosed clean regularly and lubricated once a month or so with WD-40 or a similar spray. Once a year, I clean all the blocks on my boat with gasoline (left-over outboard fuel) and re-lube them. Pretty much the same treatment applies to winches, except that when it comes to annual maintenance, disassemble them with great care, preferably with an exploded-parts diagram close at hand so you know what goes where when you put them back together again. Small winches, like the popular #10s made by most manufacturers, are very simple contraptions with few moving parts. The bits that do move, however, are very prone to escaping, and spare springs and pawls are a worthwhile addition to any spare-parts kit. Winches require greasing at least annually, and perhaps monthly if they are heavily used. I have found a water-resistant engine waterpump grease quite adequate, but there are special compounds available in chandleries for those who care enough to overspend.

Hull below the waterline

To the cruising sailor, racers never seem so eccentric as when they are painting their boat's bottom. No sooner do they coat it with a bottom paint that costs about as much as liquid gold than they rush at their work with wet-or-dry sandpaper and proceed to reduce their investment to clouds of noxious dust. The cruising sailor, on the other hand, is inclined to slap a coat of antifouling over last year's and leave it at that.

Perhaps a middle course is the most sensible. To begin with, if you care anything at all about performance, there is no question that the condition of the boat's bottom is of vital importance. A smooth, growth-free surface can make an easy knot's difference in your speed under power, and even more under sail. My own recommendation is that you use two coats of a good antifouling popular in your boating area. (There are different chemical conformations and none is ideal, but some have local advantages.) Compounds designed specifically for racing are probably not the best for the cruising sailor, as they sacrifice some antifouling property for ease in attaining a super-smooth surface.

Your object is to avoid surface roughness in the finished effort, and this means sanding with fairly coarse wet-or-dry sandpaper after the first coat of paint, and with medium-fine after the second. The idea of wet-or-dry sandpaper is that it can be hosed constantly, both to damp down the poisonous dust and to keep the paper itself from clogging; wet-or-dry costs more than the regular stuff and is well worth it.

For the first three weeks or a month, you will probably have a reasonably smooth surface. Then, as the surrounding water heats up, growth will form. If you don't scrub the hull occasionally, you'll wonder after about three months if you painted the hull at all. In warm, shallow waters, marine growth develops at an astonishing rate, and the only way to keep abreast of it is to scrub the boat's bottom about once every two weeks. This should not be too burdensome a task, since it involves only a sponge. Only if you let the weed get to the point where it has a real foothold does it become a job for a stiff-bristle brush.

Do not paint transducers or paddlewheels except with antifouling particularly designed for that application. As you are sanding the hull preparatory to painting, check the through-hull fittings below the waterline for barnacle accumulation from previous seasons. Also check around the rudder's pintles and gudgeons and the propeller shaft—indeed, anywhere you might have missed with the brush or were unable to paint.

The first and most important step toward next year's clean hull is this year's scrubdown immediately after haulout. When the boat first emerges is the moment that barnacles and weed are easiest to dislodge. Only a few days' wait and they solidify amazingly. With the boat's bottom thoroughly scrubbed, you can examine it for dings and gouges—people do run aground occasionally— and fill them with Marine-Tex or some other patching compound. If the hull has been broken through to where you can see raw fiber glass mat or cloth, allow the gash to drain for a week or so before patching. If the gouge is a large one, you may be best advised to drill a small hole into the cloth to make draining easier, but don't do this unless you observe the initial wound still visibly oozing after a week on dry land.

Interiors

Although the cruising yacht's interior lives a relatively sheltered life, it is damp most of the time and frequently very wet. Boats that are sailed in salt water soon acquire below decks a fine film of salt which tends to retain moisture and accelerate mildew and the demise of electrical parts. A proper cruising interior is made so that it can, if necessary, be hosed down, but there are very few proper interiors. Instead, you will have to go at it piecemeal, but the effort will be worth the trouble, as once mildew is established in a boat, it requires a lot of work to kill it.

Vital to a clean and dry interior are, first, an absence of leaks both above and below the waterline and, second, regular cleaning. Most fiber glass boats have relatively few possibilities for below-waterline leaks—the propeller shaft, engine water intake, and toilet and sink fittings. Although the propeller shaft can never be completely dry—nor should it be—the amount of water taken into the boat past a well-packed shaft is very small and easily contained in the usual sump. Engine water intakes are seldom a problem, nor are sink drain through-hulls. That leaves the toilet intake and outflow valves, which are, alas, the usual culprits. All through-hull pipes below the waterline ought to be fitted with seacocks—simple, positive-action valves of robust construction. Even the waterline and above-waterline pipes, often fitted with faucet-type gate valves, would be better closed by seacocks, but the savage cost of these bronze fittings makes them the first economy of price-conscious builders. Seacocks require relatively little maintenance; some have grease fittings that accept the business end of a grease gun and some must be disassembled, when the boat is hauled, in order to grease them, but this annual attention, using a water-resistant grease, is very important if the valves are not to freeze from disuse. A frozen seacock is an invitation to an impatient crew member's hammer, which will probably open it, but which is all too likely to cause leaks in the bedding compound that seats the valve base to the hull. If there is evidence—usually visible—of persistent oozing from around the base plate of a seacock or any through-hull fitting, you're being warned that the whole thing should probably be removed, examined to make sure it's still sound and not cracked, and then re-bedded and replaced.

Deck leaks, which can include ports, hatches, and through-deck fittings, are more pernicious in a fiber glass boat than leaks from through-hull fittings. Quite often, a topsides leak will manifest itself by a drip—traditionally, over the pillow of the skipper's berth—that may be many feet away from the source of the leak. The water has migrated behind the hull or overhead liner, or along the frame of a port or hatch, and it can be a maddening job to track down where the water is really coming in. Generally speaking, it's not worth your while to attack such a leak by stemming just the drip; better to devote some time and trouble to finding the source. This may involve removing some of the liner, which will then have to be replaced, and unless your boat has one of the convenient removable liners, it's a job for a professional. Finding the entry point for a hatch or porthole leak is a different matter. Nearly always it will be around the perimeter of the fitting, and one way to isolate it is to construct temporary coffer dams of epoxy putty to wall off sections of the hatch or porthole edge. These sealed-off areas can then be wetted down, one at a time, and if the water doesn't make its appearance down below, you can assume that the section in question is leak-free.

A porthole or hatch that leaks regularly even in light rain will probably have to be removed and its frame re-bedded, and so will a deck fitting—a cleat, for example—that allows water to leach past its through-deck attachments. While it is no great job to extract and replace something like a cleat, a porthole or hatch can pose a considerable problem, and unless you can easily see a method for removing it, you would probably do better to get professional assistance.

Chainplates that come through the deck and are made fast to thwartships bulkheads are especially prone to leaks, which often arise after the rig has been severely stressed; the chainplate works in time with the rig and with the bulkheads, while the deck may flex to a slightly different rhythm, and the result is that the through-deck seal is broken. The best answer is usually to remove as much of the original flexible bedding compound as you can and replace it with new material of the same type. Because many modern sealants are not mutually compatible, it's important to be sure that you are using the same substance that was originally employed, although you may have to go to the builder to find out what it was.

If you're unlucky, you may find that after a while your boat will develop leaks around the hull-to-deck joint. There are half a dozen ways of joining a fiber glass deck to its hull, but the best involve several similar elements. First, the hull and deck are so constructed that one part forms a flange or lip over the other; then, this joint is solidly bedded, either with flexible compound or by fiber glassing the two elements together; finally, the joint is locked in place by through-bolts (not screws), capped either by ordinary washers and locknuts or by locking washers and nuts. The idea, as you can see, is to create a bond that is initially leak-free and built to stay that way by being as rigid as possible. The result, of course, is to make a connection that is extraordinarily hard to work on—besides the original complexity, matters are often further complicated on the outside by a cosmetic rubrail and on the inside by a hull liner. A leak of this type in a well-built boat is probably best ignored, unless you can cure it by finding and plugging a single point on the outside where the water is entering. Other than such a quick and lucky fix, you are probably doomed.

Installing fittings

Sooner or later, every owner of a cruising boat wants to attach fittings to the deck or hull. It seems simplicity itself: Drill the requisite holes for the machine screws, slap some bedding on the outside and a piece of plywood on the inside, and there you are. In practice, however, it may not be so simple. To begin with, before you even buy the fitting in question, ask yourself seriously if you really need it and, if the answer is yes, if you know exactly where it must go. It is very easy to permanently mar a gel-coated surface with a bad installation, which you must then either live with or move to where it should have been in the first place, leaving (at best) some scars behind. If it's at all possible, you will do well to silver-tape the fitting in place first, and sail with it in that trial location until you've decided that this is the proper spot. Of course you won't be able to put any stress on (for example) a taped-on cleat, but you should be able to tell if the necessary lines will lead correctly.

Having determined the best site from the outside—or the side on which the fitting is to face—then examine the inside, to make sure that that part of the hull or deck is accessible: In fits of enthusiasm I have drilled right through the deck of a boat I owned, only to find that there was no possible way to get at the bolt in order to thread a nut over the end of it from the other side. You may have to settle for a less-than-ideal location that is accessible from both sides.

Consider also the composition of the material through which you plan to drill. Time was that a fiber glass hull or deck was just that—several layers of fiber glass cloth and mat, impregnated (you hoped) with resin. Nowadays, many decks and some hulls are sandwiches of material between two layers of glass. If the core is hard, as plywood is, you will have no trouble through-bolting anything you like, although you must take special care in bedding the attachment, to make sure that no water seeps into the core. More flexible materials, such as polyurethane foam, can easily be crushed when you tighten down on the nut. The only way to insert a through-core fitting here is to employ a metal sleeve around the bolt. You may even have, as I did, a harder substance to deal with. When installing a speedometer/log transducer through my present boat's hull, I had first to find a spot where I would not hit one of the molded-in lead plates that formed the integral ballast; then I had to cut away the inner liner and scoop out the flotation foam that also held the lead in place, before I could at last address the actual hull skin.

Many yachts that arrive with soft-cored decks will have islands of plywood core at strategic points, for the installation of deck winches and the like. You will—or should—be aware if your boat's deck is cored, and with what. If it's something like foam or balsa, then ask your dealer to show you where the plywood core area is—it may well be marked by flat, smooth, slightly raised platforms in the gel-coat deck.

Unless you have already worked on that part of the boat, it is probably a good idea to drill a pilot hole first, to determine depth, before investing in machine screws and nuts. If you're lucky, you'll be able to get standard-length machine screws that will protrude about ¼" beyond the washer. This will allow you to use an acorn or cap nut, which will make for a much less unsightly interior. Or you may employ vinyl caps that fit over standard locknuts and dress them up. In either case, try to avoid marring the inside or the exterior fiber glass—first drill narrow-diameter pilot holes and then follow up with the proper size holes for the hardware you're using.

If the fitting you're installing will take a lot of stress in the course of its job —as will, for example, a deck cleat—you should back up the fitting on the underside of the deck or cabin with some sort of plate designed to spread the load beyond the immediate area of the through-bolts and washers. The backing plate should be as large as is conveniently possible but, size aside, what's important is that the backing surface fit snugly up against the underside of the mounting structure. This can be a problem with many rough-finished under-decks, although the unevenness can be ground down to a certain extent. My own solution is to use epoxy putty between the plate and the deck, to form a temporarily flexible filling. The putty will not serve as bedding compound, since it eventually sets up hard, and so regular flexible bedding should be used between the fitting and the deck. The backing plate should have both its edges and corners rounded off, to avoid creating abrupt linear stresses in the deck.

One final word on fittings: Many novelty gadgets—hooks, holders, and racks, for instance—are sold with adhesive backing that is claimed to be adequate for actual installation. In my experience, this is seldom the case, and the device not only comes away from the bulkhead but leaves a stain behind as well. Unless a fitting can be screwed or, preferably, bolted in place, it probably has no business on a boat.

Galley stoves

When I began cruising, nearly every boat under thirty-five feet overall had a two-burner pressure alcohol stove, one of the world's supremely inefficient appliances. In more and more new boats, the old alcohol stove has been replaced—often at extra cost, as an option—by a bottled-gas stove with a small oven. The replacement would probably be nearly universal, given the tremendous advantages of the gas over the alcohol units, were it not for the Coast Guard's opposition to bottled gas. Be that as it may, the general maintenance required of gas and alcohol stoves is about the same, and consists mostly of the kind of thorough, behind-the-stove cleaning that cannot be done without removing the whole device. While you are at it, examine closely the gaskets that seal the top of the pressure alcohol tank and the fittings in the fuel line, and the fuel line itself. If the gaskets or the line show signs of age—cracks or stiffness—replace them.

The bottled-gas fuel line is even more critical, and the fittings at tank and stove must be pressure tight. My own feeling is that a solenoid safety switch is an excellent investment; it consists of an electrically activated shut-off at the gas tank, which is (or should be) mounted on deck or in a self-draining cockpit locker. The switch can be operated from the galley, and a red light is lit when the gas line is open.

If you disconnect and then reconnect the gas line, be sure to test it for pressure tightness. A properly functioning human nose is the first test instrument, followed by a slight smear of liquid soap around the joints: A bubble there equals a leak. Leaks around burners are common in older stoves employing any of the common fuels. They are probably of no significance as long as they're small and burn along with the burner flame, so that the leaked gas, kerosene, or alcohol is consumed. Leaks that allow gas or liquid fuel to accumulate at a distance from the burner flame are a different situation, however, and will sooner or later lead to explosion or fire. A stove repairman can fix them better than you can.

Plumbing

In the Northeast and Great Lakes, frozen waterpipes are a perennial problem for cruising sailors. Even a simple water system can be a monster to drain thoroughly, and even a small pocket of standing water can freeze and burst a pipe. One answer has been to fill the system with nonpoisonous antifreeze, sold for the purpose in most marine stores. Just mix it in the ship's watertank with the suggested proportion of water, then pump the mixture through the pipes until it runs from the faucets; the most popular type of antifreeze is tinted blue, so you have visual reassurance of its arrival. Grain alcohol, if you can find it, serves equally well, and it guarantees a stimulating first cruise the following summer too—but avoid wood alcohol, which is, of course, a deadly poison.

In marine toilets and the engine fresh- and raw-water cooling pipes, automotive antifreeze should work perfectly well. Before using it in a marine sanitation device, check your owner's manual to make sure that ethylene glycol, the standard component of antifreeze, will not harm the device's innards. To run antifreeze through the engine's raw-water cooling system, disconnect the raw-water intake hose at the seacock (first closing the seacock if you're still afloat, to be sure). Premix a couple of gallons of antifreeze (the usual proportions are fifty-fifty, but check the container), and stand by with a large funnel. Start the engine and, as soon as it catches, pour the antifreeze into the hose, and keep pouring without interruption until an observer, stationed at the exhaust pipe, reports a steady stream of antifreeze mix pumping out. Shut down the engine, plug the exhaust, and reconnect the intake hose, being careful to tag the closed intake seacock with a sign to indicates the engine has been antifreezed. I put a similar tag on the ignition, as well.

Many deep-keel boats with shallow bilges have sumps to collect bilgewater, and some deep-bilged boats have accidental water-trap spaces underneath metal watertanks in the keel. Ideally, all such places where water could collect, freeze, and damage the hull should be dried out before hauling, but it's not unknown for small leaks around hatches and ports to result in a considerable accumulation of water in the bilge, and so it doesn't hurt to pour a little antifreeze into an exceptionally deep or hard-to-reach sump, and replenish it periodically. One type of fitting especially prone to problems of freezing is the cockpit drain, which can become clogged by dirt or leaves, and can collect water in its tubing (which is inside the the hull) and then freeze and burst, with the consequent chance of flooding the hull. A good cockpit cover is the best insurance, backed up by regular owner inspections.

At least once a year, and probably in the spring, the whole fresh-water system should be cleaned and flushed. This simple and important procedure is becoming harder and harder to accomplish, because fewer and fewer water-tanks are being made with access ports. Without such ports, you're probably restricted to flushing and occasional prophylactic treatment of the watertanks with commercial water purifier or a small amount—about a teaspoonful—of household ammonia. This should prevent the growth of bacteria or slime in the tanks, but you can help by never allowing the water in the tanks to stand longer than necessary, especially in hot weather.

Electrical system

As I've said elsewhere, electricity and water are uneasy partners at best. Most builders of small boats have in the past minimized the potential for problems by keeping the electrical system basic, rugged, and visible, but in recent years the attempt to give even small cruisers all the comforts of a shoreside home has led to increasingly complex and vulnerable electrical systems, cosmetically concealed from sight (and repair) behind bulkheads and hull liners. It may sound cynical to say so, but if your boat has an elaborate, built-in electrical system, you will almost certainly have a certain number of difficulties because of it. And if the original system can be exasperating, its problems are likely to be minor compared with those of any add-on system installed later.

Assuming that the primary installation work has been adequately done (no small assumption, based on a lot of boats I've seen), the keys to the system's future health are the batteries, the wiring and connectors, and the fuse or circuit-breaker panel. If your boat has an inboard engine or electric-start outboard, you should have a separate battery for engine starting, aside from whatever you have for lighting and electronics. Be sure that your batteries are rated for heavy-duty marine use, and for diesel application, if that applies. It is probably too late to do anything about it now, but batteries should be located where they can easily be inspected (for clean connections and electrolyte level), serviced, and extracted. Further, they must be covered, so that a metal tool, falling across the terminals, cannot cause a short; and they must be secured against coming adrift, even in a complete rollover. Normal building practice is to chock batteries in place, usually in a ventilated plastic box, but they are seldom properly strapped down.

Your engine may or may not have a so-called battery condition meter; this is not the same as an ammeter, which indicates what the battery is doing at a given moment, but rather a gauge that shows the state of charge. Battery condition meters are not costly, and they are a good thing to have. You should check the batteries' electrolyte level and state of charge every week, as well as monitoring the ammeter while the engine is running. Aside from occasional topping up with distilled water and wire brushing of the terminals, there isn't a great deal of maintenance a wet-cell battery requires. Plan on taking your batteries home in the winter and charging them up occasionally. (Current wisdom says that leaving them on a slow trickle charge is not a good idea.) And figure on replacing them after about three years' service.

Thanks to the product liability lawsuits brought in so many fields, boatbuilders are no longer so prone as they once were to economize by using skimpy, cheap wiring. Where they are still likely to err, however, is in protection of that wire as it goes about the boat. Check once a year to be certain that wiring isn't chafing where it goes through bulkheads (it should be encased in plastic conduits in any case) or makes sharp bends, as in entering the mast, for example. Wiring should not lie in wet bilges, or anyplace else where it will be continually soaked, nor should it be any longer than required—coils of "extra" wire are always getting snagged and torn free.

Wiring problems are most likely to occur at the ends. I've found it pays to invest in a good pair of variable-sized crimping pliers and assorted terminals, so that I can replace terminals that fall off or that were unsatisfactory in size or conformation. Wiring that ends outside the hull—at running lights, mast-head gauges, and the like—is especially prone to shorts caused by water penetration. Proper terminals, taped ends, and an occasional squirt of moisture inhibitor, such as CRC 6-66, will work wonders, if not miracles. If you plan to install new electrical or electronic appliances, make sure the installation is done with function, not cosmetics, as the primary concern. Check the appliance's installation instructions for the proper wire gauge, and don't try to get away with domestic lamp or speaker wire. Even if there seems to be a convenient shelf on which the wire can lie, secure it in place with brackets or straps. At the switchboard, make certain that the fusing is of the proper size for the load imposed; you may have to double up on an existing circuit, which should offer no great problems with low-demand electronic devices.

Spend a couple of hours learning your boat's circuit boards. Most of the fuse or circuit-breaker panels for small cruisers are quite elementary, but it is far easier to learn what each component does when you're undistracted than it is when you're exhausted, furious, and trying to figure out the wiring while holding a flashlight between your teeth. Even if the system has been color-coded, you may find it helpful to letter some waterproof tags and tape them to the wires. A switchboard must by its nature be located in a dry place, and because of the need to keep the main run of wiring from the engine and batteries as short as possible, most such panels are near (often under) the companionway steps. If the board is in a place where it may get splashed or splattered, and if it has no cover, provide one. As with other electrical components, fuse and circuit-breaker panels can benefit from an occasional misting with CRC 6-66 or some other moisture-excluding spray.

Miscellany

Watching boatowners over the years, I've come to the conclusion that the ones with the best-maintained boats are those who periodically strip their craft of everything that can be removed, cleaning the gear at home and the emptied boat on the spot. Probably twice a year is normal—at commissioning and then again at haulout. What gets taken home to be cleaned or serviced, and then stored in a dry place? Food, clothing, bedding, mattresses, cushions, tools, batteries, electronics, fire extinguishers, moving fittings (blocks and cars, for the most part), rigging, sails, and books and charts. If you want to really do it right, you may also remove floorboards, stove, and even winches. Needless to say, storing all this stuff can put quite a strain on even a fair-sized attic or basement, and there is no point to the exercise unless the storage location is drier and better protected than the boat from which the gear came. There is also little point in simply stuffing the equipment away; clean it carefully, survey it to see if professional repair or replacement is necessary, and wrap it carefully for storage.

Spars

I can remember quite easily the amount of work required to maintain the wood spars of my old thirty-foot ketch. Counting spreaders, there were eight pieces of wood that had to be sanded and varnished every season, and although the total area was not large, it was the single most expensive and time-consuming job the boat entailed. I must admit, though, that the mellow glow of a well-varnished mast is terribly attractive to the eye, and while wood spars have absolutely no practical advantages over aluminum, they are marvelous to look at, preferably on someone else's boat.

Because their numbers have diminished almost to vanishing point, I won't bother with discussing the maintenance of wood spars. Aluminum will keep you quite busy enough. Any well-made spar on a boat today is anodized aluminum, and it may also be painted, usually black. Painting does add an extra protective coat to the metal's surface, but it is hardly necessary. Annual maintenance of painted or anodized aluminum is quite simple, and is very similar to the upkeep program for one's fiber glass hull. In the spring, scrub down the spars, lubricate moving parts—cheek blocks and halyard sheaves—with WD-40 or some other long-lasting coating, and then wax the surface and buff it up to a shine. If your black-painted spar has sustained a scrape that's left a shiny patch, you can darken it with a Magic Marker and wax over the ink. It's not perfect, but it will serve.

At decommissioning time, I simply repeat the process above, but with the additional steps of removing the internal halyards and replacing them temporarily with "messengers" of ⅛" flag halyard, and (after waxing) wrapping the spars in plastic leaf bags, which are then taped in place. The spars—especially the mast—must lie flat, but because of the various protrusions all around, it's almost impossible to lay them on the floor without the likelihood of damage. I keep the wrapped spar on the lawn, propped off the ground at about five-foot intervals.

My present spar has no internal wiring, which is a blessing in terms of maintenance. Generally speaking, it's more trouble than it's worth to remove running light or anemometer wires for storage, although it is a good idea to detach the lights, vanes, and spinners for a thorough cleaning and lubrication, with new gaskets when they are refitted.

Installing a new fitting on an aluminum spar is no great problem, as long as you follow a few simple rules. First, you must take pains to avoid contact between bare aluminum and galvanically dissimilar metals that will corrode it. In practice, this means avoiding bronze or brass, but most manufacturers of fittings have a full line of gear suitable for attachment to aluminum. Second, the fitting should seat cleanly and snugly against the curved surface of the spar, which can be a problem if the fitting—a winch, say—has a broad, flat base. Here again, manufacturers have anticipated the need, and you can usually find, at a good chandler's, a preformed aluminum pad, flat on one side and curved on the other, to make a proper seat. Many fittings, especially cheek blocks and cleats, have curved bases anyway, and will sit comfortably on a standard spar. Third, select the proper fastenings. If you have a new spar and plan to do a lot of work on it, you may find it convenient to buy a pop-riveting tool, which allows you to install rivets from one side only. For most of us, however, it is easier to invest in one or two taps of the proper diameter. Most marine hardware catalogs will note the correct fastenings for a given piece of hardware; for small cruisers, #10 or #12 machine screws are ubiquitous, round head, flat head or oval head being dictated by the particular application, and obvious at a glance. Winches, cleats, and other highly stressed fittings may take ¼" fittings, and of course stainless steel is the only material even to consider.

Although aluminum is a very soft metal, it is easier to drill a small pilot hole first and then follow up with a drilled hole of proper size—the tap's package will (or should) indicate the proper size drill to use with it.

The actual tapping is the trickiest part, but if you have reasonable dexterity and patience, and haven't tried to do the job on a boat bobbing at anchor, you should have no problem. I have virtually no dexterity and less patience, and I've done it successfully, so take heart. The machine screws must obviously go all the way through the spar wall, with a little to spare on the other side, but they don't need to be any longer than that—a half-inch protruding from the base of the fitting should be plenty, when you're estimating length.

Try to avoid putting any more fittings on a spar than you have to, as each set of holes does weaken the basic structure somewhat; and of course take great care in establishing exactly where a fitting should go before making it fast, because once you've drilled the first pilot hole, you're committed.

Most smaller cruisers have deck-stepped masts, which are probably not as strong as keel-stepped spars but which do make for a considerably drier boat. A keel-stepped mast will admit some water down below—there's no way to prevent it—but you can keep leaks to a minimum with a proper mast boot. If you're handy with fabric, you can make one (there's a good set of illustrated instructions in Hervey Garrett Smith's marvelous book, *The Arts of the Sailor*), or you can ask your sailmaker to run one up for you. To keep the boot truly waterproof, you'll need to caulk around it each season with flexible compound, then remove the old caulking with a solvent when the mast is unstepped. So when you buy the compound, first check the label to see what the approved solvents are, and then make sure that both are compatible with the boot fabric: This is one of the trials you must face when using modern "miracle" materials.

Standing and running rigging

Exposure month after month to acid rain and fly ash can make your boat's rigging filthy and even corroded. Once a year it's a good idea to examine and clean or replace all the rigging elements, and haulout time is probably the most logical point for this exercise. I run all my boat's rope halyards through the clothes washer, using ordinary detergent and cold water, and while the neat coils that go in are invariably reduced to incredible tangles at the end of the spin cycle, the lines themselves are thoroughly clean; they can be coiled and stowed away during the off-season in some dry place. Rope-and-wire halyards are another story, since the wire rattling about your family washer can remove a good deal of the appliance's enamel. I have found that soaking the halyards in cool water and detergent overnight, then draining, hand-washing with detergent, draining, and rinsing out the soap gets them about as clean as one can reasonably expect.

A halyard tends to wear at the mid-point, as a rule—where it goes over the sheave when the boat isn't in use. A secondary wear point is where the halyard runs over the sheave when the sail is fully raised, but this is likely to be a factor only in rope halyards. You have a right to expect at least a couple of years from your halyards, and if they seem to be chafing sooner than that, it would be a good idea to check the exits from the sheave boxes at the masthead, and nearby hardware (especially exposed cotter pins), as sources of chafe. Once a rope halyard has worn to the point where it becomes risky to hoist the sail, there is really no choice but to remove it, excise the worn section, and use the rest for docklines.

Wire normally needs little care, but you should check it for broken strands

—"meat hooks"—sticking out from the surface, and for visible corrosion or cracks in the end fitting, which is usually a Nicopressed loop. Meathooks can be cut back, but more than one or two in the same place are a warning that the wire is being bent too sharply. If the breaks come where the wire goes over the sheave when the sail is raised, then the diagnosis is very strong, and you should consider, if possible, having the sheave replaced with one of larger diameter, or changing to all-rope halyards.

Standing rigging may be wrapped to the mast when it is stored, or it may be removed, cleaned, and oiled, and stored in loose coils under shelter. In either case, be sure to check the cotter pins and replace them if they're badly twisted. Remove the turnbuckles and take them apart for a good scrubbing with kerosene or gasoline; then spray them with WD-40 or oil, wrap them to prevent their picking up dust and grit, and store them away.

If you use polyvinyl chloride (PVC) turnbuckle boots and shroud covers, these should of course be removed, thoroughly scrubbed, and cleaned with a mild abrasive. If they're waxed after that, they will pick up a little less grime next season.

I've made it a practice to remove all the removable blocks from my spars each fall. I wash and then hose the blocks down with fresh water, and some evening when there's an appropriately simple-minded movie on TV, I sit down in front of the set with my trusty spray can of WD-40 and lubricate the sheaves and bearings of the blocks, then seal them in a plastic bag for storage.

Sails

Taking care of sails on a cruising boat during the sailing season isn't easy, mostly because of the lack of room aboard. Even so, you should make an effort from time to time to rinse the saltwater and grime out of sails, to avoid mildew. Perhaps the easiest way is to come in from sailing a bit early one calm, sunny day and hose off the sails while they're hoisted, leaving them to luff gently until they dry before lowering and folding them.

There are probably half a dozen perfectly adequate ways to fold sails, and it has always amazed me how passionate some sailors—especially racers— become about the "only right way" to do it. The essential points are simple enough: Folded reasonably flat, a sail takes up far less space down below, and it acquires far fewer wrinkles; folded too flat, the fabric will tend to crack along the folds.

My own system—which is shared with thousands of other sailors—seems to work quite well. It is especially suited to mainsails with roped luffs (as opposed to luffs fitted with slides or slugs, which remain on or in the track), and these roped luffs, being cheaper and easier to make, seem to be more common each year. Ideally, you will have three people at hand: One lowers the mainsail slowly, while the other two fold it into flakes across the boom.

Furling the mainsail on its boom

1. Flake the mainsail back and forth on top of the boom; the slippery dacron will try to escape, so be sure to have several sail ties available. With about half the sail flaked, stop off the sail toward the clew.

2 and 3. With about two-thirds of the sail flaked, stop it off toward the luff. Be sure to hold the unsecured part of the sail, to keep it under control.

4. Stop the head of the sail, which should be more or less in the middle of the boom. (Try to avoid a big pile-up of roped luff next to the mast.)

5. Attach the sail cover over the stopped sail. Most inexpensive sail covers are just a rectangle with a row of eyes along one long side and a row of hooks along the other. The short ends have drawstrings. Because of the cover's shape, the sail should be furled to make a roll of even diameter along the boom.

Folding a jib

1. Flake the sail along the side deck, with the unfurled portion of sail lying loosely across the deck.

2. Work forward past the shrouds.

3. With the sail completely flaked down, start at the clew and fold it forward, making fairly tight folds.

4. The idea is to arrive at the bow with a neat package.

5. The diameter of the folded sail should be such that it will fit easily into the bag, with the tack grommet and all the snaps in a visible row.

A little experience will tell you how big the flakes should be to fit completely under the sail cover. The only drawback to this system is that in any kind of wind, the slippery sail fabric develops an incredible desire to escape from the neat flakes and go over the side. This method also works reasonably well with mainsails having slugs or slides along the luff, but it will probably be easier to employ the more traditional method of lowering the sail completely, then making a hammocklike bunt with the foot, into which the sail is flaked. Fold the stuffed bunt over the boom and secure it with a couple of sail ties before putting on the sail cover.

The easiest place to fold a jib carefully is of course on a grassy lawn ashore. Somehow, there never seems to be one where I am, and I've found that it's nearly as simple to fold the sail right on deck. You may use the system shown in the photographs on pages 234 and 235, or you may, in calm weather, lower the sail slowly, while two crew members flake it down without detaching the luff snaps. With the sail stretched out on the side deck and fully flaked, it can then be folded from aft forward; slip the bag over the folded sail, then undo the snaps.

Spinnaker folding is presumably something most people learn before they have the temerity to fly the chute in the first place, but if it has somehow missed you, consult the photographs in Chapter III.

If you have the money, you should take your sails to the sailmaker at haulout time; ask him to survey them for defects and then wash them professionally before returning them to you. You can, of course, wash your sails yourself; they will get reasonably clean and the exercise, approached in the proper spirit, can be hilarious, especially if you enjoy little pools of water throughout your home. In my experience, the best place to wash sails is in the bathtub, using a mild detergent. There are several good commercial preparations for removing specific stains, but aside from spot removal, the most important part of washing is simply rinsing out grit and salt; for that reason, a couple of good soaks are probably more important than the soaping, and I always try to finish off by flying the sail between a couple of trees and hosing it down, before letting it dry. Sails should be stored in a dry place where mice aren't likely to be able to use them as nests.

Fall is the best point at which to survey your sails, because most sailmakers are able to give their best attention to you in the autumn, and sometimes their schedules are sufficiently slack so that they'll offer a discount on work done before Christmas. If you're checking your own sails, here are some things to look for:

Headsails. Examine all the grommets, to make sure that they're still securely in place and that they haven't elongated under stress. Inspect the jib luff snaps for wear, and replace ones that seem badly eroded. Check the leech area for chafe and torn threads, especially where the spreaders hit the sail, and do the same for the foot, concentrating on the places where the sail rubs the lifelines, stanchions, and bow pulpit. Check all the seams, concentrating on the multiple reinforcements at head, tack, and clew; you're looking for seam threads that have chafed through or are in the process of doing so. Because dacron is a hard, unyielding surface, stitching tends to protrude from the surface, vulnerable to snags and wear. You may be able to repair minor problems yourself with the aid of dacron thread and sail needles, but a sailmaker will do a better job. Tears in a sail are often triangular, and while they can be temporarily repaired with adhesive-backed sail tape (you should carry two kinds—nylon for spinnakers and dacron for everything else), this is an area where a professional repair is really worth the money.

Mainsails. In addition to the seams and reinforcements, check the mainsail's slides, slugs, or bolt rope on both luff and foot. Most sailmakers use mechanically attached slides, and you should have a couple of spare slides and shackles, and perhaps half a dozen pieces of the plastic shielding that fits inside the shackle and keeps it from chafing the luff fabric. The primary areas for wear on a mainsail are the batten pockets and the places where the spreaders rub the fabric on a run. Be sure that your battens are adequately padded, and take the time now to list the sizes of your battens in case you need to replace a lost one.

Ground tackle

Most small cruisers have two anchoring rigs—the working and the storm set-ups—with anchors, rode, and chain for each. The amount of maintenance required isn't great, but since the anchor system is one part of the boat that may save your life and your vessel in a crisis, it deserves extra attention. Anchors themselves are nearly maintenance-free, unless their galvanizing has become so abraded that they're beginning to rust; while the corrosion itself isn't immediately dangerous, it can stain everything it touches. A local metal-plating shop will probably be able to regalvanize your anchor if necessary. If you employ a chain lead for your rode (and you probably should), examine it for deep corrosion and for wear in the links and in the shackles at each end. Shackles and chain should be cleaned and dried for storage, and when the rig is reassembled, the shackle pins should be rewired to prevent them from backing off.

Most of the time, the anchor rode lives in a damp hole, where it is at least protected from sunlight. The last couple of feet, however, are usually on deck, and they take an inordinate amount of abuse. I usually find that it's necessary to trim back an anchor rode by about three feet every couple of seasons, and if you anchor regularly in rocky ground, you may find that turning the whole rode end-for-end will be a better precaution. If you do so, of course, you'll need to move the length markers that indicate the amount of rode in use. Before being stored, the rode should be washed and coiled.

Take the time to check the ancillary elements in your ground-tackle system. Split tubes used as protection against chafe will themselves wear through in time, and you should carry at least two good ones. Fenders should be thoroughly cleaned, and the fenderboard should be examined closely for chafe of the ropes and for protruding screw heads, if you have faced the board with brass half-round.

Engines

Depending on your mechanical talents, the depth of your wallet, and the complexity of your boat's powerplant, you can choose to ignore your boat's engine completely, learn its operation intimately, or follow some course between the two extremes. If you have a new boat, validity of the engine's warranty may well depend on your having certain items of service performed by manufacturer-authorized mechanics, but by the time boat and engine are over a couple of years old, the warranty has almost certainly expired, and you are on your own.

The maintenance outline that follows is necessarily general and is aimed at covering the basic chores common to gasoline and diesel inboards and to outboards. Particular models of engine will have different requirements, and before doing anything, you should obtain (if you don't own one) and thoroughly read the owner's manual provided by your engine's manufacturer. Some of these manuals, notably the one for Universal's Atomic-4, are very good; others, such as the one that came with my old single-cylinder Palmer, are not very helpful; and some, including those provided by several U.S. outboard makers, seem to envision the owner's simply bringing the engine back to his dealer every fall and running it blindfold between times.

Because boating is a seasonal sport in most parts of the world, engine maintenance schedules are usually designed around an annual decommissioning-commissioning cycle. Begin with decommissioning: Most of the deterioration found in marine engines is caused not by wear but by lack of regular use; this is, of course, even more likely to be the case in auxiliary powerplants. To keep your boat's engine running properly, one of the best things you can do is run it, *under load,* for an hour or two each week; beyond that, you should check a few basic condition indicators every time you turn on the ignition. First, measure the inboard's oil level before and after running, then check the flow of raw cooling water out the exhaust of inboard or outboard, and last, observe the level of fresh-water coolant (if your inboard engine is fresh-water cooled). If your engine has what used to be the minimum number of gauges, you should monitor water temperature, oil pressure and temperature, and amperage while you're under way. Once a month, measure the level of transmission fluid in the inboard engine's gearcase.

At the end of the season, here are the basic maintenance operations for inboards. First, check the antifreeze in the fresh-water cooling system (if you have one) and top it up if necessary. Next, put antifreeze in the raw-water system, as specified above. Now, change the crankcase oil: With the engine and the oil still warm, drain or pump out the lube oil. It's a messy job, often made more difficult by the inaccessibility of the drain plug, or the problem of getting a receptacle under the drain. It will probably be easier to buy a small pump, either manual or electric (operated off an ordinary hand drill), specifically for this job. Once the oil is drained, remove and replace the oil filter cartridge, then refill the system with fresh lube oil. The reason for doing it at decommissioning time is to prevent the old oil, which is by this time full of corrosive pollutants, from eating away at the insides of your engine over several months.

At the same time, check the transmission oil. This lubricant doesn't need as much attention, and if it's up to the level mark on the dipstick and doesn't show signs of having been emulsified with water, it's probably all right. Chances are that standard automatic transmission fluid (obtainable at any filling station) is what goes in your transmission, but check the manual before adding anything.

Next, shut off the fuel line of your gasoline (*not* diesel) engine near the gas tank. Remove the flame arrester from the carburetor and, while the engine is running, slowly pour about one cup of #10 or #20 oil in the carburetor throat, letting the last couple of ounces choke the engine dead. If you like, you can use one of the commercially available fogging sprays for the same job. Don't try this on a running diesel, which can burn the oil and run wild. Do, however, fog the diesel air intake after the engine has been shut down.

Remove the gasoline engine's spark plugs and spray more oil or fogger into the cylinders. With the battery removed, crank the engine by hand to spread the oil over the inside of the cylinder walls. Make sure, incidentally, that you clean out the recesses around the spark plug bases before unscrewing the plugs, to avoid getting grit and gunk into the cylinders. With a diesel, you can remove the injectors and fog the cylinders in the same way.

While completely draining the fuel tank is perhaps the best practice, it may not be the most practicable. Now that fuel stabilizers are available for both gasoline and diesel fuel, it may be simplest to add the correct amount of one of these substances to a completely filled gasoline tank or a partly filled diesel tank. (The theory here is that a completely filled gasoline tank may burn, but it won't explode, while the fumes in a nearly empty gas tank are the ingredients of a considerable bomb.)

Remove the rubber V-belts that supply engine power to ancillary devices, such as the alternator. If left in place through a winter, they may take a stiff set. If they are worn, stretched, or cracked, replace the belts with new ones.

We've already discussed winterizing the water system of an inboard engine. An outboard doesn't retain water if it's in an upright position, but you should flush salt water from its cooling system, to prevent salt from collecting and eventually choking the tubing. Most marine stores sell attachments that allow you to flush the outboard's cooling system with your garden hose, and these are well worth their small price, as compared with the old alternative of rounding up an open-topped fifty-gallon drum and running the motor in that. After flushing the water system, drain the used lubricant from the lower unit gearcase and replace it with new oil. You may fog an outboard's carburetor and cylinders in the same way that you do for an inboard gasoline engine, and it will help to spray some moisture inhibitor, such as CRC, over the whole engine interior.

Many sailboats end the season with nicked or bent propellers. Although the dings may not appear major, they can throw off the shaft's balance and damage the bearings, besides providing a notably noisy run. If the prop is visibly marked, remove it and have your yard or the prop manufacturer recondition it. At the same time, if the boat is to be blocked up ashore, disconnect the inboard's shaft from the transmission, to keep the shaft from being bent when the boat sags—they all do—as she is chocked up. Be sure to tell the yard you've done this if they are handling the haulout, as they may otherwise be planning to move the boat under her own power.

Fitting out

Recommissioning a boat, especially a fiber glass boat, is often thought to be merely a matter of waxing the hull and painting the bottom, but an inboard engine requires more work than almost anything else connected with the vessel; you may job it out to the yard's mechanic, and in some marinas you will be required to do so, but maintaining the modern marine engine is, for the most part, something you can do yourself. To a certain extent, getting the engine ready for the boating season entails reversing all the decommissioning operations, but there are some other tricks as well.

To begin with, now is the time for a thorough visual check of the entire system, or of as much of it as you can see and reach. This means a careful examination of the entire exterior cooling and exhaust system, looking over the hoses and mufflers for evidence of severe corrosion. Take a special look at the hose clamps that lock the flexible exhaust to the exhaust pipe: There should be two such clamps (as on every through-hull connection), and they should be stainless steel—sometimes only the strapping is stainless, while the screw is ordinary steel; the rust will soon make itself evident, and the whole rig, apparently secure, can let go at any time. If you have to replace clamps, by the way, the best practice is to sock them down reasonably hard at first, then retighten them in about a week, when the stiff hose fabric has compressed a bit.

Check out the filter and/or trap on the raw-water cooling intake, and remove the gunk and scraps that accumulate here. Grease the seacocks and replace the impeller—a small, plastic paddlewheel—in the raw-water pump. Replace the V-belts and retension them (here again, a reexamination after a few hours of running is a good idea). Check the level of fresh water, if your engine has fresh-water cooling. Open and drain the raw-water cooling system of antifreeze.

Examine, both visually and by shaking them, the mechanical and electrical connections on the engine—cables, generators, fuel lines, and the like—and tighten them up if necessary. Scrape or sand corroded electrical connections to improve the contact.

The oil and transmission fluid should be fine, but it's good practice to double-check their levels, anyway. Replace the fuel filter element of a diesel —this is, after all, the source of the great majority of diesel problems—and clean the gasoline engine's filter and filter bowl.

Replace the gasoline engine's spark plugs with brand-new ones, and throw away the old ones. You should, of course, have a spare set, but they too should be new. With a diesel, check the tightness of glow plugs and injectors, using a torque wrench.

Clean off the wiring carefully, and then spray moisture inhibitor on the connections and behind the instrument panel. Take a look at the distributor cap of the gasoline inboard—if it has tiny cracks, replace it.

Lubricate the controls—the throttle and gear shift linkages—with water-proof grease.

After the boat has been afloat for a couple of days and has presumably resumed its proper hull shape, which was distorted by months of being blocked up at a few points, realign the engine and propeller shaft, using a feeler gauge for precision. (For details, see Conrad Miller's excellent book, *Engines for Sailboats,* listed in the Bibliography.)

There are two ways to approach boat maintenance, and each has its adherents (although only one has advocates). One—the faster, more efficient method —is to compose a checklist of tasks to be done, arranged in an orderly, logical fashion. This means that messy jobs come first, and that you never find yourself cleaning the same area twice; it means that tasks are arranged so that workers don't get in each other's way or need the same tools simultaneously; it means that the schedule is flexible enough to allow for a gorgeous, unseasonable day or a rotten, rainy one. And it means that you're in the water and sailing on schedule. The other system is best described as dithering. No system at all. It means leaving half the tools at home and having to go back for them; it means dropping a job halfway through in favor of one that's more fun; it means doing the same thing twice or even three times, till you get it more or less completely botched. And, to be honest, it can be a lot of fun, if that's the way you want to do your boating. Like so many aspects of cruising, a choice is involved, and no one can tell you what to do or how to do it.

XII

~~~~~~~~~~

The Social Side

For over a hundred years, yachting—both racing and cruising—was a sport with very heavy social implications. While there were a few professional watermen who raced their boats, and a few people, mostly eccentrics, who cruised alone, most yachting was a very class-oriented activity, operating within a rigid framework of rules, both written and understood. Only after World War II, when increased leisure time and the fiber glass revolution made boating a mass-participation sport, did most of the social taboos of sailing begin to fade. Even today, a relatively few old-line clubs exert a disproportionate influence on yachting generally, though they have only a fraction of the impact they once did.

The lingering reputation of yacht clubs as bastions of nautical society obscures the great changes that have overtaken many of them. The need for more members, to meet rising costs, and the changing interests of yachtsmen generally have forced considerable changes in the attitudes and policies of many clubs. At the same time, the increasing number of full-service marinas has created serious competition with yacht clubs for the sailor's dollar. As so often happens, the competitors have responded by becoming more like each other, so that sometimes it's difficult to tell when you're in a club or a marina. Or to decide which organization to keep your boat at. The choice will often come down to personal taste on the one hand and availability on the other, but it may help the newcomer to have some idea of what these and other organizations have to offer the cruising sailor.

Yacht clubs

In the United States, most yacht clubs are only social organizations with a heavy marine emphasis. They may offer swimming pools and tennis courts, and may even astound the lunching old guard with fashion shows, but their primary purpose is to facilitate the association of sailors. Because racing is the side of yachting that most benefits from good organization, nearly all old-line and middle-aged clubs offer one or more racing programs. Typically, a club will stage, during the boating season, regular weekend day races for its own boatowning members, usually with trophies for the winners and runners-up on a weekly and seasonal basis. Members of nearby clubs may also be invited to participate. Clubs with suitable memberships and sailing areas may also expand into running overnight or longer races, sometimes in collaboration with other clubs. A well-known (or aspiring) yacht club may offer to be host for class championships, or for the regional semifinals for such championships.

The standard yacht club will have a youth sailing program, which can be anything from a hard-driving training effort for youngsters' competition sailing to a waterborne babysitting service. A reasonable youth program will have its own fleet of "trainer" daysailers—tough, seaworthy small craft of some locally popular class—a trained instructor, and a schedule or curriculum that serves to advance the young people's skills.

Some clubs have cruising as well as racing programs, but since cruising people are not generally so amenable to group activities, such efforts are often confined to a one- or two-week annual cruise in company, plus the occasional holiday overnight or weekend rendezvous. A well-organized club may have an extended cruise pepped up by point-to-point day races along the way.

These are the basic services a yacht club will usually provide, but they are only a small part of what some organizations offer. As noted above, more and more clubs have tennis and paddleball courts, card rooms, a restaurant and bar, nautical instruction for adults—for those who want an activity, there's usually an organization ready to provide it. And for each activity a club offers, there's usually a charge, overt or hidden, to pay for the required personnel and equipment.

It is quite possible to have a functioning yacht club with no facilities whatever—the organization operates out of living rooms and its members keep their boats in marinas. By and large, however, at least part of the attraction of a yacht club is its base. The essentials include a clubhouse, parking lot for cars and trailerable boats (and perhaps winter storage for larger craft), anchorage and/or marina. Older yacht clubs, especially in the Northeast, can be very grand indeed, with immaculate sloping lawns, vast Victorian mansions for clubhouses, acres of tennis courts, beaches and pools. Someone has to pay for all this, and a prospective member should be aware that he may well be assessed for facilities that don't interest him in the slightest, as detailed a bit later.

Most clubs beyond the smallest have two parallel organizations, interacting and unequal. The club's unpaid officers, both elected and appointed, may well work harder than the paid staff, but this is in the nature of amateurism, and has no necessary relationship to their skill or effectiveness.

As a rule, a club has at least three elected, unpaid officers, usually called the commodore, vice commodore, and rear commodore. They're referred to collectively as "flag officers," borrowing a navy term, because their positions entitle them to fly flags of office on their boats and, when they are present, on the club flagstaff. In most tables of organization, the commodore alone has stated powers, the two others being appointed to assist him as required, or replace him if necessary. In some clubs, however, the three flag officers may divide the duties, each one having several committees that report to him. (Even in the most fully staffed club, a lot of the work is done by the membership.)

Besides the nominal flag officers, there are several other officials, usually appointed by the commodore but sometimes elected by the membership. These include the secretary, treasurer, and fleet captain (often a grandiloquent name for harbor master). In many clubs, these people also have flags of office. Committee chairmen may of course include almost any title, but even a small club will usually have a race committee, house committee, and membership committee, at the very least.

Paid staff will almost always center around the club steward or manager. Under him will be bar and restaurant staff, lifeguards, instructors, launchboys, groundskeepers, and whatever other help may be required (many of the smaller jobs are perquisites of members' children, which causes at least some of the money to move in a circular pattern).

By and large, only two aspects of a yacht club produce a positive cash flow —members' dues and the bar. Everything else is a minus, or at best a wash. At the same time, however, most yacht clubs disguise their rising costs by publicly quoting a membership fee and then quietly setting service charges on everything beyond the basic membership. This can be important for a prospective member to realize, as the $500 or so he first forks out may be just the beginning; typically, there will be additional fees for launch service, use of the tennis courts, lockers, use of the club's own boats (over and above charges for lessons or youth programs), parking, and the boat's slip or mooring space— not to mention the charge for storing the yacht's dinghy ashore. Some clubs with large but mysterious year-end deficits indulge in what they call "special assessments" to make up; the same kind of presumably one-time assessment may be levied (usually by vote of the membership) for extraordinary costs such as running a national championship or replacing an uninsured pier that washed away in the winter.

So figuring the cost of a yacht club membership may be quite complicated, and the calculation is often made more difficult by the members' tendencies to forget some if not all of the secondary fees they've paid. Perhaps the only way accurately to gauge the cost of a yacht club membership is to make a list of all the facilities you want to use and ask what each of them costs; then ask if there are any facilities you have to subsidize whether or not you use them (often there will be a minimum you must spend in the restaurant each month); and finally ask how many special assessments there have been in the past five years. Not counting the one-time initiation fee most clubs demand, you will probably find that the minimum cost will not be all that much different from what a good local marina charges for dockage and winter storage combined, although the club's fee should be somewhat lower if your boat is on a mooring and not at a pier.

The next question, of course, is how you become a member of a yacht club, and to that there is no simple answer. In areas like California, where nearly all the harbors are municipally owned and operated, yacht clubs can occupy space on the premises only by making membership available on a strictly first-come, first-served basis. In other areas, clubs may actively solicit owners whose yachts fit into an existing or developing racing fleet. In most cases, you will have to cultivate at least a superficial acquaintance with one or more members of a given club, so they may put you up for membership. You will then meet with the membership committee, and if nothing awful happens, you will in due course be asked to join, an invitation that is usually accompanied by a bill for the initiation fee, payable in advance.

If you're new in town or new on the water, it can be hard to get to know members of the clubs you're interested in. Obviously, the best place to meet is on the water, where most people tend to be more friendly than ashore, and where a well-kept boat and seamanlike crew speak for themselves. If racing has any attraction for you at all, it can be an excellent way to meet people from many local clubs. You can usually participate in local races by joining a regional or area racing association as an individual member (you may have to join the United States Yacht Racing Union—USYRU—as well), or you may race as a member of a one-design or class fleet. If you keep your boat at a marina, ask around for crewing opportunities (see the section on racing, below). Learn the appearance of local club burgees, so you can make nice to the owners whose clubs interest you: Rowing over to an anchored boat after a day's cruise and offering a discreet compliment or two will often dissolve an apparently steely exterior and get you an invitation aboard.

Because they are private membership organizations, many yacht clubs pursue restrictive membership policies, discriminating by race, religion, or (most frequently) sex. If this sort of thing puts you off—it does me—you may still be able to find a club with less insecure members and a correspondingly more relaxed admissions policy. Such establishments tend to be newer, smaller, and less well known, and while they do not usually have elaborate buildings or facilities, their fees are correspondingly lower.

Marina and boatyard

Or you may choose to short-cut the club approach to sailing and establish a strictly commercial relationship with a marina or boatyard. There are advantages and disadvantages on either side, and—apart from convenience—your own personality may be the determining factor. It will depend, I think, on whether you are more comfortable keeping your boat at an establishment where there is a straight cash-for-service relationship, or at a club where the social component is more important. As I said earlier, clubs and marinas are in many cases becoming more and more alike, and there are a number of so-called yacht clubs that are really nothing more than cooperative marinas; likewise, there are still a few old-established boatyards where the atmosphere is as *gemütlich* and inbred as at any formal yacht club.

While it would be difficult to pinpoint the difference between a marina and a boatyard, there are some attributes generally associated with one or the other. In most sailors' minds, a marina is first of all a parking lot for boats—in the water during the season, and often ashore in the nonsailing months. Its primary asset, therefore, is its system of slips or piers, and everything else is pretty much secondary. A good marina should have piers (whether fixed or floating) that are safe to walk on and strong enough to keep the boats in place even during a storm. When looking a marina over, consider the ease or difficulty of finding your way in at night or in heavy weather. If your engine quits, will you be able to sail into and away from your slip? (The former is obviously more important.) Dock cleats need not be through-bolted, although the best are, as long as the angle of pull will produce a shearing stress on them. Pilings should have cleats to hang docklines from. Padding on the face of a pier is a nice but often purely cosmetic touch.

Nearly all marinas today have both fresh water and 110-volt electricity laid on, but frequently the water lines are less than perfectly clean and the current is feeble. (A marina having a large proportion of sizable powerboats will probably have decent water and electricity.) Convenient garbage containers with secure lids are a must, as is adequate security, whether it be a guard at the main gate or locked entries to individual piers, or both.

Most marinas are capable of performing emergency repairs of a not-too-demanding nature, especially on the power or electrical systems of a cruising boat. Relatively few can handle serious woodwork or rigging problems, although most can provide adequate fiber glass work. Today's marina will, almost certainly, have a chandlery; if you're lucky, it will sell (at list price) an adequate selection of useful gear, charts and publications, and perhaps electronics. More than likely, however, it will devote too much space to costly gadgets—fenders in the shape of mermaids, plastic tumblers with code-flag humor, grossly overpriced clothing in virulent pinks and greens.

The marina may also have a restaurant and bar. I may be unlucky, but I have yet to find a really good restaurant associated with a marina, and only rarely an establishment that is even bearable. Far more valuable most of the time will be a soda machine and a dispenser for block and cube ice. A small grocery, selling mostly snack and breakfast foods, can be convenient if there's no legitimate market within walking distance.

Today's marina nearly always has a sizable parking lot, and it may even offer a swimming pool complete with lifeguard. What is more important, perhaps, is a decent restroom with good, frequently cleaned showers and clothes washers and driers.

Last and far from least, your marina should have a fuel dock.

The old-fashioned boatyard is not merely marina writ primitive. In years past, it existed to maintain, repair, and even build small craft, and its dockage facilities tended to be secondary. Because today's fiber glass pleasure boats require far less hull and underbody work than did wood yachts, and because boatbuilding has become concentrated among fewer builders, the traditional boatyard has had to change its emphasis or disappear. A few still hang on precariously, usually in backwaters where waterfront property is not at the customary premium, and if you don't care about a tarted-up ambience, such an establishment can offer the lowest prices for boat storage, on season and off. As with a marina's, a boatyard's piers and slips should be in reasonable shape, although in the latter establishment you may have to settle for nothing more than secure pilings and less than perfect walkways. The electricity and water are likely to be occasional. The yard's chandlery will probably stick pretty close to the basics in paint, tools, and hardware, although if you're lucky, the shop may have a marvelous backlog of ancient fittings, good for an afternoon's browsing anytime.

Parking in a boatyard is hit-or-miss: The antique mobile crane is usually in the way, and two or three thoroughly dead boats occupy the choicest spaces. The garbage can is an overflowing fifty-gallon drum with the head hack-sawed off, and the toilet and shower facilities are laughable only if you have an advanced sense of humor. The occupants of berths are easygoing, as well they might be, and no one is likely to object at finding most of a grease-encrusted Atomic-4 spread out along the pier floats. More than likely, skippers from adjoining berths will be down on their knees alongside the owner, offering advice and tools.

There are, of course, immaculate boatyards and shoddy marinas, but perhaps the most usual difference between the organizations is that one will offer personal, knowledgeable, no-frills service based on years of experience, while the other can make available a substitute club atmosphere, with an expanding number of ancillary facilities.

In terms of cost, the two types are surprisingly close. While the full-service marina is perceptibly more expensive, the boatyard is seldom all that cheap. Its basic costs—salaries, benefits, mortgage, insurance, taxes—are much the same as those of the marina, it is seldom able to achieve savings from modern business methods or large-scale operation, and it often has acute cash-flow anemia.

Where there is the choice, perhaps the most nearly ideal place to keep a boat is the municipal or state-operated marina, which generally has a relatively low operating cost and which is often subsidized, at least to some degree, by unknowing taxpayers. While few states have as attractive and well-designed municipal marinas as does California, most waterfront towns have some sort of boat parking arrangement for the public. The obvious problem is that municipal marinas, because of their low cost, tend to fill up first, and it can require a wait of several years—up to and over a decade, in some places—to get a berth. Humans being what they are, of course, there are ways of getting around the waiting list, for those knowledgeable enough to take advantage of them. This makes the wait even longer for the less sophisticated boatowner. For most of us, the search for a place to keep our cruiser may involve a private marina or yacht club, while at the same time working our way up the municipal list.

Where space shortages are acute, as they have become in more and more communities, sailors turn to less convenient solutions. In many places it is possible to plant a mooring in the harbor or river—perhaps in a formal anchorage area, perhaps not. Before doing so, it's a good idea to find out if the town or city has a harbor master and an official policy regarding moorings. If possible, try to conduct this research at one remove from yourself—without, that is, identifying yourself to the authorities until such revelation is proved either inevitable or harmless. It may be a question of avoiding a local fee, or it may simply be a case of putting yourself in position to do something that has not been expressly forbidden—in all too many cases, when a cautious official is asked permission for anything unusual, his instant reaction is to say no. The same person, confronted with a *fait accompli*, is most likely to ignore it. This may seem like cynical advice, but it has proven out over and over again.

If you do put down your own mooring, you will have to set up some way of reaching it, but often it can be relatively easy to find a nearby spot ashore at which to tie up a dinghy, and at the worst, you may choose to cartop your dink down to a nearby launching ramp each time you cruise.

When you arrive at this stage, however, you may consider either giving the whole thing up or investigating a trailerable boat. The latter choice requires more effort and cost than it once did, but if you're really in love with coastal cruising, you should investigate it. There are several magazines devoted to trailerable boats and the techniques they require, and a chapter in my own previous volume, *The Coastal Cruiser,* summarizes the subject. An extended, first-rate treatment is Chris Caswell's book, *Trailerable Sailboats.*

Other organizations

Besides local yacht clubs, other marine organizations may be worth your interest. As opposed to the club, which attempts to provide a whole spectrum of services for the yachtsman, other groups tend to have a limited range of aims. From the sailor's point of view, the most active and visible of these groups are devoted to one or another type of racing. They may take any of several forms, depending on the seriousness of their members' commitment to competition and the requirements of the local situation. Largest in scope are national groups, such as the Midget Ocean Racing Club (MORC, usually spoken as "more-sea"), which is described in detail below; it has both a national existence, with annual championships, and local fleets, called "stations." PHRF, mentioned previously and also detailed later, has a similar double life, but here the overwhelming emphasis is local and the national group has little visibility.

Other national, or even international, organizations include the various class and one-design organizations. To understand what they're up to, you must first become acquainted with a couple of semitechnical terms (assuming you don't already know them). In sailing, a *class* is composed of boats of similar or near-identical design. If you think about it for a moment, it's apparent that the larger and more complex a boat becomes, the harder for it to be exactly the same as another. And it is human nature for any boatowner to personalize his yacht—with or without the desire to make her go faster, but with some consequent alteration of her potential speed.

A class may include boats whose potential speeds are more or less equalized by a handicap formula. The 12-Meter sloops that compete for the America's Cup are such a group, known as a *development class,* to indicate that difference in design, within regulated limits, is permissible. A more usual type of class in small boats is the *one-design* group—Lasers, Lightnings, and many other day racers are one-designs, which attempt within extremely tight limits to make boats functionally identical. Although there are cruising boats that come under the one-design heading—J/24s, for instance—there aren't many.

Most classes, whether one-design or development, will give birth to a class association, once the number of boats involved gets beyond a very few. Most class associations are primarily interested in guiding or restraining change, so that racing within the particular class may remain reasonably equal (at least in potential), and so that necessary evolution in rig or hull takes place in an orderly fashion, to minimize the impact (both on the race course and the used boat market) on older yachts. The proprietor of a cruising yacht class is most often the boat's manufacturer, sometimes operating behind the smokescreen of an individual in his employ. His interests are, of course, commercial—competition means publicity, which generates sales—but they are helpful to the individual owners, especially the less experienced. In some cases, after a boat goes out of production and the builder loses interest in it, the class association continues to thrive for some years, helping to maintain a market in the design and providing both social and competitive opportunities for the members. Some very good organizations, such as the Triton Class Association, have regular races, rendezvous, and even a newsletter with tips for maintenance and improvement of the boats. Generally speaking, the cost of belonging to a class association is low, and the money is well spent.

On a more local level, there are area racing associations, whose membership is made up of yacht clubs—at a group rate—and individual, unaffiliated sailors. Such associations are especially effective in locales where there's lots of racing activity but a geographical spread that makes it hard for a skipper to keep up with all the activities of nearby clubs. One good example of this kind of area organization is the Yacht Racing Association of Long Island Sound (YRA of LIS), which publishes an annual list of events staged by its member clubs and in which outsiders may compete. While an area association cannot absolutely prevent conflicts—there are just too many clubs in its jurisdiction —it can help clubs to avoid accidental overlaps of scheduling and spread the season's events more evenly. Membership in an area racing association is not expensive, and it offers the beginner a credential for entering a large number of races and thus meeting many new friends.

For some reason, the United States has never had a national organization for the cruising sailor. The Cruising Club of America (CCA), which would seem organized to fill this gap, is in fact largely devoted to racing (it stages the biennial race from Newport, R.I., to Bermuda) and is very small in numbers, thanks to rigid membership restrictions. There are, however, regional cruising groups, of which the large and active Great Lakes Cruising Club is perhaps most prominent, and local clubs whose primary, if not exclusive, interest is cruising. Many of these groups function as adjuncts to local yacht clubs, rotating the meetings and rendezvous among them, and having relatively low membership fees in consequence.

Two national organizations for boatmen generally may be of interest to the cruising sailor. The U.S. Coast Guard Auxiliary is a group of civilian volunteers numbering about forty thousand men and women over the age of seventeen. While it is directly controlled by its own officers, it is also answerable to the Coast Guard in activities that impinge on government interest. The Auxiliary's local unit, the flotilla, consists of a minimum of ten members, who may own private boats, aircraft, or radio stations, or who have some skill useful to the organization. Flotillas are organized into divisions, and groups of divisions form districts, which correspond more or less to the districts of the Coast Guard's own structure. National officers and a national staff complete the pyramid.

The Auxiliary's basic aim is to assist its stepparent, the Coast Guard, and it does so in three main ways: First, Auxiliarists, using their own boats, participate in patrol and search-and-rescue missions, both individually and in concert with the regular service. Second, the volunteers offer an extensive program of classroom education in boating technique and safety, both to the general public and to their own membership. Third, the Auxiliary has for many years conducted a national program through which members inspect private pleasure craft (and some others) to insure that they are equipped and maintained up to and beyond federal safety standards.

Very few Auxiliary units are able to provide normal marine services to their members, nor are they intended to do so. On the other hand, they offer the relative novice a good source of classroom instruction in marine matters, at nominal cost, as well as the chance to meet and work with a group of skilled mariners. Unfortunately, there are relatively few sailors among the Auxiliary's members, but individual units sometimes have a nucleus of sailing people, usually owners of cruising boats. One way to find out about the local Auxiliary unit—and do yourself a favor at the same time—is to contact them (they're usually in the phone book, and any marina operator can direct you to a member) and request a Courtesy Marine Examination (CME). It costs nothing, and if your boat does not comply with the equipment regulations, the authorities are *not* alerted, but you're advised what is wrong. Nearly all Auxiliary units are very open to new members, and the slightest expression of interest will usually get you an invitation to a meeting or a class session. I was an active member of the Auxiliary for over a decade, resigning because of the press of work, and I retain a warm admiration for the membership, coupled, I must confess, with some regrets for the level of bureaucracy imposed by the government association.

Larger and older than the Auxiliary, the U.S. Power Squadrons have in recent years appeared in the news because of their long-running fight to remain a males-only organization (or as they would put it, retain their freedom of association). Recently, the USPS agreed in principle to accept female members. Like the Auxiliary, the USPS has national and district organizational echelons, but the basic element is the local Squadron. These groups have been cruelly and accurately characterized as "yacht clubs for people who don't belong to yacht clubs," and they have a dual function. First is in giving expression to the Squadrons' long-time interest in education, both of the general public and of its members (including their families). Second is the individual Squadron's social role, whose relative importance has increased in recent years, at least partly in response to the national organization's desire to prove (for legal reasons) that it is a group of genuine private clubs.

Without attempting to get into the intricacies of the legal side, which have little day-to-day effect on the membership, it seems to me fair to say that the social aspect of an individual Squadron is directly related to the locality: In the East, where yacht clubs abound, the USPS has been primarily an educational, service organization. Elsewhere in the country, where clubs are relatively few, local Squadrons are indeed genuine clubs. The best way to find out which situation obtains in your locality—and also to test the waters—is to sign up for one of the USPS public courses, which are given in most states; a schedule is available at virtually any boat show. The course will do almost anyone good (it is very much like the Auxiliary's main public course in content) and by the time it's done, you'll have been exposed to a good cross-section of the local Squadron's members.

Despite the name, USPS has a great many expert and committed sailors in its membership, and a somewhat disproportionate number of them are active and thus visible. Although I resigned from the organization on the membership question, it seems to me that USPS is worth checking out at the local level.

Cruising etiquette

Even the word *etiquette* sounds strange to our ears, reeking with pomp and stiffness and absurdity, but in any situation where people encounter each other, there must be some accepted forms of behavior. For a while toward the end of the last century and the early years of this one, the forms quite outran any reason for their existence, and in a few old-line yacht clubs today there still exist elaborate codes of dress and behavior whose purpose seems to be to make strangers uncomfortable while pointing out the insiders as persons possessed of some special grace. Everywhere else, however, the peaked-cap mentality is gone, usually replaced by a decent consideration for the feelings of others, within the limits of the nautical setting. That to me is what etiquette is all about.

On a cruising yacht, the essence of civilized behavior seems most often to involve trying to create privacy for yourself and others, while recognizing that there is very little to work with. It is easy to build yourself a nest in some part of the boat that seems unused, without realizing, perhaps, that you're monopolizing a public space. In any boat under forty feet overall, anything above a whisper will carry an amazing distance, and on a calm night at anchor, one person snoring can echo the length of the boat. What's required in this situation, I think, is not only tolerance by all hands but a willingness to make your feelings known without giving offense in the process. In a confined space, like the cabin of a cruising boat, it is very easy to get on someone's nerves without realizing it. You must be willing to suggest—for example—that someone's tuneless humming is rather annoying, before it becomes positively maddening. And the hummer, in his place, must be willing to forego some of those less than attractive habits that are barely noticed in less confined spaces.

Skippers and crews get to know each other's little ways in short order, and they adjust or change boats. The relationship between the regular crew and guests is more difficult. In most cases, guests know markedly less about the yacht—and about yachts in general—than the crew members do. Although it may sound excessively formal, it is really a good idea at the beginning of a cruise for the skipper to go over the boat with his guests, briefing them in detail about procedures, customs, and equipment. Obviously, a lot of this will wash off—even a small cruiser can be bewilderingly complex to a stranger—and it will help a guest if, before any maneuver, the skipper outlines what's expected of each person aboard. It will also help give the guests a sense of participation if the skipper and crew avoid the easiest path of doing everything themselves. Make the effort to involve your guests; it may provide some exasperating moments at first, but it will definitely make for a more enjoyable weekend.

Areas where guests commonly go astray include the head and galley, where the physical equipment resembles what's found ashore but is in use more complicated and less reliable. In my own experience, I've found that most guests aboard are terribly diffident about asking for directions on how to use the marine sanitation device (and no wonder). The best solution, to my mind, is to post step-by-step instructions, with the admonition to consult the skipper or a crew member if the apparatus seems to be giving trouble. The instructions will vary with the type of head, but nearly all marine toilets dislike swallowing large wads of paper or even quite small foreign objects. A separate trash bin, with a lid, should be easily visible.

Landsmen seldom realize how precious fresh water is aboard a small cruising yacht, and even an experienced crew can quickly empty a tank when there's pressure water and a faucet. My own rather draconian remedy in boats with pressure systems is to require users to turn the pressure water switch on the circuit-breaker panel on and off with each use.

As for the galley, the obvious danger there is the stove. One exposure to the average pressure alcohol unit is usually enough to deter the landlubber. Sometimes forever. Gas stoves are another problem, chiefly because of their location —people who use gas stoves at home almost never locate them where a strong draft is likely to blow out the burners, and of course in many galleys, a flame —gas or alcohol—is virtually invisible. Generally speaking, I think it best to keep guests away from alcohol stoves entirely, and to assign the regular cook to watch over any guests' use of the gas stove.

Electricity is not as great a problem as water on the average cruiser, but it can be a definite worry. Unless the crew are unusually boneheaded, they soon learn to turn off lights when they are not in use and to be careful about overloading 12-volt circuits. A guest cannot be expected, however, to realize that all wall sockets are not created equal, even when he or she does remember that the local power and light company is represented by a couple of 12-volt batteries under the floorboards. Again, keeping control of the master switches is the best answer for the skipper: By learning to activate circuits when they are required and shut them off at the panel when the need is done, you can bypass the problem of that forward-cabin reading lamp that cannot be seen from aft.

Good manners under way, with respect to other boats, is usually no more than a seagoing version of the golden rule. I've discussed elsewhere the advisability of giving the right of way to boats that are obviously racing and to large commercial craft. Forcing another yacht to tack for no reason or taking another sailboat's wind is merely rude and thoughtless. If you luff up to let another boat cross your bow, do it early and obviously, so he knows you're letting him pass, and doesn't have to worry that you're just unsure and likely to change your mind. In narrow fairways, it's polite to adopt the channel behavior expected of power craft—and it may be required of you, too, in a narrow fairway. As on the highway ashore, the general rule afloat is to keep as close to the starboard side of the channel as you safely can. If you must tack up a channel, try to time the tacks so you don't come about while another boat —especially a powerboat—is trying to pass.

Trying to be polite to powerboat skippers can be a tedious exercise. Although most cruising sailors have a reasonable notion of the demands of a powerboat—they are themselves powerboat skippers part of the time—few captains of powerboats have any but the vaguest idea of what a sailboat is up to at any given moment. This means, in practice if not in law, that you must be extra-careful in your actions. To my mind, it is best to watch what the other boat is doing, and to gauge what it could do, rather than to try to read its skipper's mind. In any situation, there are usually several possible courses of action open to a boat, and you should be prepared for the boat approaching yours to take any of them, no matter how irrational it might seem to you. If, for example, you see a powerboat approaching to cross your sailboat's starboard bow more or less at right angles, with some danger of collision at present course and speed, you might reflect that the other boat can head right or left, speed up, slow down, or stop. Under the rules of the road, you are required to maintain your course and heading until you decide that the other vessel's skipper has let the situation deteriorate to the point of danger.

When this point has arrived, it seems to me, you would be quite justified in sounding the danger signal—five or more blasts on your horn—if you see no evidence that the other boat is changing her course or speed at all. If the problem is simple inattention (and this will be true in a surprisingly large number of cases), causing the other skipper to wake up will solve the problem. On the other hand, the horn signal may either panic or infuriate the other skipper, with problematical results. This being likely, you should reduce your own boat's speed or stop her, until you're sure what the other vessel will do.

In most cases, you can tell well in advance which boats pose any danger by being alert for bearings that don't change. To do this, sight the approaching vessel across some fixed object on your own craft. In nearly all situations, the bearing will change appreciably, moving forward or aft as the boats close. As long as this is happening, there's no danger of collision. If, however, the two boats continue to maintain the same bearing relative to each other, then there is an excellent chance they'll collide unless one of them changes course or speed, or both. In a crowded harbor, with converging traffic patterns, you may be in some danger of collision with one craft or another a good deal of the time. For this reason, it's as well to train your crew in the elementary skill of taking relative bearings on other boats, so that they can alert you to a potential collision early on.

It's also important that you and your crew both know the basics of the rules of the road well enough so that you can apply them without thinking. The rules, which are now largely the same for inland and international waters, seem complex because of the large number of special situations they must deal with. For the most part, they are quite simple: Well over 90 percent of the potential collision situations you'll encounter can be covered by two or three rules at most. Copies of the rules are now available from the U.S. Government Printing Office at a small cost, and a digest of the more common rules appears in Appendix 4 of this book.

One of the more recent developments in right-of-way rules has been the diminishing legal stature of small craft in general and pleasure boats in particular. Because modern commercial vessels are relatively unwieldy and because coastal waters are so cluttered with recreational boats, the rulemakers (whose orientation is toward the needs of the larger vessels) have recently changed some concepts of the right-of-way regulations to favor larger craft, which are usually commercial. The situation as it now stands—and as it is described in the appendix—seems likely to continue; the only change I would foresee, in fact, is a continuing tilt away from pleasure boats.

Good manners in anchorages is partly a matter of seamanship, and otherwise just a case of behaving with the kind of consideration you'd want for yourself in any crowded neighborhood. Bear in mind always that sound travels clearly and far across still water, so that what seems like a quiet sing-along in your cockpit may be just about as loud in the cabin of a boat anchored some distance away. Another fact too often forgotten is that some sounds travel better than others: if you raise your voice to make yourself heard above your own engine, chances are excellent that your words will carry clearly to the next boat—and if you happen to be discussing that boat's appearance, let's hope you're saying something kind.

The ancient rule of the sea—which is not a part of the rules of the road— is that in anchorages the first to come has virtually all the rights. This does not apply in an area of permanent moorings (except insofar as the moorings themselves are evidence of having been there first), but rather in casual anchorages. If you're anchored first, it's up to later arrivals to keep clear of you. If you're in any doubt that they're properly anchored, raise the point—politely —if only to establish yourself in case of later problems. Contrariwise, if you decide to anchor near another boat, you should ask how much scope he has out, so that you can adjust your swinging circle to match his.

Arriving in an anchorage late or leaving it early, the considerate skipper proceeds with just enough power to maintain steerage way, in order to reduce both noise and wake. Once you've been wakened at five by some yahoo raising the anchor to a chorus of shouts, or been rolled from your bunk by an idiot waterski towboat, you'll appreciate just how golden is the silence in a proper anchorage. If there are people swimming or boardsailing (which may also involve swimming, sooner rather than later), don't flush the boat's head or dump the coals from the barbeque. And of course you won't dump garbage, even biodegradable material, because it will almost certainly wash ashore before it disintegrates. More and more owners of shoreside property have posted their land against cruising yachtsmen, and for good reason. When you do find a place that allows sailors to go ashore and picnic, it's even more important, then, to clean up after yourself. If you have rubbish, put it into a container or take it back aboard. If the area is truly deserted, you may be able to bury the trash—but dig a proper hole, don't just heap a little earth on the remains.

Different cruising people have different attitudes toward hospitality between boats. Some enjoy visiting with strangers, and some prefer to be alone—even if there are fifty other yachts in the anchorage. As a general rule, it isn't hard to tell who's feeling sociable and who isn't, just by the warmth with which

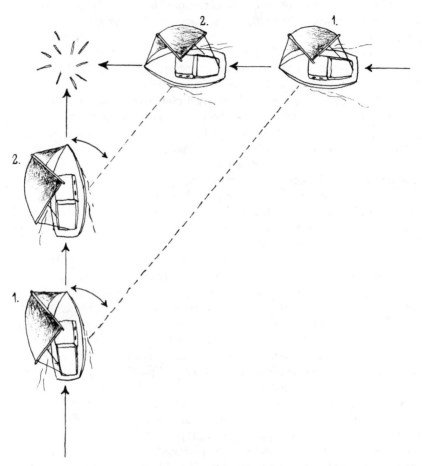

The constant bearing is an effective indicator of a possible collision in the making. Above, the two boats on a crossing course maintain approximately the same bearing from position 1 to position 2, and there is every likelihood that they will either collide or have an unpleasantly close call. At right, on the other hand, the bearing changes appreciably from 1 to 2, and the narrowing bearing (as seen from the lower boat) indicates that the other vessel is pulling ahead and will pass safely across the first craft's bow. The lower boat, in both illustrations, has the right of way because she is on starboard tack and the other vessel is on port.

they return your greetings. In former days, when there were just a few cruising boats in even the most crowded anchorage, people were more likely to invite other yachtsmen aboard for a drink, and it was a pleasant custom. It seems to have declined, however, which is rather a shame, especially since a new cruising person could learn so much from a short visit aboard a well-tuned boat.

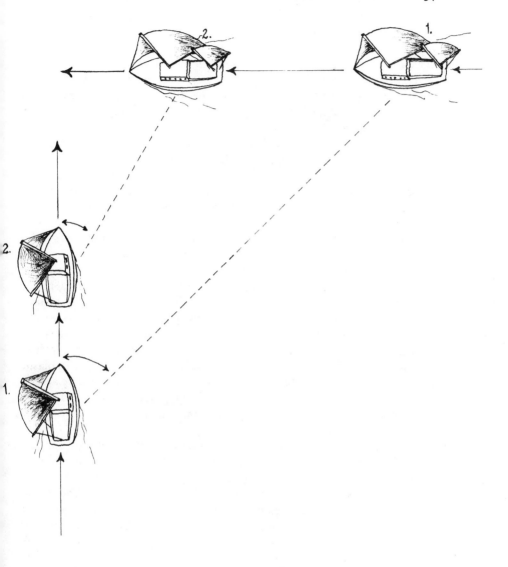

Good manners ashore

Virtually by definition, the cruising sailor is a visitor much of the time. It's fortunate that most yacht clubs and many marinas still welcome sailors from other places, although more and more clubs are financially unable to make their facilities available free of charge, in return for reciprocal privileges. Marinas are of course a different proposition, but while they are essentially commercial enterprises, for many of their regular inhabitants they are also seasonal floating colonies, more like neighborhoods than hotels. The visiting or transient skipper should remember, therefore, that he's a customer to the people who operate the place, and an uninvited guest to the regulars who inhabit it.

As a general rule, it's a sound precaution to call or radio ahead to make reservations at marinas. Admittedly, the idea of cruising doesn't suit well with rigid itineraries, but if you or your crew have your hearts set on staying at a popular place, and if it is a holiday weekend, a reservation well in advance may be vital. By the same token, do take the trouble to call the marina as early as possible if you realize that you won't be able to make it or will be arriving late. It's a courtesy that will be appreciated.

In many large marinas catering to transients there will be a staff of dock attendants, young men and women who will guide you from shore to the assigned slip and help you berth your boat. Unlike casual onlookers, these people are usually trained to give help as required without getting in the way. They will also handle registration and can tell you about such facilities as ice delivery and garbage removal. Few will be insulted if offered a tip.

Posh marinas are sometimes more clublike than a yacht club. They frown on dispays of tattered laundry in the cockpit. A marina of this type will nearly always offer, when you check in, a leaflet outlining its rules, but when making reservations in an unknown place, using a cruise guide, you can usually assume that the more facilities there are, the more like a social organization the place will be. For some reason, few cruising guides mention whether an establishment will take credit cards, and many don't. So if you plan to pay with plastic money (or with a check), make sure in advance that this form will be acceptable. And if you plan to leave early, as many skippers do, fuel up and pay up the night before, as it can often be difficult in the early morning hours to locate someone who has the keys to the cash register.

A great many people, of whom I am not one, like to spend their summer evenings sitting in the cockpits of their boats, tied up in their home marina. The visiting skipper should be aware of this; he and his crew will be the center of attention, especially if they're doing anything out of the ordinary. People who spend evenings aboard seldom stay up late, and so it's polite to keep the decibel level down after about nine. It's also polite not to peek into the portholes of yachts, even if you're reasonably certain there's no one aboard. You might be wrong.

Being a visitor at a yacht club is often very much the same as stopping at a marina, but there are likely to be nuances of behavior that are different. To begin with, even if you're asked to pay for a slip or mooring—and chances are you will be—you are still a guest rather than a customer, which implies a different attitude on both sides. The hosts will likely be more personally attentive, more interested in you as a fellow yachtsman, and at the same time you'll be expected to be more tolerant of the club's eccentricities and shortcomings, since they didn't ask for your business.

When arriving at a strange club, you will probably be greeted by one of the launch attendants; often he'll swing alongside as you enter the anchorage area.

If you belong to a club that has formal exchange privileges with the club you're visiting, you should be flying your club's burgee to alert the attendants. If you belong to another club but are not sure whether you have such privileges, fly your club burgee anyway. And if you're a member of the USPS or Coast Guard Auxiliary, don't hesitate to fly their flags, as the club you're visiting may well be home to a group of Squadron or Auxiliary members. When the launch approaches, ask if there is a guest slip or mooring, according to what you want. If there is, the attendant will probably lead you to it. The mooring may be one used only by guests, in which case its pickup line and rode are likely to be heavily encrusted with barnacles or mud. Handle it with care and, if possible, gloves, and sluice down the deck immediately after making fast, before the mud has time to set or the undersea life to smell.

The launch attendant may at this point come aboard to brief you as to costs, times of service, and facilities; or he may leave you to your own devices. In either case, it's good manners, as soon as you've tidied yourselves and the yacht, to go ashore and hunt up the club office. You may be asked to sign a guest book, or pay up, or both. You may have to buy scrip for the club's bar or restaurant, or you may be able to sign for meals and be billed (assuming you want to eat there). Although it is often a gesture of good will to eat in the club dining room—they usually need the business—it can also be risky.

As a guest of the club, albeit a paying one, you should be prepared to go out of your way to be friendly and responsive and understanding. Financially speaking, the last few years have not been easy ones for clubs, and they are almost certainly making no money on your visit. Their facilities won't equal those of a good marina, but neither will the charges, and the availability of friendly yacht clubs in the better known cruising areas is one of the delights of cruising. Sometimes it can be amazing just how friendly your hosts will be. Not only have I been warned off the club dining room, but I've even been offered the use of members' cars to find a proper restaurant.

Except on weekends, launch service may end early in the evening. Be sure the attendants know when you plan to be back. I always tip the younger club employes, just as I'd hope visitors to my yacht club would tip the people who work there.

When you're at home and a visiting yacht appears, the shoe goes on the other foot. Bear in mind how you feel in someone else's club and try to put visitors at ease. Be alert for idiosyncrasies of your club—the shower that never yields hot water after 3:00 P.M.—and warn guests. By all means invite them for drinks if you're so inclined, but be aware that they may be hungry, tired, and shy, and don't shove too much hospitality down their throats. To a stranger, every member of the host club is its representative, and as you hope the hospitality will be returned to you some day, offer the same level of friendship to your visitors.

Racing

For a great many sailors, the urge to go faster than the boat alongside is a basic element of personality. I have known very few skippers—and almost no skillful ones—who were indifferent when their boat was being passed by another yacht of even approximately equal size. It is, therefore, only natural for the competitive spirit to become channeled into organized racing, but what is remarkable, at least to me, is how relatively few cruising-boat sailors race formally. An executive of C&C, the Canadian boatbuilder whose vessels are exceptionally well fitted to serve as both racers and cruisers, once told me that fewer than 20 percent of C&C owners ever raced their boats. And if you look at the numbers of boats involved in weekend racing, as a fraction of the total number of cruising yachts, the figure remains very small.

All this is prologue to the suggestion that if you regard yourself as a cruising person, you're unlikely to enjoy serious racing. You may be an exception, of course—there are quite a few. But you're probably better advised to come to terms with the racing urge in small and inexpensive ways, at least until you're sure you've caught the bug. Fortunately, there are all sorts of races available in most sailing areas, so you can probably pick and choose among several varieties of competition.

The basic split in competitive sailing is between handicap and level racing. In the former, the unequal speed potentials of boats are balanced, at least in theory, by mathematical formulas that attempt to penalize speed-producing elements (such as sail area) and reward speed-reducing factors (such as heavy displacement). The boats still sail at the same speed as they did before the handicap was applied (so it's not the same as loading weights on a race horse), but their time to cover a given course is adjusted—or "corrected"—to reflect the boats' individual speed potentials. Ideally, if all the boats in a handicap race were sailed to their full capacities, the fleet would finish well spread out, but the corrected times would be the same. By contrast, in level racing the boats are assumed to have the same potential speeds, so no handicap is applied, and the boat to cross the finish line first is by definition the winner.

As I've suggested earlier, level racing is relatively uncommon among cruising boats; the beginning racer is far more likely to encounter some form of handicap competition. In fact, the novice's first impression is likely to be of a great number of competing systems, all supplied with alphabet-soup labels —MORC, PHRF, IOR—and each claiming to be the one true faith. If the beginner doesn't immediately decide that this is all too much to bother with (as many sailors do), he may hang around long enough to ask "how come?" There are several reasons for the plethora of handicapping systems. A cynic might suggest that the innate contentiousness of racing sailors has something to do with it, and he'd be at least partly right. More basic, I think, is that any rating system must make a compromise between precision and accuracy on the one hand, and convenience and expense on the other. Thanks to scientific measurement and calculation, it's now possible to predict with quite surprising accuracy the speed potential of almost any sailing yacht. (You'll have noted that the potential speed applies to the boat, not her crew.) The problem is that the work required to produce precise calculations is very expensive and time-consuming. You need to haul the boat from the water, having arranged for the presence of an official measurer, and spend the better part of a day standing around while he crawls over and under your yacht, taking her dimensions. The data are fed into a computer and your boat then receives an official measurement certificate, under any of several measurement rules. This certificate remains valid unless you make some substantive change in the boat, or until the rule itself is changed by its proprietors.

Another way to predict potential speed is to accumulate data on a large number of approximately similar boats until there's a bank of information that will supply a rating of reasonable accuracy for an average boat of that particular type, or a type closely resembling it. Clearly, a more casual system like this doesn't pretend to be as accurate as one that measures individual boats, and it is also easily subject to fiddling by dishonest or ignorant owners. It can, however, be operated at minimal expense, and its ratings have the accuracy produced by averaging among large numbers.

It should come as no surprise that hotshot racers generally prefer the more complicated systems first described. In larger boats, the two most commonly encountered are the International Offshore Rule (IOR) and the Measurement Handicap System (MHS). The IOR, which is managed by the Offshore Racing Council (ORC), began as a genuinely international attempt to make equitable racing possible among boats from different countries, designed in accordance with radically differing design philosophies. Unfortunately, the IOR almost immediately began to suffer from its friends—the naval architects and their clients—who inspected the rule closely for loopholes and then began to design new boats that were not necessarily faster than the old ones but that took advantage of the rule to receive better time allowances. This necessitated a series of changes in the rule, to block the loopholes, with the result that an owner might have his rating changed up or down without much warning. Measurement to the IOR was and is complicated and expensive, and the system is used mostly by international competitors who are ready to build a new boat every year or two.

As a reaction to the IOR, a group of wealthy American yachtsmen set up a project that would, they hoped, create a rule which would favor what they called "wholesome" boats, vessels that could be used for both racing and cruising, while avoiding the loopholes of the IOR. The system they produced, the Measurement Handicap System (MHS), is at present used in only a few places in the United States. Its adherents claim that it is far more accurate in predicting speed potential under varying conditions and headings than is the IOR, and that it eliminates those factors in the IOR that created—MHS claims—unseaworthy boats. For the casual racer, MHS is probably too rarified and too costly to bother with, at this point. There is, however, a move within the organization to issue series certificates for fiber glass boats, so that the costly process of individual measurement could be avoided and the cost brought down to something that would interest ordinary sailors. It remains to be seen whether this will catch on, but the history of rating rules is full of failed systems, and I for one would not put down my money till the system was well in place and had been working for a couple of seasons in waters where I sailed.

Both IOR and MHS are primarily designed for yachts over thirty feet in length. One reason for this discrimination is a purely technical one: At the upper and lower ends of the size scale, the behavior of a sailboat may change faster than a rule can adjust itself. For example, a racing yacht about twenty-five feet in length is extremely sensitive to crew weight and placement. To handicap small boats accurately, a somewhat different rule is required, and it exists in the system offered by MORC, a group I mentioned previously. Related to the IOR, the MORC rule in its basic form is similarly complex and expensive to operate, despite the club's efforts to reduce expense. Its popularity (or the absence thereof) seems closely related to geography and to the strengths and weaknesses of the local MORC stations. In the Midwest, for example, MORC remains strong on the Great Lakes, thanks largely to good organization. In the Northeast, however, MORC has limped along for some time, and it is virtually moribund in the otherwise overwhelmingly popular Long Island Sound area. In an effort to beef up its entry lists, the national organization of MORC has authorized a number of variations on the basic rule, most of which have the effect of producing a less intricate, less authoritative, and less costly measurement.

Most racing yachtsmen would agree that there are relatively few serious racing sailors, at least among those operating cruising yachts. A "serious" racer might be defined as one for whom racing is his boat's primary use; such a person, while perhaps making some concessions toward comfort and sea-kindliness (as opposed to seaworthiness), is first and foremost concerned with winning races. This goal may or may not entail coming in first, of course: A good number of dedicated racers are not terribly talented sailors, and the only way they can hope to win is by having either much faster boats than do their competition, or by having a boat of average speed with a highly favorable handicap rating. Today's truly competitive sailing yachts, however, tend to be more and more uncomfortable because they are less and less designed to accommodate human anatomy. They often resemble monstrously oversized racing dinghies, with literally dozens of complex, expensive, go-fast gadgets and sail wardrobes of great cost and variety. As naval architects become more adept at maneuvering within the confines of a handicap rule, designing their boats to take advantage of its oversights, the measurement process becomes even more complicated and involved (and expensive); in order to have a competitive boat, the serious racer finds himself spending more and more on a vehicle that less and less resembles a cruising yacht. Further, he must somehow convince a husky and talented crew to sign on for the season (which has been extending at each end), and the only boat a really hot crew wants to sail aboard is a boat that wins. The whole process becomes increasingly single-minded, and as big-league offshore racing has come to be dominated by a handful of boats, it's not surprising that serious racing—IOR, MORC, MHS —has lost its attraction for many sailors.

PHRF

What has arisen to replace it, in many parts of the country, is PHRF— Performance Handicap Rating Formula—mentioned earlier in this chapter. Since PHRF's assigned handicaps are flexible enough to allow for small differences from boat to boat, since it is cheap and easy to get a PHRF number, or handicap, and since nearly all but the most stratospheric competition uses PHRF ratings, the meteoric rise of this system is hardly surprising.

As I said earlier, a PHRF number for a given boat is arrived at by averaging the performance data for a large sample of boats from the same or similar molds. Thus, in order to be reasonably accurate, a PHRF rating must be based upon an adequate sample—which is why the system really applies only to series-built (which is to say, fiber glass) boats. An approximate rating is possible for one-off craft, especially when they closely resemble stock hulls, but the vast majority of PHRF fleets are made up of the sort of average yachts most of us own.

Within that average, of course, there are considerable differences boat for boat. Not only in skill, although that is always the most important factor, but also in amount and type of gear, stowage, trim, and maintenance. To take these local differences into account, many yacht clubs will fiddle the PHRF ratings of their own fleets to produce locally adjusted numbers which, at least in theory, will produce closer competition among the neighborhood fleet. At this point, of course, the criteria behind a rating begin to slide from the objective to the very subjective indeed. It is not unknown for local fleet politics to stretch some ratings up and others down, and the system accordingly allows for an annual reappraisal, whether or not the boat's physique or equipment has changed.

At its best, most experts agree, PHRF provides a remarkably accurate, albeit simplified, rating system. When locally adjusted, it can do what no other sailing handicap does—rate the sailors as well as the boats. How does it all work? Let us say that you're the brand-new owner of a Frimble 27, a reasonably established model advertised as a "cruising-racing sloop." (The advertising constructs "cruising-racing" and "racing-cruising" are essentially untrustworthy as guides to a boat's performance capabilities, by the way.) You observe that there are several Frimble 27s in your club's PHRF fleet, and you decide that you'd like to participate. Your normal first stop is the club's Race Committee chairman, who will supply the address of the regional PHRF authority and who may have a stack of blank PHRF rating forms. Normal procedure is to fill out one of these (see the sample illustration) and send it in,

PHRF

Yacht Racing Association of Long Island Sound, Inc.

37 West 44th Street, New York, N.Y. 10036   212-575-1019

FOR HANDICAPPER USE ONLY

SAIL NO.	YACHT NAME	HULL NO.	YR.	STD. CLASS	L	BASE	J	S	M	P	*	HANDCP.
7 3	Sporadic	73	80	AMF	21	207	5	5	5	5		207

TYPE OR CLASS	RIG	DESIGNER	STD. CLASS	% OR TYPE						ADJ.
AMF 2100	Sloop	Hood	**JIB**	149	5					0

MASTER							
Wolcott Gibbs, Jr.	**SPIN**	179		5			0

ADDRESS							
220 Bayberry Lane	**MAST**	STD			5		0

CITY	STATE	ZIP					
Westport	Conn.	06880	**PROP**	STD			5	0

HOME PHONE	ALT. PHONE		
203-226-0842	212-725-7230	**MISC**	

HANDICAPPER'S COMMENTS	TOTAL ADJ.	0

I understand that it is my responsibility to notify the handicapper of changes to this yacht which affect measurement points, handicap adjustments, or would alter her from a standard boat.

SIGNATURE OF MASTER   DATE
3/1/81

SIGNATURE OF HANDICAPPER   DATE
13 MAR 81

MEASUREMENTS

J	8'0"	**LOA**	21'1"
LP	11'9"	**LWL**	17'7"
SPL	7'10"	**BEAM**	8'0"
G	14'4"	**DRAFT**	4'0"
I	23'11"	**DISPL. lbs**	2,200 #
P	22'3"	**BAL. lbs**	850 #
E	9'0"	**MAT.**	Fiber glass

IOR RATING   MHS RATING

VARIABLES

ENG
INBOARD ☐
OUTBOARD ☑
NONE ☐

PROP INSTAL.
IN APERTURE ☐
EXPOSED SHAFT ☐
STRUT DRIVE ☐

RIG
MASTHEAD ☐
FRACTIONAL ☑
OTHER ☐

RUDDER
ATTACHED ☐
SKEG ☐
SPADE ☑

PROP TYPE
FOLDING ☐
FEATHERING ☐
SOLID 2-BL ☐
SOLID 3-BL ☐

KEEL
FIN ☑
FULL ☐
CTR. BD. ☐
DROP ☐
OTHER ☐

SPIN. GIRTH MEAS.

.5 G

FOLD ON CTR. LINE

SPL

P

I

LP 90°

E   J

PHRF form; all the information needed should be easily obtainable from the designer, sailmaker, and builder.

with a nominal fee that will not usually exceed $25. In due course, you will receive back a copy of the form you filled out, and on it a number, which represents your handicap. Let's say this number is 207. What it means in practice is that 207 seconds are subtracted from your yacht's total time for each mile in a given course. Continuing with our example, let's assume a course whose point-to-point distance totals 17.5 miles—not an unlikely length for a cruising-boat day race. Let's further assume that your boat's elapsed time over the course is 4 hours, 22½ minutes, usually written 4:22:30. Your handicap is 207 × 17.5 = 3,622.5 seconds, which is subtracted from your elapsed time of 15,750 seconds, leaving you with a corrected time of 12,127.5 seconds, or 3:22:07.

Since this particular handicap is subtractive, it is obviously to your advantage to have as high a PHRF number as possible. Other handicaps or ratings are applied and expressed in different ways, and there is not, in a book about cruising, much point in going into them in much detail. Suffice it to say that even the simplest of today's yacht racing handicaps requires at least a hand-held computer on the race committee boat—and even then there will be frequent errors, so it never hurts to check your own corrected time, using the stated length of the course as given in the race circular (it will almost certainly not be the same as the distance you actually sail, to be sure).

Although PHRF is an easygoing measurement system—or nonmeasurement system—races held under its banner may be highly regulated and stiffly competitive. Almost always, the caliber of the competition determines the formality of the race. Serious yacht racers know that a well-run contest, which demands a somewhat picky adherence to rules, yields in the long run a more satisfying regatta for everyone. So don't assume, just because you have a PHRF rating, that you'll be racing with people who are out only to kill an afternoon in a genteel manner.

PHRF has made great strides toward becoming the single rule of choice for sailors unattracted by IOR, MORC, or MHS, but there also remains a considerable number of locally devised measurement systems, cobbled together by sailors who found all the formal rules unusable or too complicated. In some cases, a local measurement system is really nothing more than a mathematical switchboard through which the ratings of several disparate handicap systems may be filtered to produce a single set of ratings compatible to a number of yachts. One such system is the New England Rule, which exists in the Cape Cod area of Massachusetts. It is not difficult to measure a boat under this relatively simple rule, which favors old-fashioned, long-keel, short-masted boats over newer designs, but one of its major attractions is that you can take another rule's measurement certificate, use some of the figures with appropriate correction, and obtain an NER rating without physically remeasuring the boat. Another unsurprising attribute of many local rules is their tendency to coddle boats that are popular in a given area or with a given group of sailors—schooners, for example, or boats with centerboards.

Level racing

Whatever the handicap system, the boat first over the finish line is not necessarily the winner. Only after the Race Committee has applied the rating can you have a corrected time, determining which yacht has really won. In some races, however, there is also a trophy for first-to-finish, regardless of rating, a prize that nearly always goes to one of the largest competitors. Such a trophy merely recognizes the perfectly human idea that the first vehicle to cross the finish line in a race ought to be some kind of winner.

In this spirit, many sailors turn to so-called level racing, where either there are no handicaps among the fleet or where all competitors, while not identical, have the same rating and are therefore on an even—or level—footing. Obviously, the simplest kind of competition to run on this basis is one-design and class racing, where the boats really are nearly equal in speed potential. It might, however, be more accurate to say that the boats are equal in theory, since even boats that come off the production line identical will soon develop speed-affecting idiosyncrasies.

There is a certain amount of class racing among cruising yachtsmen, usually very casual indeed, but relatively little one-design competition, if only because owners of cruising boats are reluctant to live within the trammels of a one-design rule, where even moving a sheet lead may make a boat ineligible. Just about the only nationally active one-design cruising class I know of is the J/24, and of course these boats are far better known as racers than as cruisers. Even though you may own a one-design boat, there's nothing that says she can only race in class events: As long as she meets or can be made to meet PHRF or MORC safety standards, she will normally be able to compete in those events, too.

The other form of level racing, where dissimilar-looking boats with similar ratings compete on an even basis, is perhaps best exemplified by the so-called "ton" class racing. This system has nothing to do with tonnage (just as a 12-Meter has no dimension that must measure 12 meters), but reflects the name of a trophy, the One-Ton Cup, which fell out of competetion and which was revived under its old name for an entirely different kind of racing.

Ton racing generally uses the IOR as the basis of its measurement, so that it can be international in scope. The competing boats are grouped according to measurement into classes—One Ton, Half Ton, Quarter Ton, and so forth. Although the boats in a given ton class are likely to be approximately the same size, they may in fact be quite unlike each other in appearance. The important thing is that each boat has an IOR rating equal to or less than a stated figure —Half Tonners rate up to 21.7, for example, Quarter Tonners up to 18 and Three Quarter Tonners up to 24.5. Because of the way the IOR is expressed, the ratings come out in feet and decimal fractions, and they are often more or less equal to a given boat's waterline length. Because of the complexity of the ton system, its use has been largely restricted to hotshot international racers.

Types of races

There are essentially three kinds of sailboat races, of which only two are of interest to the cruising sailor. (The third, match racing, is an event in which only two boats compete, and it has, accordingly, different strategies.) Cruising boats race in fleets of varying size, from half a dozen to several hundred, with larger fleets being divided into classes for administrative convenience. Generally speaking, a cruising boat will compete in either closed-course or distance races. Closed-course events are usually quite short—often the Race Committee can run several heats over the same course in an afternoon, using a mix of government navigational markers and special racing buoys to define the boundaries. Where possible, a race committee will usually try to set up a triangular course that allows approximately equal amounts of beating, reaching, and running, although many closed-course races, including the America's Cup, employ what is called an Olympic course in which beating is emphasized at the expense of the other two headings. Even when a race committee announces a "cruising canvas" race (which usually translates to "no spinnakers"), there will almost always be a running leg. The increasingly popular weekday evening races (also known as beercan regattas, from the floating trails left by the competitors) are most often closed-course events for family crews, and hence use only cruising canvas. These evening races, which normally run from about 6:00 P.M. to sunset, are an excellent place for the beginning racer to whet his appetite—or to discover if he has no taste for competitive sailing.

The distance race, which may also be known as an offshore or ocean race, depending on the locale, relies on a predetermined race course—how else could it function?—but the exact route around the course is usually less constricted, and may call for strategic decision making. Most distance races are designed to take up at least a full afternoon in average winds, and a good many are overnight affairs, starting about cocktail time on a Friday night and usually finishing in the daylight hours of Saturday. (Obviously, the greater the size range of boats within the fleet, the greater spread of finishing times will have to be allowed.) There are also the long-distance offshore races—from mainland America to Bermuda, the Fastnet off the British Isles, and the Transpac from California to Hawaii, for example—that expose the competitors to open-ocean conditions for several days and nights.

If you're new to both cruising and racing, it's a good policy to stick to day races for a season, at least when sailing your own boat; if you crew for someone else, an overnight race can be an excellent learning experience without too much pressure. The extended offshore races are not to be entered into lightly or unadvisedly, especially since the cost for racing in one may be several thousand dollars, borne mostly by the skipper.

A regatta is usually a collection of day races, held over a weekend or sometimes crammed into a single day or extended over a week; occasionally, as in Britain's world-famous Cowes Week, the individual races in a regatta are of vastly different lengths. Staging such an event is a tremendous strain on any club's race committee, and the normal regatta is run using several short courses based on the same start-finish line. The courses may utilize government marks or may rely on special race buoys dropped by mark boats.

Basic racing

There is a vast literature available for the racing sailor, and while much of it, especially in sailing magazines, is detailed tactical information for the intermediate or expert, there are also at least half a dozen excellent books for the beginner, some of which are listed in the bibliography. I won't try to preempt their coverage in a short space, but it may be useful for the sailor contemplating his first race as a skipper or crew to know some of what's happening before he invests in more literature. Whether a race is a one-hour belt around a couple of buoys or an overnight contest covering ninety miles, it can be conveniently divided into several discrete segments, the number varying with the number of legs—nominal straight-line courses—in the race. And regardless of the course, every race has three elements in common: prestart, start, and finish.

Prestart is a term of convenience that can be extended indefinitely backward before the actual starting gun. For the sake of this book, however, we'll compress it somewhat. We will assume that you have made a proper entry, and that you have a valid rating certificate, noting the handicap assigned to your boat by the appropriate racing authority. You will—or should—receive in the mail a race circular, a document that can range in size from a single sheet of paper to a printed booklet the size of a weekly magazine. In essence, the circular is a catalog. It says who's eligible, when and where the race is to take place, what the race committee's signals to participants will mean, and what rules will obtain, if any, beyond those of the United States Yacht Racing Union (USYRU). Most race circulars appear to be nearly identical, but it is absolutely vital that you read and understand everything in them; experienced racers agree that a large number of otherwise skilled competitors penalize themselves foolishly by failing to read the small print.

Assuming further that you have a well-tuned boat and a crew with whom you've sailed before, it's advisable to go over the possible courses and the general strategy with them well in advance of the race. Iron out which sails you'll use (they may be specified in the race circular), your probable course, watches (if the race will be long enough and your crew large enough to warrant them), and job assignments. I've found that it helps to have one crew member in charge of the timepiece (a stopwatch is best) and the race circular, so that there's one person to answer the inevitable questions that arise when the race committee boat starts throwing out signals.

Plan to be on the course, in the area of the start, about an hour before the scheduled start of your race. If the fleet is large enough to have been divided into divisions or classes, and if yours does not start first, it's your responsibility to keep out of the way, but at least you can get an idea of the wind strength, the wind direction relative to the course, and the composition of the fleet (this information will often be available at the start line, from the committee boat, in the form of a handout).

Loosen up the crew a bit by trying a few tacks and jibes, and make sure that the sails, sheets, and associated hardware you'll need are readily available. If the wind is light, you'll probably want to keep your engine going, just in case you have to motor back to the vicinity of the start line, but bear in mind that the starting area contains a great many boats, and a great many skippers and crews under tension, so don't be too surprised at a certain amount of aberrant behavior.

As a rule, the race committee boat will be easily identifiable by a large blue flag with the letters "RC" in white, and by some sort of framework rigged to hold the course signals, which may be letters, flags, or indeed any visual system that works; whatever it is, it'll be specified in the circular. If there's a large number of boats, or a great size disparity between classes, the race committee may use different courses for each class, and it is your responsibility to read off your course signal and understand it.

The start of a race is signaled in three stages—warning, preparatory, and start—at five-minute intervals. The ten-minute warning signal is often the starting signal for the previous class, a system that saves time and helps keep the classes precisely spaced, a convenience for the scorers. The warning is often a gun, but sometimes a horn, plus a white-colored signal on the race committee boat, and at this point your boat is allowed in the starting area, the water immediately behind the start line. Experienced racers will use the next five minutes to determine exactly how the start line is oriented to the first leg of the race; the two should be exactly at 90 degrees, but since one end of the start is usually occupied by the anchored committee boat, and since the wind—any wind—is constantly changing back and forth a few degrees, this exactitude is unlikely. The difference means that one end of the line will be favored—closer to the first, usually windward, mark, and most of the boats will attempt to cross the line there. Whether you decide to do so or not will depend on your experience, your nerve, and the size and demeanor of the fleet.

At the five-minute preparatory signal—another horn or gun and a blue-colored signal—you must shut down your boat's engine if it's still running. There are any number of ways to approach a start line, but perhaps the easiest, for a novice crew, is the timed start: At about one minute before the start, sail away from the line on a close reach for about half a minute. Then tack and come back toward the start on the reciprocal course. If you allow exactly a half-minute reaching away, you'll probably hit the line a second or two late, allowing for the time to tack, but you're unlikely to be early. Unless the start line is positively deserted, don't attempt to start except close-hauled on the starboard tack, which will give you as much right of way as possible (see the digest of rules in Appendix 5). This assumes, of course, that the start is to windward—some race committees, for reasons of their own, schedule reaching or even running starts, which offer their own problems.

Normal procedure just before the start is to have one crew member hold the stopwatch and count down the last half-minute—by five-second increments until the final ten seconds, which are counted off individually. This running time check allows the skipper to gauge whether he will be early at the line, and thus must ease sheets or luff to kill speed, or if he is on time or late, and can go for it full tilt. Most beginning skippers tend to be unaggressive at the start, on the grounds that if they are over early, they will have to restart in the teeth of the oncoming fleet.

After the start, the race falls into windward and offwind legs—the latter being any leg where competitors can sail a point-to-point course with started sheets. An old saying in racing states that a boat can win only on the windward legs, but she can lose on any leg. That is to say, boats generally gain or lose ground relative to each other on the windward legs, and more or less maintain position off the wind, unless something goes wrong or someone makes a bad decision. Since the advent of boats that are very, very fast off the wind, this is not true as frequently as it used to be, but most serious racers would still agree that a windward leg demands the most skill from the crew, particularly the helmsman.

It's not my aim to discuss tactics during a race, but there are a few general observations that will be useful whether you're competing in your own boat or as someone else's crew. To begin with, in a serious race there is little or no time for relaxing, even when you aren't actively doing something. To a cruising person, the difference in attitude aboard his boat and a racer is at first hard to believe. You'll almost certainly find the required level and period of concentration difficult to attain at first, and many very good sailors never achieve them. No one, for example, talks to the racing helmsman, except to impart vital information directly concerned with the race, and the helmsman himself will be relieved as soon as his concentration flags. Headsail sheets are trimmed and retrimmed constantly, at the order of a crew member forward whose sole job is to "call the sail"—relay to the grinder and tailer, that is, the degree of trim or ease required by every tiny change in the wind's strength or direction. And so it goes with all hands, even when most of them are draped soggily along the windward rail.

Rounding a mark and going off on a new heading is the dramatic and often tactically important moment of racing. It's approximately equivalent to the turn on a race-car track—the place for one competitor to pass another. In sailing, however, the maneuvers are more complicated, hedged by rules, and often accompanied by lightning sail changes. While experienced racers are battling each other close to the turning buoys, the beginner is often best advised to concentrate on an error-free (if not lightninglike) sail change, followed by the fastest possible settling down on the proper new course.

Even in a handicap race, the finish is an exciting place. Normally, by the time you're within a hundred yards of the line, you know whether you have a time advantage on the boats near you (their handicaps require them to "give you time") or vice versa. It is a tribute to the rating systems generally that racers so often close the finish neck and neck with boats that are very close to them in the ratings. Once finished—and once you're sure the race committee on the finish line has timed your finish—the proper move is to clear the finishing area as quickly as possible. You don't have to go far, just make sure that approaching boats have a clear shot at the line, without any wake or wind shadow from your boat.

The rules of yacht racing have become, over the years, very complicated indeed, but much of the complication consists of contingency rules to cover situations that seldom arise. The main rules, which are summarized in Appendix 5, largely parallel the rules of the road, and are not difficult to understand. If you can digest and memorize them, then you are ready to compete in easygoing club races. You may get shouted at a few times, both by experts who know more than you do and by hard-chargers who are trying to convince you that they do, but that fact shouldn't deter you. Although there are definite negative aspects to racing, the sport does teach sailors to get the most from their boats and to think coolly under stress. And many people find it an exciting and stimulating way to spend their time afloat.

Flags and boats

Few newcomers to cruising will be exposed to the level of flag etiquette nonsense that was prevalent a couple of decades ago, which is all to the good. Elaborate and essentially pointless codes of flag usage generally betray a desire by the "ins" to demonstrate their superior, arcane knowledge and/or to intimidate the "outs." Neither is a good reason for anything, and a person who spends a lot of time brooding about flags is generally best avoided. On the other hand, flags are potent symbols for many perfectly easygoing people, and have been for centuries. My own feeling, for what it's worth, is that I would not willingly hurt or offend someone by walking all over his symbols, if a little trouble on my part could avoid it. And besides, I enjoy the harmless symbolism of flags and the color they add to a boat.

Flags on sailing craft served for hundreds of years as communications. Even today, race committee boats carry their identifying banner and use signal flags for simple messages to the racing fleet. By and large, however, messages are better communicated by VHF-FM, and so flags have been relegated to a use as identifying decorations. Specifically, the flags a boat carries will normally identify her nationality, the club or association of her skipper, and, in some cases, the man himself.

The basic flag is, of course, the national ensign. In this country, yachtsmen have a choice of two—the familiar fifty-star, thirteen-stripe Old Glory, or the yacht ensign, with the normal number and arrangement of stripes, but a white fouled anchor encircled by thirteen stars in its blue canton. (A flag's *canton*, by the way, is that upper quarter of the field next to the flagpole or halyard.) No one can force you to hoist either flag, and a private pleasure craft can just as well display the one as the other. Time was when only documented yachts normally employed the yacht ensign, but those days are long gone, while the ensign itself has survived.

Traditionally, a vessel under sail alone hoisted the ensign to the peak of the aftermost sail—the *peak* being the upper after corner of a gaff mainsail or mizzen. Because of the aerodynamics of gaff sails, a flag at the peak will normally ride in a strong airflow when beating or reaching, and it will usually extend and flutter in a visible and satisfying manner. Unfortunately, the equivalent position on a Bermudian sail—two-thirds the way up the leech—doesn't work as well. The flag will fly nicely when beating in a good breeze, but most of the time it will droop unseen along the leech. The obvious solution, long adopted in Europe, was simply to move the national flag down to a short pole on the transom (the main or mizzen masthead being used by another flag, as we shall see). In American waters, this usage ran afoul of a quite useful custom whereby a vessel under both sail and power signaled that condition—and her consequent right-of-way situation—by carrying the ensign as a powerboat would, on the transom staff. Purists fumed and some still struggle, but the overwhelming majority of sailors have now shifted the national flag to a stern pole, under both power and sail.

The only other flag carried by most single-masted sailboats today is a triangular burgee (the word itself is of obscure origin) at the main masthead. This pennant is usually a yacht club flag, indicating the owner's or skipper's (when a boat is chartered) membership. In recent years, more and more sailors have shifted the burgee from its original place to a halyard running from the starboard spreader. While this location means the flag cannot be seen from one side of the boat, it does help to keep the burgee and its pole (often called a pig stick) from fouling the delicate electronic antennae that sprout on so many masts. People who care deeply about flags still shudder at seeing the burgee on a spreader halyard, but it seems to me a trend that is very likely to become accepted by just about everybody within a few years.

In some cases, skippers wish to call attention not only to their nationality and their social affiliation but to themselves as individuals. One way to do this is to hoist a so-called private signal, or house flag. This is simply a pennant, often but not always swallowtailed in shape, of a design that pleases the skipper. (It is, by the way, his flag, not the boat's.) On a ketch or yawl, the house flag appears at the mizzen masthead, whether or not a burgee is flown; on a sloop, cutter, or catboat, however, you have to make a choice. Since the house flag is your own, no one can tell you where to fly it, but it's good manners not to hoist it above an organizational flag, since by the most ancient symbolism this indicates that you have conquered the organization, or at any rate that you regard yourself as superior to it.

Most yacht clubs authorize their officers to fly special flags of office during their terms or while they are representing the club in a temporary position (such as skipper of the race committee boat). Although a few clubs authorize officers' flags that allude, by color and design, to the burgee, most use standard designs: a rectangular flag like the canton of the yacht ensign (white fouled anchor and stars on a blue field) for the commodore; the same design, but white on red, for the vice commodore; and the same design, red on white, for the rear commodore. Officers' flags replace the private signal and—peculiarly enough—the burgee as well, so that it's not uncommon to see a sloop sailed by a commodore, but no clue to what club he's commodore of.

As just about everyone knows, flags are flown from eight in the morning, local time, to sundown. On Memorial Day, the national flag is hoisted at half-mast until noon, and then mastheaded, although half-mast is nearly impossible on many yacht flagpoles. Ashore, many yacht clubs have a flagstaff that looks vaguely like a gaff-rigged mast. It's supposed to, but the boom is omitted because it's functionless. On a club staff of this type, the U.S. ensign —not the yacht ensign—goes to the peak of the gaff, the burgee appears at the masthead, and the officers' flags of commodores who are on the property are sometimes raised on hoists along the starboard spreader.

Some clubs, as well as organizations like the U.S. Power Squadrons and U.S. Coast Guard Auxiliary, have complex flag codes of their own, and if you're a member of such an organization, you will doubtless be advised of the rules. They may seem stuffy, but take it in good part, and be happy that you weren't involved in sailing when a blazer and tie were de rigueur both on and off the water.

~~~~~~~~~~~~~~~~~~

Appendices

1 Tools and Spare Parts

In a cruising yacht of any size, you're likely to accumulate enough tools, spares, and general fix-it junk to fill the whole boat, unless you make a conscious effort to keep matters under control. It helps to separate tools primarily concerned with sails, ropework, and deck hardware from those dedicated to the engine, plumbing, and the stove; a third collection consists of spares. The following list is hardly exhaustive, but it may also be more than a small yacht can carry.

ENGINE TOOLS

Socket wrench set, ⅜″ drive, metric and/or regular

Spark-plug wrench

Set of combination open-end and box wrenches, ⅜″ to ⅞″

Adjustable crescent wrench

Extra-large wrench for through-hull fittings and stuffing box nut

Hammer

Assorted screwdrivers, regular and Phillips head

Grease gun

Long-nose oil can

Vice-grip pliers

Adjustable channel-lock pliers

Long-nose pliers

Wire cutter and stripper

Battery tester (hydrometer)
Sheath knife with sheep's-foot blade
Hacksaw with extra blades
File
Tape measure
Hand drill with assorted bits
Assorted drill taps

SAILOR'S TOOLS

Swedish fid (for laid line)
Set of tubular fids (for braided line)
Sailmaker's palm
Beeswax
Cable cutters
Sail needles

LUBRICANTS AND SPARE PARTS

WD-40
CRC 6-66
Waterpump grease
Penetrating oil
Duct tape
Sail repair tape
Electrical tape
Galvanized wire (for shackle pins)
Wool (for telltales)
Assorted stainless steel screws, machine screws, nuts, and washers
Waxed whipping thread
Rubber bands for stopping spinnaker
Assorted shackles—galvanized (for ground tackle) and stainless steel (for rigging)
Assorted clevis pins, cotter pins, rings, and safety pins
Extra sail slides/slugs and plastic shielding
Extra battens
18″ length of stainless steel wire with four bulldog clips (for emergency shroud repair)
Assorted electrical wire end fittings
Fuses
Bulbs for interior and running lights
Spark plugs*
Injectors**
Fuel filter elements
Lube oil filter

V-belts for alternator and waterpump
Ignition points*
Condenser*
Distributor cap*
Waterpump impeller
Propeller
Voltage regulator
Generator/alternator
Engine lube oil
Transmission lubricant
Fuel strainer/funnel

*gasoline engine
**diesel engine

2 Publication Sources

Good chandleries and marine supply stores frequently carry some or all of the publications a cruising yachtsman needs. But if you don't have such an outlet in your area, it may be better to go to the source than to buy outdated volumes from second-rate stores.

Light List (annual); published in five volumes—I (Atlantic Coast: St. Croix River, Me., to Little River, S.C.), II (Atlantic and Gulf Coasts: Little River, S.C., to Rio Grande River, Tex.), III (Pacific Coast and Islands), IV (Great Lakes), V (Mississippi River). Superintendent of Documents, U.S. Government Printing Office, Washington, D.C., 20402.

Local Notice to Mariners (approximately weekly); free from local Coast Guard District Headquarters: 1st (Boston), 3rd (New York), 5th (Portsmouth, Va.), 7th (Miami), 2nd (St. Louis), 9th (Cleveland), 8th (New Orleans), 11th (Los Angeles), 12th (San Francisco), 13th (Seattle), 14th (Honolulu), 17th (Juneau, Alaska).

Intracoastal Waterway Booklets: Section 1 (Boston to Key West), Section 2 (Key West to Brownsville, Tex.). Superintendent of Documents, address above.

Coast Pilot (annual); published in nine volumes—1 (Eastport, Me. to Cape Cod), 2 (Cape Cod to Sandy Hook), 3 (Sandy Hook to Cape Henry), 4 (Cape Henry to Key West), 5 (Gulf of Mexico, Puerto Rico, Virgin Islands), 6 Great Lakes), 7 (California, Oregon, Washington, and Hawaii), 8 (Alaska, Dixon Entrance to Cape Spencer), 9 (Alaska, Cape Spencer to Beaufort Sea). National Ocean Survey (C44), 6501 Lafayette Ave., Riverdale, Md., 20840.

Charts; Catalogs of charts for U.S. waters are available free from the NOS (address above). Catalog 1 (Atlantic and Gulf Coasts, including Puerto Rico and the Virgin Islands), 2 (Pacific Coast, including Hawaii), 3 (Alaska), 4 (Great Lakes).

Canadian charts are available from Chart Distribution Office, Department of the Environment, P.O. Box 8080, 1675 Russel Rd., Ottawa, Ont. K1G 3H6.

The Mississippi River system is charted by the U.S. Army Corps of Engineers; charts are available as follows—Lower Mississippi to Ohio River: Vicksburg District, P.O. Box 60, Vicksburg, Miss., 39180. Middle and Upper Mississippi and Illinois Waterway to Lake Michigan: Chicago District, 219 S. Dearborn St., Chicago, Ill., 60604. Missouri River: Omaha District, 6014 U.S. Post Office and Courthouse, Omaha, Neb., 68102. Ohio River: Ohio River Div., P.O. Box 1159, Cincinnati, Ohio, 45201.

Tide Tables (annual); published by the NOS (address above) in two volumes, one each for the East and West Coasts.

Tidal Current Tables (annual); published by the NOS in two volumes, like the Tide Tables.

Tidal Current Charts; 12-chart booklets following the tidal cycle through each hour of ebb and flood. Published by the NOS for the following areas: Boston Harbor; Narragansett Bay to Nantucket Sound; Block Island Sound and Eastern Long Island Sound; Long Island Sound; New York Harbor; Delaware Bay and River; Upper Chesapeake Bay; Charleston (S.C.) Harbor; San Francisco Bay; Puget Sound; Tampa Bay.

3 Radiotelephone Procedure

Virtually all coastal cruising yachts employ short-range VHF-FM transmitter-receivers for communication with other vessels and with the shore, although a very few may carry citizens' band sets. As anyone who's watched TV or listened to a country-western song knows, CB is not so much communication as an elaborate social ritual. VHF-FM is less demanding and far more efficient, once you know a few simple rules.

In a sailboat with a masthead-mounted antenna, the standard 25-watt VHF-FM transmitter has a range of about twenty-five miles boat-to-boat and forty or fifty when sending ship-to-shore, because of the higher antennas used by Coast Guard and telephone company shore stations. Hand-held sets, which have power outputs between one and three watts, have a range that is approximately line-of-sight—say five or six miles.

All VHF-FM sets are required by the Federal Communications Commission to carry two basic channels—16, the International Distress and Calling Frequency, and 6, the Intership Safety Frequency. 16 is used to initiate ship-to-ship and sometimes ship-to-shore calls, but after contact is established, the user must shift to another, working frequency. The use of channel 6 remains somewhat obscure, but it is often used as a working frequency during search and rescue or other emergencies. Too many skippers use it as a standard working frequency, which it is not.

There are six regular working frequencies for yachtsmen to use in ship-to-ship communication; these channels are numbered 68, 69, 70, 71, 72, and 78 on your set. While they may be used anywhere in the United States, distribution among boats of individual frequencies is uneven. Except for 70 and 72, these channels may also be used for ship-to-shore communication. Channel 9 is also available for ship-to-ship and ship-to-shore use, and yachtsmen share it with commercial vessels; many marinas use 9 as a working frequency.

Ship-to-shore communication, between a vessel and a telephone company which has the facilities to patch you into a land line, is conducted on any of ten channels—24, 25, 26, 27, 28, 84, 85, 86, 87, and 88. The local phone company serving your cruising area will normally operate on at least two of these channels and can also use 16 to initiate calls. Check with the company in question before investing in specific crystals.

NOAA's continuous weather broadcasts are transmitted on three frequencies, labeled on sets as WX-1, WX-2, and (rarely) WX-3. These are receive-only channels, and the NOAA transmitters are spotted so as to cover the entire coast with minimum overlap between adjoining stations (which are on different frequencies, anyway).

There are numerous channels that are either useless to the yachtsmen or forbidden to him. A special channel that is allowable and recommended is 13, which is used to transmit and receive maneuvering information between ships and between ships and bridges that open. You may transmit at 1-watt power only on 13. Channel 22, sometimes referred to as 22A (or "Alfa") is the Coast Guard's working frequency with civilians. Call the CG on 16 and ask to switch to 22.

Normal, nonemergency communication between vessels works as follows: Turn the set to channel 16, activate the microphone, and call your party, using the name of his boat first, then the name of your boat and your FCC-assigned call letters. It might sound like this: "Iolanthe, Iolanthe, Iolanthe; this is Lizzy Borden, WXF 2230." (Repeating the called party's name three times makes it more likely that he will hear you.) He responds: "Lizzy Borden, this is Iolanthe, WXY 1313; switch and answer channel 68." (Or any of the other ship-to-ship working frequencies.) You turn to channel 68, say "Iolanthe, Lizzy Borden." He answers, and you conduct your conversation. As soon as you're done, you say, "This is Lizzy Borden, WXF 2230. Out." He says the same, substituting his own boat's name and call letters. You may call for up to thirty seconds, but if you don't connect, you must wait two minutes before calling again.

A few tips may help you over the initial awkwardness. Before transmitting on any frequency, listen to make sure no one else is in the middle of a message. Voices vary, but most people will find that if they speak a little louder than usual, pitch their voices—men especially—a little high, and hold the mike about an inch from their lips, they will have the best and clearest transmission.

If you regularly call the same people, establish the practice of beginning your call on a preselected working frequency; this eliminates extra talk on 16 and ensures you a spot on the working channel.

Do not worry about radiotelephone jargon. Most people who use it, use it wrong. Basic English is still the best, but try to outline your conversation in your head before placing the call, so as to keep this crowded party line moving.

Telephone companies ashore monitor their working frequencies regularly, so you can initiate a call on 24 or 84 or whatever, without using 16, as long as you know which frequencies a given company uses. If you don't know, they all monitor 16. Just call "Marine Operator." On weekends and holidays especially, ship-to-shore facilities get very crowded, and you may have to wait an hour or more to make a call. Make sure the marine operator at the other end has your boat's name, and then stand by on the frequency until he or she calls back. You may establish a charge account in your yacht's name, reverse charges, or charge to your home telephone—but somebody has to pay for the call you initiate. If someone ashore calls you, he must usually dial 0, ask for the *marine* operator, and then place the call to the yacht, by its name (not the skipper's). It will help if he knows what ship-to-shore frequencies the yacht's radio carries, but this is not vital, as the yacht will be paged on channel 16 if necessary.

There are three types of priority radiotelephone message. In ascending order of urgency, they are known as "Security," "Pan," and "Mayday" transmissions. Security calls are normally made by the Coast Guard, and deal with hazards to navigation and the like—a buoy adrift, for example. If you run across such a problem, call the Coast Guard and tell them about it, but there is usually no need to invoke a Security priority.

Pan calls involve the safety of a person or vessel when the problem is serious but not immediate. Your boat out of gas doesn't rate a Pan; your boat out of gas and drifting toward the breakers does. Use the word Pan twice, then send the message. If you hear a Pan call, get off the air and listen.

Most serious are Mayday messages, which indicate grave and imminent danger. To send a Mayday, turn the set to channel 16 and say "Mayday, Mayday, Mayday," slowly and clearly. This should clear all other traffic from the air. Give your vessel's name and call number, repeated three times, and wait for a response.

Most likely, the Coast Guard will come back immediately. Be prepared to tell them your boat's name and call letters; its location, preferably in reference to a charted landmark or aid to navigation; your problem and the assistance you require; what your boat looks like; the number and condition of the people aboard. If you see another vessel in obvious trouble, call the Coast Guard, but listen first on 16 to be sure someone else isn't already working the problem.

Your yacht is required to carry a radio log—most owner's manuals of VHF-FM sets contain pages for such a log—in which you must record: your boat's name and call sign, on each page; all distress calls heard or transmitted;

all Pan or Security calls transmitted; and any installation or repair work done by an FCC-licensed technician. Each entry must be signed by the person making the transmission, and logs must be retained for a year after the date of the last entry; logs containing distress traffic entries must be kept for three years.

A formal radio watch is not required on pleasure craft, but if you maintain such a watch, you must log the times it begins and ends.

4 Rules of the Road

The new Inland Navigation Rules that went into force at the end of 1981 had three immediately beneficial effects. First, the new rules virtually eliminated the many contradictions and differences among the previous sets of rules— Inland, Great Lakes, and Western Rivers (a synonym for the Mississippi); second, they made the rules of the road for inland and coastal waters nearly identical with those applying internationally, reducing the confusion that formerly occurred when ships, many with non-English-speaking crews, crossed from one jurisdiction to another; third, the new rules moved the legal regulations closer to those of the International Yacht Racing Union and other racing organizations, thus making it easier for sailors to comprehend their responsibilities under way, whether racing or not.

Cruising sailboats nearly always operate either as sailing or as powered vessels (unless, of course, they have no engines). The first thing to remember, then, is that a yacht with her engine on and in gear is for legal purposes a powerboat, even if her sails are raised and drawing. A skipper of an auxiliary-powered yacht must learn the rules for both sail and engine-driven craft, and follow the appropriate regulations.

SAILING CRAFT

When two sailboats on different tacks are converging so as to present a danger of collision, the vessel on starboard tack (that is, with the wind coming over the starboard side, and the main boom to port) holds her course and speed, and the boat on port tack gives way.

When two converging sailboats are on the same tack, the vessel to windward (closer to the direction from which the wind is coming) gives way, and the boat to leeward holds her course and speed.

When a sailboat and a powered vessel are converging, the sailing craft holds her course and speed, and the powerboat gives way.

BUT a sailing yacht gives way to the following powered vessels: commercial fishing craft engaged in fishing; vessels not under command; and vessels restricted in their ability to maneuver (definitions of these last two conditions are below).

A sailing vessel under both power and sail must exhibit a black cone shape (point down) in her rigging if she is over twelve meters (about forty feet) long, when in inland waters; she must show the same device in international waters if she is over seven meters (about twenty-three feet) in length.

In conditions of restricted visibility (usually fog, but also snow or heavy rain) a sailboat sounds one long and two short blasts on her horn every two minutes. She does not otherwise give sound signals, but may give the universal danger signal of five short blasts if collision is imminent.

POWERBOATS

When two powered craft are approaching bow to bow, they must each turn to starboard and pass port to port.

When two powered craft are crossing, and there is danger of collision, the vessel on the right of the other vessel maintains course and speed, and the other craft gives way.

Powered craft give way to sailing vessels, to commercial fishing craft engaged in fishing, to vessels not under command, and to those restricted in their ability to maneuver. Under the rule, "restricted in ability to maneuver" means a vessel whose employment or function is such that she cannot obey the rules of the road; a dredge or a towboat with an exceptionally large tow are two examples. A vessel restricted in her maneuvering ability hoists a day signal consisting of a ball, a diamond shape, and a ball in a vertical line; at night, the signal is three vertical lights—red-white-red—in addition to normal running lights. A vessel not under command cannot control her movements; she indicates this state by hoisting a day signal of two black balls in a vertical line, while at night she shows, in addition to running lights, two red lights in a vertical line.

In inland waters, a powered vessel indicates her intention of changing course by one blast of the horn (turn to starboard), two blasts (turn to port), or three blasts (engines in reverse). The same signals apply in international waters, except that they signify that the course change is already taking place—an important distinction.

In inland waters, signal the intent to overtake to starboard with one blast, to port with two blasts. Remember that the overtaken vessel *always* has the right of way.

In a narrow channel, vessels restricted to that channel by their draft have the right of way over vessels under twenty meters (about sixty-five feet), fishing craft, and sailing vessels.

Note: These are only the most important rules of the road. Every cruising sailor should be familiar with the full body of rules, which are available from the Superintendent of Documents, U.S. Government Printing Office, Washington, D.C. 20402. Ask for Public Law #96-561 (S/N 022-003-91759-0) and enclose a check for $2.25 per copy.

5 Sailboat Racing Rules

The complete International Racing Rules are available from the U.S. Yacht Racing Union (Box 209, Newport, R.I. 02840) at $3.00 per copy. Anyone planning to race seriously should have the rules booklet. What follows is a brief digest of the most important right-of-way rules; knowing these regulations will let you get started in racing without making a fool of yourself. Remember that during a race, racing yachts follow these rules instead of the normal rules of the road, but that if you, as a racer, encounter a boat that is not racing, the regular rules of the road apply between your two boats.

A yacht is considered to be racing from the time of the preparatory five-minute signal until she has either finished the race and cleared the finish line or has dropped out.

A yacht on port tack keeps clear of a yacht on starboard tack.

When overlapped and on the same tack, the windward yacht keeps clear of the leeward yacht.

The yacht astern keeps clear of the yacht clear ahead.

A yacht tacking or jibing must allow other yachts room and time to keep clear.

If you cross the start line before the starting signal (a red shape) is dropped, you must restart and you must also keep clear of all other yachts that started properly.

Before the start, if you are the leeward boat, you may luff another vessel up to windward, but you must do it slowly. After the start, you may luff the other boat as quickly as you please, until the skipper of the other yacht calls out "mast abeam" (which means that he is even with the mast of your boat). Then you must bear off to the proper course for the next mark.

At the start, a leeward boat does not have to give room to another boat that is "barging" (which means trying to squeeze between you and a start line mark to windward). But you must not try to sail higher than a close-hauled course.

When your boat is two lengths or less from a turning or finish line mark, you must give room at the mark to any yacht that has an inside overlap on you.

If your boat touches a mark, you may not continue racing until your boat has made a complete circle around that mark. If your boat touches a start line mark, you must first start, then return to make your circle.

If you consciously break a racing rule while racing, you must drop out of the race and inform the race committee, unless a lesser penalty applies in the particular race you're in.

If you see some other boat breaking a rule, call out "protest," or words to that effect, and put a red flag in your boat's rigging. Advise the race committee of the nature of your protest immediately after the race.

Bibliography

Amateur Yacht Research Society. *Cruising Catamarans.* London: AYRS, 1972.

Baader, Juan (trans. Inge Moore). *The Sailing Yacht.* New York W.W. Norton, 1979 (revised).

Bailey, Anthony. *The Thousand Dollar Yacht.* New York: Macmillan, 1968.

Bamford, Donald. *Enjoying Cruising Under Sail.* Toronto: Coles, 1978.

Bavier, Bob. *Keys to Racing Success.* New York: Dodd, Mead, 1982.

Beiser, Arthur. *The Proper Yacht.* Camden, Me.: International Marine, 1978 (2nd edition).

Benjamin, John J. *Cruising Boats Within Your Budget.* New York: Harper, 1957.

Blanchard, Fessenden S. *The Sailboat Classes of North America.* Garden City, N.Y.: Doubleday, 1968 (revised).

Boat Owners Buyers Guide. New York: Ziff-Davis, annual.

Bolger, Philip C. *Different Boats.* Camden, Me.: International Marine, 1980.

Bolger, Philip C. *Small Boats.* Camden, Me.: International Marine, 1973.

Bond, Bob, and Sleight, Steve. *Cruising Boat Sailing.* New York: Knopf, 1983.

Bottomley, Tom. *The Boatkeeper's Project Book.* New York: Motor Boating & Sailing Books, 1972.

Bowker, R.M., and Budd, S.A. *Make Your Own Sails.* New York: St. Martin's, 1959.

Brewer, E.S. *Cruising Designs.* New York: Seven Seas Press, 1976.

Campbell, Stafford. *Yachtsman's Guide to Coastal Navigation.* New York: Ziff-Davis, 1979.

Caswell, Christopher. *Trailerable Sailboats.* New York: W.W. Norton, 1982.

Chapelle, Howard I. *Yacht Designing and Planning.* New York: W.W. Norton, 1971.

Clarke, D.H. *Trimarans.* London: Adlard Coles, 1969.
Coles, K. Adlard. *Heavy Weather Sailing.* Clinton Corners, N.Y.: John de Graff, 1981 (3rd revised edition).
Colgate, Stephen. *Fundamentals of Sailing, Cruising, and Racing.* New York: W.W. Norton, 1978.
Colvin, Thomas E. *Coastwise and Offshore Cruising Wrinkles.* New York: Seven Seas Press, 1972.
Cotter, Edward F. *Multihull Sailboats.* New York: Crown, 1966.
Desoutter, Denny M. *Small Boat Cruising.* London: Faber & Faber, 1972.
Duffett, John. *Modern Marine Maintenance.* New York: Motor Boating & Sailing Books, 1973.
Duncan, Roger, ed. *The Practical Sailor.* New York: Scribner's, 1981.
Eastman, Peter F., M.D. *Advanced First Aid Afloat.* Cornell Maritime: Cambridge, Md., 1972.
Edmunds, Arthur. *Fiberglass Boat Survey Manual.* Clinton Corners, N.Y.: John de Graff, 1979.
Gibbs, Tony. *The Coastal Cruiser.* New York: W.W. Norton, 1981.
Gibbs, Tony. *The Coastal Navigator's Notebook.* Camden, Me.: International Marine, 1982.
Gilles, Daniel, and Malinovsky, Michael. *Go Cruising.* St. Albans, U.K.: Adlard Coles, 1978.
Hamilton, Donald. *Cruises With Kathleen.* New York: McKay, 1980.
Henderson, Richard. *The Cruiser's Compendium.* Chicago: Henry Regnery, 1973.
Henderson, Richard. *The Racing-Cruiser.* Chicago: Reilly & Lee, 1970.
Henderson, Richard. *Sea Sense.* Camden, Me.: International Marine, 1972.
Henderson, Richard. *Singlehanded Sailing.* Camden, Me.: International Marine, 1976.
Henderson, Richard. *Better Sailing.* Chicago: Henry Regnery, 1977.
Herreshoff, L. Francis. *The Compleat Cruiser.* New York: Sheridan House, 1956.
Hiscock, Eric C. *Come Aboard.* Oxford: Oxford University Press, 1978.
Hiscock, Eric C. *Cruising Under Sail.* Oxford: Oxford University Press, 1965.
Johnson, Peter. *Ocean Racing & Offshore Yachts.* New York: Dodd, Mead, 1970.
Kals, W.S. *Practical Boating.* Garden City, N.Y.: Doubleday, 1969.
Lane, Carl D. *The Boatman's Manual.* New York: W.W. Norton, 1979 (revised).
Leone, Nicholas C., M.D., and Phillips, Elisabeth C., R.N. *Cruising Sailors Medical Guide.* New York: McKay, 1979.
Letcher, John S., Jr. *Self-steering for Sailing Craft.* Camden, Me.: International Marine, 1974.
MacLean, William P. *Modern Marlinspike Seamanship.* Indianapolis: Bobbs-Merrill, 1979.
Madden, Anne, ed. *More Sail Trim.* Boston: Sail Books, 1979.
Maloney, Elbert S. *Chapman: Piloting, Seamanship and Small Boat Handling.* New York: Motor Boating & Sailing Books, various dates.
Marshall, Roger. *Race to Win.* New York: W.W. Norton, 1980.
Maté, Ferenc. *The Finely Fitted Yacht.* New York: W.W. Norton, 1979.

Miller, Conrad. *Engines for Sailboats.* New York: Ziff-Davis, 1978.

Miller, Conrad, and Maloney, Elbert. *Your Boat's Electrical System, 1981–82.* New York: Motor Boating & Sailing Books, 1982.

Nicholson, Ian. *Boat Data Book.* New York: Ziff-Davis, 1978.

Pardey, Lin and Larry. *Cruising in* Seraffyn. New York: Seven Seas Press, 1976.

Pardey, Lin and Larry. Seraffyn*'s European Adventure.* New York: W.W. Norton, 1982.

Robb, Frank. *Handling Small Boats in Heavy Weather.* London: Adlard Coles, 1970.

Robinson, Bill. *Cruising: The Boats and the Places.* New York: W.W. Norton, 1981.

Robinson, Bill, ed. *The Science of Sailing.* New York: Scribner's, 1961.

Ross, Wallace. *Sail Power.* New York: Knopf, 1974.

Roth, Hal. *After 50,000 Miles.* New York: W.W. Norton, 1977.

Rousmaniere, John. *Annapolis Book of Seamanship.* New York: Simon & Schuster, 1983.

Rousmaniere, John. *"Fastnet, Force 10".* New York: W.W. Norton, 1980.

Safety Standards for Small Craft. New York: American Boat & Yacht Council, various dates.

Sail Books, ed. *Best of Sail Trim.* Boston: Sail Books, 1975.

Sailboat & Equipment Directory. Boston: Sail Books, annual.

Shufeldt, H.H., and Dunlap, G.D. *Piloting and Dead Reckoning.* Annapolis, Md.: U.S. Naval Institute, 1970.

Sleightholme, J.D. *Cruising.* London: Adlard Coles, 1979.

Sleightholme, J.D. *Fitting Out.* London: Adlard Coles, 1977.

Smith, Hervey Garrett. *The Arts of the Sailor.* New York: Funk & Wagnalls, 1968.

Street, Donald. *The Ocean Sailing Yacht.* New York: W.W. Norton, 1973 (vol. 1), 1978 (vol. 2).

Taylor, Roger. *Good Boats.* Camden, Me.: International Marine, 1977.

Index